MW00910094

The Knowledge NETWORK

Designed and produced by
Aladdin Books Ltd
28 Percy Street
London W1P 0LD

First published in the United States by
Copper Beech Books, an imprint of
The Millbrook Press
2 Old New Milford Road
Brookfield, Connecticut 06804

Editor:
Brian Hunter Smart

Cover design:
David West Children's Book Design

Printed in Italy

Some of the material in this
book was previously published
in other Aladdin Books' series.

ISBN 0-7613-0779-6

A CIP data entry for this book can be
found at the Library of Congress.

The Knowledge NETWORK

Copper Beech Books
Brookfield, Connecticut

CONTENTS

Animals and Plants

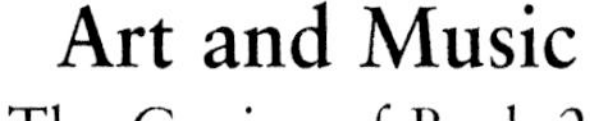

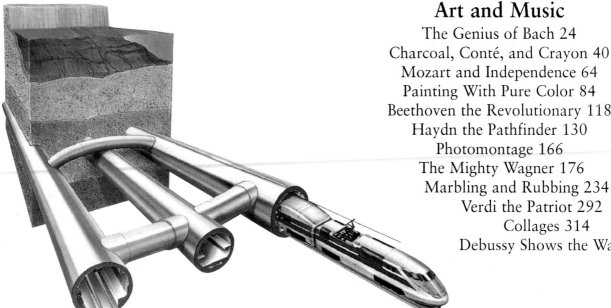

Art and Music

Beasts – Real and Mythological

Geography and the Environment

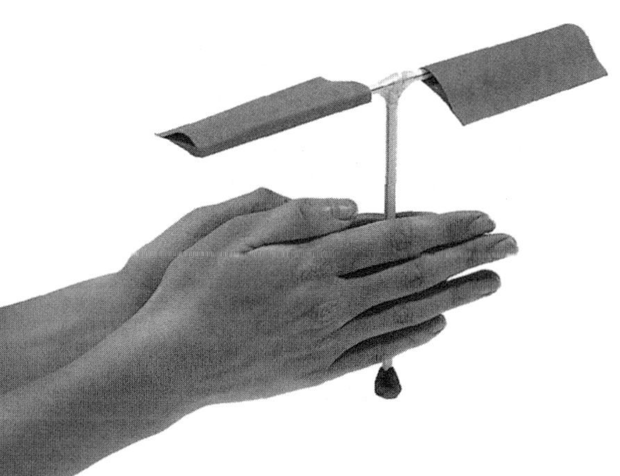

History

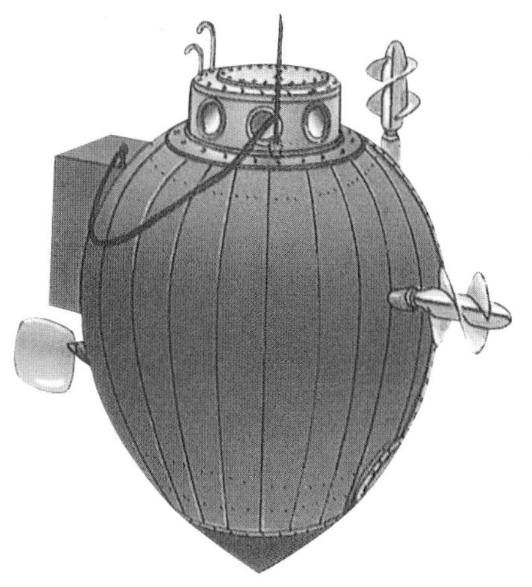

Into the Future

Science

Questions and Answers about...

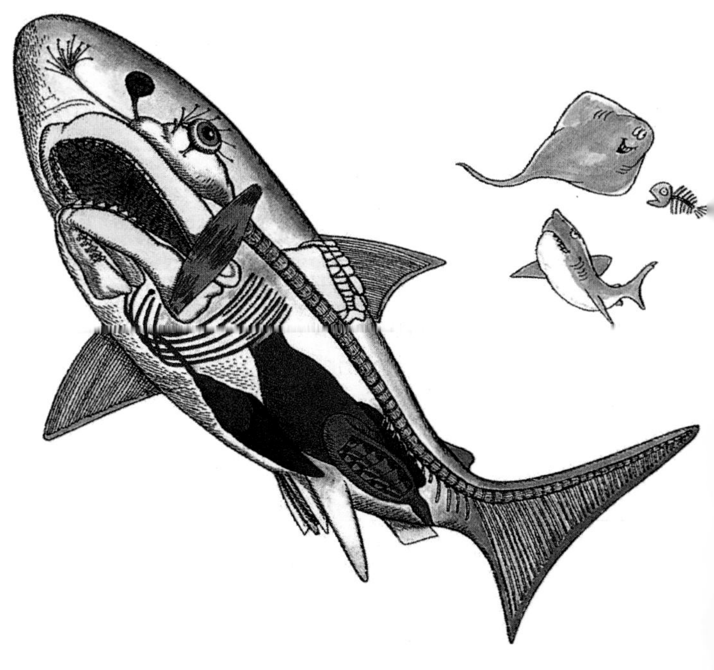

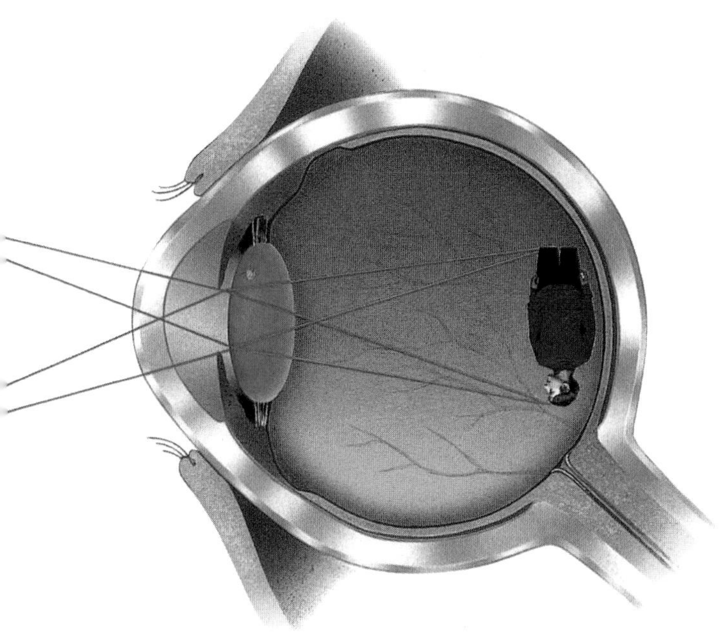

Sports

Technology

INTRODUCTION

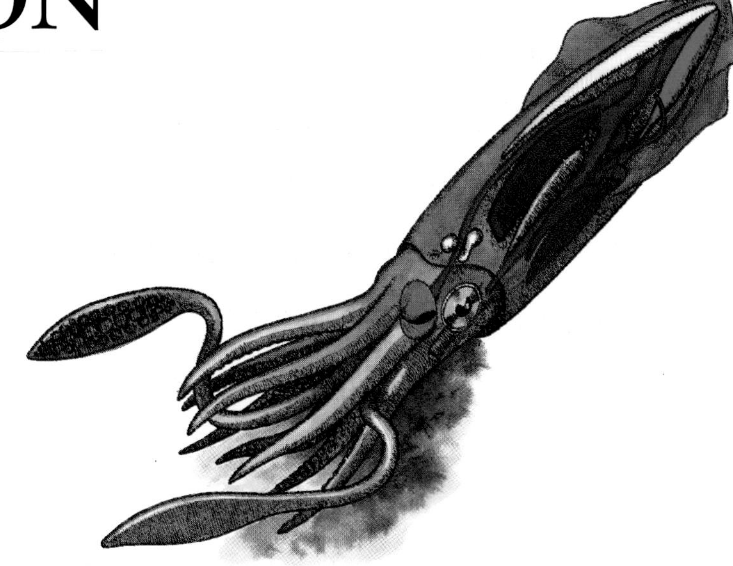

The *Knowledge Network* could just be the only book you will ever need to read. The amount of information it contains is simply enormous. It has a well defined contents and an extensive index to make it very easy for you to get to the information that you want. Your teachers, family, and friends will be shocked and amazed at the depth of knowledge that you possess; from natural history to the space race. *And* The Knowledge Network will be a very useful book for many years to come!

Animals and Plants

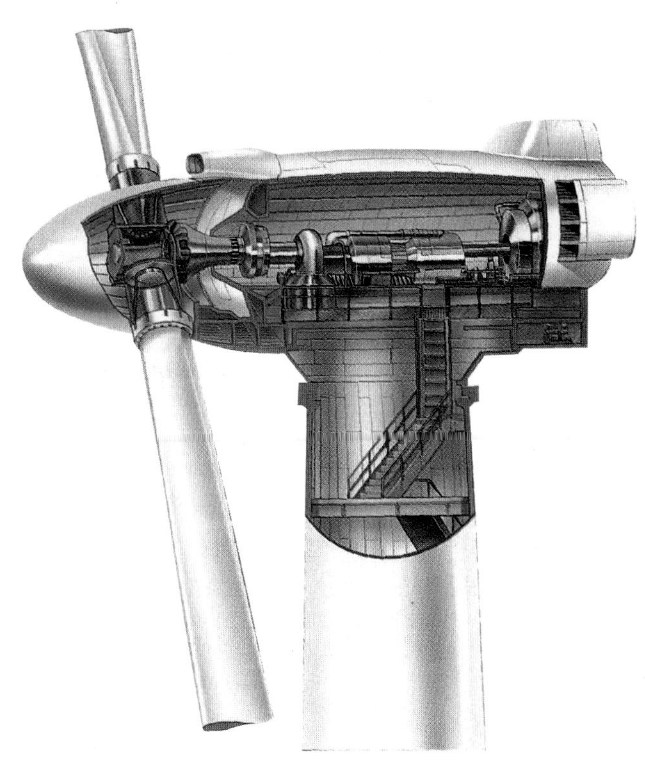

This is a huge subject that covers life on Earth from the dawn of time to the present day. It will show you how dinosaurs used to live, birds fly, and trees grow. It will also answer questions that you might not have considered, like, what if mammals laid eggs, sheep had no wool, or fish could fly!

Art and Music

Even if you are not a budding

musician, you can still read all about the most famous musicians of all time, like Bach, Debussy, and Verdi. If you're interested in art then you can find out about different art forms and how to use them, such as collages, photomontage, and marbling.

Beasts – Real and Mythological

Have you ever wondered how killer whales and wolves got their bad names? If you have then read on, and you will also find out about lions, tigers, and bears, as well as the Viking snake god that surrounds the world and bites its own tail!

Geography and the Environment

The environment is of interest to everyone. Discover for yourself, fascinating information on a wide range of topical subjects. Here you'll find out about the dangers of forest fires and avalanches as well as answers to unusual questions, such as what if we had more volcanoes and exactly what is an earthquake?

History

Did Jesse James, Dick Turpin, or Alexander the Great really exist? In this chapter you will be able to trawl through history and separate the facts from the fiction. Along the way you will discover more about the lifestyles of different peoples. You'll be able to find out about the finest swordsmen, the most notorious criminals, and the bravest explorers.

Into the Future

As we advance with newer machines and computers, will our lives change drastically or simply remain the same? Will we be able to live to 200 years old, travel to the farthest stars and planets, and see if anybody really is out there? If you want to find out, then *Into the Future* will explain it all.

Questions and Answers

The title says it all! Answers to Questions you never thought to ask is the section that is designed to keep you intrigued!

Science

This is a subject that never fails to fascinate. Even the most unscientific of readers will be glued to their seats when reading this section. On this voyage of discovery you will learn not only about fossil fuels, the water cycle, and the starry skies, but also plenty of information that you'll want to know about the human body and how it works.

Sports

What do you do during your leisure time? Do you play soccer, basketball, or go in-line skating? If you are new to these pastimes or would like to know more then here is the information you crave. Who knows – maybe you'll even find a new hobby.

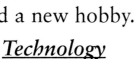

Technology

The advances in technology have increased in pace during this century and have greatly affected the way we live our lives. You'll be able to see the great inventions of the past and be able to compare them with the inventions of the present. For instance, the steam engine had a great impact on the nineteenth century, but what of the Maglev, how does it affect our lives now and what about the future? Power from space, wind energy, and glass fibers are a few of the possibilities that may affect us in future and whet your appetite to find out more.

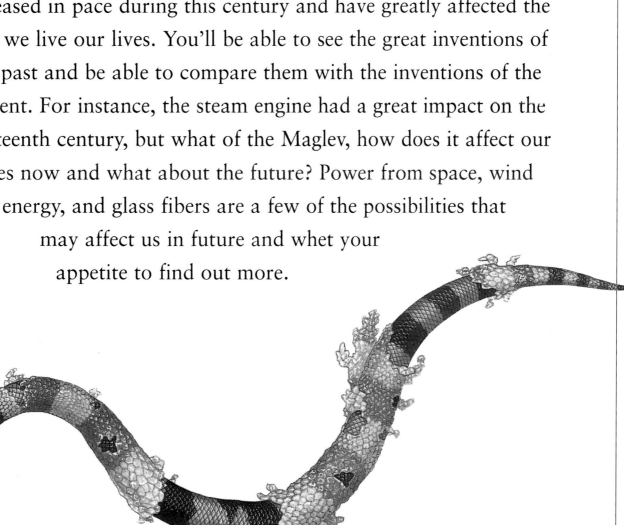

SHARK

A SHARK IS A VERTEBRATE, but it doesn't have a backbone, or any bones at all. It has a skeleton, of course, like any other fish. But this is made of cartilage, or gristle. The flattened fish called rays also have a cartilage skeleton. Together, sharks and rays make up the cartilaginous fish group.

STURDY CARTILAGE
Compared to bone, cartilage is slightly squishy and flexible, yet still durable. It is also very light, helping to save body weight.

JAWS
Sharks have sharp teeth in their mouths – obviously. But their skin is also covered with tiny, teethlike points, called denticles.

GILL SLITS
Like other fish, a shark takes water into its mouth and passes it over the gills, which absorb dissolved oxygen.

LIGHT LIVER
Sharks lack a swim bladder. This problem is partly helped by the lightweight skeleton, and also by a huge liver. This contains lots of lighter-than-water oil, to give buoyancy.

SCREW GUTS
A shark's guts are relatively short and straight. But they have a large surface area for absorbing digested food, due to the screw-shaped spiral valve inside.

ANATOMY AT WORK
TOTAL TOOTH REPLACEMENT
Sharks never need a dentist. They always have new teeth. These begin on the inner sides of the jaws, and gradually grow and move forward, to the front edges. As the shark bites and feeds, they break or snap off. But more continually grow. And more...

IT WASN'T ME, HONEST!
There are about 370 different kinds of sharks. Only 20 or so attack humans regularly. They include the great white, tiger, mako, and hammerhead. Some sharklike bites may be caused by fish such as barracudas.

SALMON

THE "FLESH" OF A FISH LIKE THE SALMON is really muscle. It's the large blocks of muscle along either side of the body, which are attached to the vertebrae of the backbone. These pull alternately to bend the body from side to side, making the tail swish, which pushes the fish along.

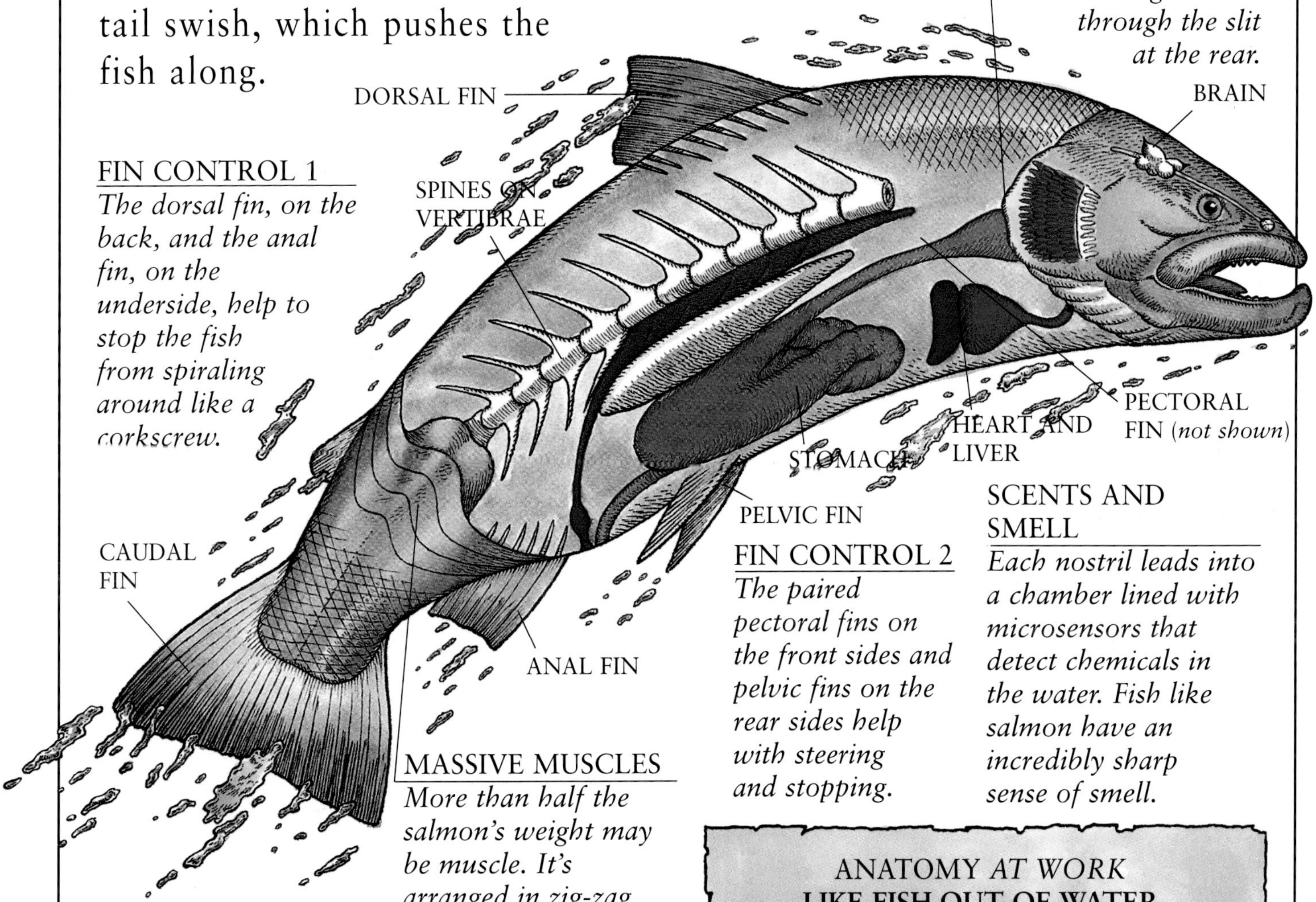

GILL COVER

This bony plate, the operculum, protects the delicate, blood-filled gills underneath. Water that has passed over the gills exits through the slit at the rear.

DORSAL FIN

BRAIN

FIN CONTROL 1

The dorsal fin, on the back, and the anal fin, on the underside, help to stop the fish from spiraling around like a corkscrew.

SPINES ON VERTEBRAE

PECTORAL FIN (*not shown*)

HEART AND LIVER

STOMACH

PELVIC FIN

CAUDAL FIN

SCENTS AND SMELL

Each nostril leads into a chamber lined with microsensors that detect chemicals in the water. Fish like salmon have an incredibly sharp sense of smell.

FIN CONTROL 2

The paired pectoral fins on the front sides and pelvic fins on the rear sides help with steering and stopping.

ANAL FIN

MASSIVE MUSCLES

More than half the salmon's weight may be muscle. It's arranged in zig-zag blocks called myotomes, which join onto the spikes and projections of the vertebral bones.

FIN CONTROL 3

The two-lobed caudal fin at the rear provides the pushing power for swimming. Oh, and it's also called the tail.

LIFE CYCLE OF A SALMON

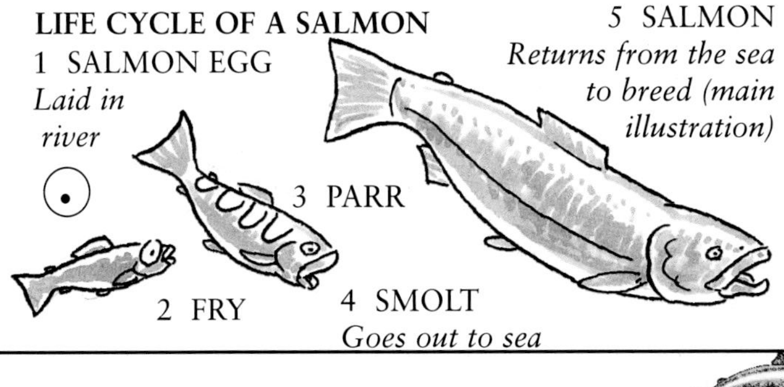

1 SALMON EGG
Laid in river

2 FRY

3 PARR

4 SMOLT
Goes out to sea

5 SALMON
Returns from the sea to breed (main illustration)

ANATOMY AT WORK
LIKE FISH OUT OF WATER

If a normal seawater fish swam from salty water into the fresh water of a river, it would take in the fresh water, swell up, and burst!

If a normal freshwater fish swam from the fresh water of a river into the sea, it would lose most of its body fluids, shrivel up, and die!

MAGLEV

THE NEW AGE OF TRAINS

Conventional trains, running on metal wheels on a track, can reach remarkable speeds - over 300 mph, in the case of the French *Train à Grande Vitesse* or TGV. But even greater speeds may be possible for trains that "fly" a few inches above the rails, supported on a cushion of magnetism. Speeds of more than 250 mph have been achieved by the German Transrapid, and the Japanese MLU and HSST prototypes. The Japanese plan is to build a 310-mile maglev track linking Tokyo to Osaka, in one hour.

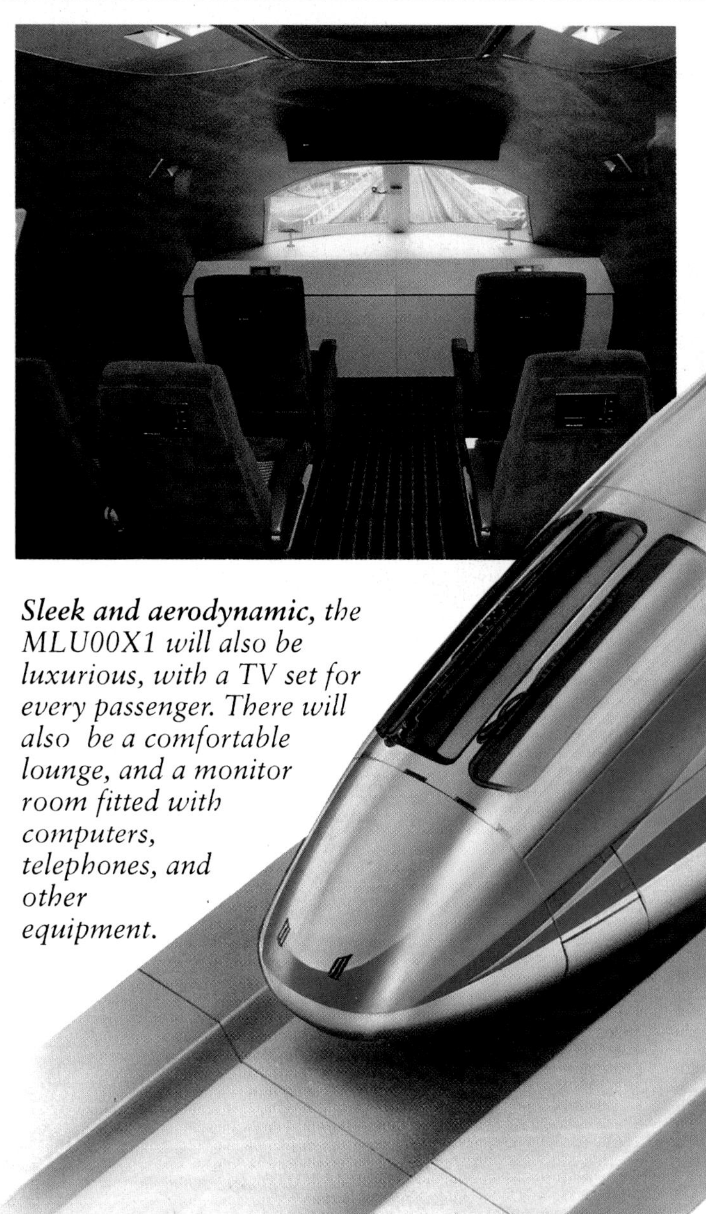

***Sleek and aerodynamic,** the MLU00X1 will also be luxurious, with a TV set for every passenger. There will also be a comfortable lounge, and a monitor room fitted with computers, telephones, and other equipment.*

***The MLU00X1 is the** latest version of the maglev train designed by the Japanese company J.R.Tokai. Test vehicles run very smoothly, with only a slight whine from the electric coils, and gentle thuds caused by air pressure in the gaps between sections.*

***Japan has developed** two distinct maglev systems. In the HSST, electromagnets in the wings of the train are wrapped around the guideway and attracted upward toward it, supporting the train in the same way. It reached a speed of 190 mph.*

The French Railways, SNCF, does not see that levitation is the future of train travel. Its TGV already links the centers of Paris and Lyons, a distance of 265 miles, in two hours, a time that cannot be matched by aircraft. The TGV Atlantique's record of 320 mph is quicker than any maglev train. When the TGV program began in 1969, SNCF assumed that levitation would be needed to exceed 150 mph, but its first experiments failed, and it turned back to traditional rails.

The MLU00X1 is fitted with eight electromagnets to every coach. At rest, the train sits on wheels, but as it begins to move, the electromagnets induce currents in coils mounted on the floor of the guideway. These currents produce magnetic fields that lift the train off its wheels and support it. Propulsion is provided by coils set in the side of the guideway, which repeatedly reverse polarity, to push and pull the train along.

ATTRACTING AND REPELLING

MOVING MAGNETS

Two electromagnets may attract one another, or repel one another: it depends on the direction of the current. In the MLU system, the high-power, superconducting magnets, mounted on the train itself, are responsible for inducing opposing currents in the coils on the guideway. When the current is flowing around both sets of coils, they repel each other, lifting the train by between 4 and 8 inches. This generous clearance makes building the guideway easier, but points are difficult to engineer. Because maglev is still being tested, a question mark remains over whether the powerful magnets will have any health effects on passengers, and how high the costs of the track are likely to be.

In the past twenty years, magnetically- *levitated trains have been developed in Japan, Germany, the U.S., and Britain. One in regular operation in Britain runs along a line just over a mile long linking Birmingham International station to Birmingham airport at a speed of only 15 mph. The German Transrapid system has electromagnets in the wings of the train like the Japanese HSST.*

JESSE JAMES

On April 3, 1882, a killer died and a hero was born – Jesse Woodson James, known as "Dingus" to his friends.

As a slim, handsome 15-year-old, Jesse rode with Confederate leader Charles Quantrill (*left*) in the Civil War. He learned how to steal horses – and kill in cold blood. In 1866, Jesse robbed his first bank. Seven years later his gang held up their first train, stealing some $2,000.

The gang proceeded to rob and shoot its way to national fame, once holding up two stage coaches in a day. Eventually, with a $10,000 reward on his head, Jesse was killed by a shot in the head.

Like the barons of Robin Hood's day, the banks and railroad companies were popular targets, and legend soon made a star of the daring young Jesse. By the close of the 19th century, already the subject of over 270 novels, he

***The railroads** are the enemy of poor farmers in many Wild West stories* (left), *and thus are a fair target for outlaws.*

THE POWER OF LEGEND. To some, Jesse James will always be the dashing youth outwitting his pursuers and fighting against injustice.

The reality is rather different. Jesse was undoubtedly brave, but he was also a cruel and violent man. For 16 years his gang survived by bullying weak officials and depending on the support of relatives to hide them. There is no firm evidence that he ever gave money to anyone in need, or that he fought for the oppressed.

Bandits and Cowboys
In the legendary Wild West, cowboys are glamorous figures who devote themselves to the fight against bandits (left).

But the real cowboys were merely cattle drovers, not high-minded amateur lawmen. Few cowboys even wore a gun!

GOOD-BYE, JESSE!

Bob Ford shot Jesse James as he was straightening a picture at his home in St. Joseph, Kansas. "The gun went off accidentally," he muttered to Jesse's wife, but he still claimed the reward. Jesse's death was front-page news all over the country (*right*). The inscription on the post over his grave read:

Jesse W. James
Died April 3, 1882
Aged 34 years, 6 months, 28 days
Murdered by a coward whose name is not worthy to appear here.

GOOD BYE, JESSE!

The Notorious Outlaw and Bandit, Jesse James, Killed at St. Joseph

BY R. FORD, OF RAY COUNTY,

A Young Man but Twenty-one Years of Age.

THE DEADLY WEAPON USED

Presented to His Slayer by His Victim but a Short Time Since.

A ROBBERY CONTEMPLATED

Of a Bank at Platte City—To Have Taken Place Last Night.

JESSE IN KANSAS CITY

During the Past Year and Residing on One of the Principal Streets.

KANSAS CITY EXCITED

Over the Receipt of the News—Talks with People— Life of the Dead Man.

"PULL THIS TRAIN UP!"

On June 2, 1899, the driver of the Union Pacific Overland Flyer saw a red lantern ahead. Two men jumped aboard and ordered him to separate the passenger cars, and move the train forward.

He refused. "Pull this train up!" the bandit snapped. Refusing again, the driver was beaten. The robbers drove the train themselves, and once over a nearby bridge, blew the safe. Minutes later, Butch Cassidy and the Sundance Kid made their getaway, richer by $30,000!

Jesse James was said to have "invented" train robbery (above) *– but in fact the Reno brothers of Indiana were the first.*

BANDITS COME TO TOWN!

Buffalo Bill's Wild West Show helped spread the myth of the Wild West around the world (*left*). To begin with, he put on costume exhibitions. But realizing that his audiences wanted more action, he staged mock fights between cowboys and indians, and even bandit holdups of trains and stagecoaches.

Colored Light

Color and light are inseparable. The eye perceives color because of three sets of receptors called cones, one for each of the primary colors. All the colors seen on a television screen are made up from colored dots of the three primary colors. The color of an object will depend on which colors of the spectrum it absorbs, and which it reflects. An object looks yellow because the yellow light rays are reflected into the eye, while the rest are absorbed. A black object absorbs all the colors of the spectrum, while a white object reflects them all.

Bright Ideas

Reconstitute white light by spinning a wheel like the one shown here. Color the wheel with colors of the spectrum and then spin it.

Make a hole in one end of a shoe box. Remove the lid and fill the box with objects of different colors. Make 2 or 3 cellophane covers, each a different color. Cover it with one of them, then shine a flashlight through the hole. Look through the cellophane. What color are the objects?

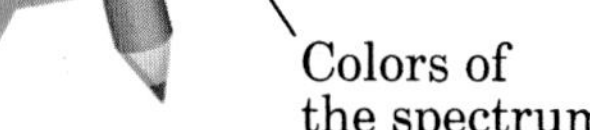

Spotlights

1 and 2. To mix colored light you will need cellophane filters in the three primary colors – green, red, and blue. Attach these filters to three long, cardboard tubes. Make sure the filters cover the end of each tube completely.

1

Why It Works

We have discovered by splitting light that each color has a different wavelength. Mixing colored lights produces new colors by adding light of different wavelengths. Colored light mixtures are sometimes called additive color mixtures or color by addition. Luminous sources of light, like color televisions, combine colors by mixing very small dots of light. Black means the absence of light because there are no colors to mix together. When red, green, and blue lights are combined, white light is the result. A secondary color is an equal mixture of two primary colors. Red and green lights shining onto a white object will make it appear to be yellow. Any two colors of light that form white light when mixed are called complementary. Other colors are formed by mixing the primary colors in different proportions.

3. Place a large sheet of white oak tag on the floor in a darkened room. Three people need to hold the tubes at right angles to the floor while shining a flashlight into the top of each. The beams of light should be directed onto the white oak tag.

4. Find out how to make new colors by positioning the three lights in such a way as to produce a variety of combinations. Where the three combine, white light is produced.

STRAIGHT AIRS

For your first air, find a small jump with a smooth, gentle landing. Practice going over the jump without taking air first. When you feel more confident, approach, or hit, the jump a little faster, and ollie (*see below*) as you get to the top. Make sure that your board is not on an edge when you take off or you will become unbalanced in the air.

Once you are used to being in the air, try some grabs — different ways of holding the board while you are in the air. As you take off, reach down with your back hand and grab in between your feet, toe-edge — this is an "indie."

HOW DOES THIS GRAB YOU?

Add a little something to your airs...

- ❄ Chicken salad – your front hand grabs between your feet and through your legs, heel-edge.
- ❄ Indie – your back hand grabs between your feet, toe-edge.
- ❄ Method – from behind, your front hand grabs between your feet, heel-edge.
- ❄ Mute – your front hand grabs between your feet, toe-edge.
- ❄ Roast beef – your back hand grabs between your feet and through your legs, heel-edge.
- ❄ Stale fish – from behind, your back hand grabs between your feet, heel-edge.

Style an air by "boning" it (left) *— straightening one leg during a trick and holding the position while you are in the air.*

1

2

OLLIEING

Before you learn to jump, you need to learn to ollie. This is a basic trick that propels you into the air, without using a launch or hit. Ollieing is a lot of fun and it's a great way to keep your balance on the board.

Before you ollie on a slope, practice on flat ground.

Start in your ready position, with your hands in front of you. Begin moving in a straight line. Rock your weight onto your back foot 1 . *Spring forward and up off the tail of your board* 2 .

Snowboarding trickery

Once you are confident and safe with the basic moves, you can try some tricks from airs to ollies. Before you start any trick or variation, remember to use your ready position — without it you are more likely to lose control when you land. Tricks also look cooler and more stylish if the rider seems to be in control, without his or her arms and hands waving all over the place!

As you develop your ability to perform tricks, you can start to polish your own style. Take a look at other more experienced riders and try to copy their moves — but only attempt what you can do safely. Make up your own tricks and moves — with names too!

FAKING IT OR SWITCHING IT? Riding fakie is riding backward (tail first) or leading with the foot that usually follows. The technique for riding fakie is similar to that for riding forward (nose first), except that you twist more with your hips. Make sure that you are looking in the direction in which you want to travel, checking that there are no people or obstacles in your way. Try to keep your weight centered, without leaning too far forward. Practice riding fakie because it will help you later to learn some harder tricks. If you start a trick, such as an ollie (above), tail first, you are riding switch.

Use your arms for balance while in the air 3*, and as you approach the landing* 4*. Land nose first* 5*.*

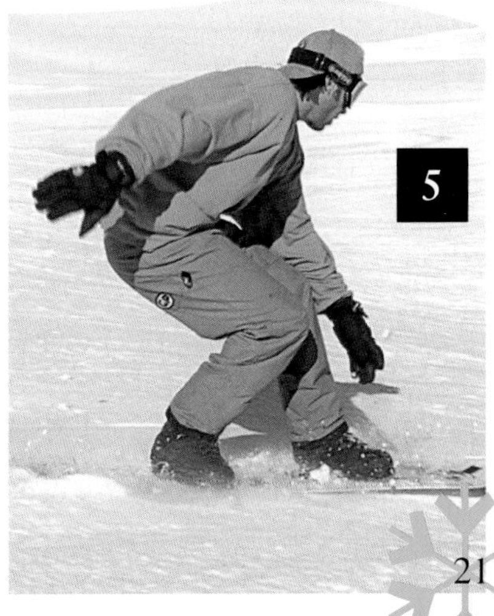

Frozen waters

"The decks broke up, the great beams snapping with a noise like gunfire." ***Ernest Shackleton, Antarctica, 1914***

The freezing waters around Antarctica can be treacherous. In summer, the seas are dotted with large chunks of floating ice (*right*) and, in winter, the water's surface freezes into one continuous sheet of ice.

Here, one of the most incredible real-life adventures took place. In 1914, Irish explorer Ernest Shackleton was sailing through the Weddell Sea, a large gulf that cuts into mainland Antarctica. Without warning, huge sheets of ice crushed his ship, smashing its beams like matchsticks. The 28-strong crew were forced to abandon ship and set up camp on the drifting ice, but gale-force winds soon ripped their tents to shreds. Surviving on penguin meat and seaweed, food supplies soon became scarce and Shackleton was forced to lead his crew on an extraordinary trek over frozen seas to Elephant Island, a tiny land mass about 620 miles (1,000 km) below South America. Leaving some men there, he continued with five others to South Georgia Island where, after a journey of almost 1,800 miles (2,880 km), he finally reached a whaling station. The station's commander who had seen them off two years before, now no longer recognized them as they looked so wild. All 28 crew were rescued.

The sinking of the *Titanic* prompted the setting up of a special Ice Patrol to warn ships of potentially dangerous icebergs.

WHAT'S IN A NAME?

*Greenland is not green (except for its coastal areas in summer), and about 85 percent of its "land" is covered by ice (*above*). The country was named by Viking explorers who wished to attract settlers. Natives sail in narrow canoelike boats that are the ideal shape for working their way through broken-up ice.*

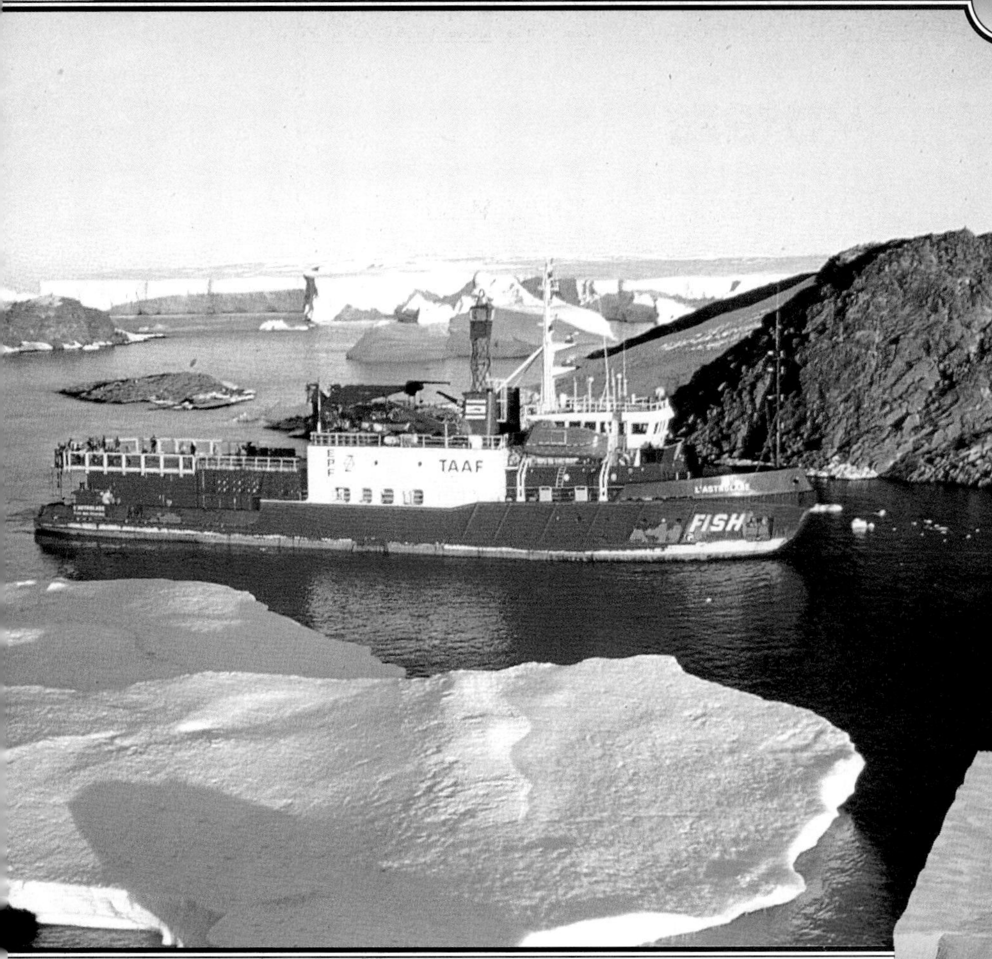

This boat sails between floating ice in Arctic waters (*above*). If a boat gets stuck, rescue boats called icebreakers may have to cut it free.

ARCTIC ACCIDENT-ZONES

*Icebergs are dangerous because they are solid and most of their immense size is hidden beneath the water (*below*). Besides icebergs, the other main danger for ships in arctic waters is floating pack ice. If a ship gets stuck working its way through the huge broken sheets (*left*), it can be crushed to pieces as the ice pushes against it.*

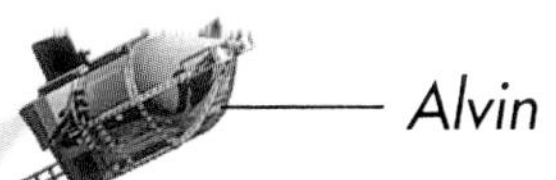

THE WRECK OF THE *TITANIC*

In 1986, the murky depths of the north Atlantic Ocean were spot-lighted by bright beams from the small, three-person submersible, Alvin *(left).*

As the mud clouds cleared, a dark shape appeared. It was the bow of the Titanic. *In 1912, this ocean liner had sunk in just three hours when it hit an iceberg on its first voyage across the Atlantic. Of the 2,220 people on board, more than 1,500 died. Many of these drowned in the icy, black waters as there were only enough lifeboats for half of the passengers.*

The genius of Bach

J.S. BACH (1685-1750)
MIXED GROUPS
Brandenburg Concertos (6)
orchestral suites (4)
Musical Offering
CONCERTOS
two violins
violin solo (2)
harpsichord (2)
SONATAS
violin (6)
flute (3)
viola da gamba (3)
SOLO STRINGS
cello suites (6)
violin sonatas and partitas (6)
KEYBOARD
French Suites (6)
English Suites (6)
Italian Concerto
Goldberg Variations
48 Preludes and Fugues
Art of Fugue
ORGAN
choral preludes (143)
toccatas
preludes and fugues (26)
CHORAL WORKS
mass in B minor
St. Matthew Passion
St. John Passion
Christmas Oratorio
over 200 church cantatas

HANS (GREAT GRANDFATHER) JOHANN CHRISTOPH (UNCLE) JOHANN AMBROSIUS (FATHER) JOHANN SEBASTIAN

J. S. Bach was the most famous member of a musical dynasty. His father taught him the violin and viola; his brother probably taught him the clavier. One very early Bach was Hans, born c. 1550.

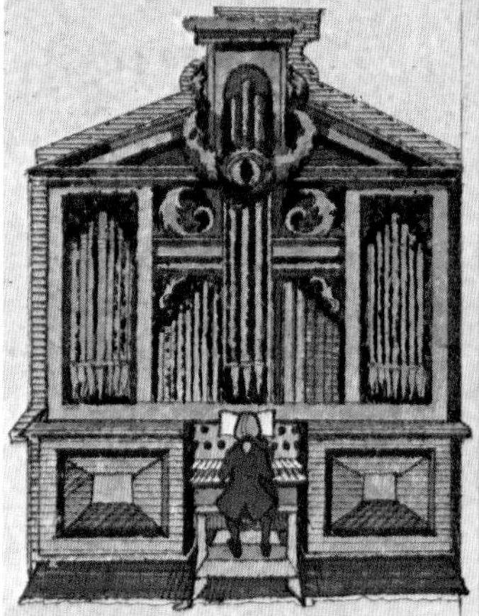

Bach's organ music, much of which was composed at Weimar in 1708-17, still forms the basis of the organist's repertory. His attitudes to his church music is shown by the initials with which he began and ended his works: J.J., standing for *Jesu, Juva* ("Jesus help me") at the beginning, and S.D.G., *Soli Deo Gloria* ("Glory to God Alone") at the end of a piece.

Bach spent the years 1717-1723 working for the Prince of Anhalt-Cöthen, writing orchestral and chamber music, and his first set of 24 keyboard preludes and fugues. From Cöthen he moved to Leipzig, where he composed his greatest choral works, among them the Mass in B minor.

Wilhelm Friedemann was J.S. Bach's eldest son. Although an extremely able musician, in later life he took to drink and died in poverty.

Johann Christian, J.S. Bach's eleventh son, is usually known as "the English Bach." Mozart, aged eight, played with him in London in 1764.

Carl Philipp Emanuel, J.S. Bach's third son, was court composer to Frederick the Great of Prussia. The king, who was ahead of his time in having pianos instead of harpsichords, was delighted when J.S. Bach came to play for him.

Almost 80 years ater Bach's death, Felix Mendelssohn (left) revived the St. Matthew Passion, and began the rediscovery of Bach.

When Felix Mendelssohn conducted Bach's *St. Matthew Passion* in Berlin on March 11, 1829, he brought into the light of day a masterpiece that had been forgotten for a century. The rediscovery of Bach was underway. Bach is now so much a part of everyday musical life – played straight, jazzed up, computerized, or turned into pop – that it seems incredible that he had to be "rediscovered" at all. Until Mendelssohn's epoch-making performance, Bach had been known almost entirely as a writer of learned preludes and fugues for keyboard. This was the way he was known to Haydn, Mozart, and Beethoven.

Johann Sebastian Bach was born in 1685 – a vintage year for composers, as Handel and Scarlatti were both born in the same year. They went on to international fame and fortune, but Bach stayed in the restricted area of northern Germany. The opera composer Handel and the brilliant harpsichordist Scarlatti looked toward the future, while Bach was rooted in the past. His attitude to music was that of a medieval craftsman, working in a long-established family tradition. "I have had to work hard," he said, adding, "anyone who works just as hard will get just as far." His portraits show a solid, respectable citizen, which is exactly what he was. From 1723 until his death in 1750, he was cantor (head of music) at St. Thomas's School in Leipzig, responsible for training the boys and for providing the music for church services. Apart from his quarrels with the headmaster of St. Thomas's and battles with the Leipzig Town Council, Bach's life was uneventful – ideal conditions for an enormous musical output that has been described as more like an industrial concern than the work of a single man.

Bach's steady attitude to his work was paralleled by a steady family life unique among the great composers. He married twice and had 20 children, three of whom grew up to become the most famous composers of their day, driving their father's memory into the shade. One of the most delightful aspects of Bach's character is shown by the *Little Clavier Books*, which he wrote for his son Wilhelm Friedemann, and his second wife Anna Magdalena. They contain simple pieces still taught today.

He combined his down-to-earth approach to composition with a deep religious faith. Bach was a Lutheran Protestant, brought up in the strong religious traditions of northern Germany. Apart from his five settings of the Passion story, of which only two (the *St. John* and *St. Matthew Passion*) survive, he wrote sets of church cantatas for every Sunday in the calendar.

Before his final move to Leipzig, Bach had a varied musical career. At the age of 18 he was appointed organist at Arnstadt, where he gained his mastery of church music and, on one occasion, was reproved by the authorities for inviting a "strange maiden" into the organ loft. He spent nine years as court organist at Weimar, and at the end of his time there was imprisoned for a month for "stubbornly forcing the issue of his dismissal." He spent six happy years at Cöthen as *Kapellmeister* (musical director), writing the six masterly *Brandenburg Concertos* and the first of his two books of keyboard preludes and fugues that make up the *Well-Tempered Clavier* ("clavier" means simply "keyboard").

His amazing skill as an improviser was shown most vividly toward the end of his life, in 1747, when he visited King Frederick the Great of Prussia. Frederick was a keen flute player and amateur composer. When Bach arrived at the court in Potsdam he was given no time to change his clothes, but was asked by Frederick to sit down at one of his pianos and improvise on a theme the king himself had written. Bach obliged with a three-part fugue straight out of his head. On his return to Leipzig, he composed a set of canons and fugues on the royal theme, together with a sonata for flute, violin, and keyboard, which he sent off to Frederick as his *Musical Offering*. In this work learning and grace go hand in hand. Bach's "last will and testament," musically speaking, was the gigantic *Art of Fugue*, in which he summed up a lifetime's mastery of counterpoint (the skill of combining horizontal lines of music). He died before the work was finished.

Bach's sons composed in a new, lighthearted style known as the *galant*, and their father's learning went underground for a while. But it soon burst forth again. "Johann Sebastian, mighty Bach," as the poet Dylan Thomas called him, now rules unchallenged as the most all-embracing intellect in musical history.

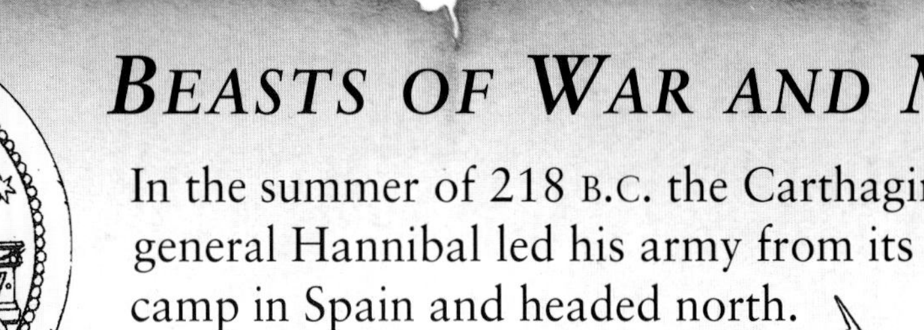

BEASTS OF WAR AND MYTH

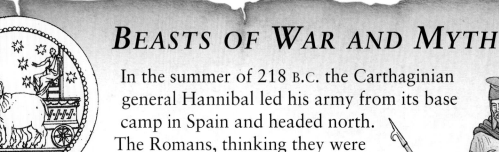

In the summer of 218 B.C. the Carthaginian general Hannibal led his army from its base camp in Spain and headed north. The Romans, thinking they were safe for that campaigning season, launched an attack across the Mediterranean on Hannibal's Spanish headquarters. It proved to be a disastrous mistake.

Hannibal took his 30,000 men, horses, and 37 elephants (see coin, *above*) across the Pyrenees and crushed the Gauls. In October, to everyone's amazement, he decided to take the Little St. Bernard Pass into Italy and launch a surprise attack on Rome itself. Fifteen days later he was in Italy, elephants and all!

Assisted by his war beasts, Hannibal won a series of brilliant victories. But in the end, deprived of support and reinforcements, he had to return home without capturing Rome.

STEEDS OF MYTH. The importance of horses to humans is reflected by their appearance in numerous legends. The mythical centaurs were half human, half horse inhabitants of the wooded foothills. They have been popular figures in folklore since the time of the ancient Greeks.

***Pegasus** was a mythical winged horse born out of the blood of the monstrous snake-haired Medusa.*

THE TROJAN HORSE

The world's most famous horse appears in a story from Homer's epic poem, *The Odyssey*. It was a huge model built by the Greeks for their enemies, the citizens of Troy. Odysseus and his Greek warriors hid inside the horse while the Greek army sailed away. Then the Trojans pulled the horse into the city.

Quick Victory
Once the horse was inside the walls, the Greeks opened the city gates. Troy fell soon afterward.

THE MYTHICAL UNICORN is a beautiful white horse with a single horn growing from its forehead (depicted *right* in the film *Legend*). Drinking from the horn was believed to give protection from illness.

Trunk Route (left)
The passes were blocked by snow when Hannibal led his war elephants through the Alps into Italy, fighting off local tribesmen as he went.

HANNIBAL'S HEAVIES

Once on the Italian plain, the elephants proved a useful shock tactic. But they needed to be cared for and were too slow and cumbersome to win a battle on their own.

THE SWEET SMELL OF SUCCESS!

In a story told by the Greek historian Herodotus, when Cyrus the Great of Persia's army met that of the Lydian king Croesus, the horrible smell of Cyrus' camels terrified the Lydian horses!

When their horses ran away, the Lydian cavalry were forced to jump down and fight on foot, and were soon beaten by Cyrus' troops.

Conquering Camels (right)
Camels were also used by the Arab soldiers of the 7th-8th centuries A.D. They built a vast Muslim empire stretching from Spain to Persia.

BLACK HOLES • Doors to other universes or deadly dead ends?

Above *Cosmic researcher, Stephen Hawking, thinks the universe is peppered with black holes of all sizes, large and small.*

When we launch a rocket into space, we need to make it move fast enough to escape the pull of the Earth's gravity. If Earth were heavier or denser (more tightly packed), our rocket would need to go faster. Now imagine an object that is so heavy and dense that not even light — the fastest thing in the universe — can travel quickly enough to escape it. An object like this is called a black hole.

DEAD STARS

Black holes aren't just science fiction — scientists think they really do exist. They could be formed when massive stars die, for example. Dying stars collapse in on themselves to leave super-heavy, super-dense remains. The remains could become so tightly packed, they form a black hole.

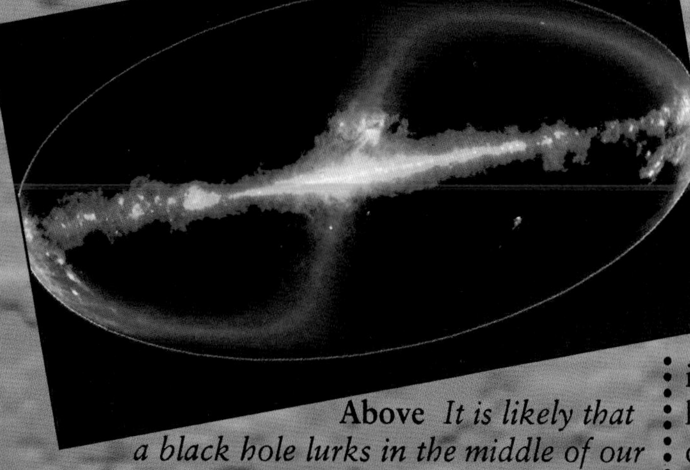

Above *It is likely that a black hole lurks in the middle of our own galaxy, the Milky Way. Recent telescope images have shown that many stars are being pulled toward an invisible object at the center.*

TOMORROW IS YESTERDAY

Some theorists have imagined how black holes could work like time machines. The gravity around a black hole could be so great that it would cause time and space to fold back on itself, creating a loop. If you traveled into this loop, you could find that time doesn't go forward as usual, but doubles back on itself. So you'd end up going back in time!

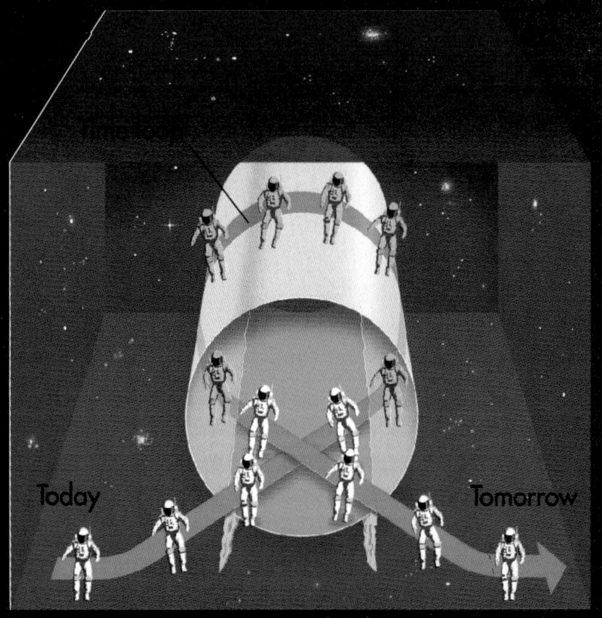

IN THE DARK

We will never be able to see a black hole as light cannot escape from it. But we can spot a black hole in action. As it creates a huge gravitational force, it pulls gas clouds and other stars toward it. Matter spiraling into a black hole heats up, giving off X rays that we can detect.

People have come up with lots of imaginative ideas about travel through black holes. Some suggest they could be gateways to other times or universes (see box *above*). But Stephen Hawking offers a word of caution. He doesn't think anyone could survive such journeys, even if they were possible.

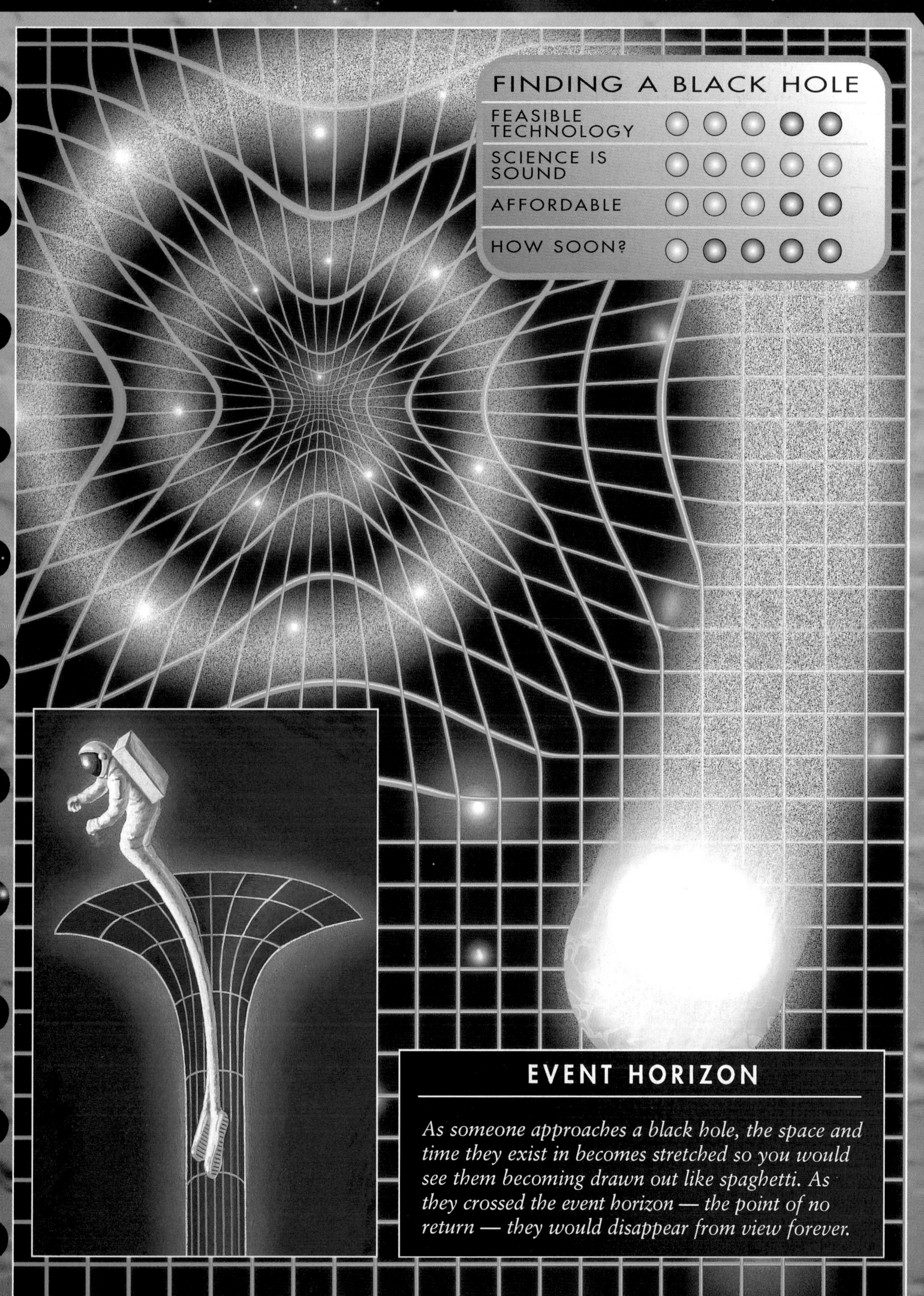

EVENT HORIZON

As someone approaches a black hole, the space and time they exist in becomes stretched so you would see them becoming drawn out like spaghetti. As they crossed the event horizon — the point of no return — they would disappear from view forever.

CANALS, BRIDGES, AND TUNNELS

All forms of transportation are faced with natural obstacles, and engineers have had to find ways of overcoming them. The ancient Greeks built canals across land as shortcuts for ships and the Romans invented aqueducts – bridges that carried water across valleys. The Romans also coined the word "engineer" from the Latin word *ingenium,* meaning genius. Modern engineering began in the 18th century with the Industrial Revolution. New materials such as iron and steel began to replace stone and brick. The first bridge built entirely of iron (*right*) was finished in 1780 at Ironbridge, England.

EARLY CANALS
The ancient Egyptians (*above*) built canals to irrigate crops in areas that received very little water. Their knowledge of canal-building spread throughout the Middle East to Europe.

towpath

CANAL BOATS
Before boats were fitted with engines, they were towed by horses, who walked alongside on paths known as "towpaths" (*above*). Until the railroads, canals were vital for the transportation of heavy and fragile goods.

CANALS FOR COAL

Canals and rivers carry huge barges carrying thousands of tons of cargo – an inland country such as Switzerland relies on the Rhine River to take goods through Germany to the ocean. Some canals were originally used to transport raw materials like coal, and are now used mostly for canal-boat vacations.

THE SUEZ CANAL
The 114-mile- (184-km-) long Suez Canal (*below*), opened in 1869, cuts through Egypt to link the Mediterranean Sea with the Red Sea. This great feat of engineering took ten years to build. It cut thousands of miles off the trip from India and the Far East to Europe. Today it is a vital route for oil tankers.

LESSEPS

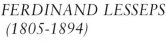

FERDINAND LESSEPS (1805-1894)
A brilliant French engineer, Lesseps forwarded the idea of the Suez Canal after visiting Egypt. On its completion he was acclaimed as a great hero.

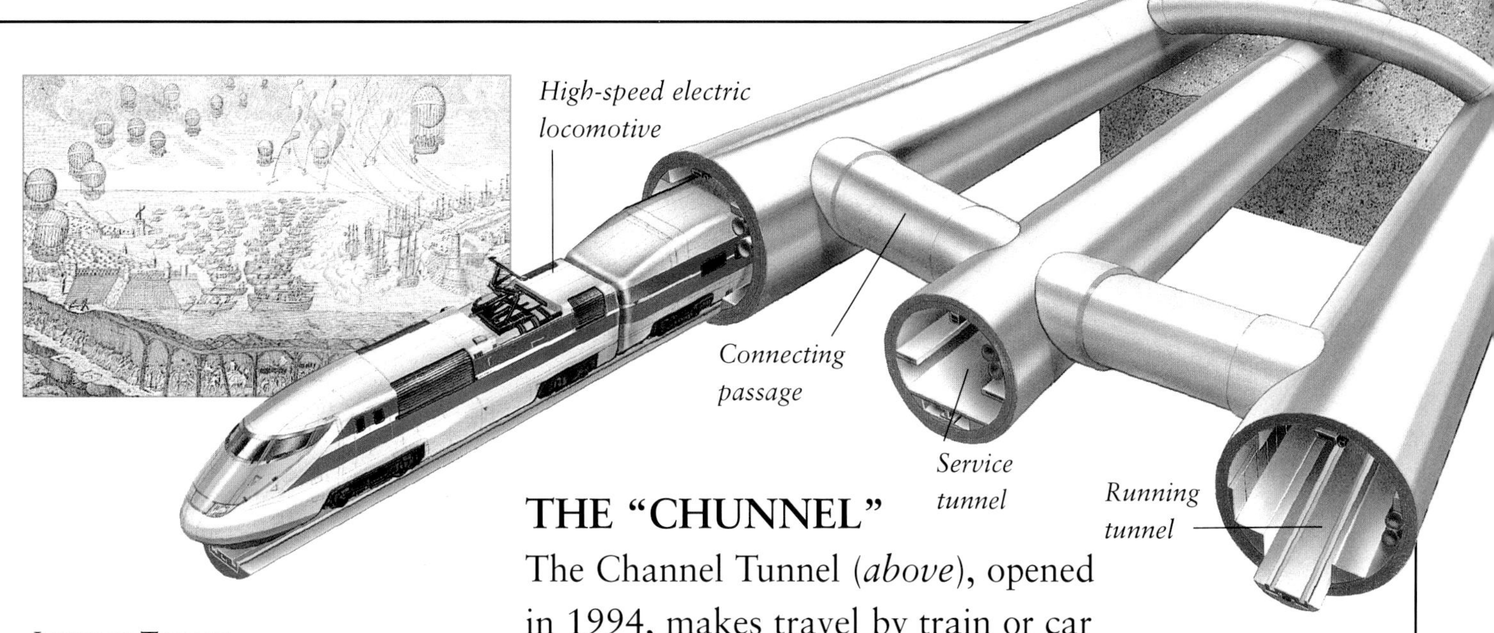

THE "CHUNNEL"

The Channel Tunnel (*above*), opened in 1994, makes travel by train or car between Britain and France possible in about 30 minutes. The tunnel is 31 miles (50 kilometers) long – just 3.5 miles (4 kilometers) shorter than the longest tunnel in the world, at Seikan in Japan.

INVASION THREAT
The first attempt to bore under the English Channel was in 1880 – but progress was halted because of the supposed threat to British defenses (*above left*)!

TOWER BRIDGE
Tower Bridge, London (*left*), is a famous example of a bascule bridge – one in which the bridge tilts upward to let ships pass. Cars drive across when the bridge is down.

FROM LOGS TO SUSPENSION

The first bridges were made of pieces of wood laid across streams. As road travel and railroads increased, bridge building improved. The longest bridges – suspension bridges, such as this one in Normandy, France (*right*) – are held in place by cables supported by towers at each end. San Francisco's Golden Gate Bridge, opened in 1937, has a span of 4,200 feet (1,280 meters).

BUILDING BRIDGES
Long bridges are built in stages (*left*). The weight of each section is supported by intermediate piers crowned with towers, from which parallel cables are suspended.

BUTTERFLIES AND MOTHS

Butterflies and moths are called Lepidoptera, which means scale-wings. Their wings are covered with tiny scales, arranged like roof-tiles. Some scales have beautiful colors, and others bend light, like crystals, to give a rainbow sheen. Butterflies are generally more colorful than moths. They fly in the daytime, and hold their wings together upright when resting. Their antennae are club-shaped. Moths are active at night. They hold their dull-colored wings flat over their backs when resting. Some male moths have feathery antennae. Butterflies and moths undergo complete metamorphosis.

Owl butterfly (*Caligo oileus*)

Siderone galanthis

Butterfly mimics

The colorful markings on some butterflies' wings are warning colors, to deter predators. Poisonous insects advertise their distastefulness in this way. Birds soon learn to recognize these species and avoid them. Different species of poisonous moths or butterflies from the same region reinforce the message, by having very similar patterns and wing shapes. In Peru, two poisonous species, of heliconius and podotricha butterflies, look alike. This is called Mullerian mimicry (imitation). Some other butterflies which are not poisonous 'cheat' by mimicking the warning patterns of poisonous species. In North America, a species of harmless viceroy butterfly looks very like the poisonous monarch butterfly. This is called Batesian mimicry.

Podotricha telesiphe

Heliconius telesiphe

Viceroy

Monarch

Butterflies and moths, like all insects, are cold-blooded. Their body temperature is about as warm or cold as their surroundings, since they cannot generate their own body heat, as warm-blooded mammals and birds can. Butterflies spread their wings in the sunshine to warm up and hide in the shade when they are too hot. Moths have furry bodies to retain the heat they absorb during the day, so that they can fly at night.

Disgusting disguises

The young of many moths and butterflies camouflage or disguise themselves as inedible objects, to avoid being eaten by predators. Geometer moth caterpillars look like twigs, and position themselves on branches so as to complete their disguise. The European black hairstreak chrysalis and the hawkmoth caterpillar from Central America (right) pretend to be unpleasant bird droppings.

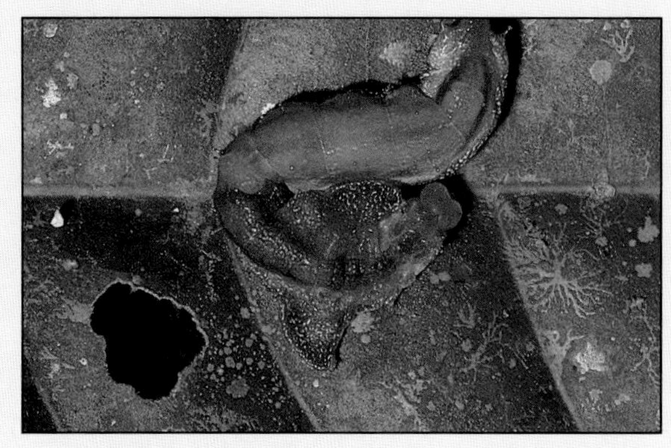

Large elephant hawkmoth

Morpho butterfly (*Morpho menelaus*)

Dasyopthalma rusina

Adapting to industry

The peppered moth is an example of how, over many generations, some species of insects are able to adapt their camouflage to fit in with a changing environment. The normal form of the peppered moth is creamy with dark speckles, difficult to see on the bark of trees. But following the Industrial Revolution in the 19th century, a new form of dark moth became common, which could hide on sooty bark.

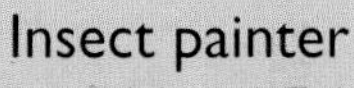

Insect painter

Jean Henri Fabré (1823-1915) lived in Provence in France. He was a village school teacher before he turned to entomology, the study of insects. But he did not collect dead insects, like many naturalists of the time. He studied their habits by watching them in the wild.

Fabré wrote many books on insect behavior, describing each detail of their lives. He also left behind many beautiful watercolor paintings of the species he had studied.

Madame Butterfly

The opera *Madame Butterfly* was written by an Italian composer, Giacomo Puccini, in 1904. It tells of a tragic love affair between an American naval officer, Pinkerton, and a Japanese girl, Butterfly. They marry, but Pinkerton leaves, and returns years later with a new wife. Puccini's beautiful melodies convey the drama, passion and tragedy of the story.

WARTIME

The fighting took place in theaters of war, such as the Western, Eastern, and Middle Eastern Theaters. Africa and the Far East staged side shows.

Machines mattered more than muscles. Shells crumpled the landscape, gas poisoned the air, and the earth spat bullets. Gray battleships patrolled the waves, submarines slinked below. The best soldiers could do was survive. Eight million failed.

When it began, World War I (1914-1918) seemed an over-by-Christmas type of war. When people saw what it really was, it was too late to stop. The team rosters read:

Team A (round hats)	***Team B (pointed hats)***
France, Britain, Russia, United States (1917), Italy, and friends.	*Germany, Austria-Hungary, Turkey, and friends.*

The war involved everyone. Everyone made or threw bombs or had them fired at them. Both sides sat in muddy trenches waiting for the other to give up.

If someone cheated by trying to move, they were stopped dead. Since no one wanted to give up, the war went on for four years.

Helped by the United States, Team A finally overwhelmed Team B. By 1918, B's citizens were starving, too so their politicians made peace.

MAKING TRACKS

The troops stored their water in metal tanks. When these were empty, the British put them on caterpillar tracks, attached engines and guns, and chugged about in them.

Team A met at Versailles and decided the war had been Team B's fault. Their money and new countries like Czechoslovakia were taken from them. A Winners' Club (League of Nations) was formed, but the United States refused to join.

JAZZ TIME

HAPPILY EVER AFTER?
In his fairytale "The 14 Points," President Woodrow Wilson explained in 1919 how the world could be happy and safe forever and ever. But politicians and generals just didn't want to listen.

Gangster's Paradise
When the United States banned the manufacture and sale of alcohol (1919–1933), gangster Al Capone grinned all over his scarred face. Criminals made a killing from the illegal liquor trade.

Bright young things held a 10-year party to forget the war and the famine and disease that followed. They swapped long faces for short skirts and roared into the 1920s on a high of jazz and champagne. Because they had behaved like men during the war, women were allowed to continue to do "manly" things like wearing pants and voting.

Peace-loving governments bought blackboards, indoor toilets, and stethoscopes.
Factories turned out little black cars instead of big black bombs. Theaters (*below*) sold an evening of fairyland, silent at first, but soon with music and talking (1927).

Americans held the biggest party. We had more cars and theaters – but no champagne because we had given up drinking along with everything else European. All we wanted with the Old World was to sell it cornflakes and little black cars.

The Germans of the easy-going Weimar Republic came late to the party. They were broke because no one wanted suitcases stuffed with their cheap money. Soaring inflation meant that a loaf of bread cost a wheelbarrow full of marks.
In the late 1920s, they cheered up, dressed up in leather shorts, and joined in the fun.

By 1929, World War I seemed just a nasty dream.

ELECTRICITY AND MAGNETISM

There are many natural sources of electricity and magnetism on planet Earth that have existed since the beginning of time. In Greek mythology, lightning, which is a form of static electricity, was used by gods such as Zeus (above) to impose authority on mortals. A magnetic field called the magnetosphere surrounds the Earth, stretching over 36,000 miles (60,000 kilometres) into space. The Earth's magnetic poles move a few inches each year – over millions of years, their positions have even reversed direction!

Finding your way

A compass needle is a tiny magnet, which always points to the Earth's magnetic poles. A map does not tell you which direction you are traveling in, but with the help of a compass, you can find your way. To use a compass with a map, place the compass on top of the map. Turn the map around until the north arrow on the map points in the same direction as the compass needle.

Magnetic Earth

Scientists believe that the Earth's magnetic field is produced by the molten iron core at the center of the Earth. This metal core has melted because of the very high temperatures there. As the Earth rotates (below), electric currents are created in the core. This produces the magnetic field. Scientists believe this works in a way similar to producing electricity in a power station.

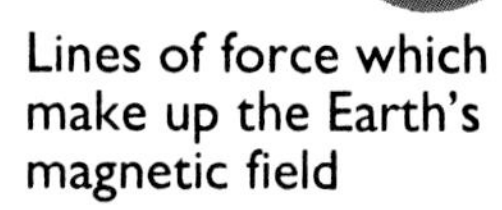

Lines of force which make up the Earth's magnetic field

Clues to the past

Over millions of years, hot liquid rock rising and sinking beneath the Earth's continents has caused them to drift about the Earth's surface. This liquid rock has broken through the surface along ridges in the middle of the ocean floor. As the liquid cools down, magnetic material in the rock lines up with the Earth's magnetic field. The rocks have set in opposite directions, providing evidence that over time the Earth's magnetic field has changed direction (right).

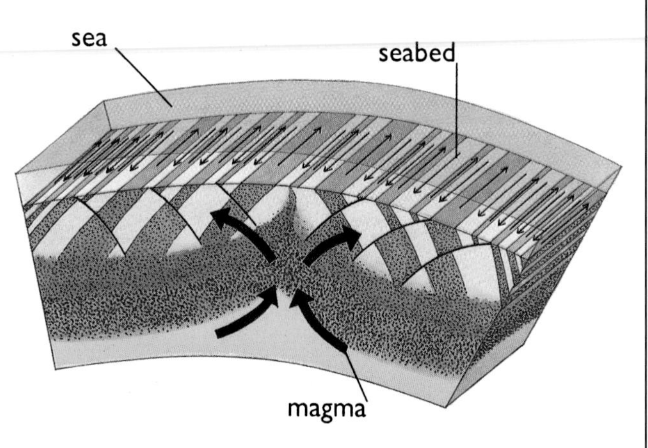

Electric fishes

About 500 species of fish produce an electric field from special muscles with columns of waferlike cells, which are a bit like tiny living batteries. Species such as the elephant nose fish give off almost continuous electric charges to help them navigate and communicate. Electric eels, rays (left), and catfish have large electric organs, which can give off powerful bursts of electricity, enough to stun a person or kill a small fish. Sharks (right) pick up electrical signals from the muscles of fish. They can home in on their prey with deadly accuracy.

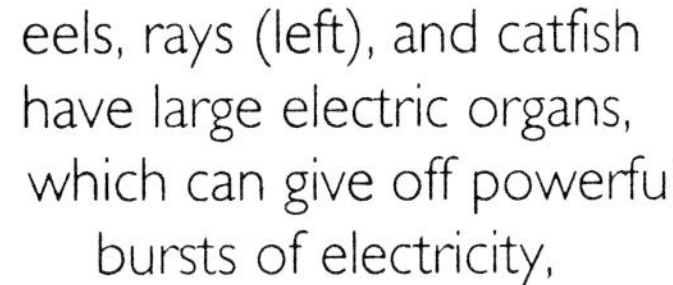

Electricity in the sky

Lightning is a huge spark of static electricity. It builds up inside storm clouds when small drops of water and ice rub against each other. Storm clouds build up either positive or negative charges as their particles are rubbed in different ways. When negative and positive clouds get near each other, giant sparks jump between them. These can leap to the ground, producing a flash of lightning. An American inventor called Benjamin Franklin (1706-1790, right) showed that a bolt of lightning was really a spark of electricity. In 1752, he flew a kite during a storm. Lightning flowed down the kite string, making a small spark on a metal key at the bottom of the string. This dangerous experiment led to the invention of lightning conductors – metal strips running from the top of a building to the ground. If lightning strikes the building, they carry the electricity safely to the ground. The top of a conductor (left) can be bent by the lightning's heat.

Animal migration

Many animals make long migratory journeys to find food or to avoid bad weather. They can sense the Earth's magnetic field, which helps keep them on the right course. In Australia, compass termites protect their nests from the Sun's heat by building them facing north to south.

Force fields in space

Other planets in our solar system also have magnetic fields. Space probes sent out from planet Earth have discovered magnetic fields around the planets of Mercury, Jupiter, Saturn and Uranus.

The magnetic fields around Jupiter (left) are about 4,000 times greater than those around the Earth. These huge magnetic fields trap clouds of particles.

GOLF

In the 14th century, *kolven,* a game with a stick and a ball, was widely played in the Netherlands. This was probably the first kind of golf. Shortly afterward, bandy ball *(see below)* was invented in England.

Modern golf originated in Scotland in the 15th century, from where it was taken to Europe by King James VI (James I of Britain). The first golf club, Saint Andrew's in Scotland, was founded in 1754. Women began to play golf in the 19th century, and it soon became equally popular among men and women.

THE HASKELL BALL
In 1902, Coburn Haskell invented a ball made of rubber strips wound around a rubber core, a design that is still used today. The dimples on the ball increase the distance and accuracy of its flight.

WOODS
Different golf clubs are used for different shots. Woods, which are designed to hit the ball for long distances, are made of wood – or plastic, graphite, or metal!

IRONS
There are nine different types of irons, designed to give the ball height.

JOIN THE CLUB

By the end of the 19th century, modern golf was popular throughout Europe and Scottish emigrants had brought the game to the United States and other countries. Golf was mainly popular among wealthy people, because they had the time to spend whole days playing and because club membership and golf equipment were expensive. Unfortunately, this is still true today. Modern golf courses are carefully designed and maintained, and there are thousands worldwide, with new courses opening every day. The longest course is the International Golf Club in Massachusetts. Players have to travel 25,200 feet (7,612 m) to play its eighteen holes!

BANDY BALL
The game that seems closest to golf is bandy ball *(above)*, played in 16th-century England, but it was probably more like hockey. Players used curved sticks to hit a ball into a goal.

LOOK OUT!
Early golfers wore a red coat or shirt *(below)*, to avoid hitting each other with the balls. Today, players shout "fore!" as they make a shot, to warn other people on the course.

Tee

Rough

Fairway

Wedges
These are needed when the ball lands in a sand bunker (ditch). The player uses a wedge to "chip" the ball up and over the edge of the bunker.

Putters
These are flat-ended clubs for rolling the ball over short distances on the green (where the hole is located).

The Genteel Sport
Croquet *(right)*, in which players use a long mallet to hit a wooden ball through a series of hoops, originated in Ireland in the early 1800s and soon became a very popular garden game. Today, croquet is played as an organized sport in South Africa, New Zealand, the United States, Australia, and England.

Competitive Play
Golf competitions are now very important. Every two years since 1927, professional golf players in the United States and England have played in the Ryder Cup competition. A European team replaced England in 1979. Top golf players can earn huge amounts of money for winning a contest – sometimes as much as $350,000 – and through sponsorship deals from various

WHAT TO WEAR

Early players wore formal outfits, but since the 1930s people have worn much more casual clothes. Modern golfers wear brightly patterned sweaters and pants and a visor or cap to keep the sun out of their eyes. They wear a glove on their left hand to help them grip the club firmly, and special shoes *(left)* to stop their feet from slipping while they take their shots. Professional golfers usually display sponsors' names on their clothes.

JOYCE WETHERED
(b. 1901) *Wethered is regarded as one of the best golfers ever. In five English Ladies' Championships in a row, she played 33 matches – and won every single one. She made similar achievements in many other contests. Her amazing power and accuracy revolutionized women's golf.*

The Course
Most golf courses have 18 holes, with obstacles such as bunkers, water-filled ditches, and trees. Players have to hit the ball into each hole. The winner is the player who completes the course by taking the fewest strokes at the ball.

Bunker
Green
Pin (hole)

CHARCOAL, CONTÉ, AND CRAYON

Getting a grip
How you hold your drawing implement makes a big difference to the kind of line you produce. In general, if you hold your implement in the middle in a relaxed way, your arm muscles will relax, and the line you produce will be relaxed, too. If you hold your implement near the point, you can get harder, more intense marks. Try holding it at the end, to produce freer, looser marks.

Sharpening your pencils
Pencils and crayons can be sharpened with a pencil sharpener or with a sharp knife, preferably one with a safe, retractable blade. You can also use sandpaper to vary the point you get: a sharp point for thin, fine lines, and a flat edge for broad, thick lines.

Getting some support
Even if you buy your drawing paper in a pad, it may not be stiff enough to give you proper support by itself. You will need to rest your paper on a board of some kind. You can get one from an art store, or simply buy a piece of plywood or fiberboard from a hardware store.

Charcoal
Charcoal is made from burnt wood, usually willow, and is always black. It is available in sticks of various thicknesses, which are brittle and can tend to break. Charcoal is also available in *compressed* form, in a straight, hard stick, or in pencil form, encased in a paper cylinder that you can gradually tear away.

Fixative
Finished drawings, especially charcoal and pastel ones, need to be protected from smudging. This can be done by spraying them lightly with fixative.

Erasers
There are many different kinds of erasers. For chalk or charcoal drawing, it is best to use a kneaded eraser, a soft gray eraser that you can squeeze like clay into any shape you want.

Conté

Conté is a hard form of pastel compressed into a thin stick. It comes traditionally in black, white, and shades of brown, although other colors are now available. Drawing with brown rather than black conté can produce a softer, warmer drawing. Conté can be blended by rubbing it with your finger.

Wax crayon

Crayons are bold, simple sticks of color that come in many forms and prices. They can sometimes be dissolved with turpentine or mineral spirits, and applied with a brush or even with cotton. Used on a textured surface, crayons produce a grainy effect that can add considerable interest to your drawings.

What kind of paper?

Cartridge paper is fine for most pencil or ink drawings. Try out other kinds too, including colored paper. Textured paper is good for use with pastel, crayon and charcoal.

AQUATAIN

THE FLYING BOAT

For years, Western intelligence officials were bewildered by a strange craft, half plane and half boat, which appeared on satellite photographs of the Soviet Union. Now the Cold War is over, its Russian developers have unveiled details of how the craft works. They call it an "ekranoplane" (from the Russian for surface, *îekranoï*) and claim that its high efficiency and low fuel costs come from exploiting something that the early flyers were familiar with – gaining extra lift by flying close to the ground or the sea. Dubbed the "Caspian Sea Monster" by American intelligence experts, the flying boat can skim the surface on an air cushion, something like a hovercraft, but can also soar thousands of feet high to avoid bad weather. Jane's Defence Weekly published the first photographs of this Wing in Ground Effect craft (WIG), and it was immediately recognized as a spectacular piece of technology. The "ekranoplane" can fly over water, land, or ice.

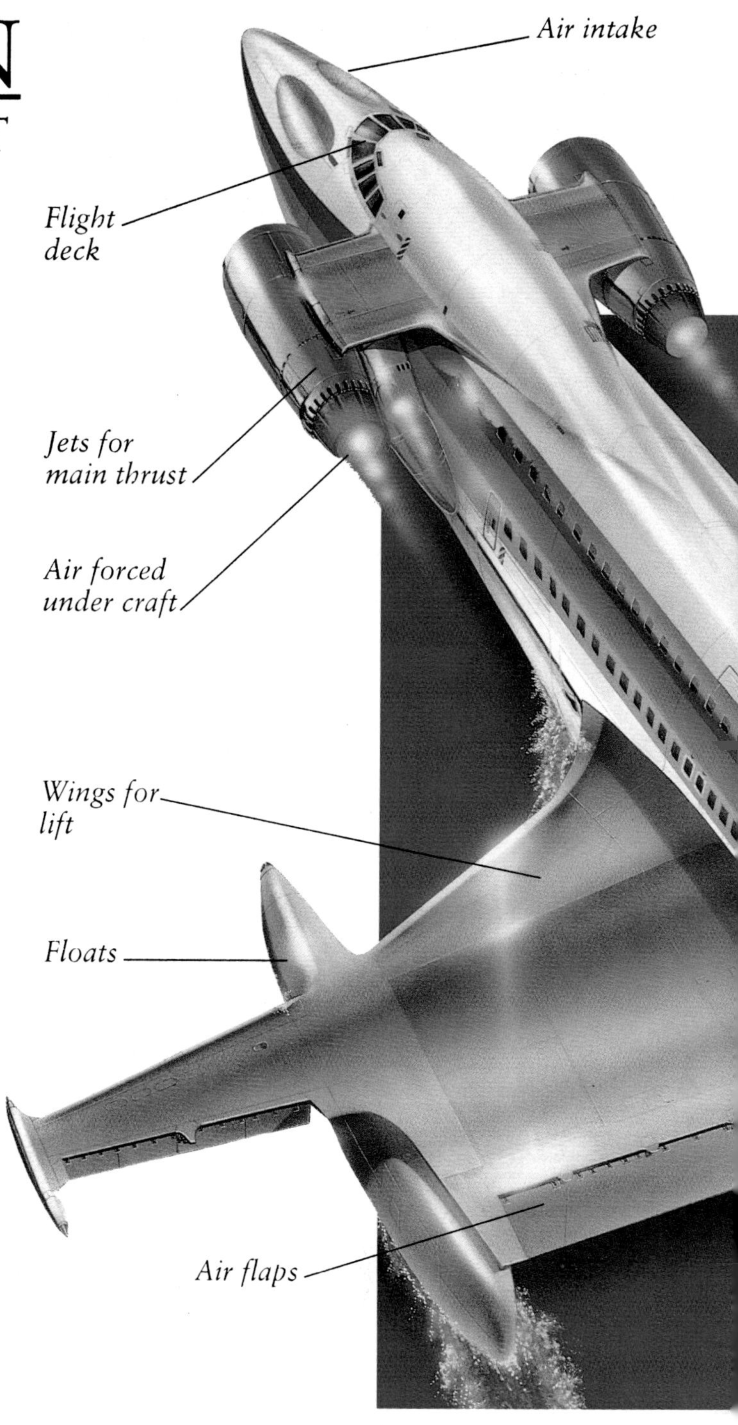

The Airfoil is a new type of boat that is currently being developed in Germany. It uses the same kind of principles as the Aquatain. *Short wings on either side of its hull create lift, and help the craft to rise out of the water altogether and fly through the air!*

***Aquatain would be 240** feet long, and have a wingspan of 180 feet. Carrying 400 passengers, it could be used for short hops such as crossing the Channel, or for longer-haul flights. One problem is licensing the craft, since nobody has yet decided if it is an aircraft, or a boat. Although there are models and videos, the craft has yet to be seen in the West.*

A CUSHION OF AIR

HOW THE AQUATAIN FLIES

As designed, Aquatain could fly above water, land, or ice. It uses two sets of engines, one to provide forward propulsion and a second set angled downward to direct thrust under the wings. For takeoff, a set of deep flaps, called screens, are lowered from the back of the wings, trapping the exhaust gases from the second set of engines and creating a region of compressed air, that has the effect of lifting the aircraft away from the water. The forward engines are started, and the craft moves forward, enabling the lift engines to be switched off. The short, broad wings maintain the air cushion on which the craft floats at a height of 45 feet. If necessary, Aquatain can fly much higher, like a conventional aircraft, to avoid storms, but then it is no more economical than any other aircraft. Because few people have ever seen this craft actually fly, some believe that a prototype may have stalled and sunk during a trial flight.

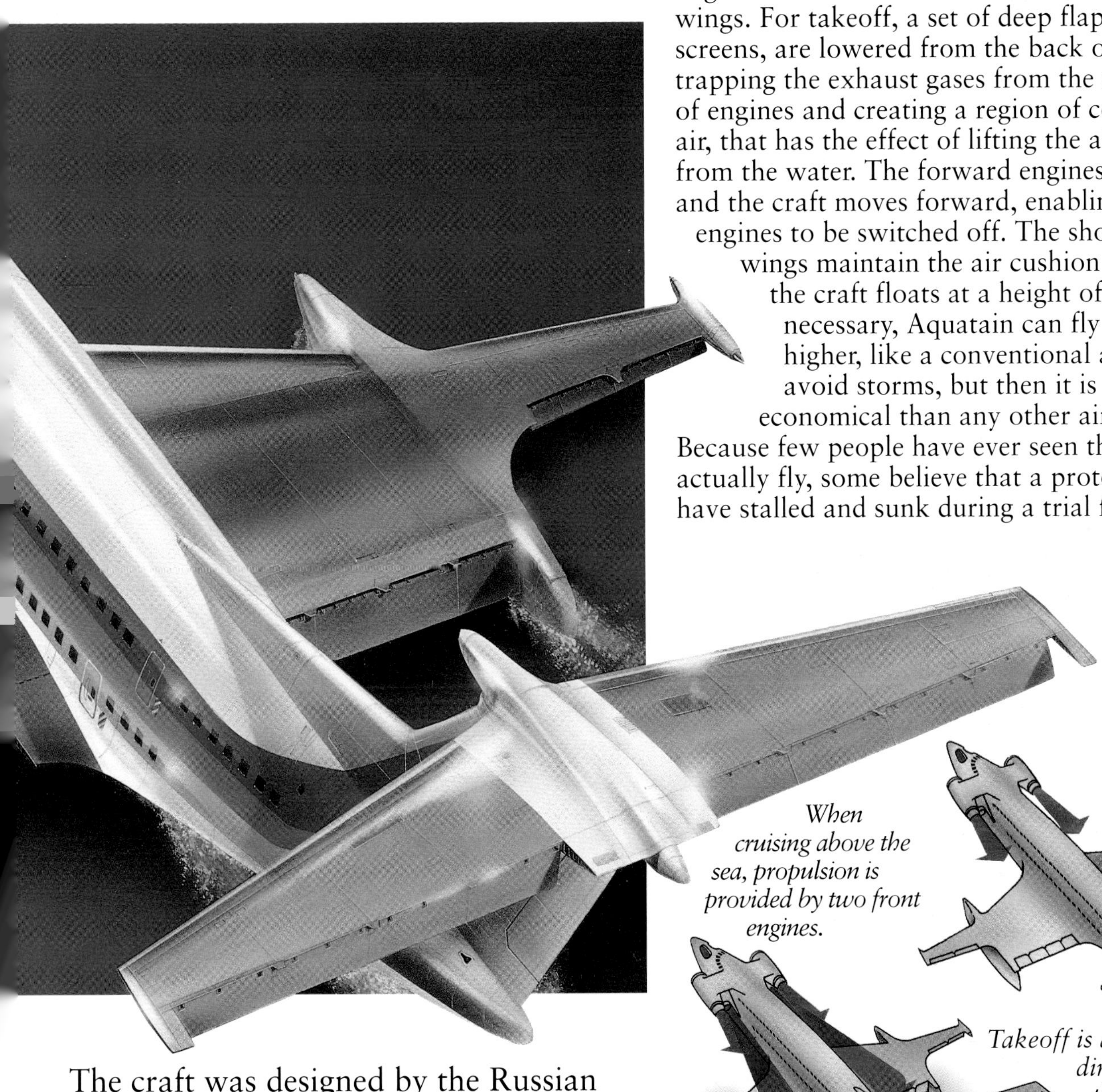

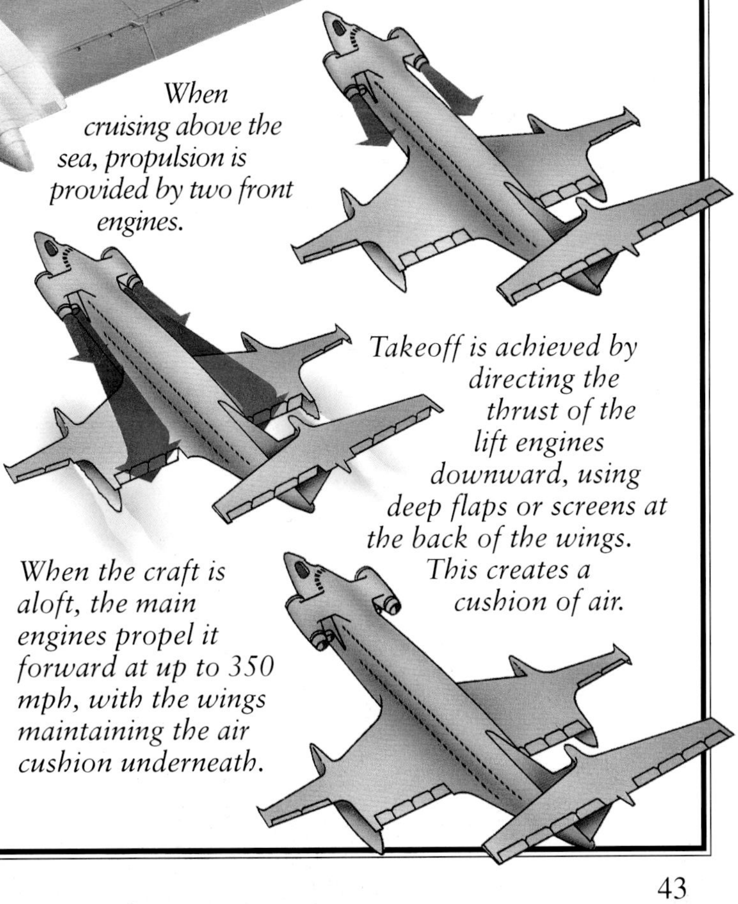

When cruising above the sea, propulsion is provided by two front engines.

Takeoff is achieved by directing the thrust of the lift engines downward, using deep flaps or screens at the back of the wings. This creates a cushion of air.

When the craft is aloft, the main engines propel it forward at up to 350 mph, with the wings maintaining the air cushion underneath.

The craft was designed by the Russian Hydrofoil Research Center, and the Soviet Navy has designed several versions. Now the designers want to create a 250-ton craft able to carry 400 passengers at 300 mph, over distances of up to 10,000 miles. This is possible, according to designer Dr. Boris Chubikov, because the craft uses only a fifth as much fuel as a conventional aircraft.

PROFESSOR PROTEIN'S HINTS AND TIPS ON *personal hygiene*

WHAT'S IN SKIN?

UNDER YOUR SKIN Like the rest of the body, skin is made of microscopic cells. On the skin's surface the cells are flat, hard, and tough for protection, like tiles stuck on a roof. As you move around, sit, walk, wash, get dry, and sleep in your bed, these cells are worn away and rubbed off your body. On average, you lose about 50,000 every second. Scratch your cheek – there go another few million! But don't panic, your skin won't disappear. Just under the surface, more cells are multiplying like mad, to replace the ones that have been rubbed off.

AT THE SURFACE

The outer layer of skin is called the epidermis. The hard, flattened cells on its surface are not very lively. In fact they are dead, ready to be rubbed away.

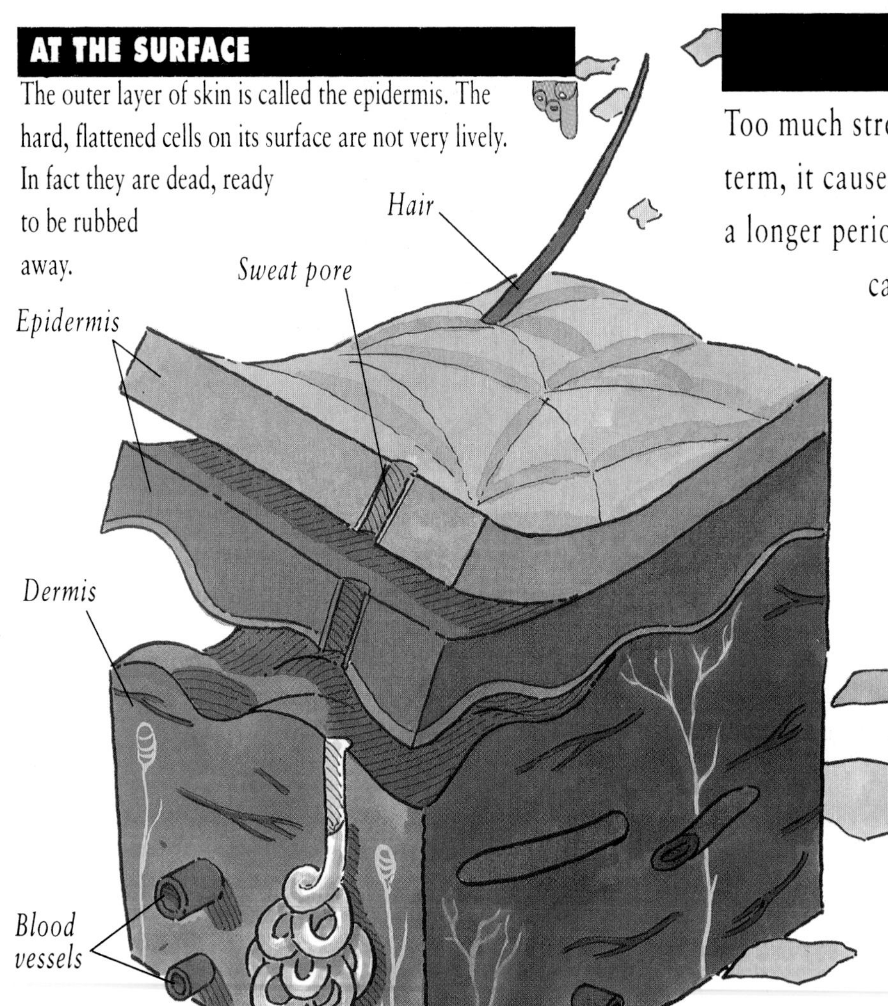

EVEN DEEPER UNDER THE SURFACE

The lower layer of skin is the dermis. It contains millions of microscopic touch receptors, nerves, blood vessels, hairs, and sweat pores.

BIG TIP CARE IN THE SUN

Too much strong sunlight damages skin. In the short term, it causes the soreness and pain of sunburn. Over a longer period it may trigger skin growths and cancers. So Slip-Slap-Slop. Slip on a shirt or top, slap on a wide sunhat, and slop on the sunscreen lotion.

JUST UNDER THE SURFACE

At the base of the epidermis, cells are busy multiplying. They move upward, and get filled with keratin which makes them very hard. After three weeks they reach the surface to replace those that have been rubbed off.

PROFESSOR'S FACT SKIN IS THIN

• Your skin's thickness varies on different parts of the body. On the soles of the feet it's more than 1/20th inch (five millimeters) thick. On the eyelids it's less than 1/100th inch (half a millimeter) thick and very delicate. So don't try walking on your eyelids!

PROFESSOR PROTEIN'S HINTS AND TIPS ON *personal hygiene*

KEEPING SKIN CLEAN'N'SHINY

HAVE YOU HAD A BATH TODAY? No? Eeek! Human skin is not self-cleaning, like an oven. It needs to be washed, all over. To do this, use soap and warm water, as found in most bathrooms. Splash the warm water onto your skin, rub on the soap to make a bubbly lather, scrub well, and wash off the sweat, dirt, and grime. If you've never seen soap before, it usually comes in small bars or lumps, often green or pink,sometimes with writing. Or use gel or a similar soapy substitute.If you don't use them, your skin will get dirty, grimy, sore, spotty, and smelly.

PROFESSOR'S FACT HOW SOAP WORKS

• Tiny pieces of dirt clump together in larger sticky lumps, which you can see. Soap is a type of chemical substance called a detergent. It surrounds each tiny piece of dirt, making it come away from the main lump and away from your skin. Gradually the dirt clump is broken into millions of specks that float away when they are rinsed off.

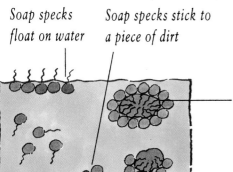

Soap specks float on water

Soap specks stick to a piece of dirt

Soap specks surround a piece of dirt

DON'T GET OLD SWEAT

Skin makes sweat, a watery, salty fluid with an important job – to keep the body cool in hot conditions. It also makes sebum, the natural waxy oil which makes skin supple and water-repellent. But as sweat and sebum dry, they become smelly and attract dirt. A good reason to bathe regularly.

TOP TO BOTTOM

Wash all over, not just the parts that show! Especially under arms, between legs, and in folds of skin. Sweat and dirt are more likely to collect here, trapping dirt and causing smells.

USING A SPONGE

Dunk the sponge in the water, and squeeze it to get the air out and water in. Then rub it on the soap, and rub it on you.

Dick Turpin

No highwayman is more famous than Dick Turpin (*left*). In numerous stories, ballads, and movies he is the ideal "gentleman of the road" – a handsome figure on his noble mare, Black Bess, dashing along the highways, robbing the greedy of their money, and the women of their hearts.

The real Richard Turpin was nothing at all like this. He was a butcher by trade, 5 feet 9 inches tall with a pock-marked face. He did not have a horse named Black Bess, nor did he make a famous ride from London to York to escape capture. He stole from both rich and poor, and rather than wooing women, he tortured them.

Born in 1706, Turpin gave up his butcher's business in favor of poaching and burglary. In time, he became a murderer and highway robber with a reward of $120 for his capture. He was eventually caught when his writing was identified, and he was hanged at York in 1739.

Turpin Leaps the Tollgate

Legend says that Dick Turpin rode his mare, Black Bess, from London to York in twelve hours (main picture, *right*). Exhausted by the ride, the horse died just before reaching their destination. This supposedly impossible feat gave Turpin the perfect alibi for a robbery he had committed.

This story is an excellent example of how facts become confused. The marathon ride to York was first attributed to "Swift John Nevison." A report from 1676 claims Nevison carried out a robbery at Gad's hill in Kent at 4:00 A.M., then rode to York by 7:45 P.M. that evening.

The Beggar's Opera. The romantic hero of John Gay's *Beggar's Opera* (1728) is Macheath, highwayman, robber, and womanizer (*left*).

This ever-popular musical illustrates perfectly the English people's sympathetic attitude toward their highwaymen.

In 1773, angry magistrates called for the show to be banned!

JONATHAN WILD

Jonathan Wild (*left*) was the craftiest criminal of his age. Titled the "Thief-taker General of Great Britain and Ireland," he lived by catching criminals for reward and selling back to people their stolen property.

Yet it was Wild who organized the robberies, and the villains he handed over had refused to obey him! In the end, the law caught up with Wild and he was hanged at Tyburn, London in 1739.

***Blueskin Blake**, a London criminal, was so furious at "Judas" Wild for betraying him that he tried to cut the Thief-taker's throat* (above, right).

Frenchman Claude Duval (right) *certainly pretended to be a gentleman of the road, dressing and speaking with great style. He was irresistible to women.*

It is reported that in the middle of a holdup, he took time to dance with a lady on Hounslow Heath, (near London, below left)*! Sadly, he performed his final dance on the end of a hangman's rope.*

GENTLEMEN OF THE ROAD

A few highwaymen were genuine "gentlemen of the road." These were generally bankrupt young men who turned to crime to restore their fortunes. Two famous gentlemen highwaymen were Old Etonian William Parsons and James Maclaine, a minister's son.

After a dissolute life, including some rather amateur highway robbery, Parsons was executed for running away from a penal colony. Maclaine conducted a number of brave but non-violent robberies before he too was caught and executed.

OSTRICH

THE BIGGEST BIRDS ARE THE OSTRICH from Africa, the emu from Australia, and the rhea from South America. They are too heavy to fly. But these flightless birds, called ratites (pronounced ray-teetz), are suited to life walking and running on the ground.

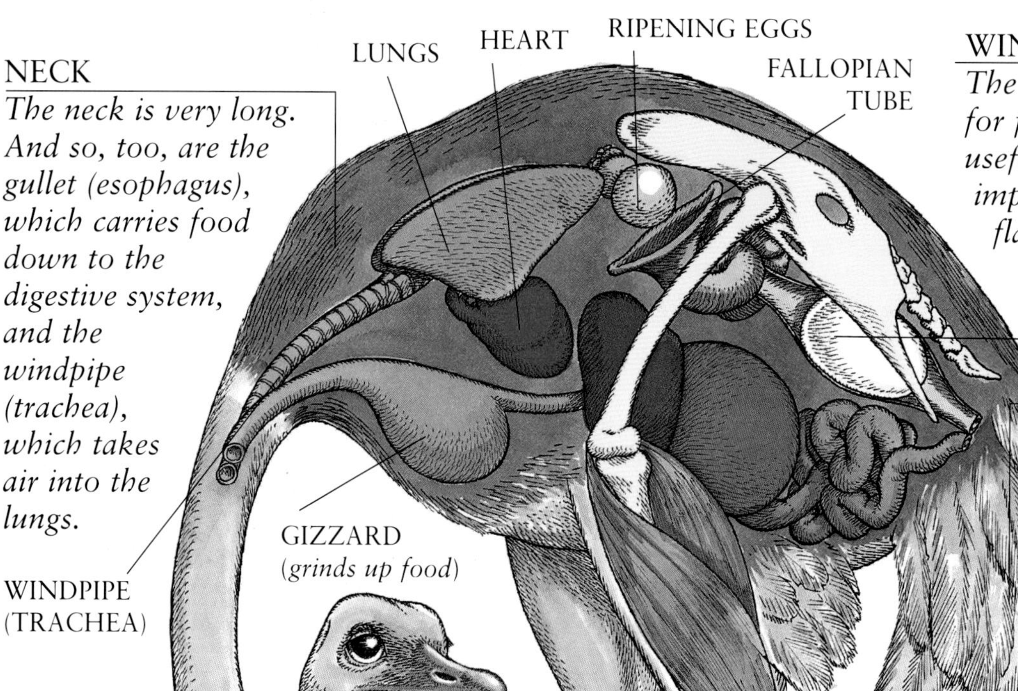

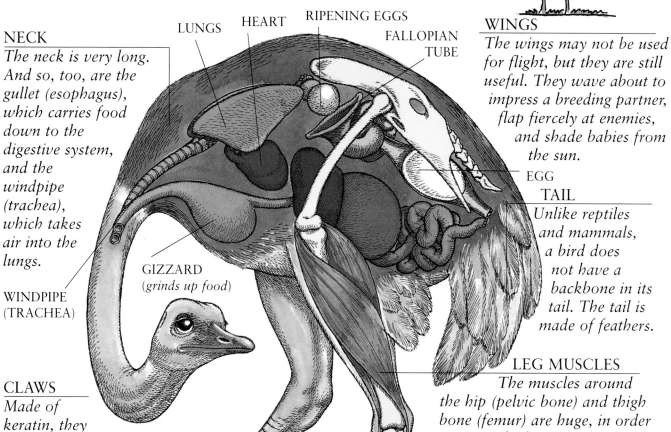

NECK

The neck is very long. And so, too, are the gullet (esophagus), which carries food down to the digestive system, and the windpipe (trachea), which takes air into the lungs.

WINGS

The wings may not be used for flight, but they are still useful. They wave about to impress a breeding partner, flap fiercely at enemies, and shade babies from the sun.

TAIL

Unlike reptiles and mammals, a bird does not have a backbone in its tail. The tail is made of feathers.

CLAWS

Made of keratin, they are designed to be strong for self-defense, and for scratching around to find food.

LEG MUSCLES

The muscles around the hip (pelvic bone) and thigh bone (femur) are huge, in order to move the long legs back and forth for running at over 31 miles per hour.

CAN I COME TOO?

An ostrich doesn't really need to fly. It can find food and defend itself very well. On its two long, strong legs, it runs faster than most four-legged animals. It can kick out with its big clawed feet. And peck very hard, too. Ouch!

ANATOMY AT WORK

BIGGEST AND SMALLEST

The mother ostrich produces about a dozen of the biggest eggs in the bird group. Yet they are also the smallest eggs in the bird group – in relation to the mother's size. Each one weighs the same as about 25 ordinary chicken's eggs.

PENGUIN

PENGUINS ARE DESIGNED FOR LIFE in cold seas. Their flipper-shaped wings and webbed feet are ideal for swimming. And they are never troubled by polar bears because penguins live in the South Atlantic Ocean and Antarctica, while polar bears live at the other end of the world, in the Arctic north.

COLD FEET

The feet and flippers are designed to be cold. As blood from the warm central body goes into them, it flows next to cooler blood coming back, and is cooled. This reduces heat loss from feet and flippers into the sea, while the returning blood is warmed.

DOWN, DROWN

Like any bird, a penguin needs to breathe fresh air regularly into its lungs. If it is kept underwater for more than a few minutes, it drowns.

FLAPSTROKE, NOT BACKSTROKE

Penguins can fly – not in the air, but through water. They flap their flipperlike wings up and down, just like any other flying bird, and speed along faster than any human swimmer. However, they cannot do the backstroke.

ARTERIES (red)

VEINS (purple)

AIR SACS

BONES

MUSCLES

WINDPIPE (TRACHEA)

SALT GLANDS *(for ridding the blood of excess salt)*

FAT IS FINE

The penguin's stout, body has a thick layer of the fatty substance, blubber, just beneath the skin. This helps to keep the cold out. It also makes the body's outline smoother and more streamlined, for swimming.

SNAPPER

The strong, stout, sharp-edged beak is ideal for snapping and catching prey such as slippery fish and squid, and hard-cased shellfish.

ANATOMY *AT WORK*
STOMACH

After the mouth, gullet, and crop, the next part of a bird's gut is the gizzard, or stomach. This has very thick, muscular walls. Birds cannot chew, so it's the gizzard's job to grind up food.

DISASTER STRIKES

When a landslide begins its descent, huge quantities of soil, mud, rocks, and smaller debris hurtle down a hillside. Whole villages are buried alive, and their inhabitants and livestock are swept along on a tide of mud and debris. Trees are uprooted, houses are flattened or swamped, and communications are cut off.

The mountainous regions of Nepal in Asia are prone to torrential rains. Here, the water-saturated soil has been eroded, exposing the layers of rock beneath. This erosion is worse in areas where large numbers of trees have been cut down. The hillsides are stripped of protection against the falling rain, and of tree roots to anchor the soil in place. Landslides glide over the smooth rock at speeds of up to 60 feet per second.

Following an earthquake in the Andes Mountains in Peru in 1970, a devastating mudflow swept through the Peruvian town of Yungay. Almost 18,000 people were buried alive as a giant wave of mud and debris about 263 feet high swamped the town.

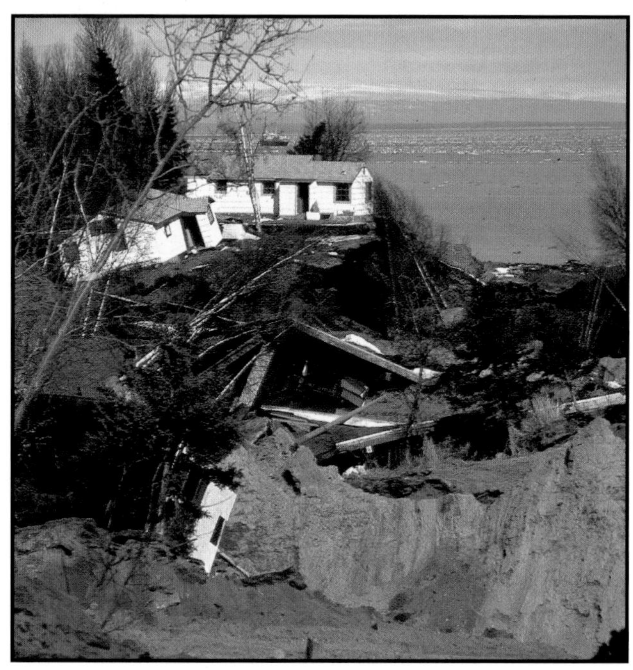

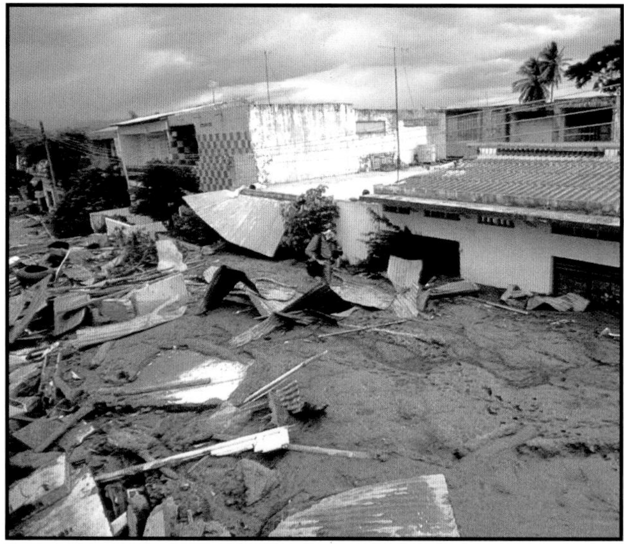

►▲▲ Shockwaves from the 1964 Alaska earthquake caused a mudflow of clay to engulf the town.
►▲ Mud and floodwaters wreaked havoc in the streets of Armero, Colombia, after the 1985 volcanic eruption there.
► The 1970 mudflow in Yungay, Peru, caused severe damage to railroad lines and roads (right).

◀ In 1969, in the area around Los Angeles, about 44 inches of rain fell in just 42 days. These rains, some of the heaviest ever recorded in the area, washed down mud and gravel from the San Gabriel Mountains. As a torrent of mud, debris, and water swept over the suburb of Glendora, over 100 people were drowned and 15,000 people had to evacuate their homes. The landslide also blocked the main highway into Los Angeles.

THINKING MACHINES

Computers can do many things brilliantly, but they cannot "think" for themselves. "Artificial intelligence" is the next goal for computer science: the creation of computers that can learn and teach themselves.

Above Chess-playing computers can beat human opponents — but they would not react if there was a fire.

FUZZY THOUGHT

Until now, computer chips have worked on a binary principle — they make simple yes/no decisions. The chips of the future will use what is called "fuzzy logic" to choose between "almost" or "nearly" right or wrong — like a human.

Below *Neural networks are computer systems that "learn." Their circuitry is based on the connections made in the human brain. They have learned how to drive a truck by copying a human driver.*

SURVIVAL OF THE FITTEST

Scientists also want to develop "genetic" software, which will be able to start from a few basic principles and learn as it goes. It would crash (destroy) any programs that are inefficient.

Right *Computer chips of the future may be specially prepared so that, instead of simply being programmed, they can "grow" like a living creature. Will we then have to start thinking of computers as living things?*

LIVING CHIPS

FEASIBLE TECHNOLOGY	○ ○ ○ ○ ○
SCIENCE IS SOUND	○ ○ ○ ○ ○
AFFORDABLE	○ ○ ○ ○ ○
HOW SOON?	○ ○ ○ ○ ○

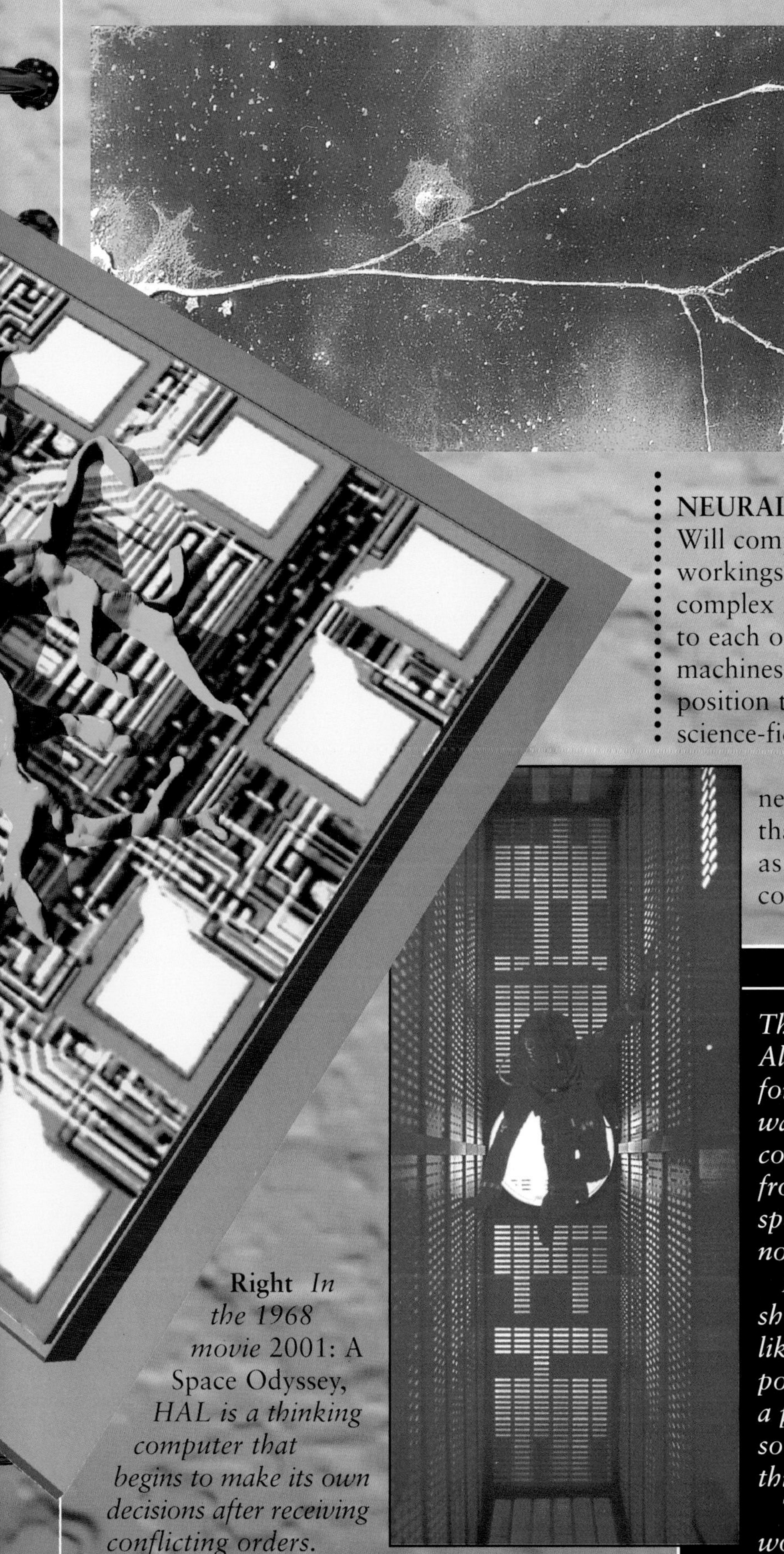

NEURAL NIGHTMARE?

Will computers one day be able to copy the workings of the human brain, with its vastly complex network of neurons passing messages to each other? If they could — would machines that think for themselves be in a position to take over the world, as many science-fiction writers have imagined?

Perhaps not, as computers would need to be connected to machines that could actually do things (such as missile launchers). Even then, we could simply pull out the plug.

Right *In the 1968 movie* 2001: A Space Odyssey, *HAL is a thinking computer that begins to make its own decisions after receiving conflicting orders.*

Today, experts are often surprised at the decisions that computers make, even though they know how they reached them.

LET'S TALK

The British computer pioneer, Alan Turing came up with a test for deciding whether a computer was "intelligent:" It would have to convince someone talking to it from another room that they were speaking to another human. So far, no machine has passed the test.

However, some scientists think we shouldn't build computers to think like us. They argue that the most powerful use for them is to create a partnership with human brains, so that two very different ways of thinking are working together.

This is an extension of how we work now. People think in different ways, so two brains can be better than one.

MOTORCYCLES

U.S. Militaire (1914)

The first motorcycle was a wooden bicycle fitted with a gas engine. Invented in 1885 by a German engineer called Gottlieb Daimler, it was only slightly faster than walking. By 1900 several firms were making motorcycles and, by 1914, the United States was taking the lead in technical development with bikes like the Militaire (*above*). Motorcycles were used by soldiers in wartime and are used by police officers and messengers today. But for many enthusiasts motorcycles are one of the most thrilling forms of transportation in the world.

Grooved tires increase grip

Twin-cylinder Royal Enfield bike (1960)

Honda Super Blackbird

Twins and "Super Bikes"

From the 1940s, some bikes were built with twin-cylinder engines for improved performance (*above*). Modern "super bikes" can perform as well as Formula-One racing cars. This Japanese Honda *Super Blackbird* (*right*) is the world's most powerful bike. Its top speed is 188 mph (300 kmh) and it can accelerate from 0-60 mph (0-96 kmh) in 2.5 seconds.

SCOOTER CRAZES

Scooters are an Italian invention, first produced by Vespa in 1947. These simple motorbikes are still popular with young people in Europe. In the 1960s scooters were favored by teenagers called "mods." Some of them embellished their scooters with extra lights and mirrors (*left*). These "mod" bikes are now valuable collectors' items.

Bike Safety

Safety is now an important issue in motorcycle manufacturing. Designers make handling easier by improving suspension and steering systems. Some of the most expensive bikes use air-sprung shock-absorbers to reduce the impact of bumps.

HARLEY-DAVIDSON

The famous American "Harleys" are ridden by the U.S. Army, most U.S. police forces, and thousands of other people – including the notorious "Hells Angels" (*left*). The first Harley bike was built in 1907. In 1965 it introduced the Electra Glide – one of the most luxurious motorcycles ever produced. Recent models have a five-speed gearbox, disk brakes, and a rubber-mounted engine. The firm is one of the few U.S. motorcycle companies to survive competition from Japanese manufacturers today.

GOTTLIEB DAIMLER (1834-1900)
Daimler, a German engineer and inventor, is most famous for his automobiles. But he built the very first motorcycle before he built cars. His motorcycle was made mostly out of wood, and his son Paul rode 6 miles (9.5 km) on it to become the first motorcyclist.

MOTORCYCLE POLICE
Motorcycles are vital to the police (*left*). Motorcycle outriders escort ambulances and important people such as prime ministers and presidents.

SEATED SIDE BY SIDE

During World War II (1939-1945), Germany equipped motorcycles and sidecars with machine guns, while Britain and America used bikes mainly for staff work (*above*). After the war, sidecars were used before automobiles became widely affordable. Sidecars are now made in small numbers, and high-tech ones can cost as much as cars; this German model (*right*) costs $51,000!

FARMING QUADS
Quads are motorcycles with four large wheels used for riding across rough terrain (*right*). They are useful for farmers, but many people also enjoy the excitement of cross-country racing.

WHAT IF SHEEP HAD NO WOOL?

Humans have been using animals, such as sheep, cows, and pigs, for thousands of years. These domesticated mammals have been supplying us with meat, milk, and materials. If sheep didn't have any wool, then not only would they be cold, but we would not be able to use their fleece to make our woolen clothes.

Sheep's wool is sheared, washed, cleaned, and woven into clothes, rugs, and many other woolen products.

Mammal products

Mammals produce a wide range of products that humans use directly or convert into other substances. The milk of mammals such as cows, goats, and camels is made into butter, cheese, and yogurt. We eat the muscles, or red meat. We crush and melt bones and hard pieces into glues and fertilizers. Clothes and textiles are made from the wool (mammal fur) of sheep, goats, vicunas, rabbits, rodents, and many others.

Chamois leather is the skin of the chamois, a type of goat-antelope. It is very soft, flexible, and absorbent.

A-hunting we will go

Although hunting for sport takes place in many places throughout the world, several groups of people rely on hunting mammals to survive. For example, the Inuit (Eskimo) of the far north hunt whales, walruses, and seals for their meat, bones and fur to make food, clothing, and utensils.

Bizarre pets

For as long as people have been using mammals for food, they have also been keeping them as pets. Since this time we have bred many different animals. Some of these were bred for their ability to work, such as sheepdogs, but now they are mainly for company or for show. The result has been some very strange-looking animals, such as the bulldog, whose nose is so short that it can only breathe through its mouth, the hairless sphinx cat, and the shaggy rough-haired guinea pig.

Cows provide most of our ordinary leather. They also give us a lot of meat and make most of the milk that we drink.

Arks or prisons?

Zoos have become the center of debate between many groups of people. Some people believe that keeping wild animals captive in cages is cruel.

However, zoos can play a positive role in the conservation of many species. Conservationists can breed rare creatures such as the giant panda, golden lion tamarin, and rhinoceros, to release them back into the wild and save them from extinction.

Zoos have not always been successful in saving species. Some animals, such as the quagga from Africa and the thylacine from Australia, have become extinct, despite having some specimens kept in zoos.

Pigs yield many products, from meat to pigskin for shoes. They are used to make drugs and body organs for transplants.

THE ROMAN ARMY

The rapid expansion and incredible success of the Roman Empire was largely due to the Roman army. It was first formed to defend the city of Rome, but it went on to conquer a vast empire. The early Roman army was made up of volunteers. General Marius (see below) reorganized it into a well trained and better equipped force. Soldiers became paid professionals who joined up for 20-25 years. People from lands conquered by the Romans were also recruited into the army ranks.

A legionary's uniform

Over a woollen tunic, a legionary wore a breast plate made of metal strips, scales or rings. He also had a helmet of leather or metal. During cold weather, the thongs of his heavy, studded sandals were stuffed with wool and fur and he was given a thick, hooded cloak, called a *Birrus britannicus*, to keep him warm. A foot soldier was armed with a short sword, two metal-tipped javelins and a rectangular shield of wood and leather. On the march, a legionary had to carry all his equipment on his back. Each man had a heavy pack which contained his tools, food and so on. Fully-laden legionaries were nicknamed "Marius's mules" after the general and consul, Marius (157-86 B.C.)

Breast plate

Copy of shield

Emperor

Legatus

Tribune

Centurion

Signifer

Legionary

Auxilary

The order of ranks in the Roman army is shown on the left. Senior offices, such as Legatus and Tribune, were usually held by members of the upper classes.

A Roman legion

A Roman legion was divided up into separate units. Ten sections of eight men made up a century. Six centuries made a cohort (480 men) and there were ten cohorts in a legion. There were also about 120 cavalrymen attached to each legion. Each legion had as its standard a silver eagle, the symbol of the Roman Empire.

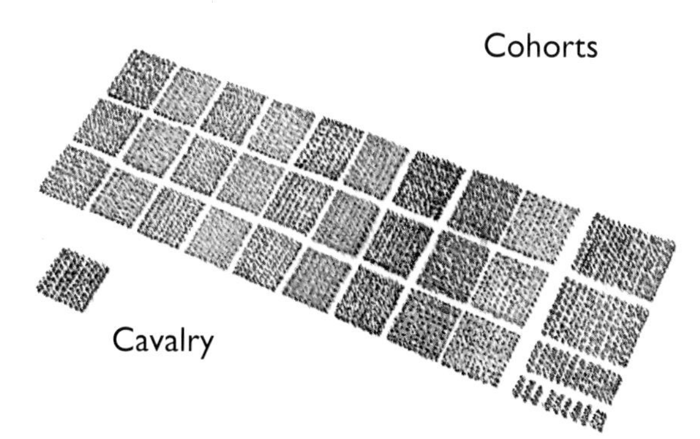

Signifer

Aquifer

Auxilary cavalry

Centurion

Praetorian guard

Fighting talk

Many of the words that we use today come from Latin.

A corduroy consisted of logs laid side by side to form the foundations of a rampart. The pattern of lines on corduroy cloth resembles the logs.

A praefectus was a high official in Rome. Today, the word prefect means someone with authority.

Gladius is the Latin word for sword. From it comes the words gladiator and gladioli.

Ballista is the Latin word for catapult. Today the word ballistics is used in connection with weapons.

Tortoise technique

The Romans devised many new military techniques. The "tortoise" formation involved soldiers holding their shields above their heads as protection against arrows, stones and other missiles hurled by the enemy. The raised shields resembled the pattern on a tortoise's shell and offered a similar type of protection, hence its name. The Romans also used assault towers and battering rams as a way of storming enemy territory.

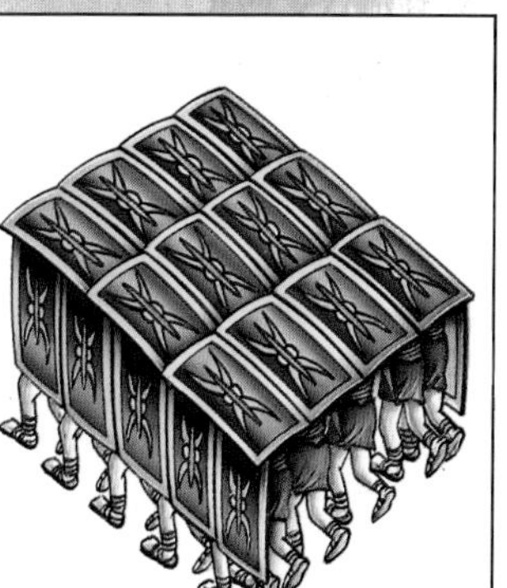

The Spectrum

In 1666, Sir Isaac Newton used a prism (a triangular block of glass) to demonstrate how white light can be split up into lots of different colors. These colors are called the spectrum. With a second prism, he showed how white light could be re-formed by mixing the colors. Prisms can be used to make beams of light turn corners inside periscopes. The Frenchman, Augustin Fresnel, introduced the use of glass prisms to collect the light rays from a lighthouse into one powerful beam. When a light ray strikes a prism, light is refracted. Raindrops act as prisms under certain conditions, creating a rainbow across the sky. Try making your own rainbow.

Bright Ideas

Look all around you for examples of white light being split up – take particular notice of glass objects. You can learn the correct order of the colors in the spectrum and in a rainbow by using the initials of each color in a name like ROY G. BIV.

Why It Works

Water acts like a prism, splitting light into its different wavelengths and producing a spectrum of seven colors: red, orange, yellow, green, blue, indigo, and violet. The spectrum occurs because as the light is refracted (bent) by the water, each color is bent at different angles, splitting the white light into colors. Raindrops falling while the sun is shining can cause refraction and reflection of white light. Colored rays of light spread out across the sky to create the curved band of a rainbow.

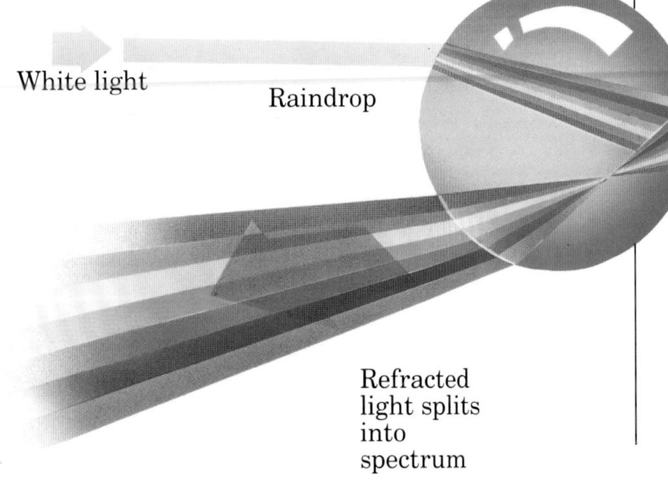

Colors of the Rainbow

1

1. Seal the edges of a mirror with tape. You will need two clips that are joined together like the ones shown here.

2. Half fill a glass container with water, and use the clips to hold it in the water at an angle. You may have to alter the angle later.

2

3. Find a piece of black oak tag, large enough to block out the light source completely. With sharp scissors, cut out one long, narrow strip as shown here. This will allow the passage of light from the light source to the mirror.

4. Rest the flat mirror at an angle in the container of water so that the light entering through the slit will strike it. Place a smaller piece of white oak tag beneath the slit in the black oak tag. Adjust the mirror's position until a rainbow appears.

3

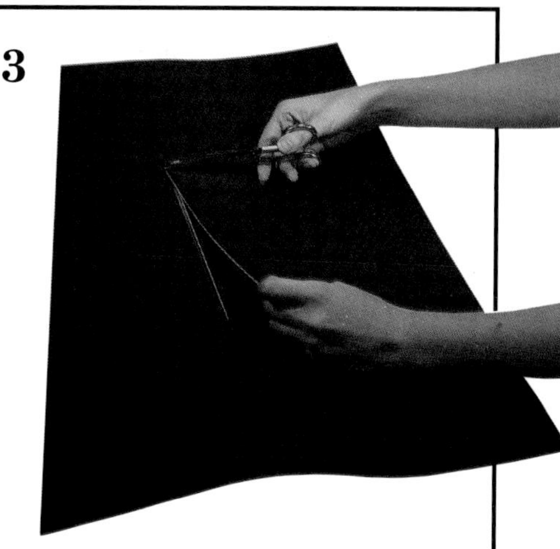

4

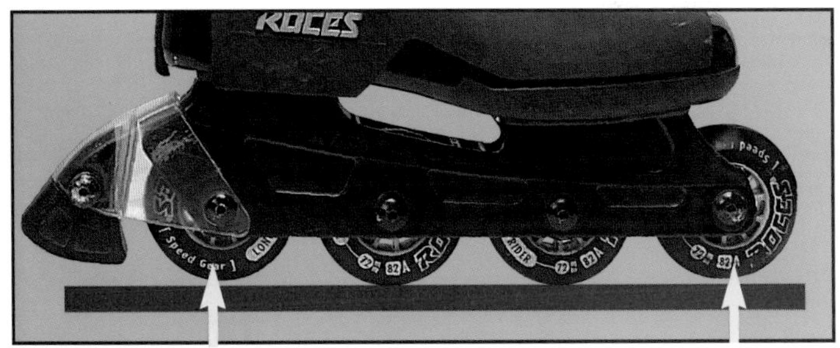

ROCES

“Rockered” system

ROCES
ROCES

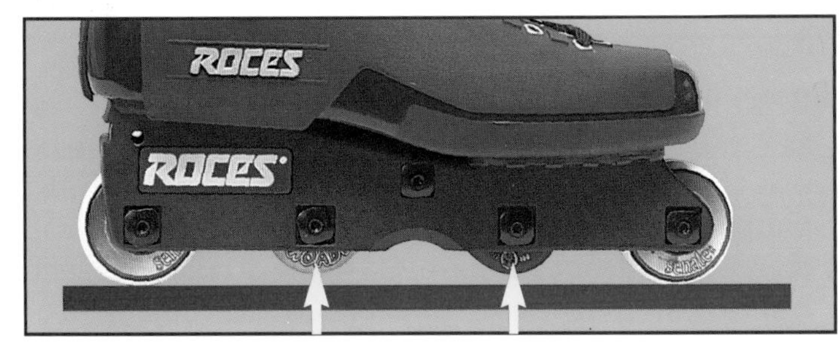

“Anti-rockered” system

ROCKING AND ROLLING

On most skates you can adjust the height of your wheels to create different skating effects. Lower the two center wheels to create a “rockering” effect which allows you to turn more effectively.

With all the wheels flat, you can turn less easily, but you gain more speed. Raise the two middle wheels or replace them with smaller wheels for “anti-rockering.” “Aggressive” skaters use this to “lock on” better to rails when grinding.

KNOW YOUR SKATES!

❋ The chassis, or frame, is the part of your skate which is fixed to the underside of your boot and holds the wheels. It may be made from aluminum, plastic, or hard acrylic.

❋ Soft boots, a very popular type of “rec” skate, are soft, like a sneaker, with no outer boot.

❋ Other boots have a hard exterior or shell made from molded plastic *(main illustration)*. A soft inner boot fits within this. Stitched boots, such as hockey boots, are usually made from plastic and leather stitched together.

❋ Some boots have holes, or vents, cut into them to allow air to circulate and cool your feet.

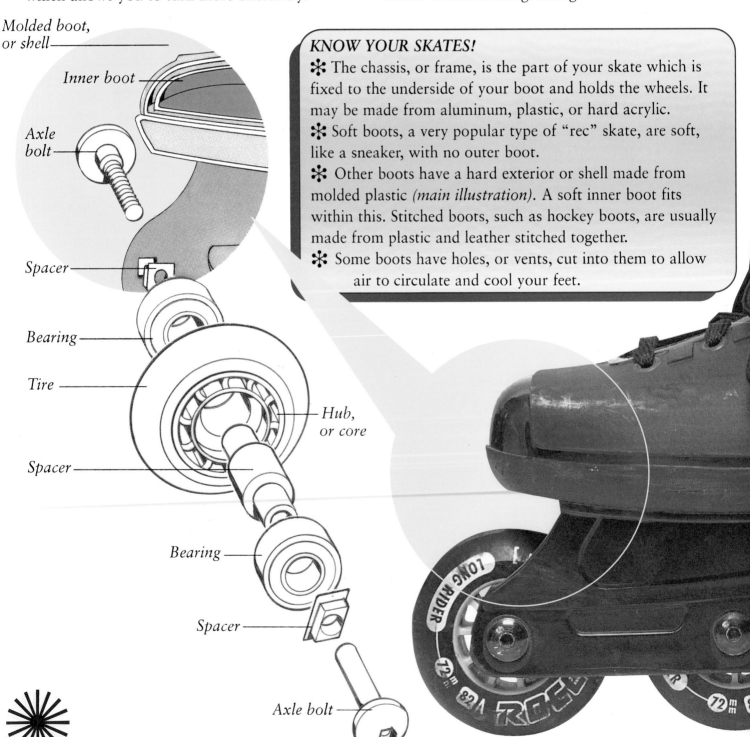

Molded boot, or shell
Inner boot
Axle bolt
Spacer
Bearing
Tire
Hub, or core
Spacer
Bearing
Spacer
Axle bolt

LONG RIDER
72mm
82A
ROCES

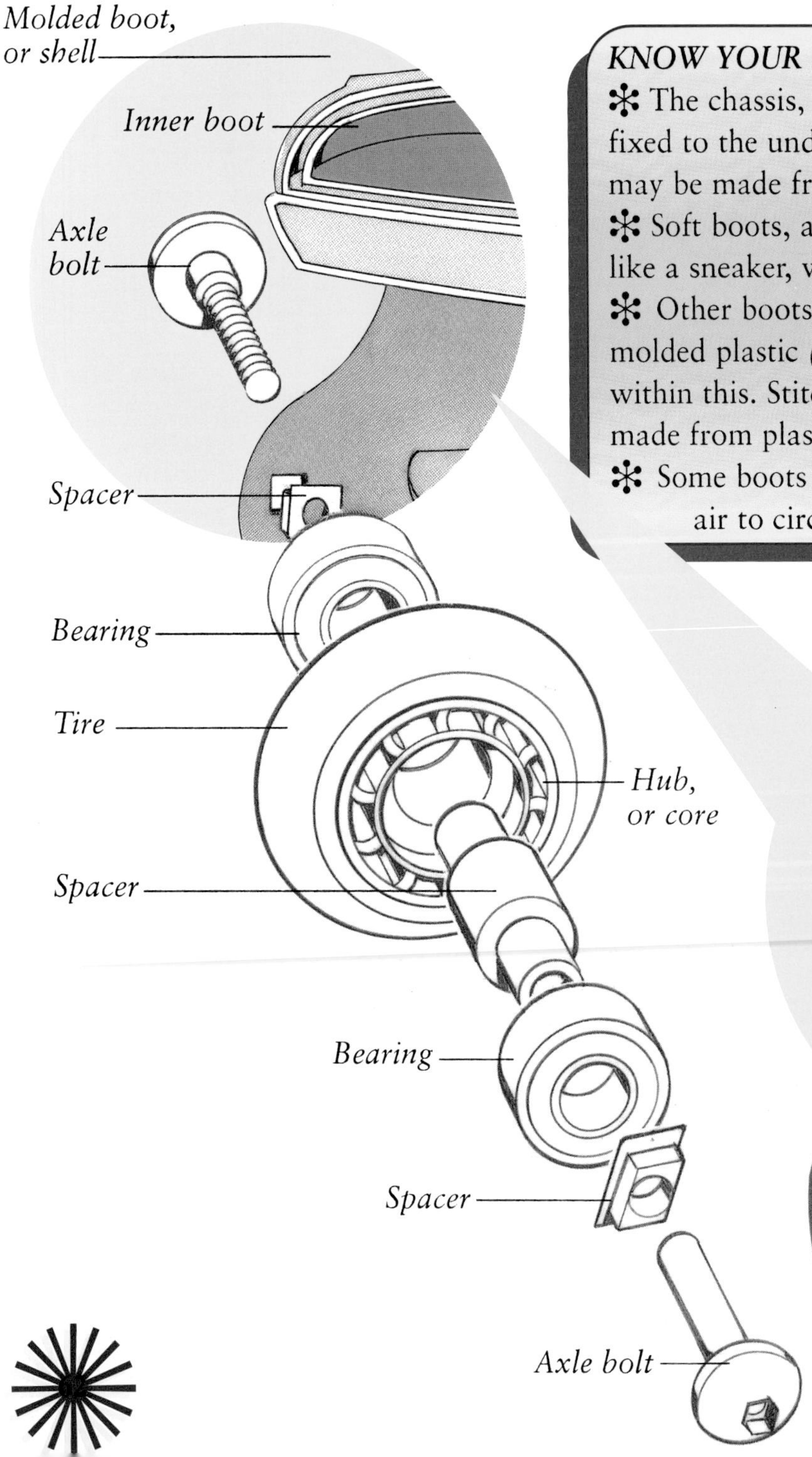

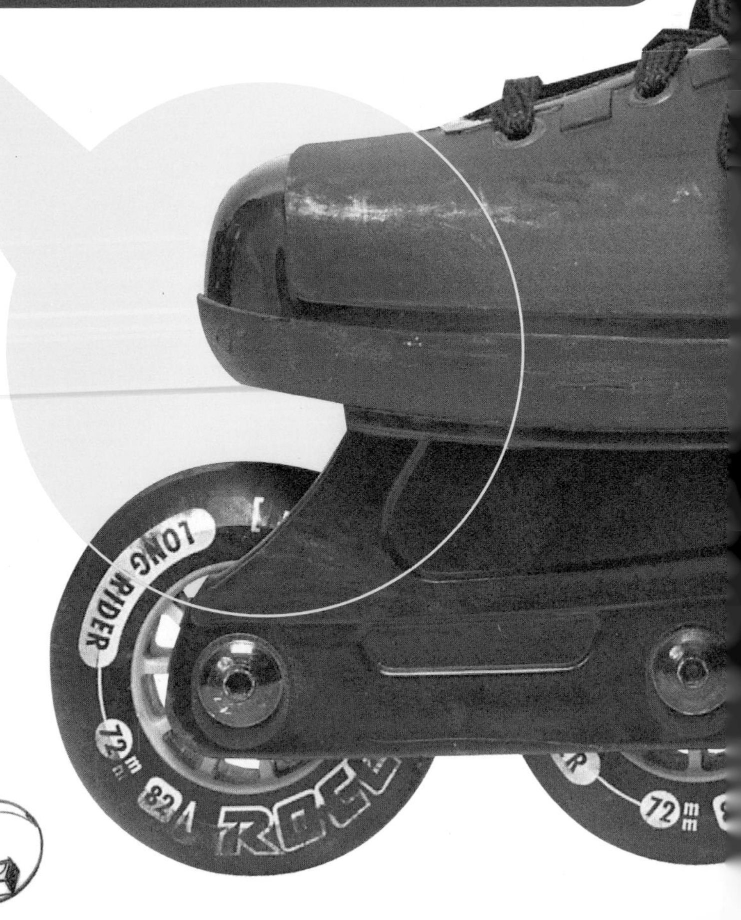

Skate Equipment

In-line skates have been specialized to suit each type of skating. There are, however, some general principles which apply to most in-line skates. The skate pictured on this page is a two-piece "rec" skate, with an ankle cuff hinged to the lower boot.

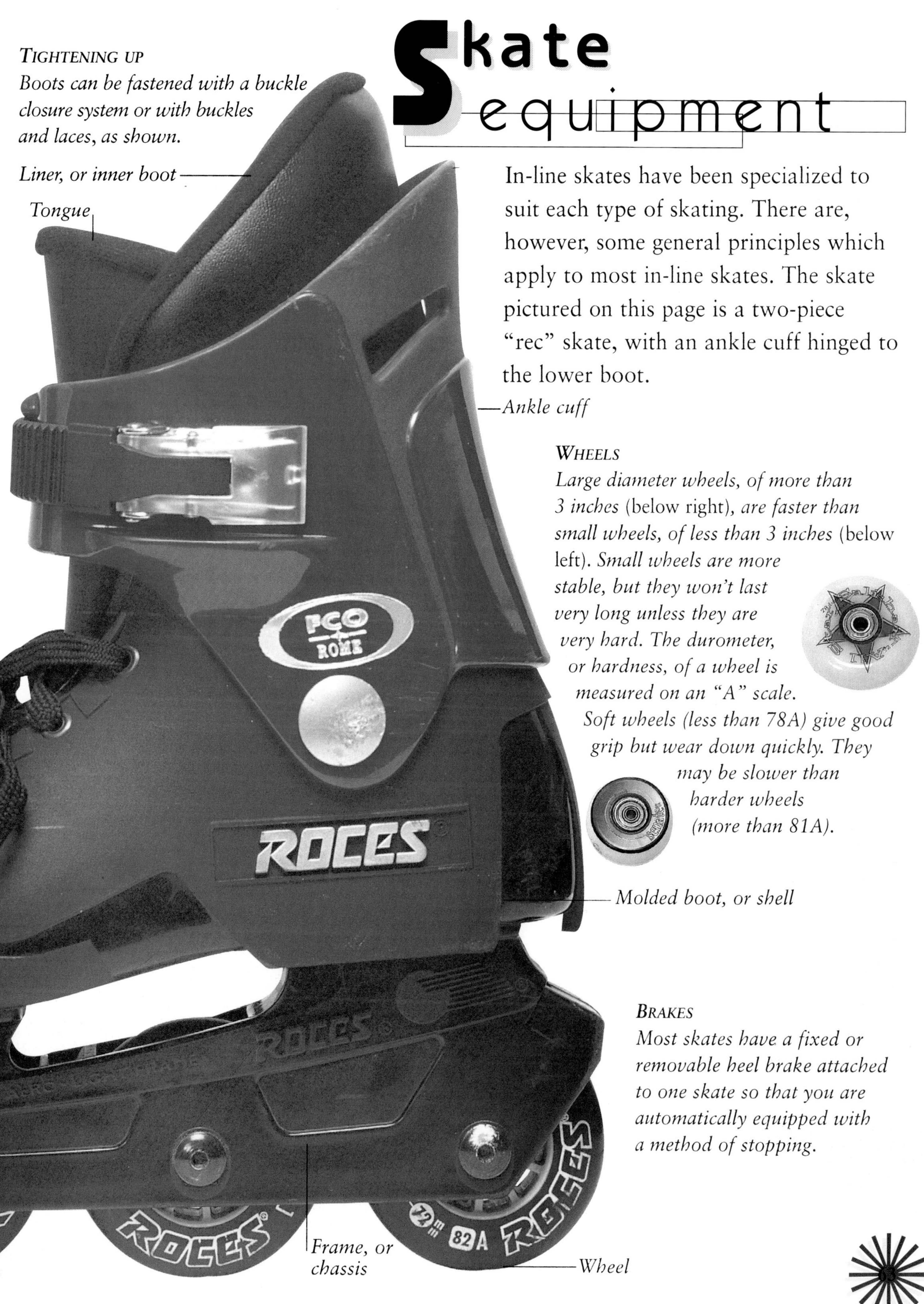

WHEELS

Large diameter wheels, of more than 3 inches (below right), *are faster than small wheels, of less than 3 inches* (below left). *Small wheels are more stable, but they won't last very long unless they are very hard. The durometer, or hardness, of a wheel is measured on an "A" scale. Soft wheels (less than 78A) give good grip but wear down quickly. They may be slower than harder wheels (more than 81A).*

BRAKES

Most skates have a fixed or removable heel brake attached to one skate so that you are automatically equipped with a method of stopping.

Mozart and independence

MOZART
(1756–1791)

MAIN WORKS

SYMPHONIES (41)

concertos:
for piano (27)
for violin (6)
for flute (2)
for clarinet
for bassoon
for horn (4)
for flute and harp

Sinfonia concertante for violin and viola

Serenade for Thirteen Wind Instruments

quintets:
for strings (6)
for clarinet and strings

quartets:
for strings (27)
for piano and strings (2)
for oboe and strings

trios:
for piano and strings (8)

sonatas:
for violin and piano (28)
for piano (19)

operas (23)

masses (19)

Wolfgang Amadeus Mozart was born in 1756 into an ordered and settled society. But by the time he died 35 years later, the world had been shaken, first by the American War of Independence in the 1770s, and then by the shattering upheaval of the French Revolution. During his lifetime, the intellectual movement known as *Sturm und Drang* ("Storm and Stress") provided the mental background for those who, like Mozart, questioned the fossilized social framework into which they had been born.

His father, Leopold, was one of the leading violinists of his day, and made sure that his son met and learned from the most talented people in Europe. As a young man in the service of the Archbishop of Salzburg, Mozart became increasingly critical of the system of patronage under which he and his father lived. He despised his colleagues, whom he described as "those coarse, slovenly, dissolute court musicians," and commented bitterly that, although he sat below the valets at table, he "had the honor of being placed above the cooks." His headstrong character led to his dismissal in 1781. From then on, Mozart was on his own.

At first, things went well. As the finest pianist in Vienna, he filled the concert halls. But he found, to his cost, that the day of true independence for composers had not yet dawned. Mozart's blunt speaking cannot have done much for his popularity, but he was so aware of his own genius that he had little

MOZART'S JOURNEYS

Leopold Mozart, knowing that his five-year-old son Wolfgang was a genius, took him on short tours to Munich and Vienna. The first Grand Tour began in June 1763 and continued for over three years. In Paris, Mozart met Madame de Pompadour (above). At this time, his first sonatas were already being published.

In London, he played for the king and queen and, under the influence of Johann Christian Bach (below), he wrote his first symphonies.
During his great Italian Tour, 1769-1771, Mozart received the Order of the Golden Spur from the pope, and was elected a member of the Bologna Philharmonic Society.

As a young man, on his last Grand Tour in 1777, Mozart met his cousin, Maria Thekla (above). Later, they poured out their high spirits in letters to each other. But Mozart's gaiety was short-lived. While in Paris, in 1778, his mother fell ill and died in his arms. Overcome with grief, he returned to Salzburg to become the archbishop's organist.

Mozart, at the age of six, sitting between his father, Leopold, and the Archbishop of Salzburg (below) during a visit to Vienna in 1762.

Mozart's works are noted by "Köchel numbers" ("K" for short). Ludwig von Köchel (left) was an Austrian who studied the chronology of Mozart's works and systematically cataloged them. As nearly as possible, he put them in the order in which they were written.

patience with lesser musicians. He remarked of Muzio Clementi, the famous Italian composer whose piano works were later admired by Beethoven: "Clementi is a charlatan, like all Italians ... he has not the slightest expression or taste, still less feeling."

After a few years of success in Vienna, Mozart began to find himself in financial difficulties. His wife Constanze needed expensive medical care, and some experts claim that although he made plenty of money, he lost much of it in gambling. He failed to complete commissioned works, and his applications for various regular posts and the subscription concerts he planned (the usual way of raising money at the time), were unsuccessful. In his last years, Mozart was forced to send letters to his friends, begging for money; and when he died, on December 5, 1791, he was bundled into an unmarked pauper's grave.

Yet while Mozart was at the lowest ebb in his struggle against poverty, he was writing music of unruffled calm and beauty. It is astonishing that he could have composed a work as graceful as the Clarinet Quintet (K581) under such circumstances. Although many of his works, such as the D minor Piano Concerto (K466), are passionate and tragic in inspiration, Mozart's music breathes a spirit of joy and accepts sorrow as a necessary contrast. Haydn once said to Leopold Mozart: "Your son is the greatest composer known to me either personally or by name." No other composer has seen more deeply into the human heart than Mozart, or expressed his thoughts in music of such unerring beauty and grace. Now that more than 200 years have passed, Haydn's judgement still stands.

MOZART–FREEMASON

Mozart was born a Roman Catholic, and wrote many Masses and other works for the Church. Yet his deepest beliefs lay not in orthodox religion but in Freemasonry with its emphasis on universal benevolence and the brotherhood of man. As a Freemason, Mozart was the equal of his fellow Masons, many of whom were Viennese aristocrats. He became a Mason in 1784 and from then on composed many works for Masonic ceremonies – there were cantatas, and instrumental works such as the splendid Masonic Funeral Music. Because Freemasonry is a secret society, it makes much use of symbols and emblems (above). *The Magic Flute*, the opera Mozart composed in 1781, is based on the private initiation rites of the Freemasons (below) and is full of this kind of secret symbolism. Music played an important part in Freemasonry at this time. Since the number three was significant in Masonic ritual, the music was often in three-time, and as all members of Masonic Lodges were men, the choruses were for male voices only.

Mozart chafed under the system of servitude, and loathed having to follow his master wherever he chose to go. He wrote a letter of resignation but before it could be presented to the archbishop, Mozart had an argument with the court chamberlain, Count Arco, who kicked him down the stairs of the palace.

THE PHONOGRAPH

"And this week's number one in the pop charts, with over a million sold, is *Fifty-Three-and-a-Half*, by Dave 'n' Steve!" The record charts, along with vinyl records, cassettes and compact discs, and the whole area of recorded music and speech, began with "Mary had a little lamb."

It's him again – Thomas Edison. In 1877, he had the idea of recording sound so that it could be played back afterward.

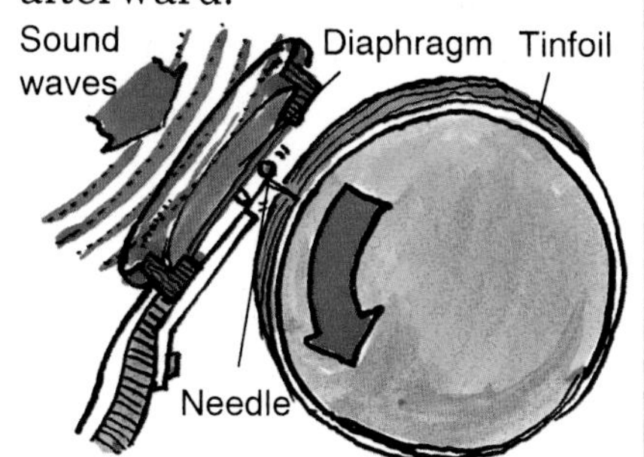

Edison designed a machine in which sound waves hit a thin, flat, metal sheet called a diaphragm. The waves made the diaphragm vibrate. The vibrations passed into a stylus or "needle." This pressed on a sheet of tinfoil, which was turning round on a cylinder. As the cylinder turned, the stylus pressed harder or softer for the different sounds, and made an up-and-down groove in the tinfoil. This was the recording.

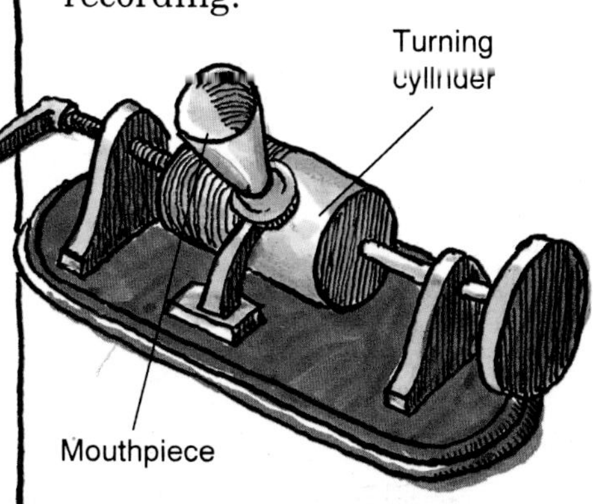

Groovy sounds

The recording in the tinfoil was changed back into sound waves by reversing the process. The cylinder turned, and the grooves made the stylus vibrate. These vibrations passed to the diaphragm, which shook the air around it, to make the original sounds.

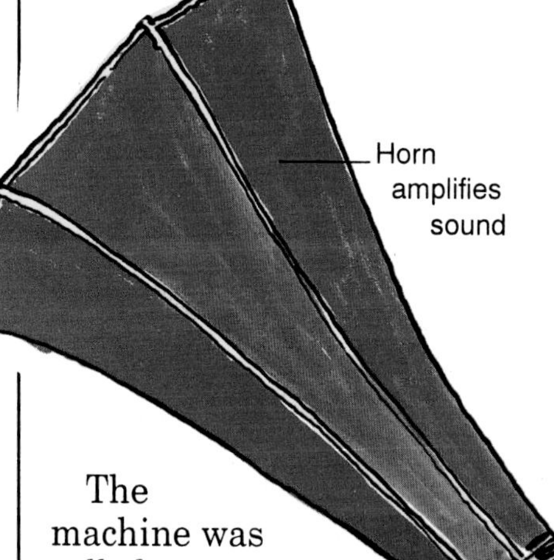

The machine was called a phonograph. Edison spoke into it for a test recording: "Mary had a little lamb." It worked!

Other inventors saw that the phonograph could be used for music and entertainment. In 1885, they used a cylinder covered with wax, instead of tinfoil. Lots of copies of one recording could be made, by pouring hot wax into a mold, which was shaped like the cylinder with its groove.

Cylinder to disc

In 1887, Emile Berliner came up with a flat disc, instead of a cylinder. The stylus was in a wavy groove and vibrated from side to side, rather than up and down as in Edison's version. Again, many discs could be made from one original recording.

Needle vibrates

Groove in disc

Berliner did not want his version to be confused with Edison's phonograph, so he called it the Gram-o-Phone. He gradually improved the sound quality. Soon people were buying the first recordings of songs. The "charts" had begun!

LPs to singles

Early record discs went round 78 times each minute, or 78 rpm (revolutions per minute). The discs were made of shellac. Vinyl records were introduced in 1946.

In 1948, the first successful long-playing records came out. They had much narrower grooves, went round at 33⅓ rpm, and lasted up to 30 minutes on each side.

Soon after, smaller vinyl discs came out. They usually had a single song on each side, they were seven inches across, and they went round at 45 rpm. They became known as "singles" or "45s."

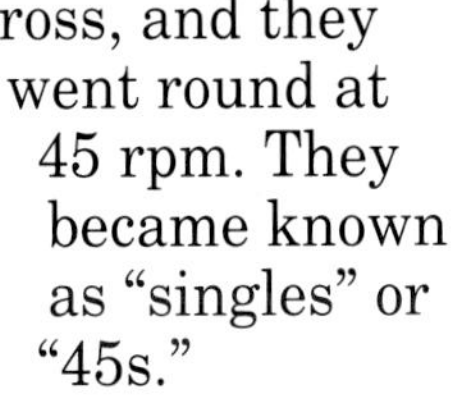

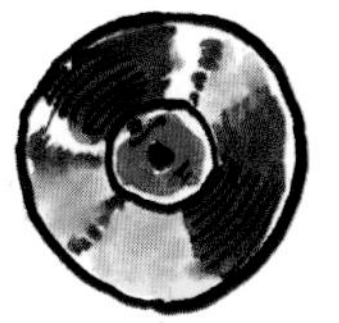

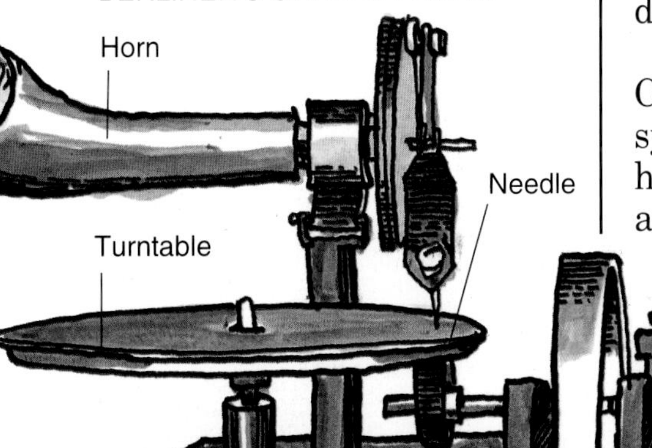

Tapes big and small

In the 1950s, enthusiasts recorded sounds as patterns of tiny magnetic patches, on a long tape. The big tape reels were awkward to handle, and they took a long time to wind up.

In the 1960s, the Philips company brought out much smaller magnetic tapes, in little plastic cases or "case-ettes." They were neat and easy to handle. You could buy them already recorded, or make your own recordings. The cassette had arrived.

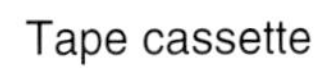

In the 1980s, compact discs began to take over. They had patterns of microscopic bumps and pits, detected by a laser beam.

If Edison could see all the CDs, cassettes, LPs and hi-fi systems today, he would be amazed!

Aaaah, nice little dog

• The world-famous sign of HMV Records is a dog listening to the sound from a gramophone. This was a real dog, that lived in about 1900. Its owner had made a gramophone recording, but then died. When the recording played, the dog came over and sadly listened to – His Master's Voice.

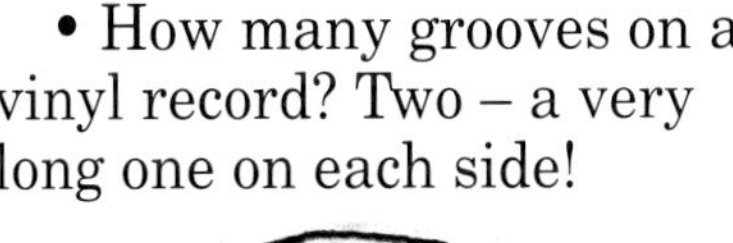

• How many grooves on a vinyl record? Two – a very long one on each side!

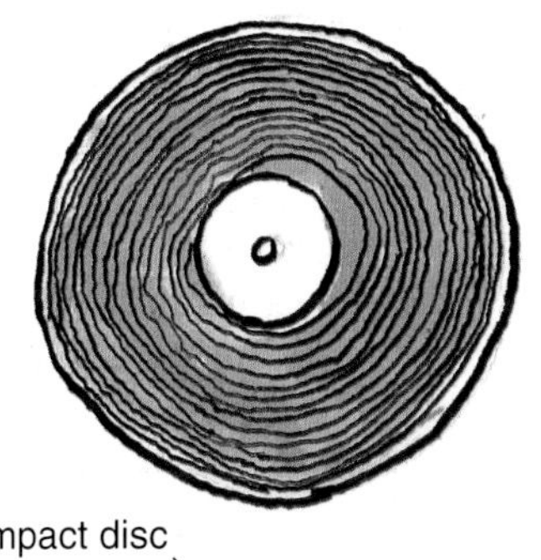

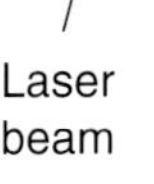

ANIMALS IN WATER

From seas and oceans, to rivers, lakes and ponds, the waters of the Earth teem with all sorts of animal life. Fish live in water all the time, while animals, such as frogs, are amphibious (specially adapted to living on land and in water), and only spend part of their life-cycle in water. Some of the largest animals in the world, such as the whale, can only live in water, because it supports their massive body. Ocean currents carry sea mammals, fish and microscopic animals, called zooplankton, around the world. Most animals are adapted to either fresh or salt water, but a few, such as eels and salmon, can survive in both.

Water birds
Ducks, geese and swans have webbed feet which help them swim. Rails and coots have long toes to walk over soft mud without sinking in. Long legs allow herons and storks to wade in deep water.

Animals in shells
Shellfish, such as crabs, limpets and mussels, have strong, hard shells to protect their soft bodies. Crabs are scavengers, eating almost anything edible from the seabed or seashore.

Insects
Water bugs, such as water boatmen and water beetles, inhabit freshwater ponds, slow-moving streams and still pools.

Fish
Roach and bream are freshwater fish which live in lakes and rivers all over Europe. Eels can survive in both salt and fresh water.

Sea mammals
Dolphins, sea cows and whales, like this humpback whale (left), spend their whole lives in the water. Thick layers of fat, called blubber, help to keep them warm. They come to the surface to breathe air through a blowhole on the top of the head. Other sea mammals include seals, sea lions and walruses.

Dolphins and porpoises have a smooth, sleek, streamlined shape. Water flows past them easily, allowing them to swim faster.

Mermaids

Mermaids have appeared in stories about the sea for hundreds of years. The top half of a mermaid is like a woman, and the bottom half is like a fish. People used to believe that mermaids lured sailors to their deaths with their beauty and enchanted singing.

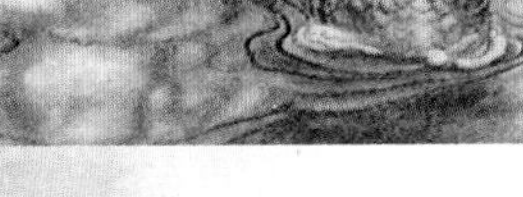

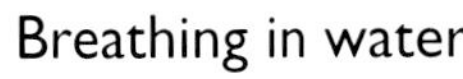

Breathing in water

All animals need to take in oxygen, which allows them to release energy from their food. There is oxygen dissolved in water which fish absorb by gulping in water and forcing it over tiny, feather-like structures called gills (shown right). Gills are rich in blood vessels, and oxygen is absorbed directly into the blood and carried around the body. Like other animals which breathe oxygen, fish produce carbon dioxide as a waste product. It passes from the blood through the gills and into the water. Gills, or gill-like structures, are also found in molluscs (animals in shells), crabs and water insects, such as mayfly nymphs.

Gill

Otter

Mammals

Otters are specially adapted to living both in and out of water. They have soft underfur which traps air, keeping water out and body heat in, and webbed feet for swimming.

Leeches and medicine

Doctors once believed that too much blood in the body was the cause of some diseases. They put water animals, called leeches, on a patient's body to suck out some of the blood. When a leech feeds, it produces a chemical that stops blood from clotting (thickening). A single leech can rapidly take in three or four times its own weight in blood.

Reptiles

Most reptiles live on land but some, such as sea-turtles, crocodiles and alligators, spend much of their lives in the water, coming to land mainly to lay eggs. Turtles swim with their paddle-like flippers, while crocodiles and alligators use their powerful, flattened tails for swimming.

Crocodiles and turtles are ancient reptiles which have lived in the world's seas and rivers for thousands of years.

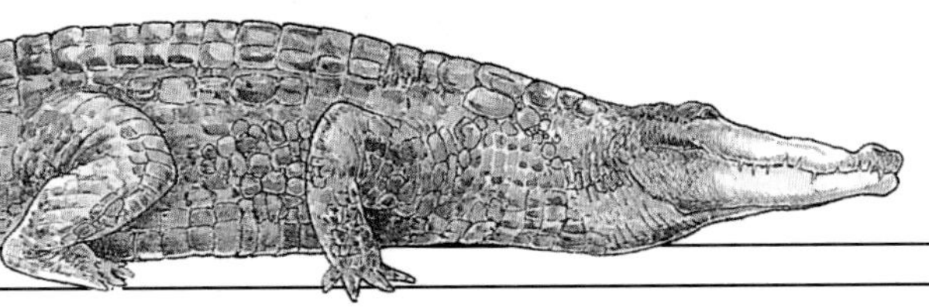

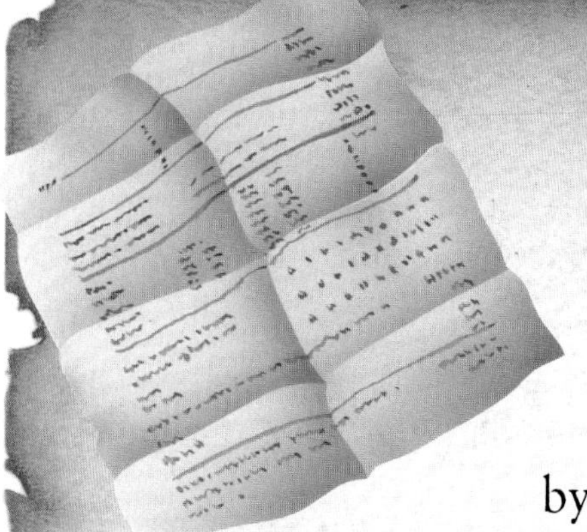

Secret Words

As soon as people learned to write, they wanted to keep others from reading what they had written. The ancient Egyptians, Greeks, and Romans all devised means of disguising written information. An 11th-century Chinese manual describes how pre-arranged messages could be sent by using the beginning of a line of poetry! By the 16th-century it was common for European diplomats to communicate all sensitive information in code, and many of them employed a full-time "cipher secretary."

The invention of radio demanded new cipher skills – or good luck. During World War I, a German radio broadcast was thought to be just a test signal, until a recording was played slowly on a phonograph and it was found to contain a secret message!

Today, the invention of the computer has taken codes into a world that writers of Egyptian hieroglyphs could not even have dreamed of.

Silky Codes
In World War II, codes for sending messages back from occupied France were printed on silk that could be folded tightly for concealment (top).

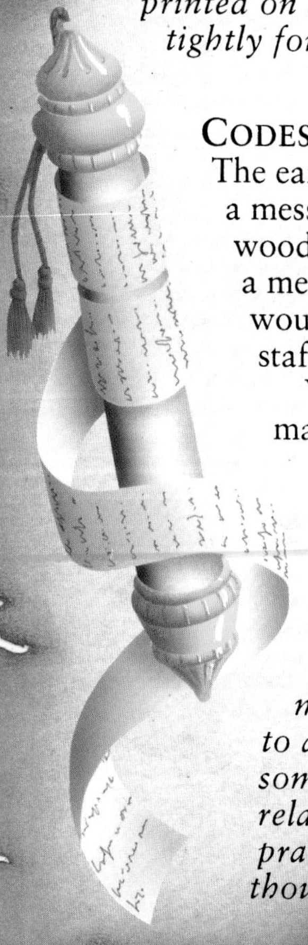

Codes and Ciphers

The earliest device for encoding a message (cryptography) was a wooden staff. The sender wrote a message on a strip of material wound in a spiral around the staff (*left*).

When unwound, the writing made no sense. But the recipient read it by simply wrapping it around a similar staff of his own.

Secrets on the Wing
However subtle, an intercepted message written in code is likely to arouse suspicion. To avoid this, some agents use carrier pigeons to relay vital information (right) *– a practice that has continued for thousands of years.*

Samuel Pepys' Diary

Between 1660 and 1669, Samuel Pepys (*left*) kept the most famous diary in the English language. During his lifetime, England was alive with scares and rumors of plot, rebellion, and invasion by the Dutch. In such an atmosphere, it is easy to see why he wanted to write in code rather than in a normal script.

As a result, Pepys wrote in a shorthand that was not deciphered for another 150 years. His diary was finally read for the first time in 1825.

The Enigma

In the 1930s, German scientists developed a brilliant coding device called Enigma. Unknown to them, in 1939 British agents gained access to the secrets. Copies of Enigma (below) *were made to speed up the decoding.*

A Body of Evidence

During World War I, Russian sailors discovered the drowned body of a German navy officer (left). *Death had made the corpse rigid, and in its stiff arms were clasped two books.*

One book contained one of the main codes used by the Germans to send radio messages. The other had detailed maps of the entire North Sea. The books were sent to the British Navy, and for the rest of the war, they were able to decode virtually every German wireless message.

Morse's Dots and Dashes

American Samuel F.B. Morse invented the telegraph, the first means of sending a message down an electric wire. But to make use of his invention, he also had to devise a simple means of transmitting language. The result was the Morse Code, which translated the letters of the alphabet into dots (•) and dashes (—).

INTERNATIONAL MORSE CODE

A	•—	J	•———	S	•••
B	—•••	K	—•—	T	—
C	—•—•	L	•—••	U	••—
D	—••	M	——	V	•••—
E	•	N	—•	W	•——
F	••—•	O	———	X	—••—
G	——•	P	•——•	Y	—•——
H	••••	Q	——•—	Z	——••
I	••	R	•—•		

The best-known message is the call for help: ••• / ——— / ••• Can you work out this spy warning? •—— / •— / •—•• / •—•• / ••• // •••• / •— / •••— / • // • / •— / •—• / •••

Anatomy of a Mountain Bike

A mountain bike, like any other bike, consists of a frame to which wheels and other components, such as brakes, gears, and pedals, are attached.

The parts that make a mountain bike look different from other bikes are its large tires, its set of three chainrings, which gives it low gears for hill climbing, and its flat handlebars, fitted with powerful brake levers.

MOUNTAIN BIKE BRAKES

To make the brakes on a mountain bike powerful enough to stop the bike quickly and to allow the bike to be ridden through mud without jamming up, the brakes are fitted to a specially welded part of the frame.

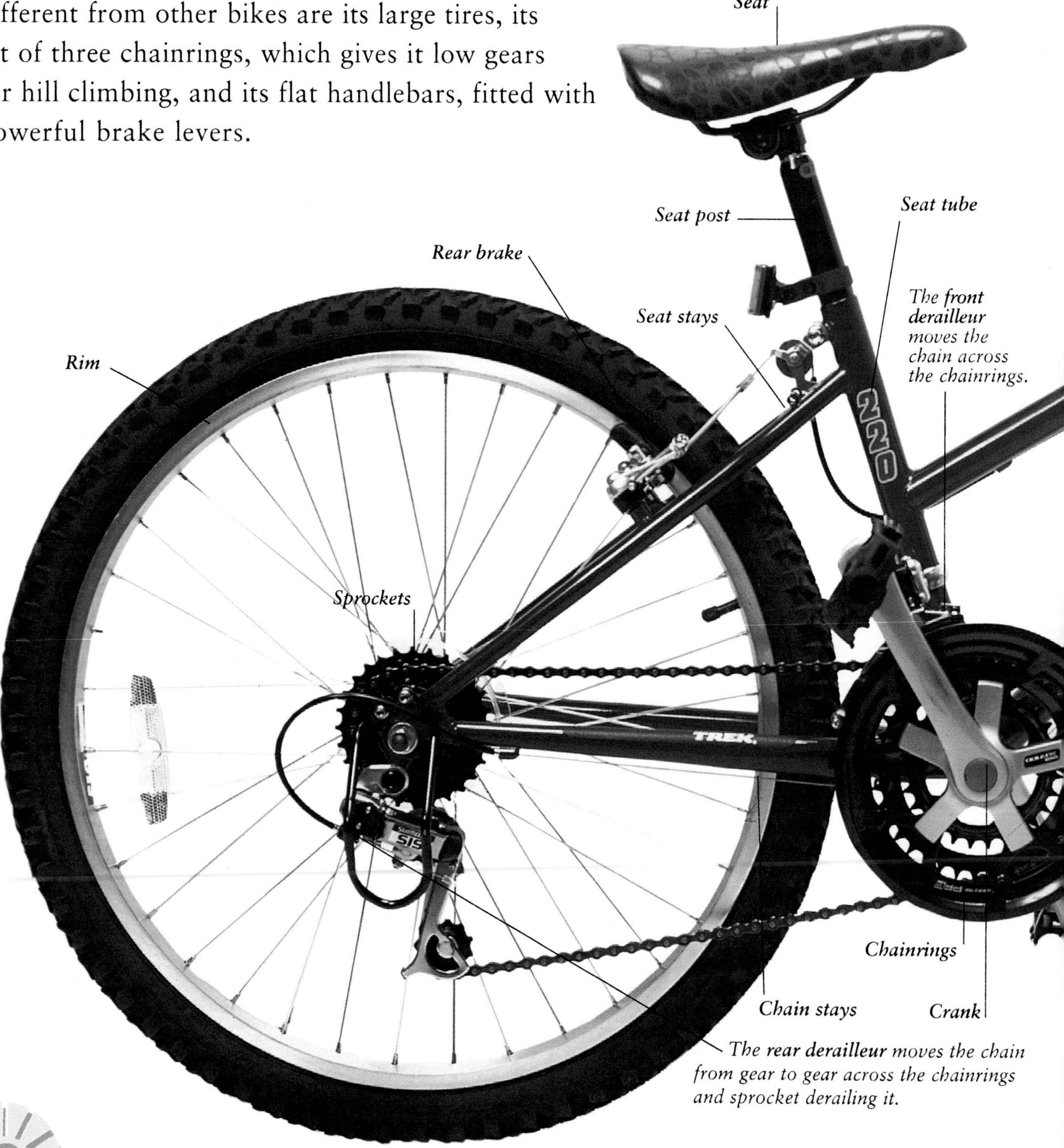

GETTING IN GEAR

The mountain bike pictured has gear shifters, operated by the rider turning the handlebar grips. Other mountain bikes may have push button gear shifters or simple gear levers.

HISTORY

In the 1960s, motorcyclists were banned from speeding down California dirt roads. The riders continued — but on bikes. The earliest mountain bikes, such as the *Stumpjumper* (*below*), were fitted with motorcycle handlebars.

*The **hub** contains the axle and bearings to keep the wheel in place.*

DINOSAUR COURTSHIP

Did dinosaurs live in families, and how did they talk to each other? How did they lay their eggs? New work in North America and in Mongolia has shown that dinosaurs were able to pass complex signals to each other, partly through sight, and partly through sound. The males and females often looked quite different from each other. The males seem to have had larger horns and crests which they may have used in fighting for mates, and for displaying, just as with deer and antelope today. After the males and females had paired off, the mothers made large nests in the ground, and laid their eggs. It seems that dinosaur societies were probably just as complicated as any mammal community today.

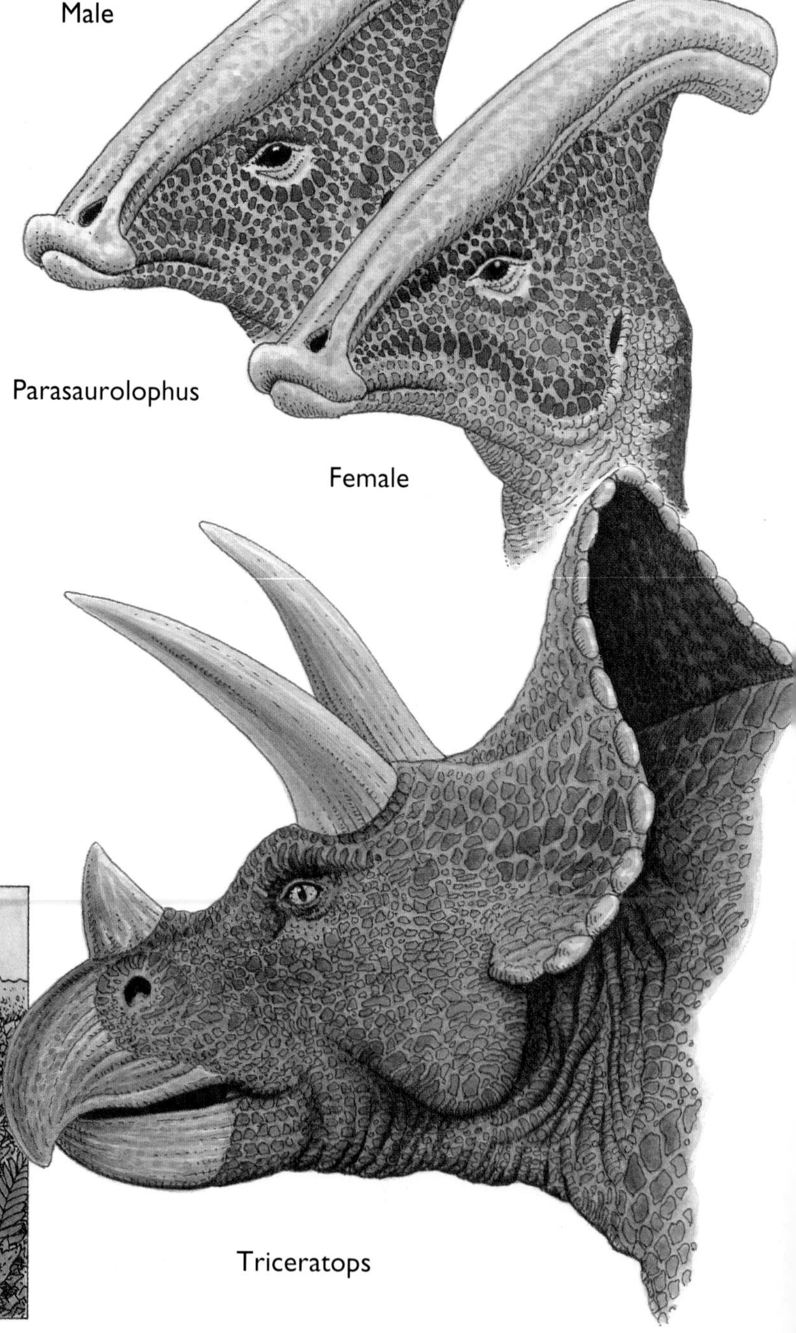

Males and females

Some of the biggest differences between males and females are seen among the plant-eating, duckbilled dinosaurs, like *Corythosaurus*, *Parasaurolophus*, and *Tsintaosaurus*. When many skeletons are found together, half of them may have tall crests, and the other half smaller crests. The horned dinosaurs, like *Triceratops*, also seem to show differences in the length of the horns over their eyes. The horns of the meat-eater *Ceratosaurus* may have been larger in males, who probably used them to establish territory.

Dinosaurs laid ten to thirty eggs at a time, often arranged in regular circles, in an earth nest on the ground. They covered the nest with leaves and mud to protect the eggs. After a few weeks the young hatched out. Some parent dinosaurs then fed the young after hatching.

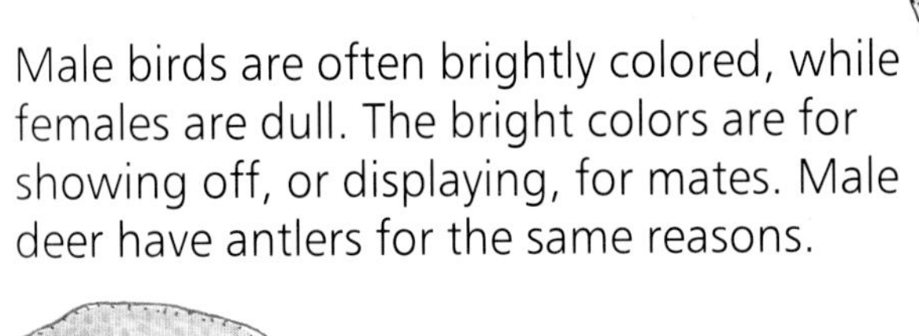

Male birds are often brightly colored, while females are dull. The bright colors are for showing off, or displaying, for mates. Male deer have antlers for the same reasons.

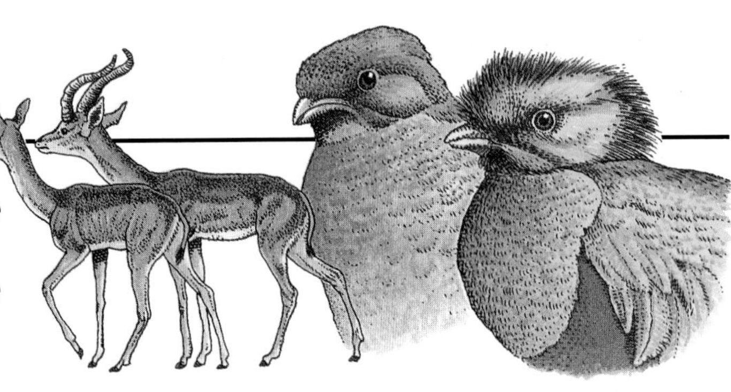

Corythosaurus

Tsintaosaurus

Ceratosaurus

John Sibbick

One of the best-known modern dinosaur artists is John Sibbick. He painted a series of pictures of all the major dinosaurs for a 1985 book, and he is now one of the most famous dinosaur painters.

Musical crests

Inside the crests of the duckbills, air passages were found linking the nostrils to the throat. When air passes through a tube, it causes it to vibrate, producing sound waves. Try blowing down a long, coiled tube. This is how trumpets produce sound. When these dinosaurs puffed out hard, they whistled and produced trumpeting sounds.

SURVIVE THE COLOSSEUM
INTRODUCTION
The scene here shows the Colosseum packed with Romans lusting for blood. The giant canopy has been pulled out to protect them from the sun, and gladiators are fighting wild beasts in the arena.
Imagine you are a gladiator. Have a go at the puzzles and see if you can survive the tough training and the horrors of the wild beast show before escaping from the arena. Good luck – the answers are at the bottom of page 77!
1 ANIMAL TRACKER
If you're going to have to fight against wild animals, it's worth knowing their tracks so you can tell what's hiding around the corner. Which tracks *below* should tell you to watch out?
a
b
c
d
e
f
XI
VIII
7 TIME TO ESCAPE!
Now you've worked out the secret message, can you escape from the maze of corridors beneath the Colosseum? Be quick, because the *fugitivarii* (slave catchers) will soon be after you!
6 MIRROR MESSAGE
Safely beneath the arena, you find this message telling you how to escape the maze of tunnels (*left*). Using a mirror, write down these instructions:
To escape, you must avoid the
guards and the wild animals.
But once you get a sword from
the center of the maze, you can
fight past the lion and escape.

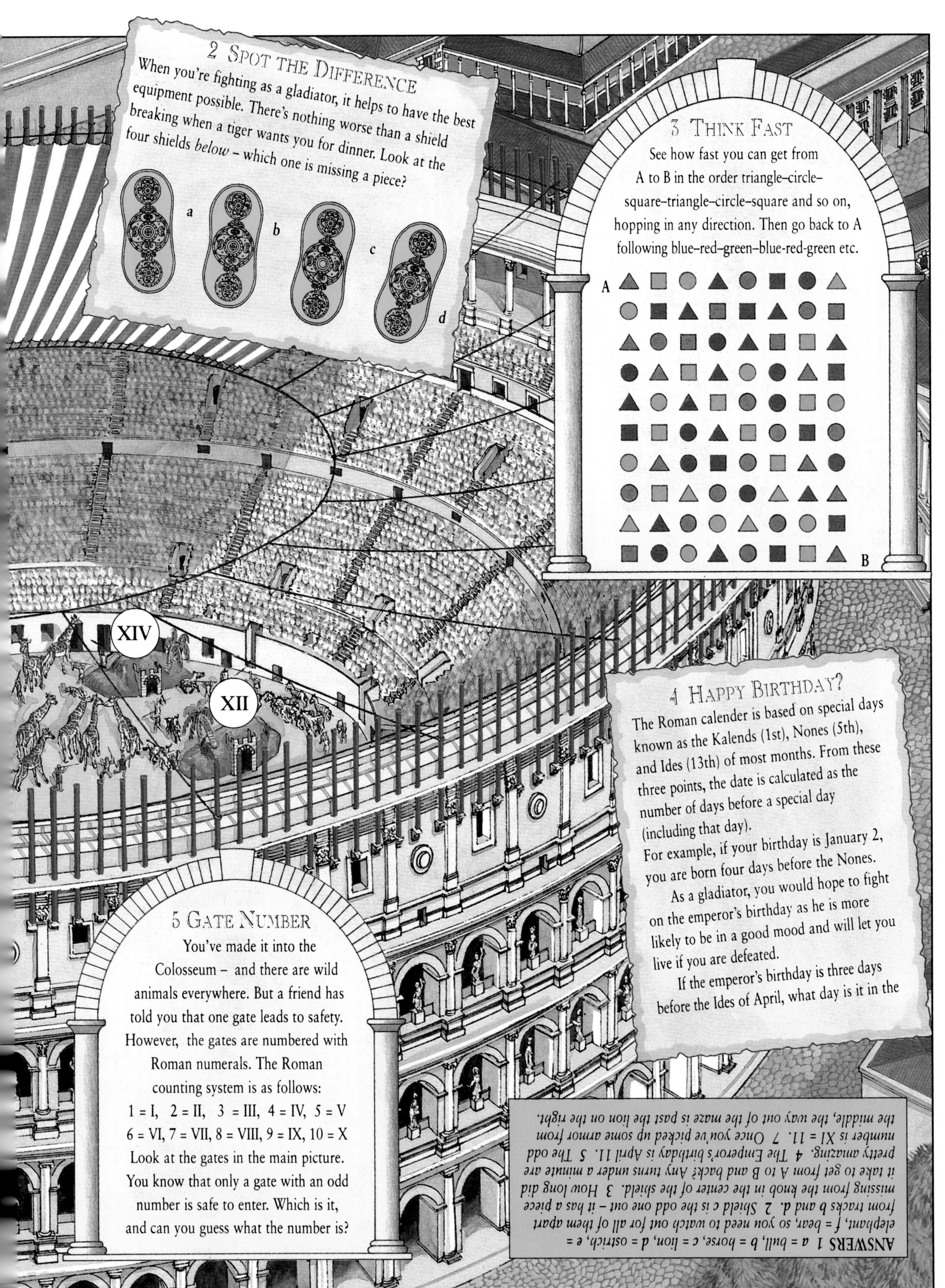

2 Spot the Difference

When you're fighting as a gladiator, it helps to have the best equipment possible. There's nothing worse than a shield breaking when a tiger wants you for dinner. Look at the four shields *below* – which one is missing a piece?

3 Think Fast

See how fast you can get from A to B in the order triangle–circle–square–triangle–circle–square and so on, hopping in any direction. Then go back to A following blue–red–green–blue–red–green etc.

4 Happy Birthday?

The Roman calender is based on special days known as the Kalends (1st), Nones (5th), and Ides (13th) of most months. From these three points, the date is calculated as the number of days before a special day (including that day).

For example, if your birthday is January 2, you are born four days before the Nones.

As a gladiator, you would hope to fight on the emperor's birthday as he is more likely to be in a good mood and will let you live if you are defeated.

If the emperor's birthday is three days before the Ides of April, what day is it in the

5 Gate Number

You've made it into the Colosseum – and there are wild animals everywhere. But a friend has told you that one gate leads to safety. However, the gates are numbered with Roman numerals. The Roman counting system is as follows:

1 = I, 2 = II, 3 = III, 4 = IV, 5 = V
6 = VI, 7 = VII, 8 = VIII, 9 = IX, 10 = X

Look at the gates in the main picture. You know that only a gate with an odd number is safe to enter. Which is it, and can you guess what the number is?

ANSWERS 1 *a* = *bull*, *b* = *horse*, *c* = *lion*, *d* = *ostrich*, *e* = *elephant*, *f* = *bear*, *so you need to watch out for all of them apart from tracks b and d.* **2** *Shield c is the odd one out – it has a piece missing from the knob in the center of the shield.* **3** *How long did it take to get from A to B and back? Any turns under a minute are pretty amazing.* **4** *The Emperor's birthday is April 11.* **5** *The odd number is XI = 11.* **7** *Once you've picked up some armor from the middle, the way out of the maze is past the lion on the right.*

BIOSPHERE 2
THE GREENHOUSE EARTH

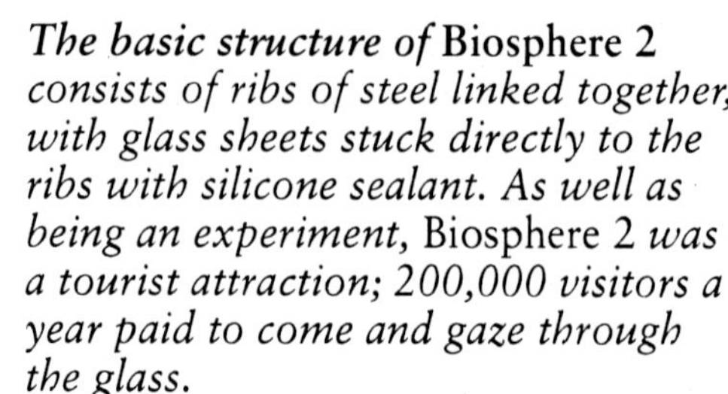

The basic structure of Biosphere 2 *consists of ribs of steel linked together, with glass sheets stuck directly to the ribs with silicone sealant. As well as being an experiment,* Biosphere 2 *was a tourist attraction; 200,000 visitors a year paid to come and gaze through the glass.*

In the desert,40 miles north of Tucson, Arizona, a model of the earth has been created inside a huge greenhouse. *Biosphere 2* was home for two years to eight volunteers who survived – more or less – on what they could grow within the 130,000 sq ft of the building. Their aim was to prove that life was sustainable inside the sealed mini-world, and to carry out research for the possible construction of future space colonies.

Abigail Alling prepares to dive into the Ocean biome *(above). Not everything inside was hard work, however. The occupants had a recreation room (below) where they could relax, talk, and play games.*

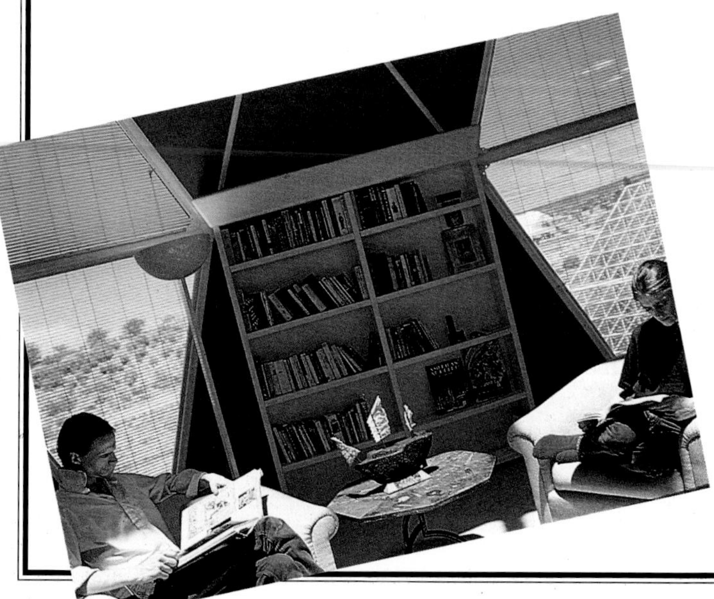

Inside *Biosphere 2* were small-scale copies of the oceans, grasslands, forests, marshes, and deserts found in Biosphere 1 – the earth itself. The eight "Biospherians" shared the space with 3,800 other plant and animal species, designed to create as balanced an eco-system as possible. They had problems, from crop failures to mites, and all of them lost a great deal of weight.

Biosphere 2 *consists of two linked glasshouses, the circular domed agricultural space and the pyramidal section housing the artificial habitats. To allow for air inside to expand and contract with the changing temperature,* Biosphere 2 *was connected to a "lung" – a huge rubber bag in a dome – that could fill and empty.*

The most serious problem was a steadily declining level of oxygen inside *Biosphere 2*, which exposed its occupants to conditions similar to those experienced 15,000 feet up a mountain. The plants ought to have created enough oxygen, but for reasons so far unexplained, were unable to do so. Eventually, more oxygen was pumped in, breaking the original promises, but preventing the Biospherians' health from suffering permanent damage. Remarkably, there was only one serious argument in the whole period.

***The savannah biome is** the area inside* Biosphere 2 *where the world's grasslands are modeled. 45 species of grass were planted. Colonies of ants and termites provided a natural balance. The other biomes were a rainforest, an ocean with a coral reef, and a desert. Many species died, but some survived.*

TRACK EVENTS

Track competitions include running and walking races. Both the ancient Greeks and Romans held running races, and various types of races have been popular ever since. Marathons, or long-distance road races, have mythical origins. One Greek legend tells of a messenger, Pheidippides, who ran 26 miles (43 km) from Marathon to Athens with news of a great victory – then died of exhaustion! This distance is still used for modern marathons. Race walking also covers long distances – up to 30 miles (50 km). Walkers try to reach a speed of 9 miles (15 km) per hour.

THE IMPORTANCE OF TIME
Before stopwatches were invented, there was no proper timing of races and competitors simply raced against each other. Electronic timers which can read times to thousandths of a second *(left)* have replaced traditional stopwatches. This is vital when a split second can make the difference between winning or losing, or can set a new record.

A CHALLENGING EVENT
Hurdling *(below)* became a competitive event in the 1870s. The idea came from cross-country running, which often involved jumping over fences and walls. Ten hurdles must be cleared in as short a time as possible.

ON YOUR MARK...
The 100-m sprint is one of the fastest, most exciting races of all. The sprinters start from special blocks *(left)* so that they can take off easily and reach a high speed in a short time.

EDUCATED ATHLETES
In the 19th-century, English schools and colleges invented various forms of cross-country running *(right)*. Paper chases were led by a single runner who scattered a trail of paper – but the sport was stopped by an anti-litter law! Cross-country running is still a popular sport both for amateur and professional athletes.

THE SPIRIT OF THE OLYMPICS

The modern Olympics were first held in 1896 to promote world peace. The rings on the flag represent the five continents, linked in friendship, and at least one of the colors is shown on every flag in the world. New sports, like synchronized swimming and snowboarding, feature in the Olympics every year, but the Games still include events with ancient origins, such as gymnastics.

SPORT FOR ALL
Disability does not prevent athletes from taking part in all events. The Paralympics for disabled athletes are held every four years, while athletes with disabilities have competed and won medals in the Olympics and the Commonwealth Games. Athletes in wheelchairs compete in all the major marathons.

WOMEN'S GYMNASTICS
Only women perform on the beam *(right)* and uneven parallel bars. Until only recently the Russian womens gymnastic team dominated all the major competitions, including the Olympic Games.

MEN'S GYMNASTICS
Men's gymnastics became an Olympic event in 1900. Only men perform on the parallel and horizontal bars, rings, and pommel horse *(above)*.

THE LIFE OF A CHAMPION
Gymnastics requires a huge amount of training and great physical strength. Gymnasts, like all athletes, must devote themselves to their sport.

OLGA KORBUT (b. 1956)
Seventeen-year-old Korbut, from the former Soviet Union, shot to fame with her brilliant performance at the 1972 Olympic Games. She was loved by the public for her breathtaking gymnastic skills and warm personality. Her fame greatly increased the worldwide popularity of gymnastics.

Korbut

City fires

“All the sky were of a fiery aspect, like the top of a burning oven...” ***John Evelyn, diarist, on the Fire of London, 1666***

In Pudding Lane, London, at two o’clock in the morning on Sunday September 2, 1666, a baker and his family were awakened by smoke and flames coming from their bakery. They managed to escape by clambering over the roofs of their neighbors’ houses, but the fire spread quickly from house to house. Soon, whole streets were ablaze — the flames fanned by strong winds. London, like most large towns of the time (including Nuremburg in Germany, *above*), was full of wooden houses packed tightly together. Their roofs were thatched with straw and coated with pitch (a highly flammable substance) for waterproofing. Following a hot, rainless summer, the timbers and straw were dry as a bone. Small fires were commonplace, but this, the Great Fire of London, was something else. There were no official firefighting forces at this time so disorganized bands of ordinary people were left to pass buckets of water to the flames. Houses were blown up to stop the fire from spreading, filling the air with the sound and smell of gunpowder. Nothing could stop the raging blaze until, after four days, the wind dropped and it began to die down.

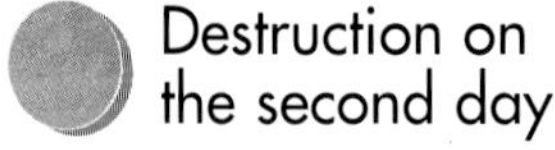

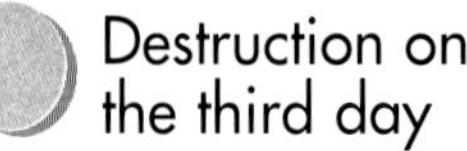

FIGHTING FIRES WITH WATER PISTOLS

*The first known fire engines were invented by the ancient Romans. They were like large buckets on wheels (*below*), with two hand-operated pumps on either side that produced a jet of water.*

Similar engines were still being used during the Great Fire of London in 1666. The hoses were not powerful enough to shoot water to the tops of buildings. Hand-held pumps, which worked like large syringes, or water pistols, were also used — but were equally ineffectual.

ROME BURNS

The mad Roman Emperor Nero ordered the burning of Rome in 64 A.D. *(*below*), so that he could expand his palace. Gangs of thugs attacked those who tried to put out the flames, which burned for six days.*

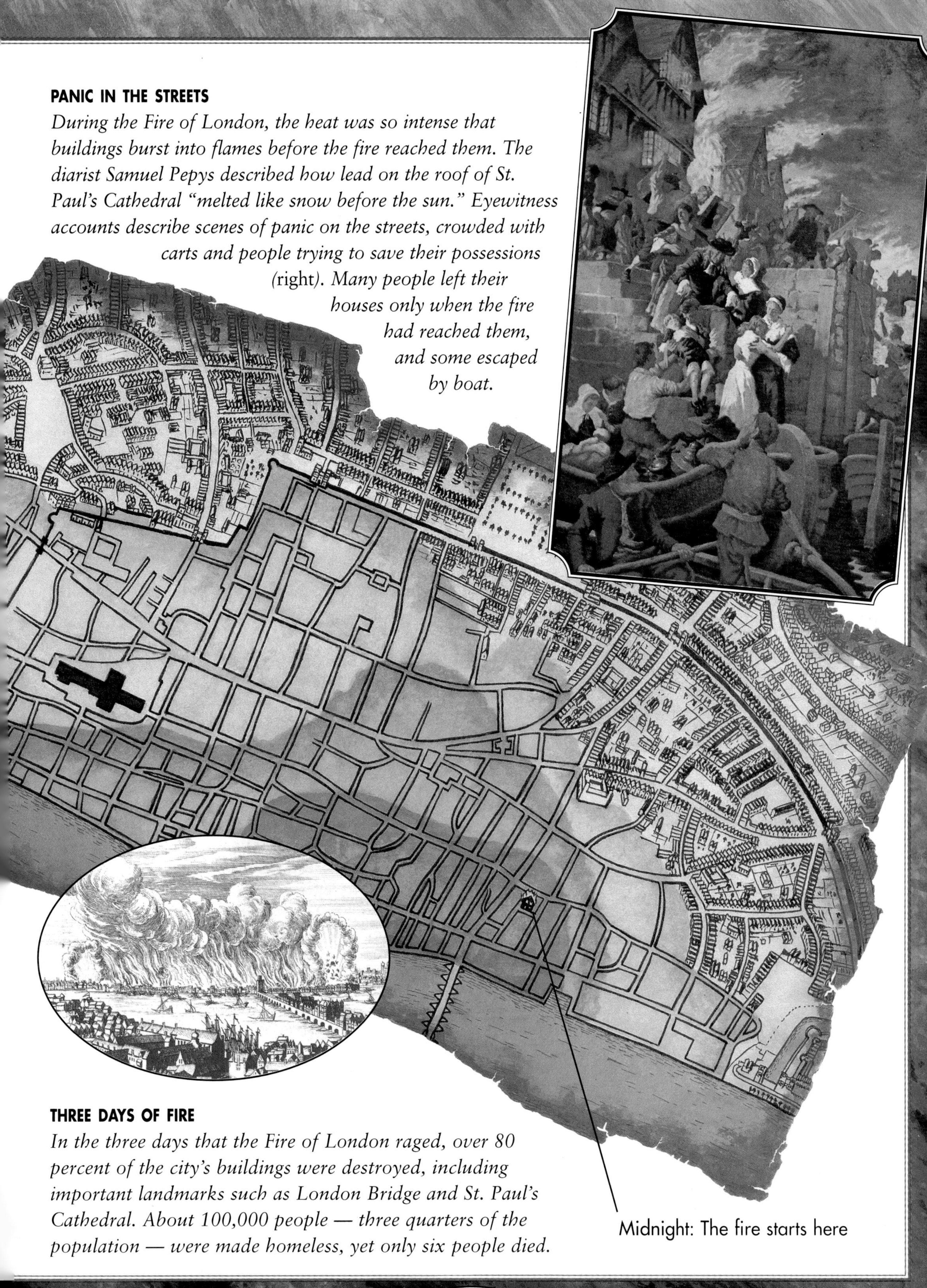

PANIC IN THE STREETS

During the Fire of London, the heat was so intense that buildings burst into flames before the fire reached them. The diarist Samuel Pepys described how lead on the roof of St. Paul's Cathedral "melted like snow before the sun." Eyewitness accounts describe scenes of panic on the streets, crowded with carts and people trying to save their possessions (right)*. Many people left their houses only when the fire had reached them, and some escaped by boat.*

THREE DAYS OF FIRE

In the three days that the Fire of London raged, over 80 percent of the city's buildings were destroyed, including important landmarks such as London Bridge and St. Paul's Cathedral. About 100,000 people — three quarters of the population — were made homeless, yet only six people died.

PURE COLOR

This project is to give you a chance to get to know the colors in your tubes or paintbox and to practice using them *flat*, in their pure form, without mixing them together.

If you look around you, you will see all kinds of colors, some bright, some dull, some easy to name, and some neither one nor the other. The world can look very complicated when you start trying to paint it. Some painters avoid looking at real things and just make things up! But most people like to paint what they see, at least from time to time.

Choosing your subject

Make a collection of everyday objects that correspond as closely as possible with the six pure colors from the color wheel (bottom right). Don't forget to include something to use as background – a bright curtain, perhaps, or a piece of colored paper. Find something red, blue, green, yellow, orange and purple. Take some time arranging everything in a group so that you can see all the objects clearly and they aren't in each other's way. Your painting will turn out very bright and cheerful.

You may like the bright colors so much that in future you may paint things brighter than they really are. Keep the colors clean when painting by using a different brush for each new color or by making sure you clean your brushes thoroughly between colors.

▽ ***"For the painting below I first made a simple drawing in pencil. I spent some time deciding where the colors would go. You can see that some of the marks look a bit like the ones I made on the previous page. Paint several pictures of this subject and choose the one you like best."***

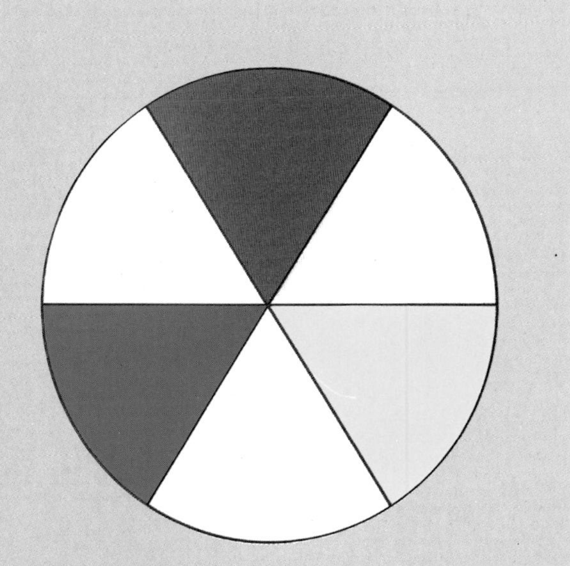

Primary colors

Here are the three basic or *primary* colors and their position on what is called the "color wheel." There are many kinds of red, yellow and blue but the primaries are the purest you can get.

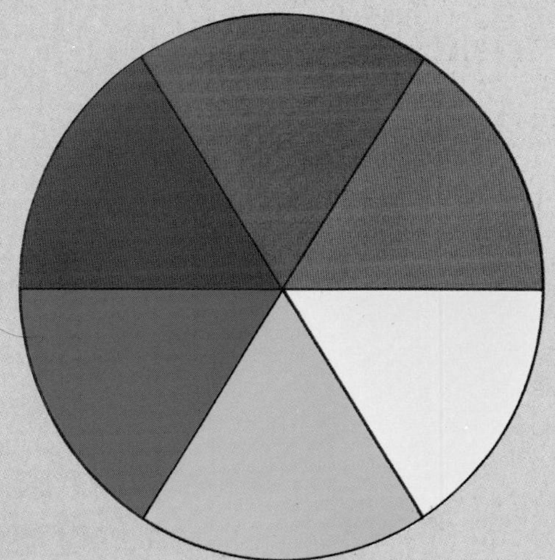

Secondary colors

Here are the primaries again with their neighbors: orange, green and purple. These are the *secondary* colors, mixed from the two primaries on either side of them. Experiment with painting the color wheel yourself.

Helicopter Action

As any object falls through the air, the air pushes against it. Many trees have winged seeds that use this push to make them spin. The wings are shaped like airfoils, so as they spin they stir up low pressure above them. Higher pressure from the blanket of air below slows their fall as they drift away from the "parent tree." Helicopters also get lift from twirling airfoils. Their rotor blades spin so hard that the low pressure creates enough lift to carry them into the air.

WHIRLIGIG

1 Make two small airfoils from two pieces of oak tag, 4in by 3in. Fold each piece with an overlap.

1

2 Push the overlapping edges together and tape them together. One side will curve up like a wing.

2

3

3 Spread a little glue onto each end of a stiff straw or thin stick. With the curved side of the wings pointing up, glue them onto the straw so that they face in different directions.

4

4 Tape another straw to the one holding the wings. Use a piece of modeling clay to weigh down the end. This keeps the whirligig level.

5 To send the whirligig spinning, hold it between the palms of your hands. Brush your hands together, pulling one toward you and pushing the other away. As your hands come apart, the whirligig is released, twirling as it flies.

5

BRIGHT IDEAS

Make another, bigger whirligig by doubling the size of the blades. Do larger blades give more lift because they create more low pressure? Therefore do you have to spin the whirligig as hard as before?

Try fixing the wings of your whirligig at different angles. Notice how this affects the lift. Drop your whirligig. Does it spin as it falls?

WHY IT WORKS

As you twirl and release your whirligig the wings give it lift. Their airfoil shape cuts through the air smoothly, but the "bulge" in the top stirs up the air, creating low pressure above. The air pressure beneath the wings, higher by comparison, pushes the whirligig skyward. A fast spin creates a big lift, greater even than the pull of gravity. But as the spin slows down, the lift is lessened and gravity wins, pulling the whirligig to the ground.

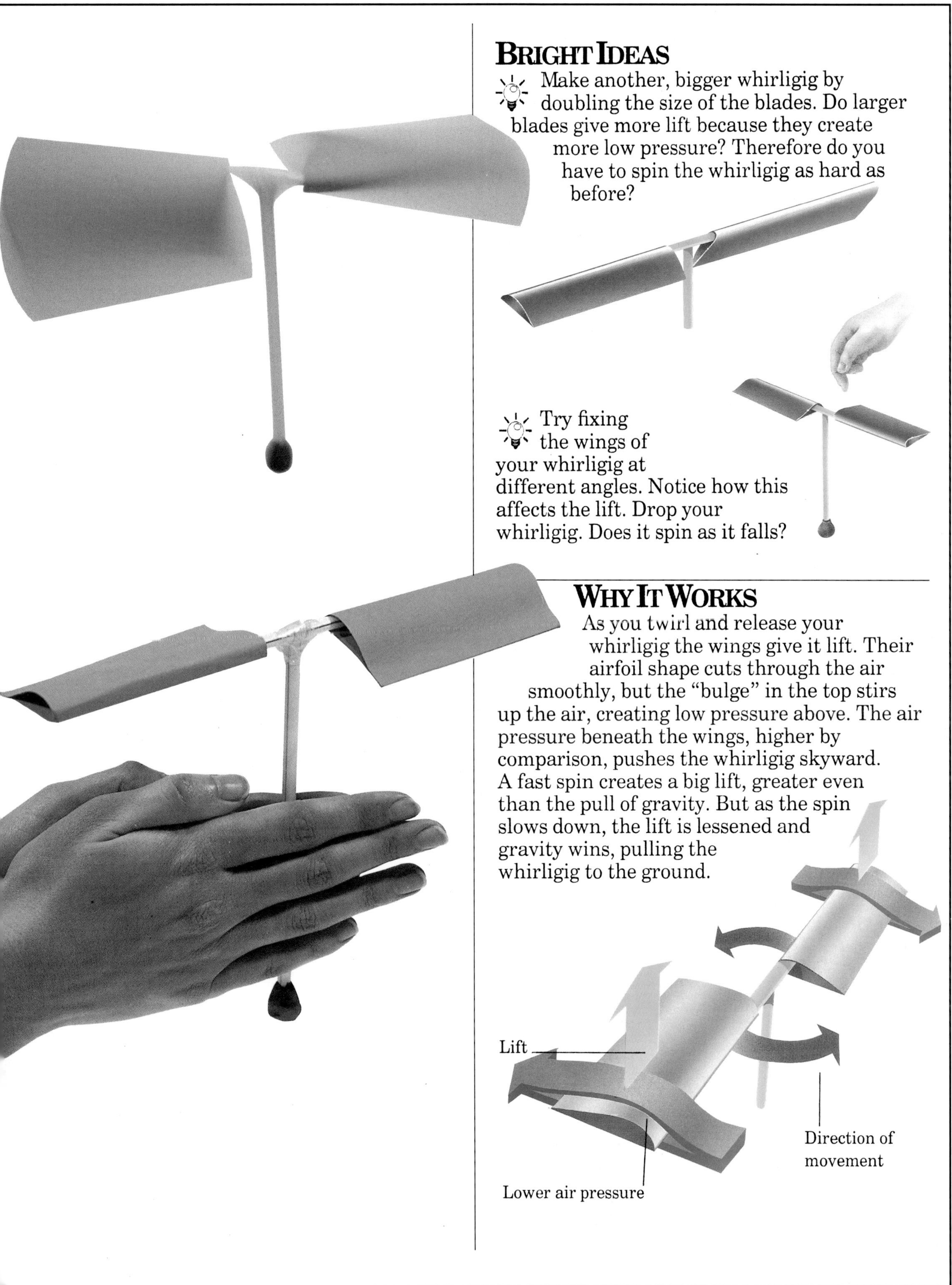

Why are most plants green?

Plants make much of their food by a process called photosynthesis. This involves absorbing sunlight and using the energy to manufacture its food. The light is absorbed by a special pigment called chlorophyll, which is green. Red seaweed has a red pigment that helps out, but it is the green chlorophyll that actually does the photosynthesis.

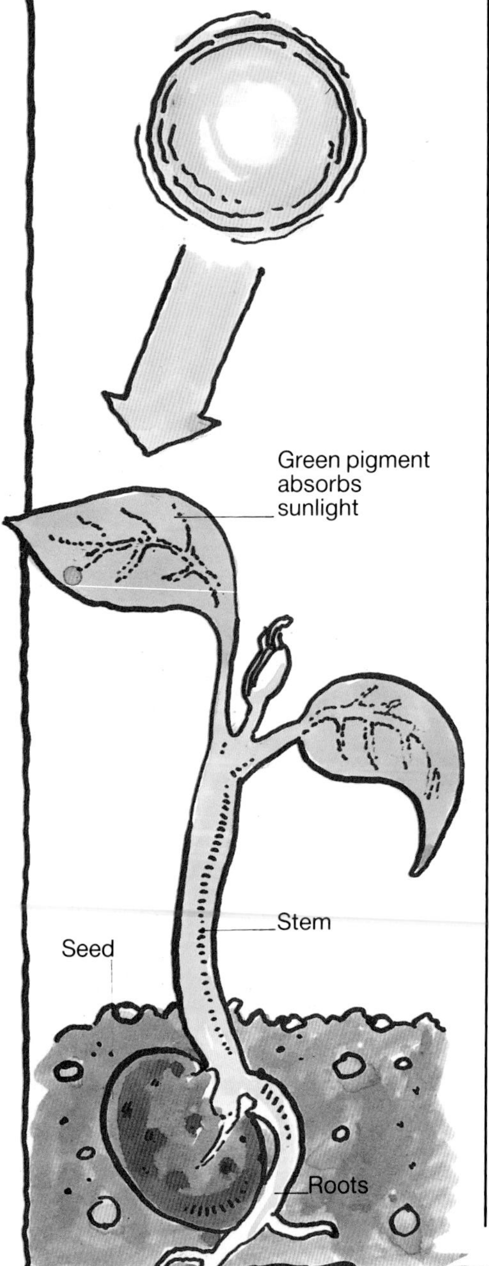

Why are some plants carnivorous?

Carnivorous plants, like the sundew, butterwort, pitcher plant, and Venus's flytrap, live in marshes and bogs. The soil in such places is lacking in nutrients, especially nitrogen. Nitrogen is very important for making proteins and similar substances. To make up for the poor soil, these plants catch and digest insects. Insects contain plenty of nitrogen (because they contain a lot of protein), as well as other minerals.

How do seedless grapes reproduce?

Seedless grapes have no seeds to produce new plants. They only can reproduce by human intervention. Cuttings are taken from a seedless grape vine and grafted onto the stem of another sort of grape. This is, in fact, how most grape varieties are reproduced by farmers.

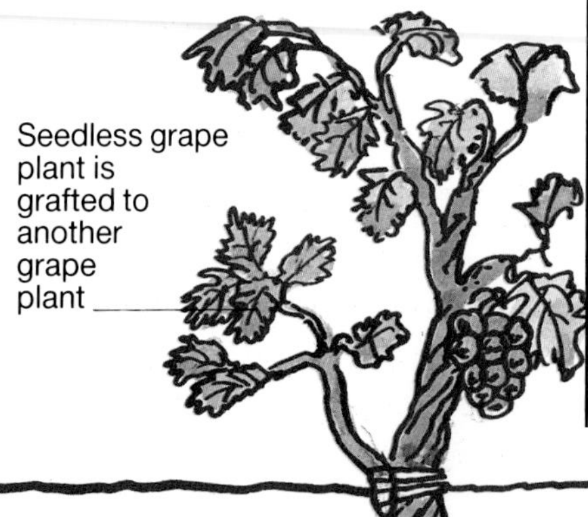

Why does a Mexican bean jump?

A Mexican bean (also called a jumping bean) does not move on its own. Inside the bean is a caterpillar. A moth lays an egg in the bean and the caterpillar hatches out. The caterpillar feeds off the inside of the bean. Its movement makes the bean move. Mexican beans usually roll around more than they really jump.

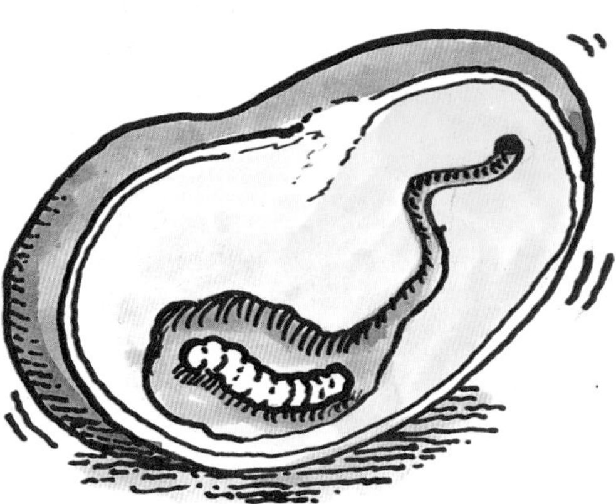

Why do cacti have so many thorns?

Cacti live in areas of the world where there is very little water. They deal with this problem by storing a lot of water inside them. Animals living in the same areas also have a problem with getting enough water. A juicy cactus is a tempting snack to them, because it holds a lot of water. Cacti are quite soft, so they need thorns to stop themselves from being eaten.

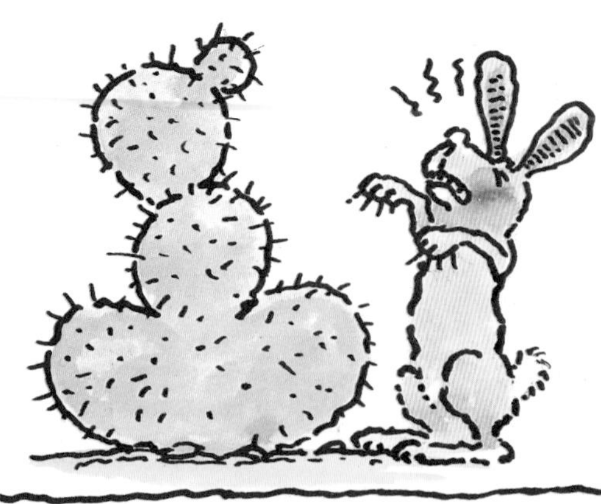

Why do trees lose their leaves in winter?
In the summer, trees are always drawing water out of the ground, and as they do so they evaporate water from their leaves. As the water evaporates, more water is pulled into the leaves from tubes in the branches and trunk. These in turn pull water up from the roots. In winter, the water in the ground is often frozen, and so trees cannot draw it into their roots. If a tree did not lose its leaves, it might lose too much of its water and die. Some trees in hot climates lose their leaves in the summer to save water.

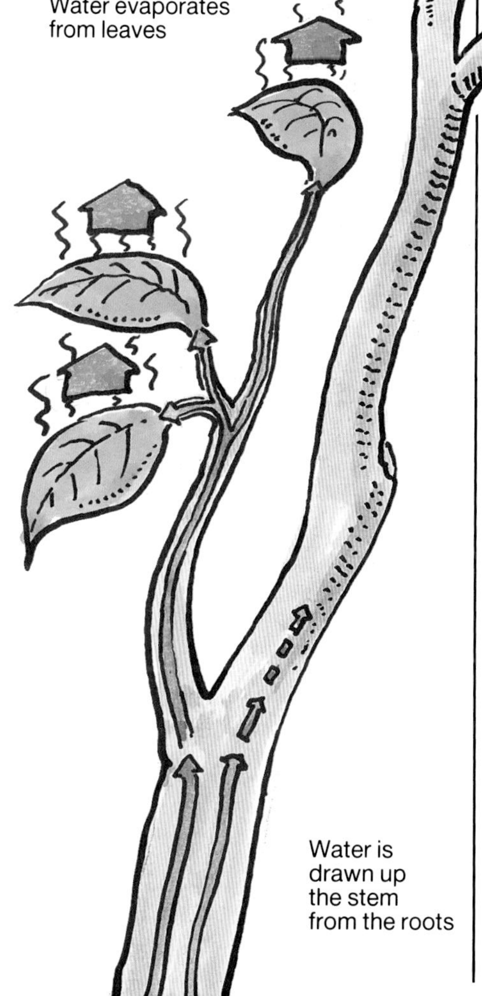

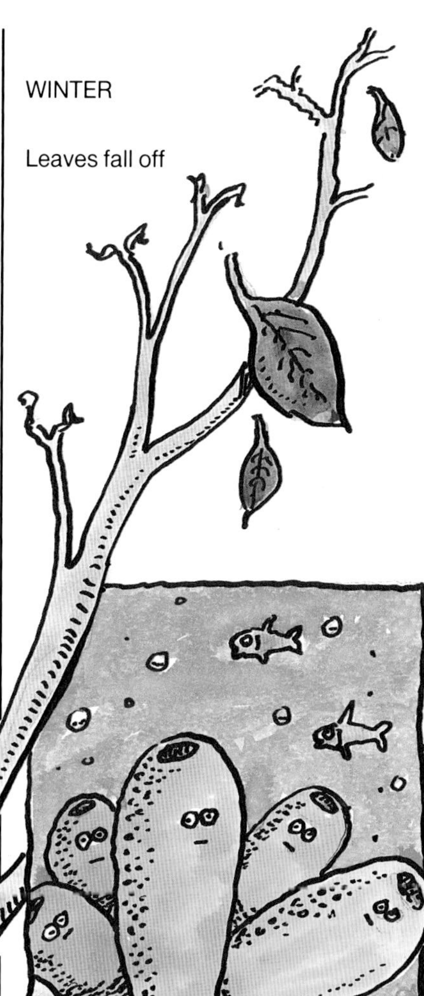

Is a sponge an animal or a plant?
People used to think that sponges were plants. Like a sort of seaweed, they live attached to the sea bed and never move. Sponges are, however, animals. They can have quite complex shapes, but internally are very simple. There are no special organs, and they have nothing like a head or a nervous system. In many ways, each sponge is more like a colony of tiny individual animals. If you break up a sponge into individual cells (by putting it through a fine sieve), the cells will join together to form a new sponge.

What is the oldest living thing on Earth?
Trees live much longer than any other type of plant or animal. It is possible to know the age of a tree by counting the rings in its trunk. One ring grows each year. The oldest living tree, and so the oldest known living thing, is a bristlecone pine in California. It is over 4,600 years old.

JEANS AND GREENS

After World War II, a new breed of human appeared – the teenager. It was developed by democrats wanting new consumers.

Teenagers tried hard to be themselves, which meant hanging around in herds and looking just like every other teenager – i.e. pimply and quarrelsome. They wore flashy clothes, very long (or short) hair, and obeyed fashion rather than their parents.

Other people started to look and behave more and more like each other, too. Uni-culture music, from Elvis Presley and The Beatles to Jimi Hendrix and Michael Jackson, thumped around the world. Saharan tribes changed 1000-year-old habits to watch T.V. soap operas. Swingers everywhere wore jeans, spoke English, and ate burgers that tasted like rubber.

By the 1990s, *Homo* streetwalker was supreme. Thriving on noise, crush and rush, it jammed together in "ant-nest" cities. Leisure – once associated with doing nothing in particular – became an industry, led by entertainer Walt Disney (1901–1966) of Hollywood. From the huts of Calcutta to the mansions of Manhattan, the square box in the corner became neighbor, entertainer, teacher, and babysitter.

MEANWHILE...
As films and photographs became more realistic, artists like Pablo Picasso (1881–1973) pointed out that some people looked better with a nose on the side of their face.

Elvis Presley (1935–1977)

Superheroes

Jimi Hendrix (1942–1970)

Walt Disney

The new world uni-culture dressed everyone in ready-made suits.

Peaceful prophets like Indian Mahatma Gandhi (1869–1948) and American Martin Luther King (1929–1968) pointed out that all people were also the same inside. This led to "wishful-thinking" laws. These said that all races were equally important and color mattered only on an artist's brush.

***Homo* streetwalker put individual rights before duties.** Men and women (now equal) wanted everything: health, homes, happiness, and their own cars.

BATON CHARGE

When muscle mattered, men conducted the human band. In the modern world, brain was more important than brawn. Women such as Eva Perón (Argentina 1929–1953), Margaret Thatcher (Britain, 1925–), and Indira Gandhi (India, 1917–1984) conducted the "history symphony" just as skillfully as any male maestro.

The age of the gleaming dream machine was born. Camels, horses, bikes, llamas, and even railroad engines stepped aside as *Homo* streetwalkers stopped walking – and drove happily to supermarket heaven.

Mother Earth did not like the way her child, Homo sapiens sapiens, was behaving. It swallowed up her stocks of fish and trees quicker than she could replace them. It polluted her air and her seas.

It bullied its animal brothers and sisters, driving some to extinction. Mother Earth felt hot, dirty, and untidy. Had her super-brainy baby, she wondered, been such a good idea after all?

Sensitive human beings noticed the Earth's distress. They felt guilty and anxious. Their history was now at a vital crossroads. It could go on only when (and if) the light turned green.

Hoping they hadn't left it too late, people began to cut down their smoking, *(right)* chat with whales, and re-cycle the mess in their backyard.

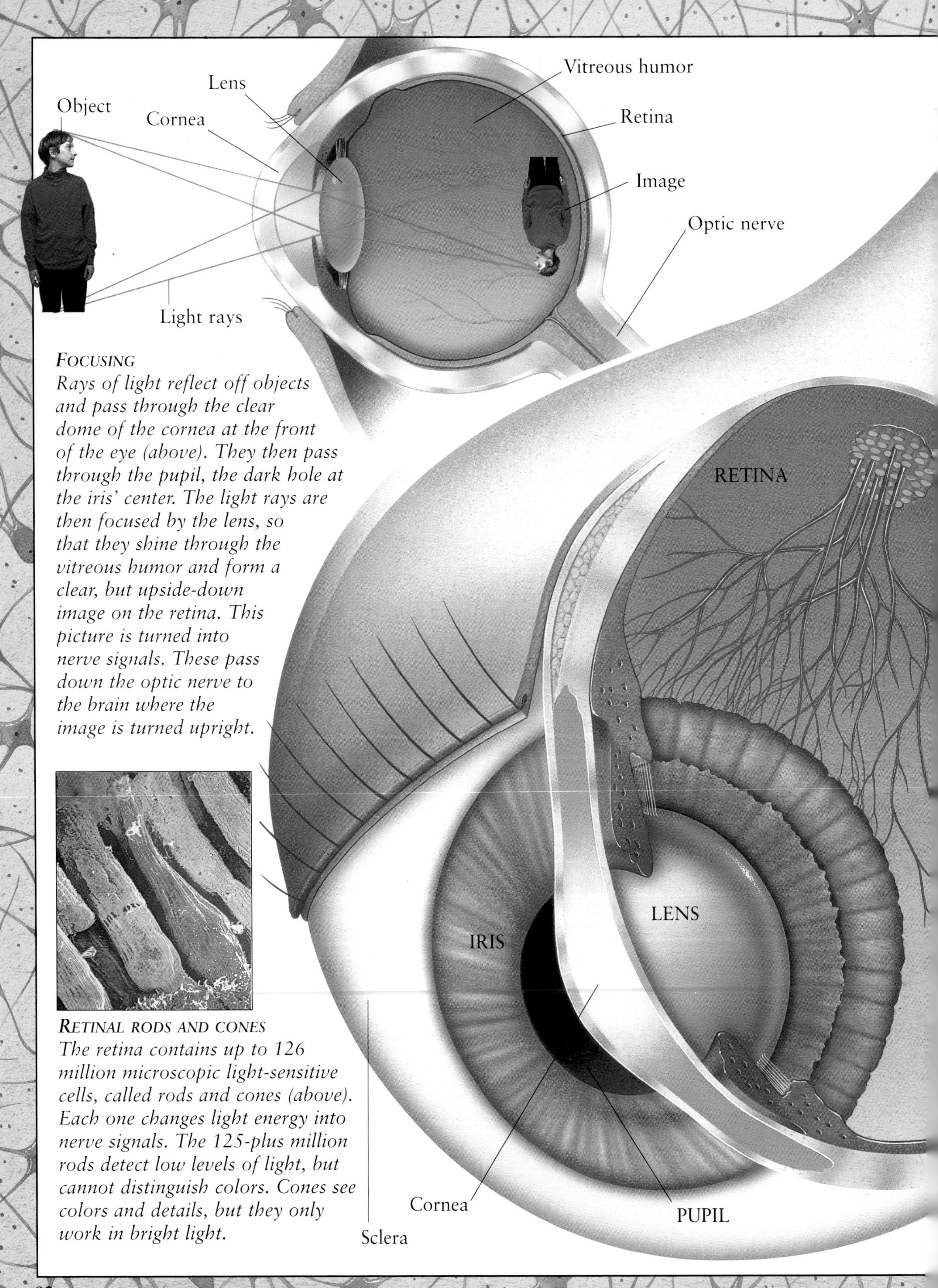

FOCUSING
Rays of light reflect off objects and pass through the clear dome of the cornea at the front of the eye (above). They then pass through the pupil, the dark hole at the iris' center. The light rays are then focused by the lens, so that they shine through the vitreous humor and form a clear, but upside-down image on the retina. This picture is turned into nerve signals. These pass down the optic nerve to the brain where the image is turned upright.

RETINAL RODS AND CONES
The retina contains up to 126 million microscopic light-sensitive cells, called rods and cones (above). Each one changes light energy into nerve signals. The 125-plus million rods detect low levels of light, but cannot distinguish colors. Cones see colors and details, but they only work in bright light.

INSIDE THE EYE

EACH EYEBALL is covered with a tough outer sheath called the sclera, except for the colored part at the front. This colored circle on your eye is called the iris. At its center is the black pupil. The iris changes size to let more or less light through the pupil and into the eye.

Most of the eye's interior is filled with a clear jelly, the vitreous humor. The part that detects light, the retina, lines the rear of the eyeball. This very delicate layer provides the detailed moving pictures of the world that you experience in your brain.

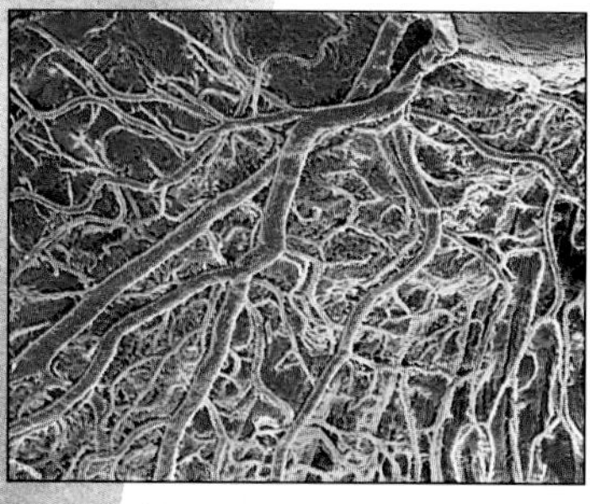

BLOOD VESSELS *The back of the eye is covered by branches of blood vessels (above), which supply the retina with nutrients.*

OPTIC NERVE

BLOOD VESSELS

Tear duct

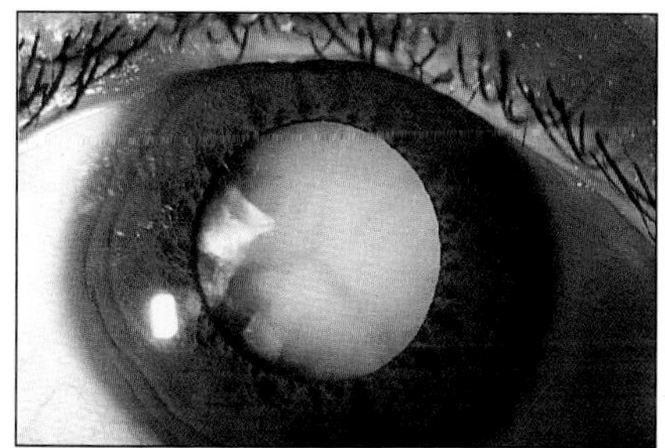

Cataracts affect millions of people around the world and are a major cause of blindness in less-developed countries. This misting or haziness in the lens (left) obscures sight. As it worsens it can cause total loss of vision. Surgery to remove the misty portion or the whole lens, and insert a plastic artificial version (above) or implant, can drastically improve eyesight.

FAR SIGHT *The eye is too small compared with the power of its lens, so the image cannot be focused (right). Convex lenses will focus the image on the retina.*

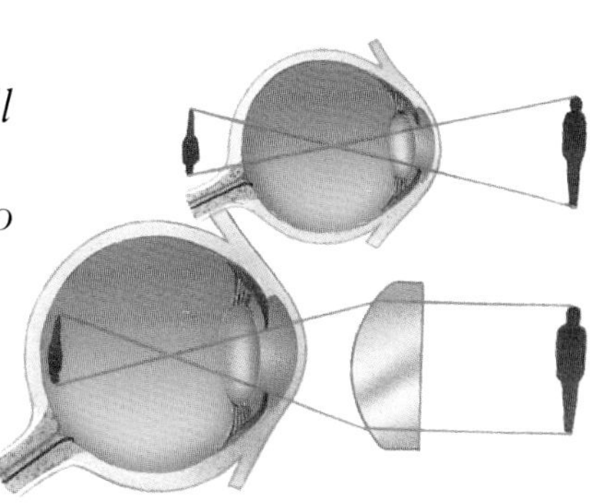

SHORT SIGHT *The eye is too large compared with the focusing power of its lens. Concave lenses diverge the light rays before they reach the eye's own lens.*

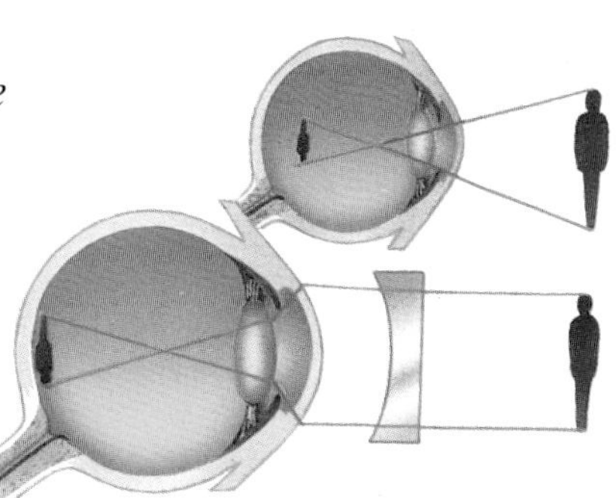

TEARS *The tear gland makes salty tear fluid. This flows onto the eyeball, where the eyelids wipe it across the surface. It helps remove dust and germs. When we cry (below), we produce a lot of tears.*

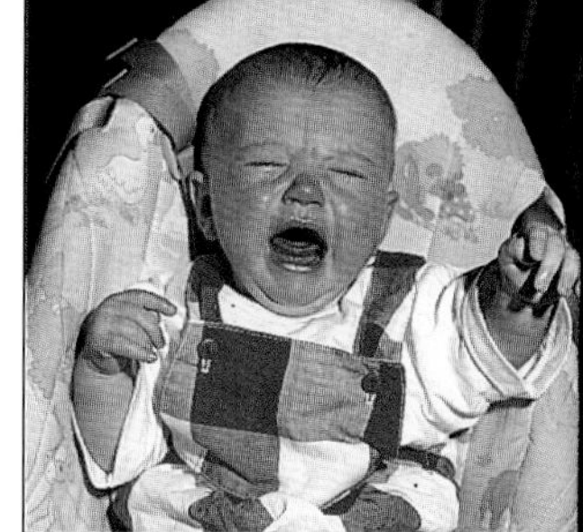

ARACHNOPHOBIA

Few beasts are more hated than the spider. The very sight of one paralyzes some people with terror – or sends them screaming from the room! Their fear is largely groundless. Of the 35,000 types of spiders, only a very few are dangerous to human beings.

The hairy tarantula, for example, is a shy beast whose bite is usually less painful than a wasp sting. The bite of the larger (and hairier!) "false" tarantula (*above right*) is even less venomous. Instead of despising the humble spider, we ought to thank it for feeding on genuine pests, such as germ-carrying flies and bugs.

Paralyzed with Poison
Spiders have eight legs and a front end that is head and chest combined. Some of them have eight eyes!

Spiders grab other creatures with their chelicerae (claws), paralyze them with venom, then store them in a silk picnic basket until mealtime.

Black widow

WEB SITES

Many spiders, such as the common garden spider, weave fantastic webs (*above right*) to trap their prey. Each thread is stronger than steel wire of the same thickness. Silk is made by glands in the spider's body. The silk is liquid at first but hardens into a thread when it is pulled out by little tubes called spinnerets.

Spiders living underwater spin bell-shaped webs. They fill these with air by collecting bubbles.

Danger under the Sheets
A popular scene in films is the sight of a huge spider crawling toward its victim (main picture). *Such movies suggest that large spiders like the bird-eating spider* (left) *have a deadly bite. But the real killer is the tiny but deadly black widow spider.*

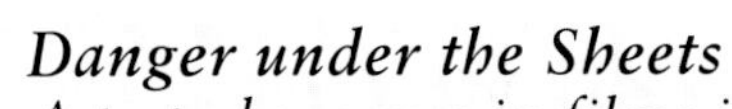

Crazy Cure
The inhabitants of medieval Italy believed the bite of the tarantula drove people crazy. The only cure for their hysteria was a wild dance (right). *The mythical cure stopped being used years ago – but the dance survives as the tarantella.*

YARN SPINNING. Spiders are both good and bad in mythology. Christians believed it was the devil, because it trapped the innocent. The African Asanti, who had a Trickster Spider, did not think much of it either. But the ancient Egyptians, Hindus, and Buddhists were more fond of it. Focusing on its amazing spinning, they linked it to Creation. It was the Great Weaver or the creature that drew the web of life out of itself. Native Americans believed the spider wove the first alphabet.

The Inspirational Spider
According to legend, King Robert the Bruce of Scotland failed to defeat the English six times. Hiding in a barn, he watched a spider trying to fix its web onto a beam (right). *After seven attemps, it succeeded. The lesson inspired Bruce to make one more attack. The real king won a great victory at the Bannockburn in 1314.*

SUPER-SPIDERS
On a desert plateau near the town of Nazca, Peru, stands the world's largest piece of art – gigantic outlines of beasts (including a 164-foot spider!) between dead-straight lines. As the monstrous shapes can only be properly seen from the air, it has been suggested that the ancient Nazcas (500 B.C. to A.D. 900) must have had balloons long before anyone else.

MUTANT HEROES. Compared with most creatures, big-brained humans are a puny lot. But all this changes in the world of fantasy, where Spider Man (*right*) slings his web and swings from one building to another, while the super-fast Wolf Man has razor-sharp claws of steel!

THE HARVEST

Traditionally, crops were harvested by hand *(left)*, either by picking them from trees and bushes or by cutting them with scythes *(right)*. This is still the case for some crops, such as tea, grapes, olives, and rice. However, massive combine harvesters usually do all the jobs needed to gather a variety of plants. They can do the work of hundreds of people in a fraction of the time and in most conditions.

ANCIENT HARVESTS
Images of the harvest are found among all ancient civilizations. They were often put in places of worship, as offerings to the gods in return for a good crop the next year. Many religions still hold harvest ceremonies.

Bronze Age sickle

Iron Age sickle

CUTTING THE CORN
Scythes and sickles have been used since ancient times. The scythe dates from at least the Roman era and was used to cut a crop in a single, strong stroke. The sickle *(above)*, a smaller, lighter version, has been used since prehistoric times. Sickles are still used widely today, despite the development of machinery, because they are cheap to make and easy to use.

Handle

Grassnail

THE SCYTHE
This consists of a long, straight handle made of wood with a metal blade, supported by a metal *grassnail*. Originally, scythes were sharpened with a *straik (below)* – a piece of pitted wood smeared with mutton fat and soft or stony sand, depending on the sharpness needed.

Straik

THRESHING

Threshing (separating) grains from stalks and winnowing (blowing) the husks from the grains were done by hand until 1780, when Andrew Meickle of Scotland built the first machine. Early threshers worked by horse power. The horses walked on a treadmill *(right)* to turn the machine. This was replaced in the mid-1800s by steam-powered engines.

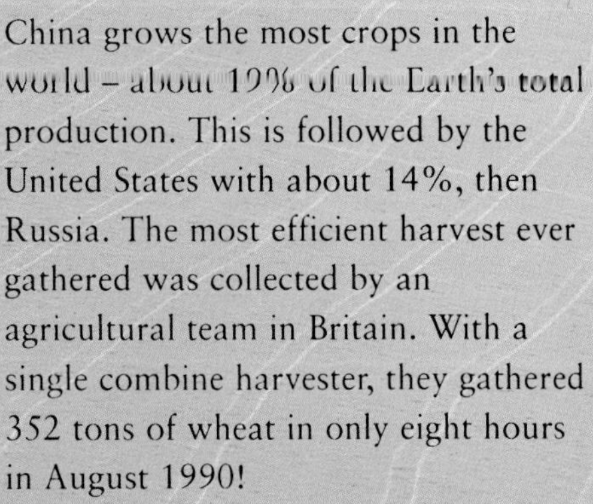

FARMING... ON A MASSIVE SCALE!
China grows the most crops in the world – about 19% of the Earth's total production. This is followed by the United States with about 14%, then Russia. The most efficient harvest ever gathered was collected by an agricultural team in Britain. With a single combine harvester, they gathered 352 tons of wheat in only eight hours in August 1990!

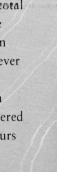

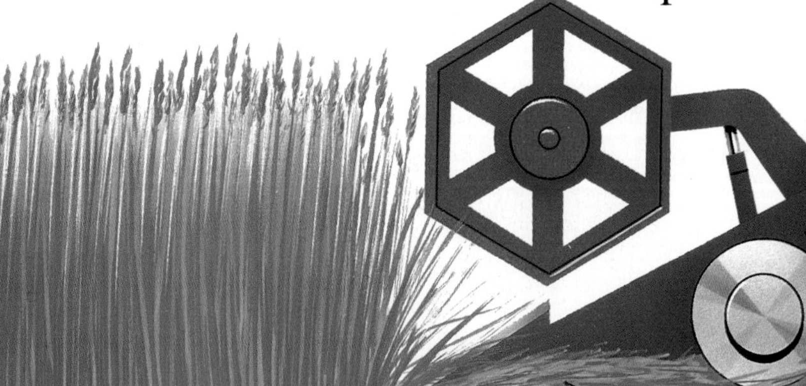

PATRICK BELL (1801-1869) *Bell, a Scottish clergyman, invented a mechanical reaper in 1827, but it did not catch on quickly. In 1834, Cyrus Hall McCormick of Virginia saw one of the reapers. He produced a similar machine adapted into a combined reaper and binder.*

MULTI-PURPOSE MACHINES

In the early 1900s, work began on a combined reaper and thresher. It had an engine which worked the moving parts *(above)*. Today, combines come in many sizes, to suit different crops and fields. They have special attachments to harvest crops other than cereals, such as soybeans and cotton. Some are designed to harvest unusual crops like trees or potatoes. Most are self-propelled, although the smallest may be pulled by tractors.

HOW THE COMBINE WORKS

1. A cutting bar cuts the stalks with a moving knife.
2. The stalks fall onto a platform and are carried by a feeder to a threshing drum. This revolving cylinder separates the grain from the stalks, then the stalks are discarded and used for straw.
3. The grain passes through sieves and the husks are blown away by a fan.
4. The grain is fed into a tank. From here it is poured into trucks or sacks and taken away for storage.

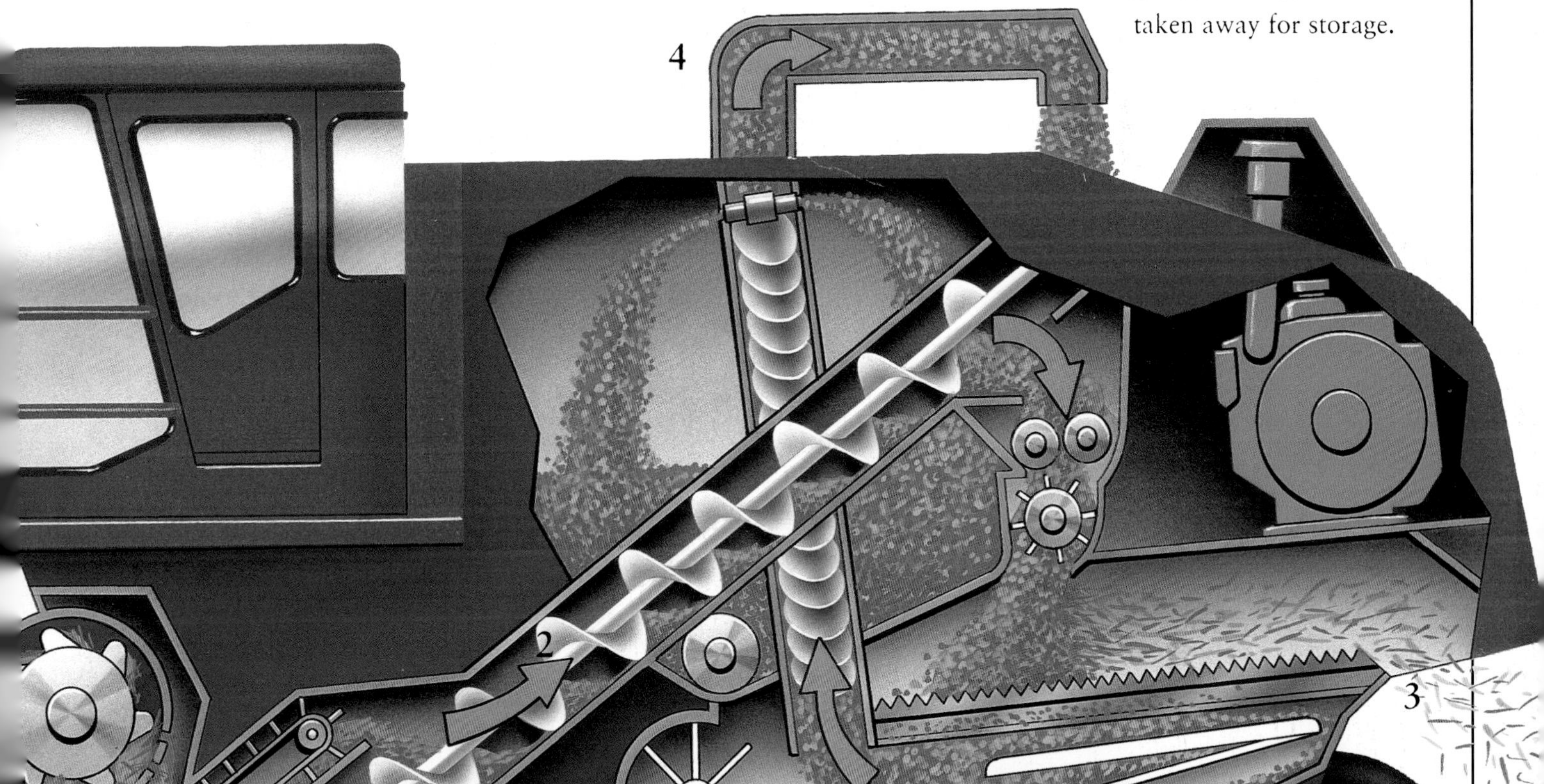

TURTLE

AMPHIBIANS LIKE FROGS must return to water to breed. Their eggs are soft and jelly-coated, and soon dry out on land. Reptile eggs don't. They have tough waterproof shells, so they can spend all their lives on land. Except those who choose to live in water, like the turtle.

SHELL
This has two layers. On the outside are thin, light scutes – curved plates made of horn (keratin). Underneath are thicker, heavier osteoderms – or plates of bone.

LUNGS
These are under the highest domed part of the shell. Some turtles can hold their breath and survive underwater for more than two hours.

BODY ARMOR
For extra strength, the scutes and osteoderms (see left) are different sizes and patterns so their joints overlap.

BRAIN IN TWO BOXES
The brain is well protected inside the thick, bony skull, which is also protected when drawn into the shell. The parts dealing with sight and smell are well developed.

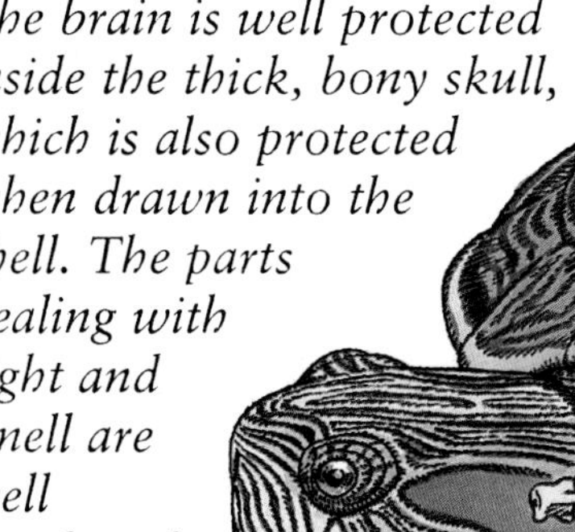

BEAK
Turtles and tortoises lack teeth. They bite with the hard, sharp jaw edges. They cannot chew properly either, so food often falls out before it's been swallowed.

GUTS
A plant-eating turtle has an intestine seven times longer than its body. It is coiled into the dome of the shell.

SKELETON
The main part of the backbone is joined to the underside of the upper shell. So are some of the upper limb bones, and the ribs.

ANATOMY *AT WORK*
HOW THE TURTLE HIDES

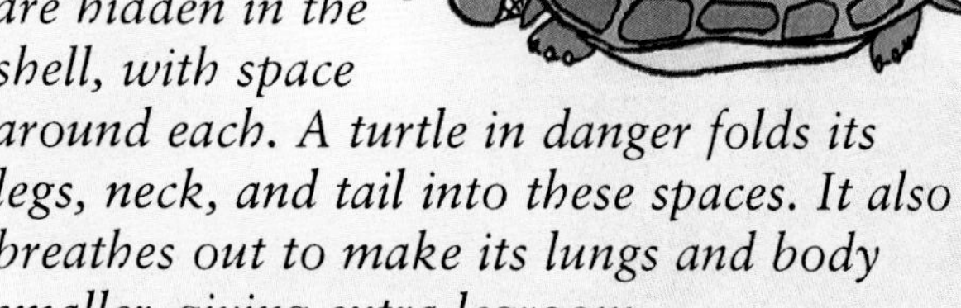

A turtle's legs are longer than they seem. The upper parts, or thighs, are hidden in the shell, with space around each. A turtle in danger folds its legs, neck, and tail into these spaces. It also breathes out to make its lungs and body smaller, giving extra legroom.

HELLO, GORGEOUS
Turtles have good eyesight for finding prey and mates. But sometimes unnatural, human-made objects which are designed for the same purpose – protection – can trick them.

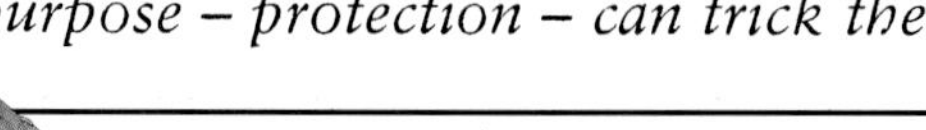

CROCODILE

REPTILES INCLUDE TURTLES AND TORTOISES, snakes and lizards, alligators, and crocodiles. The croc's gappy "smile" means death for its prey, since its bite is one of the most powerful in the animal kingdom. It drags land animals underwater, for death by drowning.

TWO-SPEED SWIM

A croc swims quickly by sweeping its tall, narrow tail from side to side, while holding its legs against its body. It swims slowly by kicking with its rear webbed feet, using its tail to steer.

SKIN AND SKELETON

The skin has horny plates, or scutes, on it, and bony plates, or osteoderms, in it. The bones of the skeleton are strong and heavy, pulled by powerful muscles.

GUTS (INTESTINE)

LUNGS

WINDPIPE

This tube, called the trachea, carries air into the lungs when breathing. After the oxygen is absorbed into the blood, the stale air comes back out along it.

BONES

BRAIN

BIG BELLY

The stomach is very stretchy. It can expand to hold most of an antelope. The croc often swallows stones, which help to steady it... and may also aid digestion!

BABY!

LIVER

WINDPIPE

HEART

CLOSED TO DIVE

The crocodile heart has four nearly separate chambers, almost like a mammal's. When it dives, a flap inside diverts low-oxygen blood to the less-vital guts and other inner organs. The important brain and heart continue to receive oxygen-rich blood.

ANATOMY *AT WORK*
COLD BLOOD?

Animals like reptiles are sometimes called "cold-blooded." Mammals are warm-blooded. But a crocodile basking in the sun may have blood hotter than yours! They control body temperature by basking in the sun or cooling off in the shade.

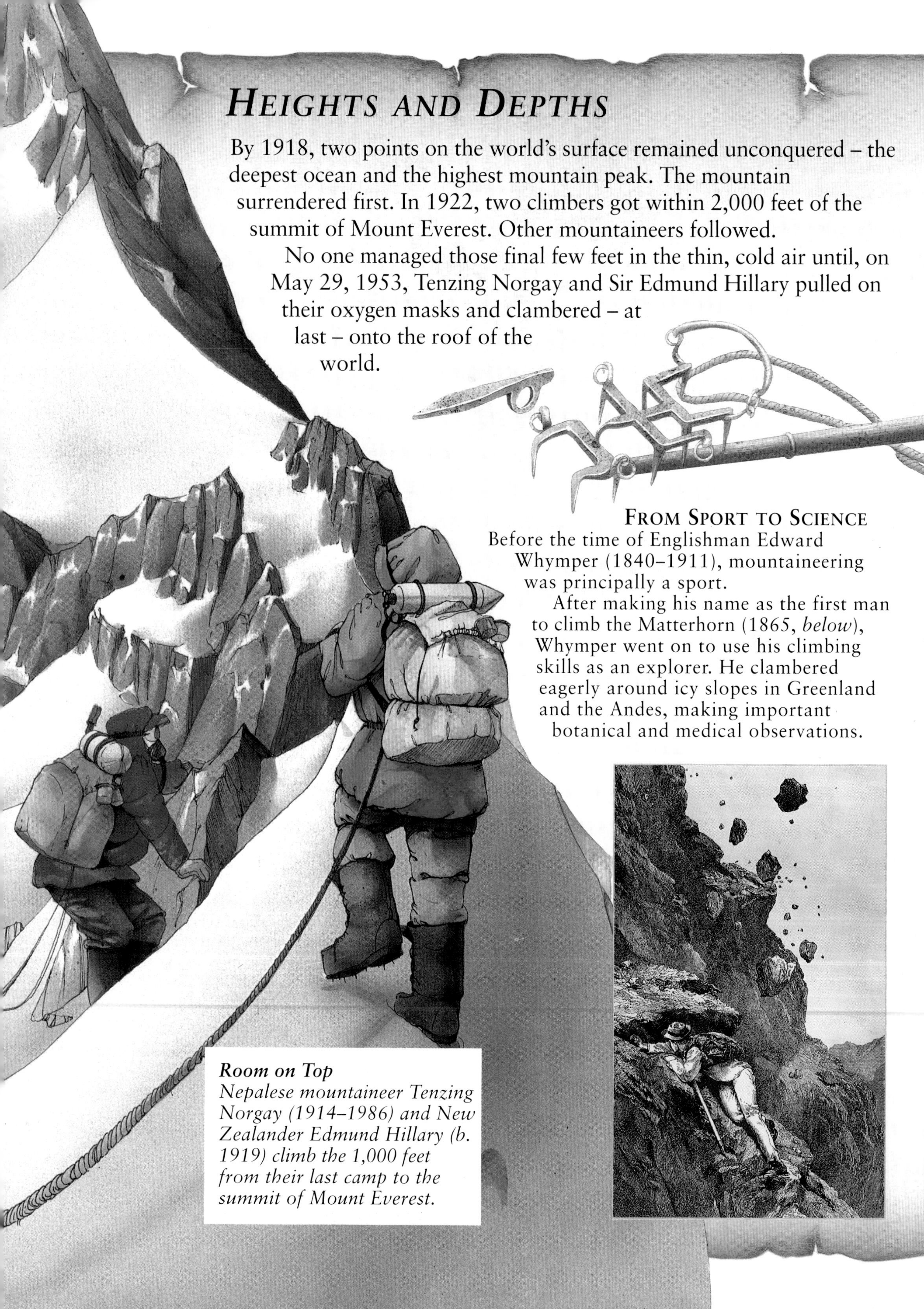

HEIGHTS AND DEPTHS

By 1918, two points on the world's surface remained unconquered – the deepest ocean and the highest mountain peak. The mountain surrendered first. In 1922, two climbers got within 2,000 feet of the summit of Mount Everest. Other mountaineers followed.

No one managed those final few feet in the thin, cold air until, on May 29, 1953, Tenzing Norgay and Sir Edmund Hillary pulled on their oxygen masks and clambered – at last – onto the roof of the world.

FROM SPORT TO SCIENCE

Before the time of Englishman Edward Whymper (1840–1911), mountaineering was principally a sport.

After making his name as the first man to climb the Matterhorn (1865, *below*), Whymper went on to use his climbing skills as an explorer. He clambered eagerly around icy slopes in Greenland and the Andes, making important botanical and medical observations.

Room on Top
Nepalese mountaineer Tenzing Norgay (1914–1986) and New Zealander Edmund Hillary (b. 1919) climb the 1,000 feet from their last camp to the summit of Mount Everest.

Into the Abyss

When mountaineer Edward Whymper camped on the slopes of Cotopaxi Volcano in Ecuador, he found the rubber groundsheet on the floor of his tent was melting! That night, he scrambled to the very rim of the volcano and peered down at the glowing, molten mass below. However, no one has yet journeyed into the 2,200° F heat of a live volcano (*top*).

Get a Grip
Two vital pieces of moutaineering equipment are ice picks and crampons (worn on the boot) (left).

Verne's journeys. Frenchman Jules Verne (1828–1905) produced an incomparable series of fantasy exploration novels. They include *Journey to the Center of the Earth* (1864), *Around the World in Eighty Days* (1873), and *Twenty-Thousand Leagues Under the Sea* (1870).

Terrors of the Deep?
The movie of 20,000 Leagues Under the Sea (above) *began a mini-cult of deep-sea adventure films, of which* The Abyss *(1989,* right*) is one of the most recent.*

Dive, Dive, Dive!
The Turtle (right), *built by American David Bushnell, was one of the first submarines.*

Going Down

The bathysphere *Trieste* (*below*), in which Jacques Piccard and Don Walsh sank to the deepest point in the ocean, the Marianas Trench, in 1960. The men sat in the tiny capsule at the bottom.

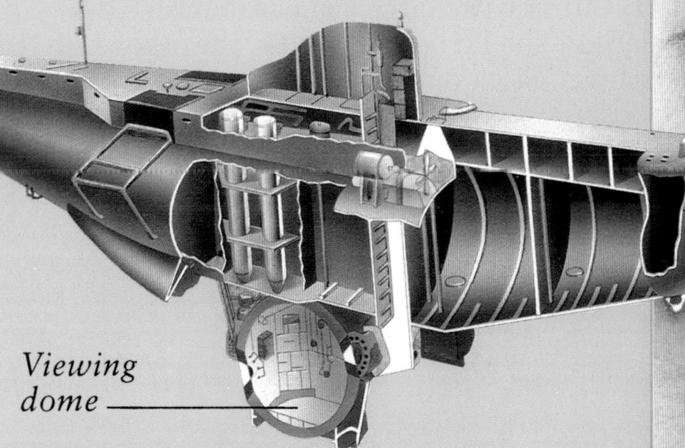

Viewing dome

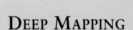

Deep Mapping

Investigation of marine life and geological structure on the ocean floor began in the 18th century. Three 20th-century developments gave it added importance: (1) the discovery of undersea oil fields; (2) the realization that the Earth's surface comprises gigantic moving plates; (3) the need to monitor ecological changes.

As a result, a variety of submarines, submersibles (such as *Deep Flight One*, *right*), and satellites have now mapped the underwater world almost as accurately as the surface.

Measuring Time

Before the invention of the clock, people had to rely on nature's timekeepers – the Sun, the Moon and the stars. The daily movement of the Sun across the sky provided the simplest unit, the solar day. The time period of a year was estimated by watching the seasons, and the constancy of the lunar cycle led to the division of each year into months. Traditionally, calendars were controlled by priests. They were devised either by counting days or by following the phases of the Moon. Nowadays, the Gregorian calendar is most common. This was worked out by Pope Gregory XIII in the 1580s.

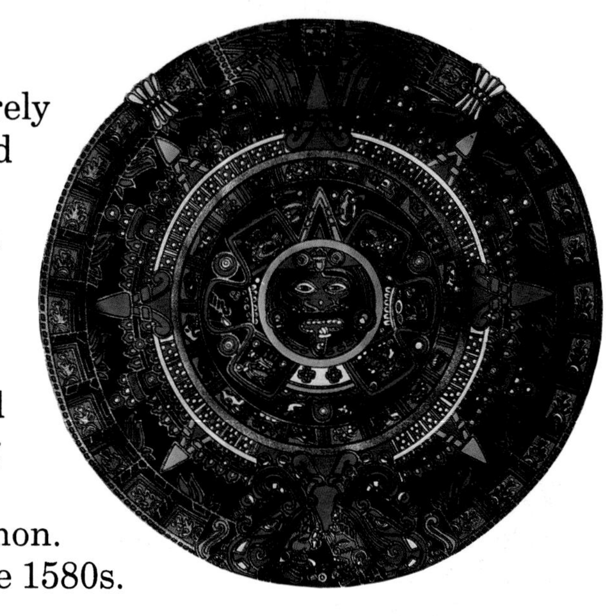

Day by Day

1. Cut out two circles of cardboard. The largest should be 12in across, the other 11in across. Stick one on top of another and divide into 12 equal pieces to indicate the months.

1

2

2. Cut out 12 paper circles of 0.5in across. Find out the number of days for each month and write them around the edge of each small circle. Now stick them in order around the large circle. The first day of the month should be nearest the edge as shown.

3. Cut another cardboard circle 10.5in across. Cut a hole, radius 0.5in, to correspond with the position of the paper circles. Cover the hole with stiff, transparent plastic. Attach a red arrow marker, as shown.

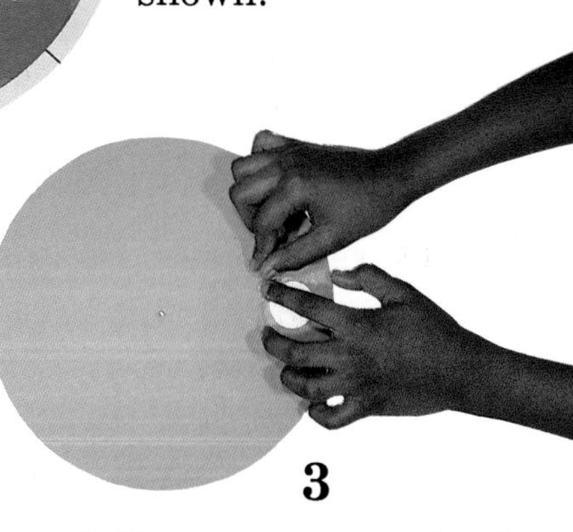

3

4. Cut out a cardboard circle, radius 0.5in. Carefully make a tiny "window," to view the date through. Position it over the 0.5in hole, and fix it to the plastic with a paper fastener, so it turns.

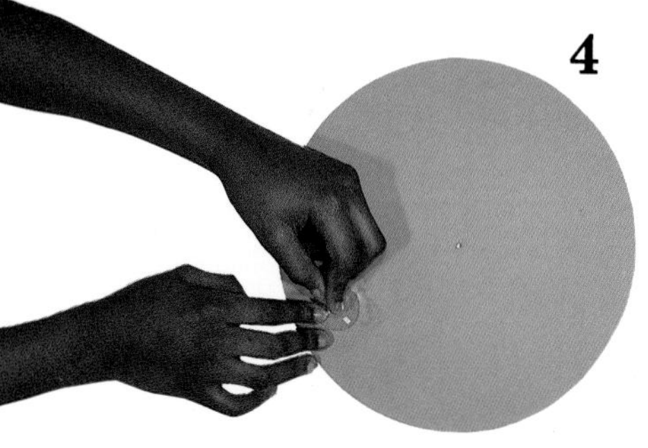

4

5

5. Decorate your calendar before joining the separate sections together. Position the smaller circle centrally over the larger circle and join them together with a paper fastener. Rotate your calendar until it is set on the correct day for the current month.

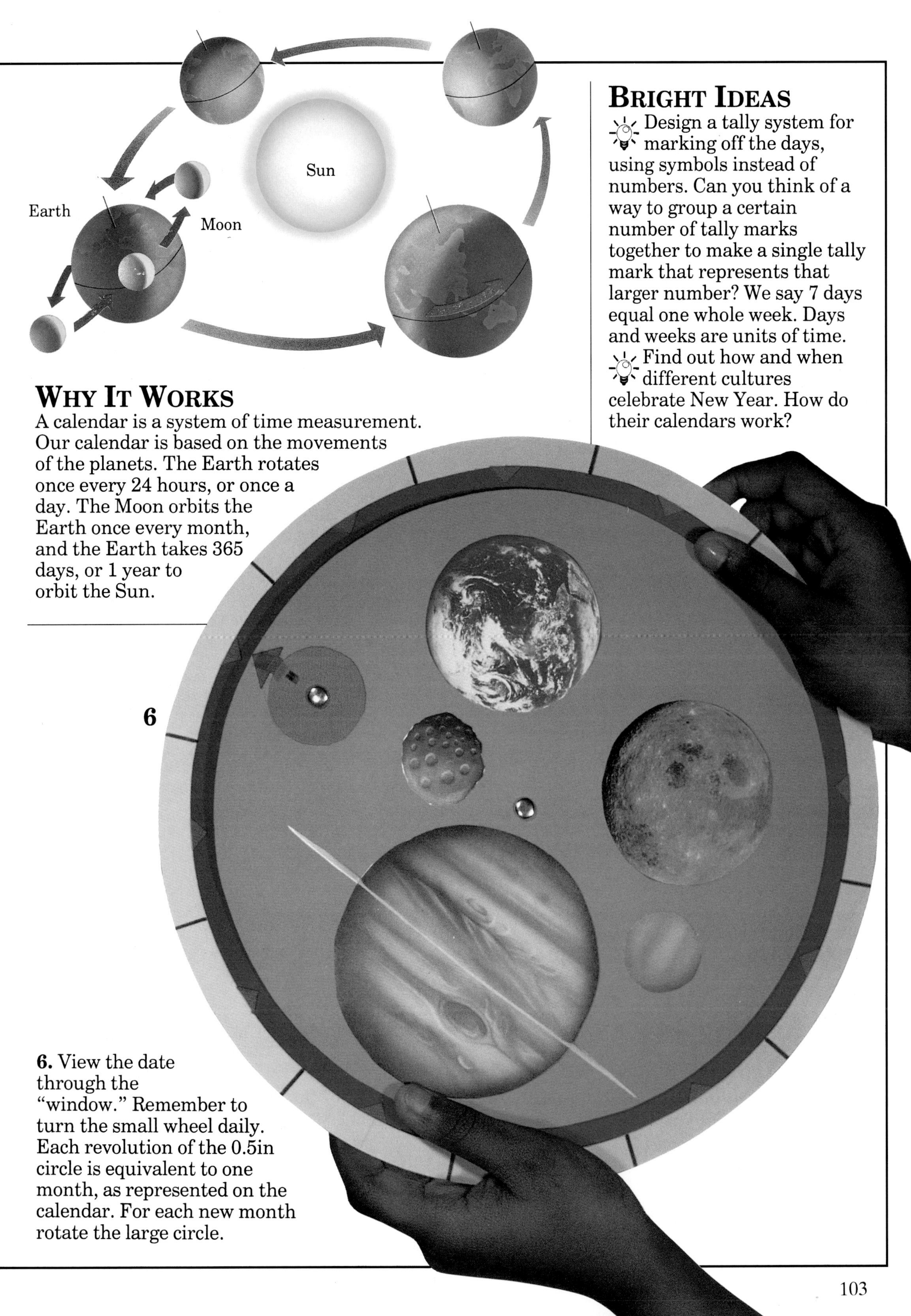

Bright Ideas

Design a tally system for marking off the days, using symbols instead of numbers. Can you think of a way to group a certain number of tally marks together to make a single tally mark that represents that larger number? We say 7 days equal one whole week. Days and weeks are units of time.

Find out how and when different cultures celebrate New Year. How do their calendars work?

Why It Works

A calendar is a system of time measurement. Our calendar is based on the movements of the planets. The Earth rotates once every 24 hours, or once a day. The Moon orbits the Earth once every month, and the Earth takes 365 days, or 1 year to orbit the Sun.

6. View the date through the "window." Remember to turn the small wheel daily. Each revolution of the 0.5in circle is equivalent to one month, as represented on the calendar. For each new month rotate the large circle.

SNOW, ICE, & HAIL

High in the sky, where the air temperature is below the freezing point of water, droplets of water in the clouds turn into ice crystals. More water then freezes on to the ice crystals, which grow bigger. As these crystals fall down through the cloud, they bump into other crystals and may form snowflakes. If the temperature near the ground is below freezing, snow falls from the clouds. But if is above freezing, the snowflakes melt and fall as rain or half-melted snow, called sleet. Icebergs are huge lumps of ice that break off the polar ice caps.

Icy hazards

An avalanche can bury a village in seconds and smash trees as if they were matchsticks. It can happen when fresh snow falls on top of an icy layer on slopes. Avalanches can be triggered by a rise in temperature, a strong wind or even a loud noise. Icebergs are also a hazard. The passenger liner, Titanic, sank in April 1912 after hitting an iceberg. Lumps of ice that fall off icebergs are known as bergy bits, and even smaller lumps are called growlers.

Jumping hailstones

Hailstones are hard lumps of ice formed in cumulonimbus clouds when crystals of ice are thrown up and down by strong air currents. Ice builds up in layers around the ice crystals. Clear layers build up in the lower part of the cloud where it is warmer and the water freezes slowly; frosty ice layers form when the crystal is higher up in the cloud. By counting the layers, you can tell how many times a hailstone was tossed up and down inside a cloud.

This hailstone was tossed up and down five times in a cloud

Tracks in snow

Animal footprints in fresh snow provide clues to the variety of wildlife in an area. They show something of how the animals moved and what they were doing before you arrived on the scene. Can you guess which animals made these tracks? The answers are at the bottom of the page. You may find similar tracks in mud.

C. Domestic cat D. Mouse

Each snowflake is different although they all have six sides. The shape and size of snowflakes depends on the height and temperature at which they are formed and the amount of moisture in the cloud. In cold air, they are needle or rod-shaped; in warmer air, they are star- or plate-shaped.

Frost forms when the temperature drops below 32°F

Jack Frost

The legendary Jack Frost is an elf-like figure who is supposed to leave his icy fingermarks on windowpanes. Beautiful patterns sometimes form on windows when water vapor turns directly to ice as it touches the freezing glass. The legend of Jack Frost probably comes from Norse Mythology, where Kari, god of the winds, had a son called Jokul (meaning icicle), or Frosti (meaning frost).

Jack Frost

The Ice Man

In September 1991, hikers in the Alps came across the body of a man who turned out to be over 5,000 years old. He was preserved by being sealed in an airtight pocket beneath the ice of a glacier and the intense cold stopped his body decaying in the usual way. He was still wearing a boot stuffed with grass and his brain and internal organs were still intact. Bodies caught in glaciers are usually crushed and torn by the ice, so the fact that this body was preserved was pure chance. Scientists think the ice man froze to death after falling asleep. He may have been a mountain shepherd who had lost his weapons and was collecting material to make new ones.

The Ice Man

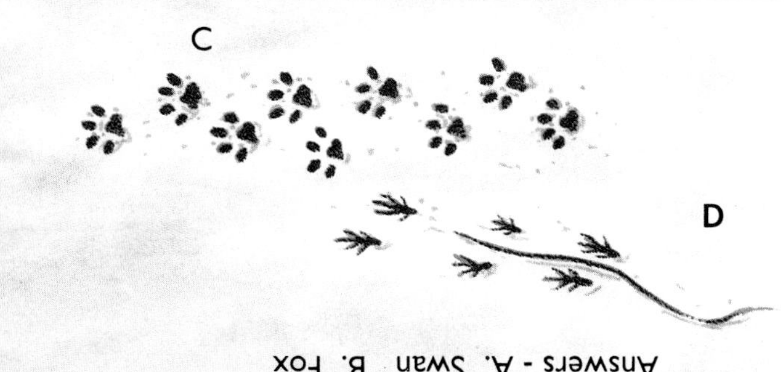

Claws from the Sky

In Medieval Europe, it happened every year, as surely as spring followed winter. The eagles came hunting the lambs. Armed only with slings and bows, there was little the shepherds could do to guard their sheep. One minute the flock would be grazing peacefully and the next – a beating of wings, a chorus of terrified bleating – and another lamb was carried off to eager beaks in a distant aerie (*main picture*).

Eagles are not always as bold and fierce as they look, however. Most will eat the easiest meal available, including carrion (dead animals). They generally avoid humans and will only attack if cornered, especially when defending their nests.

Snatch!
Daylight hunters – such as falcons (left), *buzzards, hawks, merlins, and kestrels – circle or hover above their prey, waiting for the chance to strike. Peregrine falcons drop from the sky at incredible speeds (up to 220 mph), snatching their prey with clawed talons.*

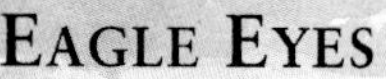

Eagle Eyes

All hunting birds have remarkable hearing and eyesight. The night-hunting owl can detect the scuffling of a mouse many feet away, and its unusual, forward-facing eyes allow it to zero in on its target with deadly precision. A single pair of owls will clear a wide area of thousands of rats and mice.

Kings of the Air

Although only a few of the 8,500 species of birds hunt living mammals, the power, speed, and grace of these creatures are awesome. The golden eagle with its 7-ft wingspan, is widely seen as the king of birds. Since ancient times, people have trained captive eagles (*left*), hawks, and falcons to hunt for them.

Poised for the Kill
Until firearms were used to scare them off, eagles were a problem at springtime (below).

Holy Hawks
All cultures respected the swift hawk (right). *To the ancient Greeks and the Aztecs, it was a messenger for the gods. Some Native American peoples believed a hawk helped to create the world. The Ainu of Japan sacrificed hawks with the prayer: "Divine hawk, you are an expert hunter, let your cleverness fall on me."*

A Sign of Strength

Because the mighty eagle was thought to be able to fly nearer the sun than other creatures, and even look at it without blinking, it became a symbol of power and victory.

Not surprisingly, many peoples made it their emblem. Roman soldiers were prepared to die for their eagle standards (*left*). Russian and Austrian emperors also used eagles as their symbols, and the United States chose the bald eagle as its national bird in 1782.

PAINFUL PUNISHMENT. According to Greek legend, Prometheus was punished by Zeus, king of the gods, by being chained to a mountain and having his liver pecked out by an eagle (*right*). As his liver grew again during the night, his horrible ordeal was repeated day after day!

The Hunter Hunted
Humans have long admired birds of prey, but today many species, such as the Java hawk and the Monkey-eating eagle, are under threat as their forest homes are destroyed. Though eagles are protected in most countries, they are still hunted illegally for sport.

The First DIVERS

People have been diving in the sea for thousands of years, to search for valuable sponges and pearls or fish and other food. The earliest divers had no equipment, but with practice could dive to 60–100 feet (20–30 m) while holding their breath. As the centuries passed, curiosity and the hope of finding treasure or defeating enemies led to the development of all kinds of diving aids. Even the Italian artist and inventor Leonardo da Vinci (1452–1519) designed a device for breathing underwater, although he never tried it. Today, thousands of people enjoy diving as a sport.

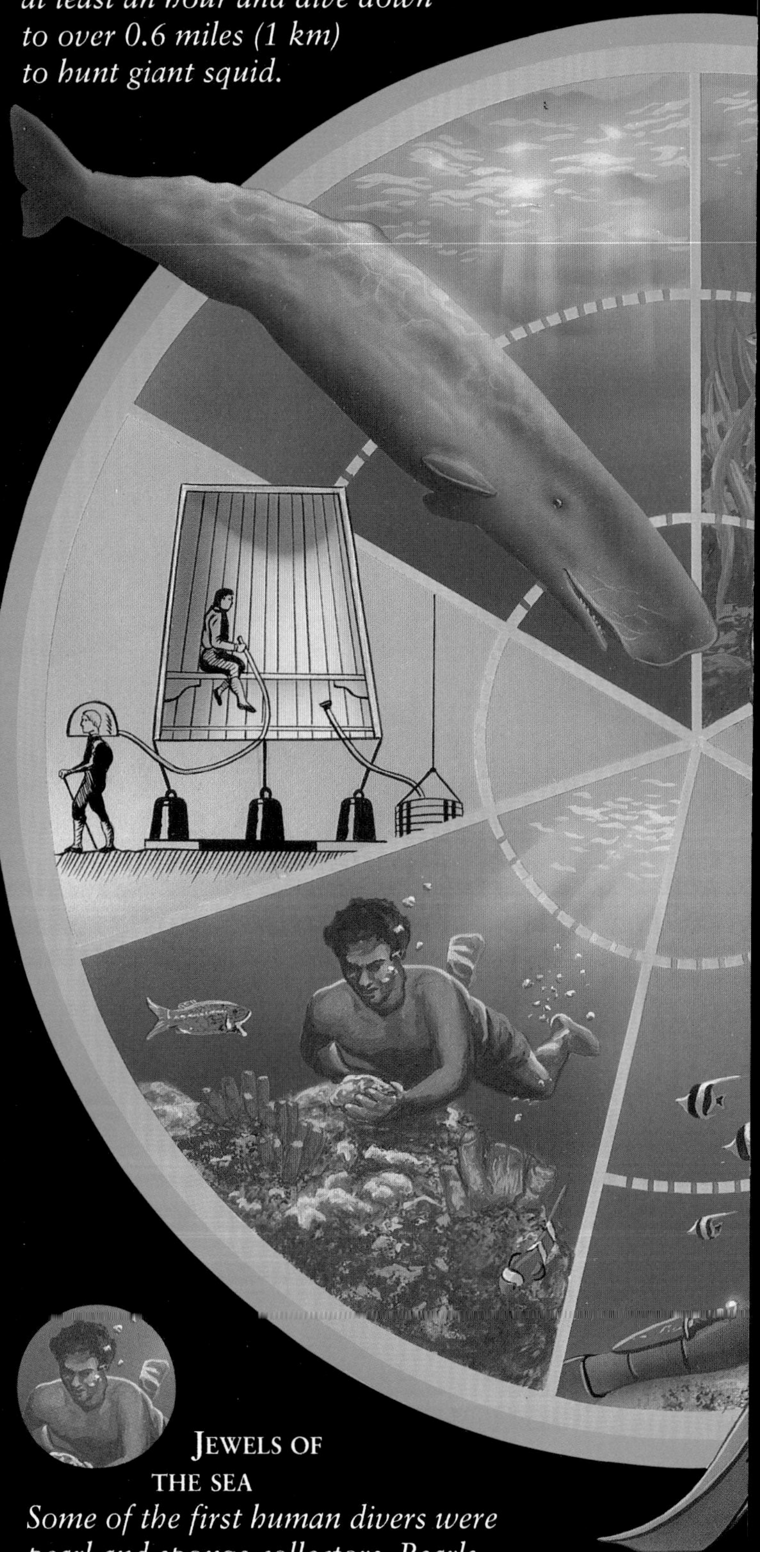

NATURE'S DIVERS

Human efforts to explore the oceans must seem puny to the great sperm whales. They can hold their breath for at least an hour and dive down to over 0.6 miles (1 km) to hunt giant squid.

Where do pearls come from?
A pearl is formed when an irritating particle of sand gets into a shell. It is covered in smooth *nacre* (mother-of-pearl) to stop the itch. Many shellfish can form pearls, but valuable pearls come only from tropical seas. The biggest pearl ever found weighs over 13 lb (6 kg) and came from a giant clam.

JEWELS OF THE SEA

Some of the first human divers were pearl and sponge collectors. Pearls have been gathered in the Arabian Gulf since at least 3000 B.C. Early divers wore tortoise-shell nose clips to keep water out of their nostrils.

UNDER THE SEAS
The astronomer Edmund Halley invented the first diving bell in 1690. Divers sat in a wooden cask with an open bottom. As the cask was lowered, the air inside was squashed by the rising water, so extra air was pumped in from wooden barrels. Divers could walk outside the bell with small casks over their heads.

THE HELMET SUIT
The first diving suit was developed in 1837 by Augustus Siebe from Germany. The watertight rubber suit had a heavy copper helmet which kept the diver on the seabed. Air was pumped down from the surface. This allowed divers to work at over 300 feet (90 m) deep. A very similar but lighter suit is now used by commercial divers.

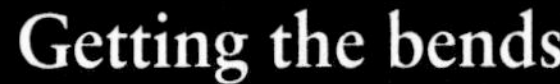

Getting the bends
Early divers suffered from a strange, often fatal disease – decompression sickness, or the bends. If divers surface too fast, the decrease in pressure makes the nitrogen gas in their blood form bubbles, which block the blood's flow. Dive computers can work out the safest ascent speed. Divers with the bends go into decompression chambers (right), with high air pressure to make the gas dissolve.

DIVING ALONE
In 1865, Benoît Rouquayrol and Auguste Denayrouze invented a diving set that did not need an air hose from the surface. Air was carried in a canister and fed through a valve in the helmet. But the set could be used only in shallow water at low pressure.

DIVING TODAY
Modern SCUBA (Self-Contained Underwater Breathing Apparatus) gives divers great freedom. The Aqua-Lung, the first breathing device to let people dive independently, was invented in the 1940s. The explorers Jacques Cousteau and Frédéric Dumas developed the demand valve, which gives air to divers when they breathe in (rather than all the time, which wastes air).

WHAT IF FISH COULD FLY?

Most fish move by swimming through the water, either by wiggling their body from side to side, or by waving their fins. A few have learned how to use their fins to walk on land. Other fish have developed the ability to leap from the water and swoop and glide above the surface for several feet, before plunging back down into the waves. They are called flying fish.

Take off
If they are threatened by a predator, such as a shark, flying fish will gather speed, up to 20 mph (32 km/h), and shoot above the waves.

What if you could ride a sea horse?

Sea horses are true fish, cousins of pipefish and sticklebacks, but with a very strange body shape. The face resembles a horse's head, with small pectoral fins sticking from the neck, one dorsal fin on the back of the stiff body, and a curly tail to wrap around plants or rocks to hold the fish in place. Instead of getting forward movement by swishing its tail, the sea horse waves its dorsal fin very quickly to move itself forward. By swimming at a modest speed, the sea horse can suck or snap any food into its small, tube-shaped mouth.

Swooping to safety
Once the flying fish becomes airborne, it can glide for more than 330 feet (100 m) and up to 20 seconds on its outspread pectoral fins. This will take it far away from any danger.

Flapping fish
The freshwater hatchetfish of South and Central America (above) is able to fly through the air by rapidly flapping its pectoral fins, in much the same way as a bird flies.

How to swim

Although all fish swim, they don't all swim in the same way. The majority of fish, such as tuna and sharks, get the power for their forward movement from their tails, or caudal fins. Fish also need a variety of other fins around their body to control their movements. Dorsal fins keep the fish upright, while steering and braking are provided by the pectoral and the pelvic fins.

Tuna swim at more than 44 mph (70 km/h) by moving their tail from side to side. The front of the body remains fairly still.

Sharks and dogfish swim by swinging their tail from side to side, while the rest of the body curves in the opposite direction.

Eels move through the water by bending their body in curves, like a snake.

ALEXANDER THE GREAT

As the city states squabbled and fought each other after the Peloponnesian War, the kingdom of Macedonia in the northeast grew more powerful. In 353 B.C., Philip II of Macedonia launched a successful campaign to gain control of Greece. Philip planned to lead a combined army of Greeks and Macedonians against the Persians but he was assassinated in 336 B.C. His son, Alexander, came to the throne. He led the army into Persia, and within 13 years he had conquered a vast empire which stretched from Greece in the west to India in the east.

The racing chariot on this gold coin from Philip II's reign refers to Philip's success in the Olympic Games of 356 B.C.

A gold coin from the reign of Alexander the Great which commemorates the victory at Salamis.

Battle of Issus 333 B.C.

Battle of Gaugamela 331 B.C.

332 B.C. Battle of Tyre

SYRIA

Alexandria 332 B.C.

323 B.C. Alexander dies in Babylon.

KEY

Alexander's route

EGYPT 332 B.C.

Extent of Empire

ARABIA

Philip II came to the throne in 359 B.C. At that time, Macedonia was very poor and split by political differences. Over the next 25 years, Philip reorganized the army into a tough fighting force, united Macedonia and transformed it into the greatest power of the day. Greek independence ended in 338 B.C. when they were defeated by Macedonia at the Battle of Chaeronea.

Alexander's empire was larger than any previous ancient empire, a third bigger than even the mighty Roman Empire. Alexander defeated the Persians in 333-331 B.C. By 326 B.C., he had reached northwest India but was forced to turn back by his battle-weary army.

Philip's tomb

In 1977, over 2,000 years after his death, Philip's tomb was discovered in the royal graveyard at Vergina, Macedonia. His cremated remains were found in a gold casket. Experts were sure it was Philip because the skull had a hole near the right eye socket. Philip had been hit in his right eye by an arrow.

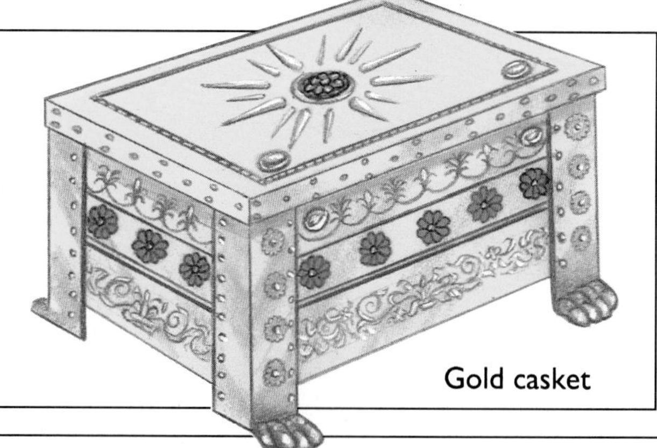

Gold casket

Bust of Alexander the Great

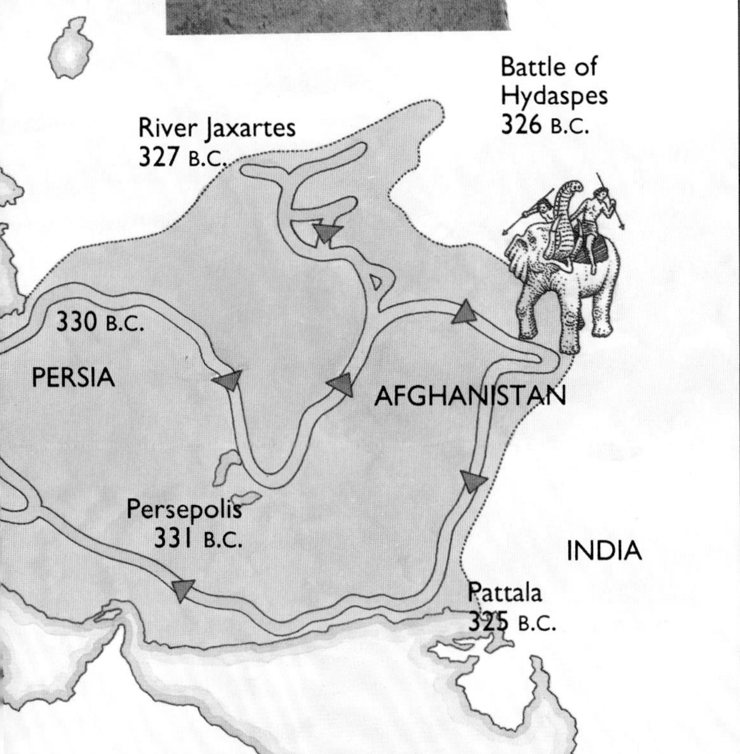

A town called Alex

Alexander founded many new cities throughout his empire. He called all of these "Alexandria." The most famous Alexandria was in Egypt. Under Ptolemy, Alexander's successor in Egypt, it became the country's capital. Its great marble lighthouse, the Pharos (right) was one of the seven wonders of the world.

Alexander wanted the people he conquered to feel part of the empire and not to resent their Greek rulers. To strengthen the ties between the Persians and the Greeks, Alexander took to wearing Persian dress, and married a Persian princess, Roxane. He tried to persuade his soldiers to marry Persian wives. He also wanted the Persians to take part in the government of the empire and in the army. Alexander was a great leader who was respected by his soldiers because he marched as far and as hard as they did. When Alexander died of a fever in Babylon in 323 B.C., the empire was left in a state of chaos and uncertainty.

Greek influence on India

As Alexander's empire spread, so too did Greek culture, ideas, and style. They continued to influence the places conquered by Alexander long after his death. In India, Greek styles influenced art and sculpture (below), especially in the region known as Gandhara, in north-west India. Statues were carved with flowing robes, similar to those which appeared on Greek statues.

Persepolis palace

The ruins of the ancient city of Persepolis lie near Shiraz in modern-day Iran. Persepolis was one of the greatest cities of the Persian Empire. It was founded in 518 B.C. by Darius I. During his reign, a splendid palace was built at Persepolis. Each year, festivities were held at the palace to celebrate the religious holiday of the New Year. At these festivities, the king would renew his divine right as king, and would receive gifts from representatives of all the peoples within the Persian Empire. When Alexander captured the city in 331 B.C., he burned the palace to the ground.

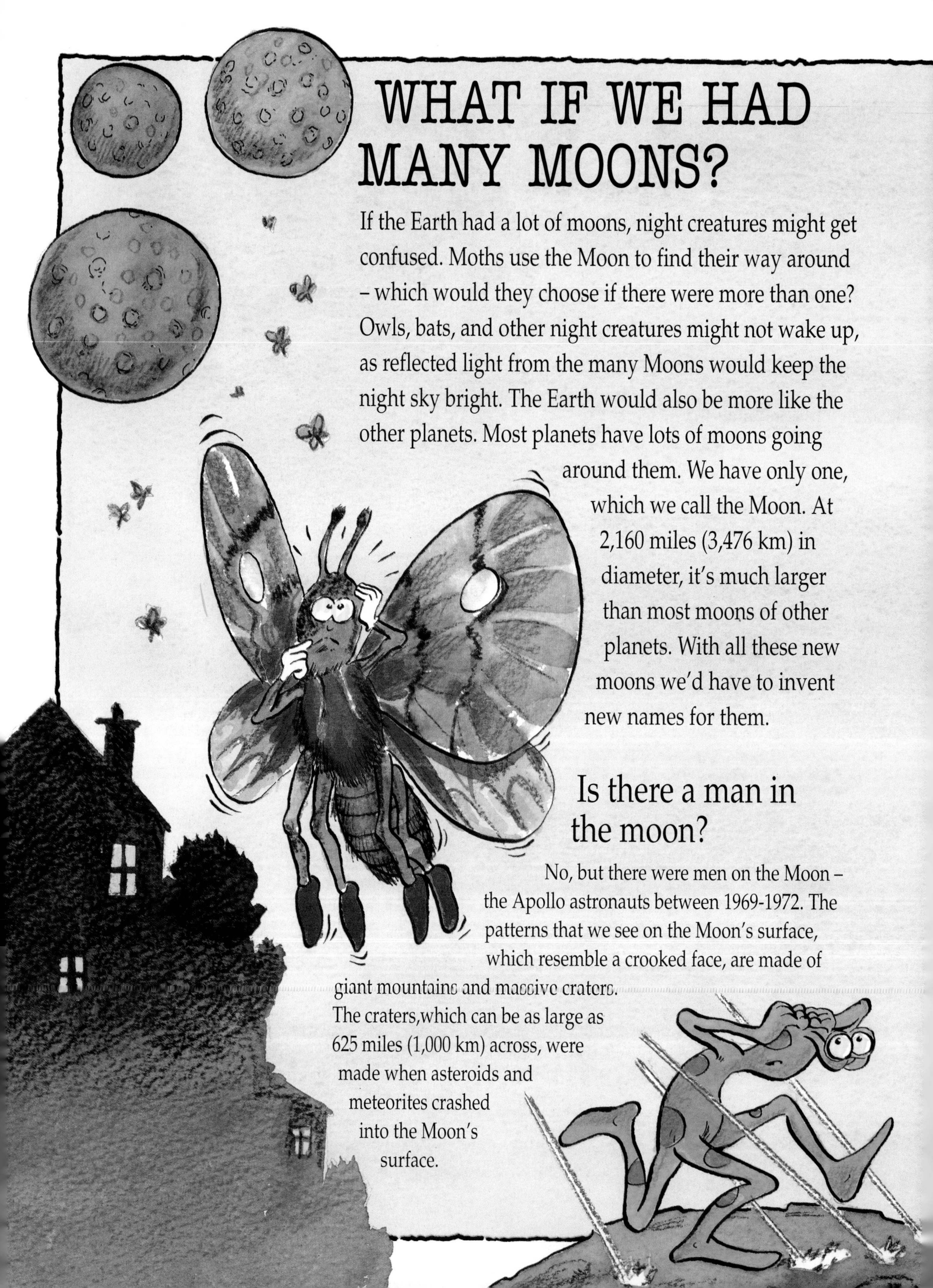

WHAT IF WE HAD MANY MOONS?

If the Earth had a lot of moons, night creatures might get confused. Moths use the Moon to find their way around – which would they choose if there were more than one? Owls, bats, and other night creatures might not wake up, as reflected light from the many Moons would keep the night sky bright. The Earth would also be more like the other planets. Most planets have lots of moons going around them. We have only one, which we call the Moon. At 2,160 miles (3,476 km) in diameter, it's much larger than most moons of other planets. With all these new moons we'd have to invent new names for them.

Is there a man in the moon?

No, but there were men on the Moon – the Apollo astronauts between 1969-1972. The patterns that we see on the Moon's surface, which resemble a crooked face, are made of giant mountains and massive craters. The craters,which can be as large as 625 miles (1,000 km) across, were made when asteroids and meteorites crashed into the Moon's surface.

The birth of a moon

Some scientists believe the Moon was probably formed at the same time as the Earth, from rocks whirling in space. Others think it was made when a planet crashed into the Earth, throwing up masses of debris, which clumped together to form the Moon. The moons of other planets may have been asteroids captured by the planet's gravity.

Which planet has the most moons?

At the moment Saturn has the most, with 18 moons as well as its colorful rings. This is followed by Jupiter with 16, and then Uranus which has 15. However, as telescopes get bigger and better, more moons may be discovered, so these numbers may change.

What happens if the Moon goes in front of the Sun?

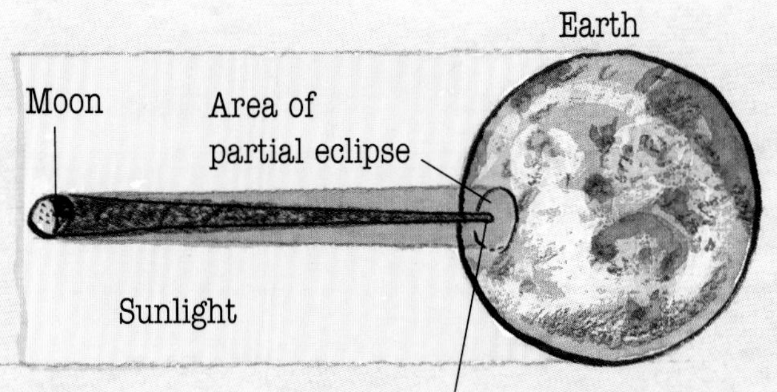

It blocks out the Sun and casts a shadow on Earth, and we get a solar eclipse. But this does not happen all over the world. The total eclipse, with all the Sun hidden, is only in a small area. Around this is the area of partial eclipse, where the Sun appears to be only partly covered.

What's on the far side of the Moon?

The Moon goes around the Earth once every 27 days 8 hours. It also takes 27 days 8 hours to spin on its own axis. So the Moon always shows the same side to us. The far side of the Moon was first seen by the spacecraft Luna 3 in 1959, which sent back photographs of a lifeless moon, with no partying aliens!

RAILROADS

The first steam-powered trains were built in the early 1800s by Richard Trevithick in England and Oliver Evans in the United States. In 1830, George and Robert Stephenson's *Rocket* managed a speed of 20 mph (32 kmh). At first people thought that the force of such speeds would harm passengers! The railroads, however, expanded rapidly over the 19th century and brought far-away places closer.

SIGNALING
In the early days of the railroads, signals were given by flags (*above*).

EARLY RAILROADS
Before steam locomotives, horses were used to pull trucks along short railroad lines linking coal mines to canals and ports (*above*).

COAST TO COAST
Railroads were vital to the expansion of the United States in the 19th century. Many U.S. steam trains had "cow catchers" on the front (*below*) to reduce the impact of collisions.

CITY RAILROADS

As cities grew in size at the start of the 20th century, new forms of rail transportation were developed. Electric trains are well-suited to urban areas: They can stop and start quickly; they are quiet and, unlike steam trains, they produce no soot. The world's first public electric railroad was opened in Germany in 1881. To avoid congestion, some urban trains run underground or, like the automated, driverless trains of the Docklands Light Railway in London (*above*), travel overhead.

STATION TO STATION

The British were thrilled with the railroads. By 1900 more than 18,641 miles (30,000 kilometers) of railroad line had been built in Britain alone. The United States now has over 200,000 miles (320,000 kilometers). Cathedral-like railroad stations (*right*) were built in many cities. Waterloo-International (*below*) is a spacious new station in London that services the Eurostar trains that run through the Channel Tunnel to France.

HIGH-SPEED TRAINS (*BELOW LEFT*)
The first steam trains traveled at a horse's pace but, by the end of the 19th century, some trains reached 100mph (160 kmh). The fastest steam train is *Mallard*; it reached 126 mph (202 kmh) in 1938. Modern high-speed trains, like Germany's Intercity Express (ICE) and France's TGV, travel at 186 mph (300 kmh).

ORIENT EXPRESS
The world's most luxurious train, the *Orient Express*, ran from Paris to Istanbul in the early 20th century. It began running again in the 1980s (*above*).

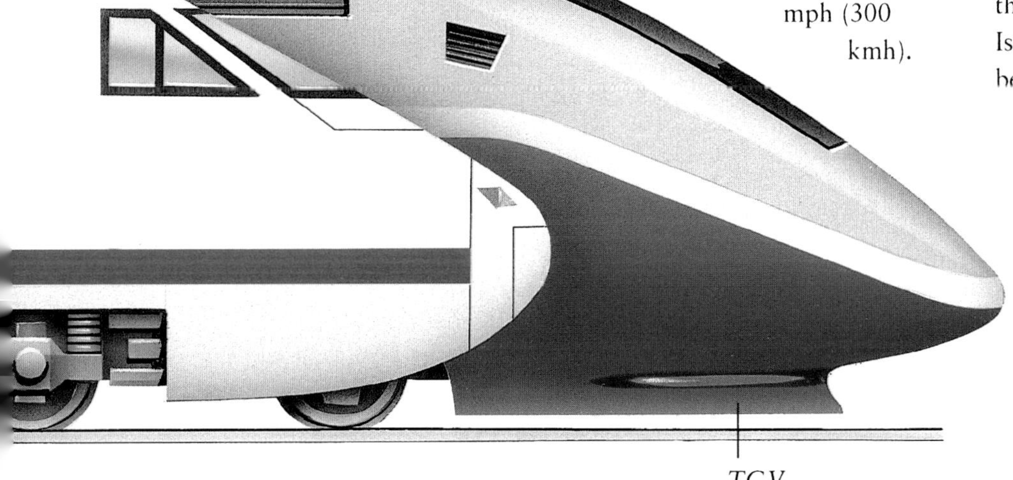

TGV

GEORGE STEPHENSON (1781-1848)
Called "the father of the railways," Stephenson was a self-educated engineer whose Rocket (above) *won a competition in England for the best locomotive. He helped to prove that railroads could be successful. He also showed how railroad lines could be built almost anywhere.*

FREIGHT TRAINS

The development of train travel meant that fresh food could be transported cheaply into cities. Lengthy freight trains are common in the United States and Canada (*below*) where the huge distances make rail freight economical. The longest freight train, which ran in South Africa, had 660 cars, 16 locomotives, and was 4.5 miles (7.3 kilometers) long!

Beethoven the revolutionary

BEETHOVEN (1770-1827)

MAIN WORKS

- symphonies (9)
- overtures (11)
- piano concertos (5)
- violin concerto
- quintet for strings
- quintet for piano and wind
- string quartets (17)
- piano trios (7)
- violin sonatas (10)
- cello sonatas (5)
- piano sonatas (32)
- *Diabelli Variations*
- *Fidelio* (opera)
- mass in C major
- *Missa solemnis*
- Ninth Symphony (choral)
- *Choral Fantasia*

Of all the great composers, Beethoven alone can fill the world's concert halls unaided. This has been true almost since the day of his death, and the reason for it lies in the universal quality of his music. Mozart has more ease and grace, and Bach more intellectual power, but Beethoven's music has a toughness that no amount of hammering can spoil. Mozart, played badly, is no longer Mozart; but Beethoven remains recognizably himself, however badly orchestras or soloists treat his music. Beethoven's music comes from the turmoil of battle – not a battle with an external enemy, but with the inner enemy of deafness.

Ludwig van Beethoven was born in Bonn in 1770, the year after Napoleon's birth. In his early years he was a fanatical admirer of the French Revolution and all its ideas. His gigantic *Eroica Symphony*, completed in 1803, was originally dedicated to Napoleon. Beethoven's own ideas, which he copied into a friend's album, were: "To help wherever one can; love liberty above all things; never deny the truth even at the foot of the throne."

Beethoven's early music was in the direct tradition of Haydn and Mozart. When he first arrived in Vienna, in 1792, he even took a few lessons from Haydn, although he later said they were of no use. The quartets, sonatas, and symphonies of the years up to about 1800 continue the classical tradition. In them, Beethoven was flexing his musical muscles, before the tremendous expansion of the so-called "middle period" of his creative life.

Shortly before writing the *Eroica*, Beethoven realized that he was going deaf. He poured out his despair in the "Heiligenstadt Testament," a letter written in 1802 at a country spa outside Vienna. Addressed to his brothers, Karl and Johann, it begins with an appeal for understanding from "men who believe or declare that I am malevolent, stubborn or misanthropic." It ends with a heartbroken postscript: "As the leaves of autumn fall and are withered, so, too, my hope has dried up." Yet Beethoven roused himself to compose his master works: the mighty Fifth Symphony (whose opening four notes made the Victory V rhythm, dot-dot-dot-dash, broadcast by the BBC during the World War II), the three Razumovsky' string quartets and the "Emperor" Piano Concerto.

If defiance of deafness gave these works their impetus, the revolutionary works of Beethoven's later life were only begun after an exhausting three-year lawsuit, in which he gained custody of his wayward nephew Karl. His renewed creativity produced the great works of his "third period," some of which have only recently begun to be understood. Toughest of all is the *Great Fugue*, written as the last movement of the String Quartet in B flat, which for many years was thought to be virtually unplayable.

BEETHOVEN'S DEAFNESS

Beethoven was only 26 when his hearing began to go. Carl Czerny, who became his pupil in 1799, noticed that Beethoven's ears were stuffed with cotton, although his hearing seemed normal.

By 1800, Beethoven's ears buzzed constantly. He pounded his piano until the strings broke in his effort to hear them.

His grief found its most moving outlet in the "Heiligenstadt Testament" (right), in which the composer expresses his sense of loneliness, cut off from his friends and from his music.

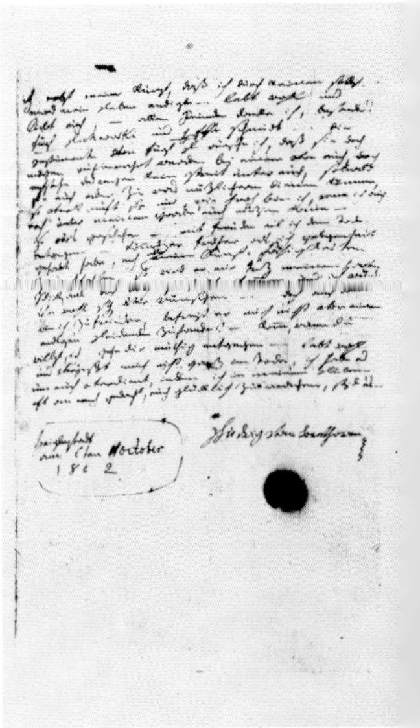

Beethoven, inspired by the democratic ideas of Napoleon (left), dedicated his Third Symphony (the *Eroica*), to him. But when, in 1804, news reached Vienna that Napoleon had crowned himself emperor, Beethoven felt betrayed. He flew into a rage and cursed the new ruler as a "tyrant." He scratched Napoleon's name off the *Eroica* score (below).

The last five quarters still require complete concentration on the part of the listener. The same is true of Beethoven's final piano sonatas, especially the enormous *Hammerklavier* Sonata, which lasts the best part of an hour and ends with a fugue that remains one of the most difficult pieces ever written for the keyboard. The title of this sonata, which means simply "keyboard," reflects Beethoven's growing interest in the establishment of German music. But he did not spend all his time on such lofty creative heights. The boisterous side of his nature was also reflected in his music, which is full of rough good humor. His letters to his publishers display the same qualities of earthy commonsense. In fact, Beethoven was the first composer to make publishers run after him, instead of the other way around, as was usual.

Although as a young man Beethoven had been something of a dandy, with increasing deafness and isolation from the world he neglected his appearance. Weber visited him in 1823 and described the sordid conditions in which the great man lived: "The room was in the greatest disorder: music, money, clothes, lay on the floor, linen in a heap on the unclean bed, the open grand piano was covered in thick dust, and broken coffee-cups lay on the table."

Beethoven shared his love of the country with Wordsworth, and spent much of every summer going for long rambles through the country-side, with a notebook at the ready to jot down thoughts that occurred to him. The best loved of all music depicting nature is his *Pastoral Symphony*, which is true scene painting. But all Beethoven's greatest works reflect his belief in the beauty and goodness of nature. Alongside this belief went a faith in the eventual brotherhood of all mankind, expressed in the last movement of the Ninth Symphony, a choral setting of Schiller's *Ode to Joy*. "All mankind will be brothers" is the message of the work, which Beethoven passed on to future generations as no other composer has done before or since.

Beethoven's early works were largely a continuation of the formal classical tradition, in the style of Haydn and Mozart. Yet, with regard to the way in which he expressed his innermost feelings in his later works, he is a forerunner of the later, romantic composers.

Beethoven's deafness increased at an alarming rate. At first, he used an ear trumpet, but soon this was useless. When he conducted his Seventh Symphony, in 1814, he could not hear the soft passages and ended several bars ahead of the orchestra. Eventually, he had to use "conversation books" (above), in which his friends wrote down their questions and remarks for him.

In May 1824, he conducted the very first performance of his Ninth Symphony. His deafness was so bad that he could not tell when the work had finished, or hear the audience's applause.

POWER
FROM THE SKIES

Clouds and nightfall limit the amount of sunlight reaching the earth. In space, there are no such limits; a solar cell in space would receive 10-15 times as much sunlight as one on earth.

To take advantage of this, American engineer, Peter Glaser, has proposed the concept of a solar power satellite (right). A large number of solar cells in geostationary orbit (orbiting above the same point on the earth's surface) would generate electricity from sunlight. The electricity would be converted into microwaves, beamed to a collector on the earth's surface, and converted back into electricity. In the United States, studies by the space agency NASA, show that such a system could, in theory, supply enormous amounts of electricity day and night.

***The satellite would be** built in space, and placed in orbit 23,000 miles above the earth. In this orbit, the earth would block the sun from the satellite only one percent of the year.*

The satellite would consist of solar cells to collect the sunlight, and a transmitter to send it to earth. An alternative would be to place the whole system on the moon.

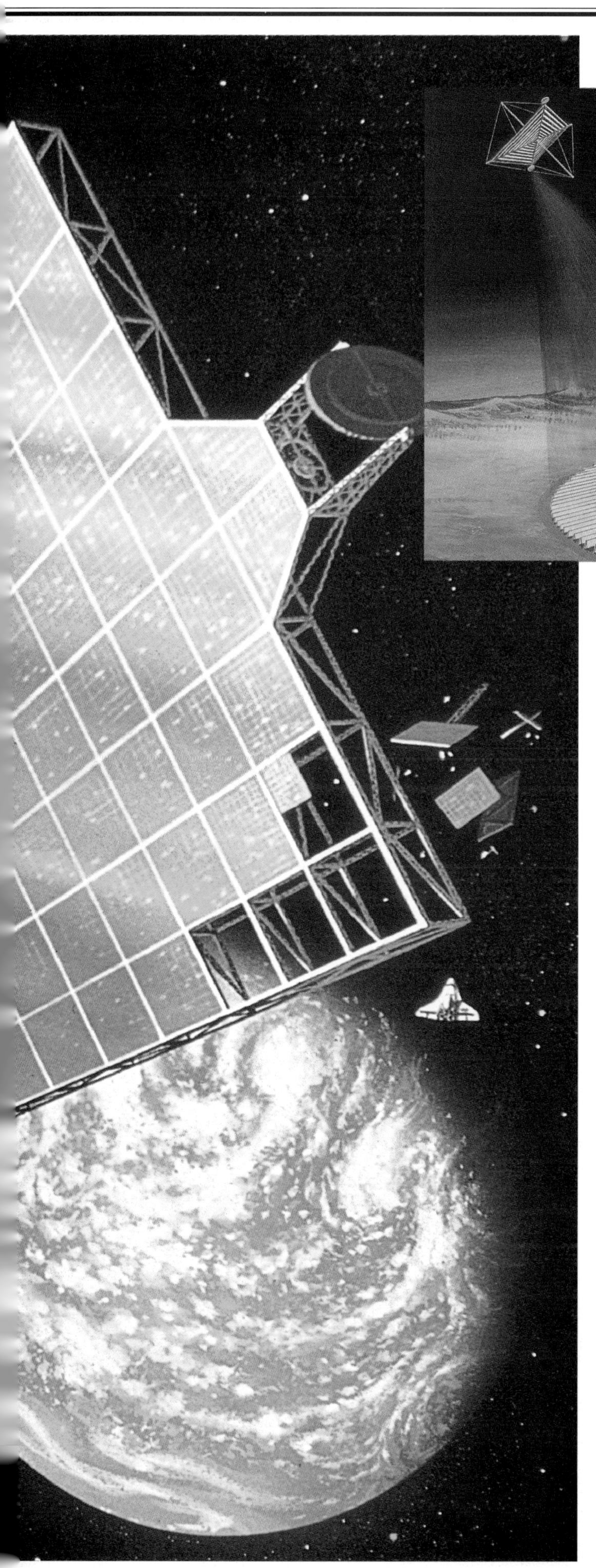

Reliable methods exist *for converting electricity into microwaves; people use them daily in microwave ovens. Microwaves travel through space and easily penetrate the atmosphere. Precise aiming of the beam is important to ensure that it does not stray over populated areas. The collectors (above) could be built in remote areas, or float in shallow water.*

SPACE POWER

BUILDING THE SATELLITE

All the technology needed to build the solar power satellite exists, but the scale of the project is enormous. In space, millions of solar cells would have to be assembled into huge collectors. The equipment to transmit the microwaves or laser beam would have to be at least half a mile across. On earth, a collector for the incoming beam would have to be over 36 square miles in size. This would have to be built in a remote place or on a platform over an expanse of water. It would be capable of generating electricity for two million households. The possible effects on health of exposure to the microwave beam need careful investigation, but exposure should be no greater than from radar sets or industrial processes, where no ill effects have been seen. Solar power satellites might be hit by meteorites, and would be difficult to protect in a high-tech war. But they would be pollution free, inexhaustible, and capable of almost indefinite expansion.

BUGS

Bugs are a particular group of insects that share a common feature: they all pierce their plant or animal food, and suck the juices with mouthparts formed into a beak or long nose, called a rostrum. The front pair of wings in many bugs is divided into two halves, a hard front part and a delicate, transparent back part. This gives the group its scientific name, Hemiptera or half-wing. Cicadas, hoppers, aphids, and scale insects are all members of the family. Bugs undergo incomplete metamorphosis, and the young look very similar to adults. Many bugs are serious pests. Some, such as aphids, devastate plants; others carry disease, such as the assassin bugs of South America.

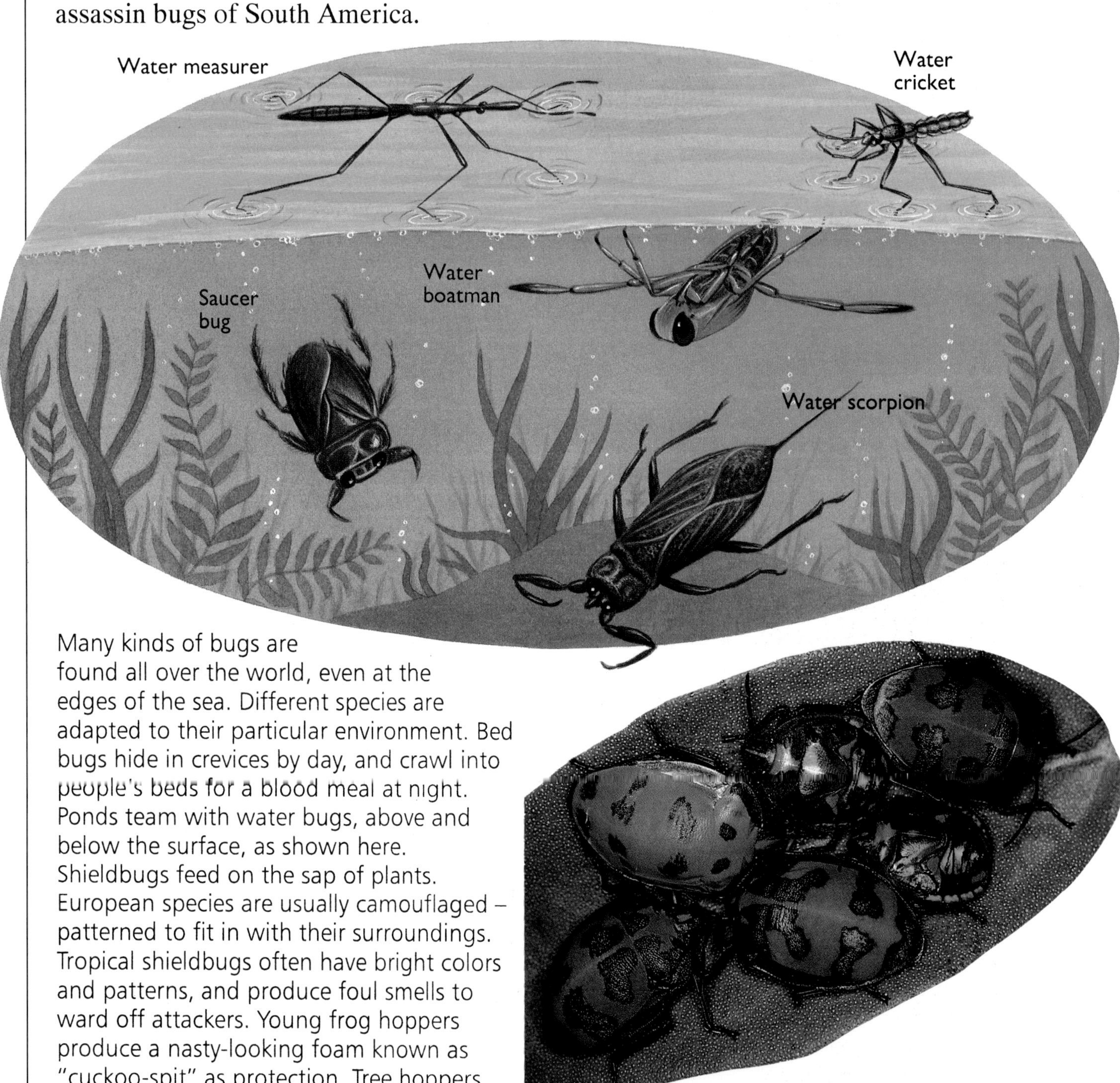

Many kinds of bugs are found all over the world, even at the edges of the sea. Different species are adapted to their particular environment. Bed bugs hide in crevices by day, and crawl into people's beds for a blood meal at night. Ponds team with water bugs, above and below the surface, as shown here. Shieldbugs feed on the sap of plants. European species are usually camouflaged – patterned to fit in with their surroundings. Tropical shieldbugs often have bright colors and patterns, and produce foul smells to ward off attackers. Young frog hoppers produce a nasty-looking foam known as "cuckoo-spit" as protection. Tree hoppers disguise themselves as thorns.

Many species of bugs live in or on the surface of fresh water. Water crickets and water measurers have water-repellent feet which do not penetrate the surface of the water. They use their feet and antennae to sense the ripples caused by a drowning insect. Once a victim is located, it is stabbed with the insect's piercing mouthparts and its juices are sucked out. Different species of water bugs prey on tadpoles, beetle larvae, and other small creatures at different depths in the water.

Insects that live underwater must still breathe air. The water boatman solves this problem by trapping a layer of air in a bubble around its body.

Great diving beetles store air beneath their wings, which can then be taken into the body through the spiracles. The water scorpion (above) has a long siphon, like a snorkel, on the end of its tail, which it extends up above the surface of the water to breathe.

Opposite page:
This group of harlequin bugs from Australia consists of three red males, a yellow female and two nymphs.

Virgin birth

In the spring, aphid eggs hatch into wingless females. To save time, these insects do not mate or lay eggs, but give birth to live babies. Producing young without mating is called parthenogenesis. It is quite common in insects. Later winged males and females (right) are born. They fly off to mate and lay eggs for the following year.

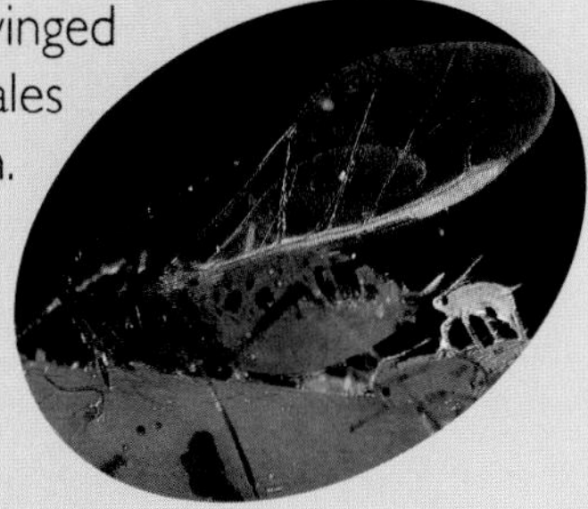

Song of the cicada

On warm summer evenings in tropical lands, in Mediterranean countries, and North America, the song of the male cicada is heard. The organ producing the sound is a "click box," like the wing mechanism located in the insect's abdomen. An area of hard cuticle is pulled in by a muscle and 'clicks' out again. Long streams of clicks are produced at different pitches. They are amplified by air sacs in the abdomen. Cicadas have ears on their abdomens so that they can hear others singing. The males sing to attract a mate. Females respond by seeking out the best singer, other males respond by singing louder.

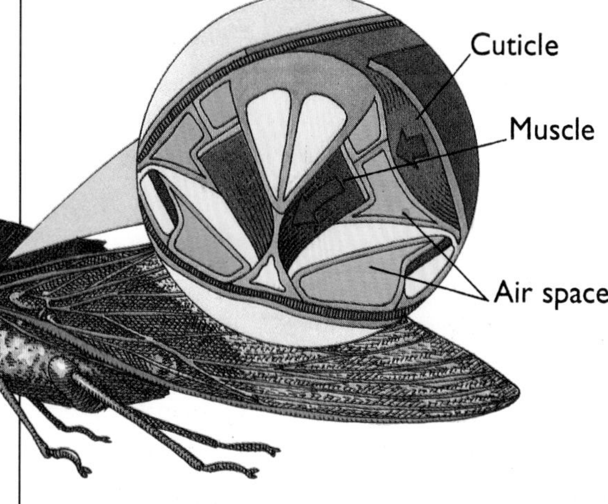

Outlaws Of The Marsh

Where could you meet with Black Whirlwind, Marvelous Traveler, and Ten Feet of Steel Hu? In medieval China, among the lofty mountains rising above the Liangshan Marsh, in Shandong province. They are heroes of *Outlaws of the Marsh* (or *The Water Margin*), one of the great bandit tales.

The novel was written by Shi Nai'an, who witnessed massive peasant unrest during the fall of the Yuan Dynasty, and based his stories on the activities of real-life bandits. Outlaw leader Song Jiang and his followers fought for honesty and fair government under the slogans "Pursue the Way of Heaven!" and "Wipe out Tyranny!"

Shi tells of the formation of the bandit gang under its 108 glorious officers (seven are shown *below*), its battles with corrupt officials (notably the wicked Gao Qiu), and its betrayal. The adventures of the bandits, officials, gentry (*above*), and peasants are described with humor and great detail. When they are finally overcome, the reader is left in no doubt about who the real criminals were – not the Outlaws of the Marsh!

Cai Xing
(Lone Flower)

Duan Jing Zhu
(Golden Hair Dog)

Lin Chong
(Tiger's Head)

OUTLAWS OF THE MARSH was so popular that its sequel was banned by the Qing dynasty rulers as they thought it might encourage a peasant revolt!

During the Ming and Qing dynasties, over 48 different plays were written using themes from the original story, and today dozens of local operas use characters from the book (*left*). So this work of fiction may well have encouraged generations of real bandits!

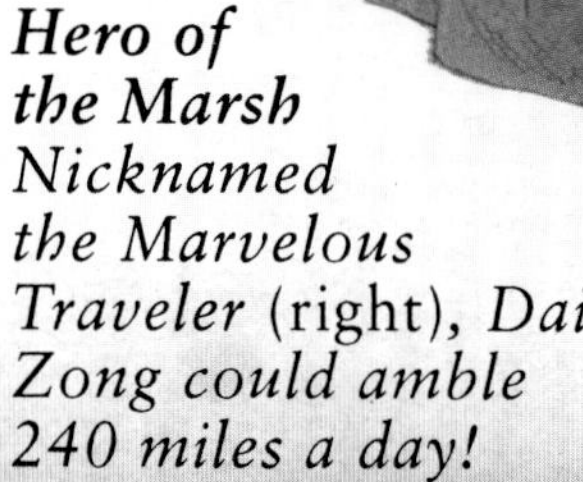

Hero of the Marsh
Nicknamed the Marvelous Traveler (right), *Dai Zong could amble 240 miles a day!*

Hero Hua Rong (below) *He could shoot out the eye of a flying bird!*

REBELLIOUS TALES. Many of the tales used by Shi Nai'an in *Outlaws of the Marsh* came from the time of the Song Dynasty (960-1279). By the 12th century, the dynasty was beginning to lose power and there was widespread rebellion and banditry. Taking advantage of this, the Mongols, a tough, warlike people from the north, conquered China by 1279. Under Kublai Khan, and then Genghis Khan (*right*), they remained in power until 1367. This change in leadership had little effect on the mass of peasants, however, and China was soon plagued by bandits again.

HEAVEN'S MANDATE

A ruling Chinese dynasty was said to hold power through "Heaven's Mandate" (or blessing). To oppose it was to oppose the way of Heaven. This did not mean that a dynasty stayed in power forever. Sometimes a series of disasters, such as floods, coincided with unrest and widespread banditry. This was a sign that a dynasty's Mandate might be coming to an end, and rebellion was justified.

Zheng Tian Shou *(Pale Face)*

Zou Run *(One Horn Dragon)*

Sun Xin *(Little Yuchi)*

Tong Meng *(Big Oyster)*

RISINGS AGAINST THE MONGOLS

Revolts began in 1335. To make matters worse, in the 1350s eastern China was devastated by floods. To many Chinese it was now clear that the Yuan Dynasty had forfeited Heaven's Mandate.

Chu Yuan-chang emerged as the principal rebel leader. Overcoming his rivals in 1368, he set up a dynasty of his own – the Ming. Within 20 years, the Ming had driven out the Mongols, and to keep them out, fortified the Great Wall (*left*). The Ming's chief task was now to drive out banditry and get the country back on its feet.

Questions and Answers about...

Why do we get goose pimples when we are cold?
All of our skin, except our lips, palms of our hands and soles of our feet, is covered with hair. The hairs may be too small to be seen easily, but nevertheless they are there. When we are cold, a tiny muscle at the end of each hair pulls it erect and the hair stands on end. In animals with fur, the erect hairs trap a layer of air, making an insulating layer. Our hairs are so short that this really doesn't do any good. When the hair is erected, the muscle pulls the surrounding skin into a tiny pimple.

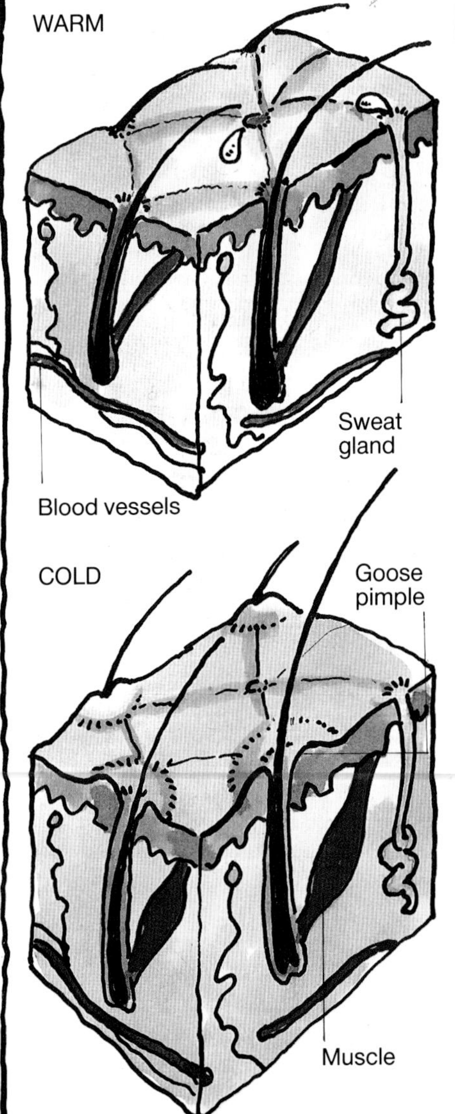

Why do we sweat when we're hot?
To make us cooler. When you are hot after exercise or if you have a fever, tiny glands in your skin release sweat. This is a slightly salty liquid containing 99 percent water. The water evaporates, and while doing so absorbs heat from your skin and cools you down. In hot humid places water does not evaporate. It runs off in drops, and so in these climates sweating is not as effective at cooling us down.

Why do some people turn brown in the Sun?
When people expose themselves to the Sun, cells in their skin produce the substance melanin. This gives them a suntan, and the darker skin is not so easily harmed by the Sun's rays. But too much Sun still can cause nasty burns.

Why do we blush?
When you blush your face turns red and you can feel it getting hot. The more you think about it, the worse it gets. You turn red because extra blood flows in the tiny blood vessels just under the skin. The cause is often emotional—perhaps you feel embarrassed or very shy. Also, drinking alcohol or eating spicy food can make people look flushed. A hundred years ago blushing was thought to be attractive, and young women used to pinch their cheeks to make them pink.

Why do we get a fever when we're ill?
Sometimes when you're ill, your body temperature goes up above the normal of 98.6°F (37°C). This rise in temperature is called a fever, and it is triggered off by the germs that cause the illness. They release chemicals that act on the part of the brain whose job is to control temperature. This in turn produces other chemicals that make you feel cold. Your body reacts by increasing its temperature.

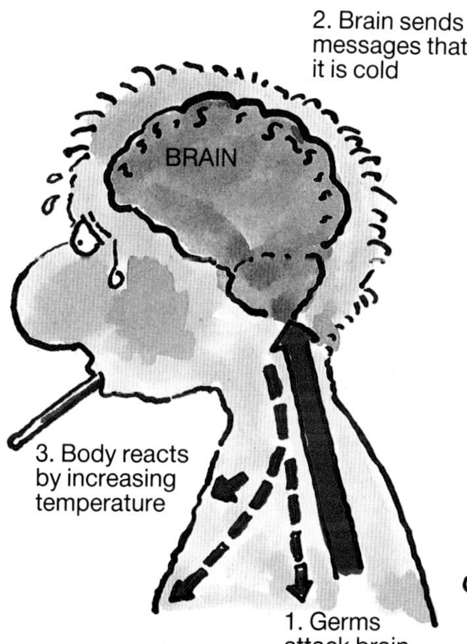

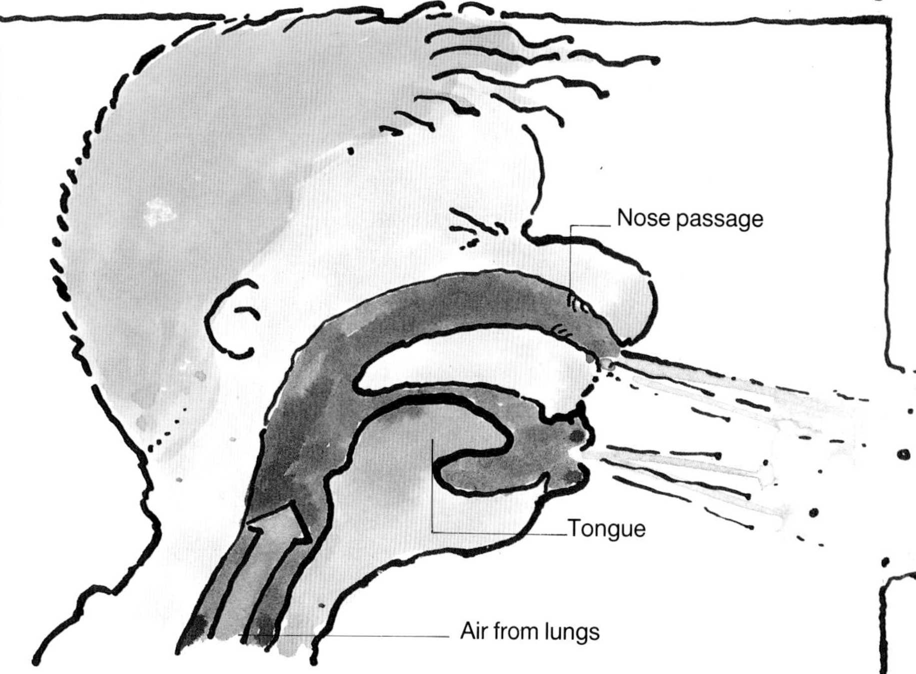

What makes us sneeze?
Sneezing is an automatic action to remove something that is tickling inside our nose. The tickling may be caused by dust, or by the inflammation that goes with a cold or hay fever. Some people also sneeze when they look into a bright light. When we sneeze, the back of the mouth is blocked by the tongue and breath is forced violently out of the nose. Droplets of water are sprayed into the air at speeds of up to 100 miles (150 kilometers per hour). Sneezing can spread colds. The world record for sneezing is held by an English girl who sneezed nonstop for more than 32 months.

Why is there no cure for the common cold?
Colds are caused by one of a number of different germs. The germs are viruses, which change all the time. As with other virus diseases, there is no specific cure for a cold, only medicines to relieve the unpleasant symptoms. Even if scientists could develop a vaccine against a particular form of the cold virus, it would be of no use against the many other cold viruses.

There are too many types of cold viruses for vaccines to be effective

What makes us yawn?
Yawning may be brought on by tiredness, lack of sleep or fresh air, or simply boredom. It also may be caused by seeing somebody else yawn. Like sneezing, yawning is an action you cannot control. Your mouth opens wide as you first take a deep breath in, and then breathe out. Some people think yawning is a way of exercising our lungs.

LONG-LIFE HUMANS

Why do we grow old? The secret may lie in our genes. These chemicals, found in every cell, tell our bodies how to grow, how to work, and how to stay healthy. But certain genes stop working after a set number of years. If scientists can find out how to keep aged genes working, one day we may all live to 150 — or longer!

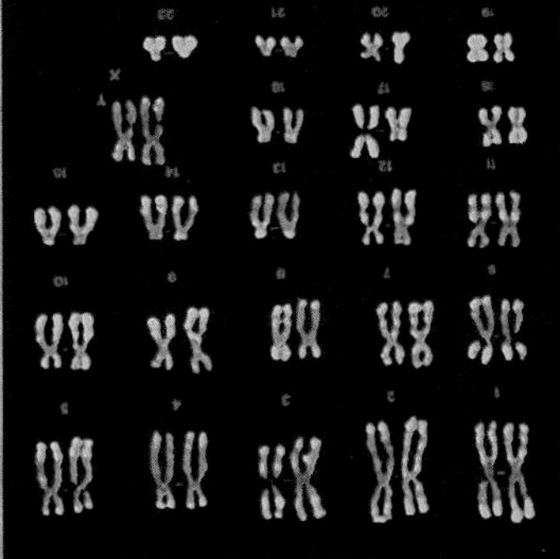

Right *Genes are found on long, coiled threads called chromosomes. Shown here are the 23 pairs of chromosomes found in each human cell. In every pair, one chromosome comes from our father, the other from our mother.*

GENETIC MIX-UP

In the 1986 movie, The Fly, *a scientist uses a machine that can transport his body to a different place. When a fly accidentally gets caught in the machine, their genes are mixed up. The result is a creature that is half-human, half-fly* (below). *But today's scientists are a long way from mixing genes.*

IT RUNS IN YOUR GENES

Cells are the tiny living blocks that make up our bodies. Inside each cell are genes, chemicals that tell the cell what to do. Genes contain codes passed on from your parents that determine the color of your hair and eyes, and even whether you will have sweaty feet!

The codes are created by just four chemicals inside genes, called A, C, G, & T.

GENE GENIES

Since 1988, scientists working on the worldwide Human Genome Project have been plotting the exact location of every gene — a bit like giving each one an address. Once they learn where a particular gene lives, doctors will know exactly where to go if it's damaged. One day we will even track down sweaty feet genes!

Inside a chromosome

LONGER, LONGER-LASTING GENES

The latest research studies the tips of genes. Over the lifetime of genes, the tips get shorter. Scientists have found that keeping the tips long appears to make genes live longer.

In experiments, drugs have been used to preserve the tips, extending the life of human cells by 30 percent — at least in a test tube.

GENOME PROJECT

FEASIBLE TECHNOLOGY	○	○	○	○	○
SCIENCE IS SOUND	○	○	○	○	○
AFFORDABLE	○	○	○	○	○
HOW SOON?	○	○	○	○	○

WRINKLE FREE

"Free radicals" are molecules that move around inside our cells, causing damage that can lead to wrinkles.

Scientists believe that getting rid of free radicals would make us healthier when we get older. Some experts say we should eat plenty of fruit and vegetables, since these foods are rich in substances that may soak up free radicals and take them out of the body.

So, eating prunes may stop you from looking like one!

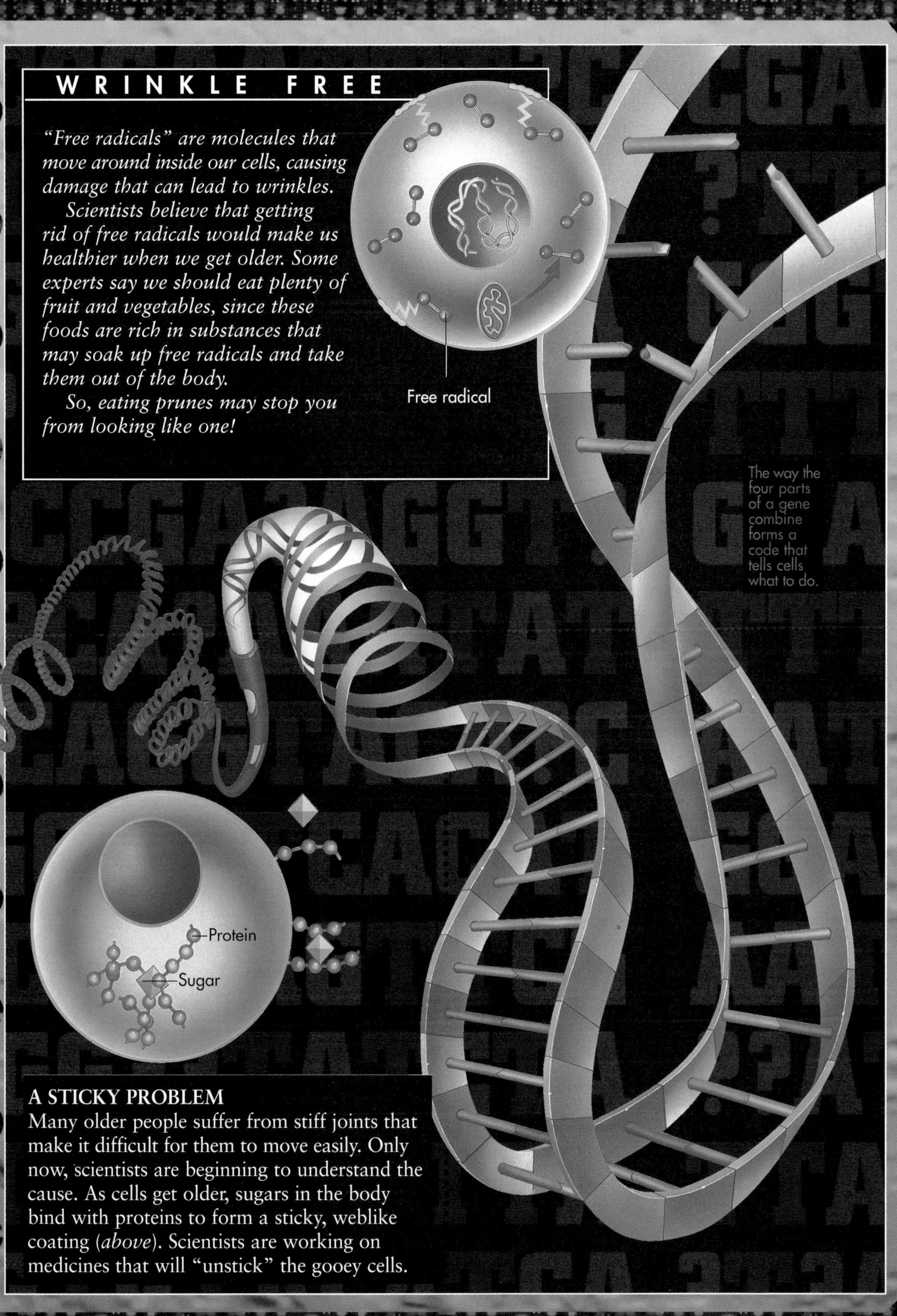

The way the four parts of a gene combine forms a code that tells cells what to do.

A STICKY PROBLEM

Many older people suffer from stiff joints that make it difficult for them to move easily. Only now, scientists are beginning to understand the cause. As cells get older, sugars in the body bind with proteins to form a sticky, weblike coating (*above*). Scientists are working on medicines that will "unstick" the gooey cells.

Haydn the pathfinder

HAYDN (1732–1809)
MAIN WORKS
symphonies (104)
cello concertos (2)
trumpet concerto
string quartets (83)
piano trios (32)
trios for baryton, viola, cello (126)
piano sonatas (62)
operas (24)
masses (12) including *Maria Theresa*, *In Time of War*, and *Nelson*
oratorios (4) including *The Creation*, *The Seasons*, and *The Seven Last Words*

When the 77-year old Haydn lay dying in Vienna in May 1809, Napoleon, who had just conquered the city, posted a guard outside the composer's house to make sure that he was undisturbed. There is no better illustration of Haydn's status as the Grand Old Man of classical music. By the time of his death his symphonies were being played as far afield as America, and his beautiful oratorio *The Creation* had taken a permanent place alongside Handel's *Messiah*.

Joseph Haydn was unique among composers for the high regard in which he was held from the start of his career. His first adult years in Vienna, where he studied theory and began to make his name as a composer, were a struggle. But at the age of 26 he was given his first salaried post, with an aristocrat, Count Morzin, and for the rest of his life he never needed to worry about money.

In 1761 he was employed by the Esterházy family as assistant conductor at Eisenstadt, outside Vienna, and remained there until he resigned as an old man, in 1804. The Esterházys, the wealthiest landowners in Hungary, were also lavish patrons of the arts. Under the terms of his contract. Haydn had to train the singers and orchestra and write compositions for the exclusive enjoyment of the prince. Although he had to wear livery, like the other court servants and officials, Haydn was quite happy with a situation that Mozart came to regard as little better than slavery. He contentedly turned out symphonies, string quartets, and operas, first for Prince Pàl Antal Esterházy, and then for Prince Miklós, known as "the Magnificent."

In the early 1760s, Miklós built Esterháza, a palace that rivaled Versailles in splendor. It included a theater with seating for 400 people, for which Haydn wrote many of his operas. Prince Miklós not only appreciated music: He played it as well. His favorite instrument was the baryton, an extinct string instrument, for which Haydn wrote over 120 works. The year that Esterháza was completed, Haydn became the prince's *Kapellmeister*, or musical director. The help and encouragement that the composer gave the court musicians quickly won him the affectionate nickname "Papa," by which he was known for the rest of his life.

THE "FAREWELL" SYMPHONY

Prince Esterházy did not allow the families of his musicians to live at Esterháza, his palace in the country, because it was too small for them all. But in 1772, the prince stayed at Esterháza longer than usual, and the players were missing their families. Although Haydn was exempt from this ruling, he sympathized with the musicians. As a gesture of solidarity with them, he wrote the *Farewell Symphony*. The orchestra played it in the winter of 1772.

After the four movements of a conventional symphony, the prince must have been surprised to hear the beginning of yet another movement, and a slow one at that. As the movement went on, the musicians snuffed out their candles one by one, and walked quietly off the platform: first, the wind instruments, then the strings, until only two violins remained to complete the movement. Playing with their mutes on to soften the tone, they ended the symphony pianissimo, and walked off, leaving the platform completely empty. Fortunately, the prince took the hint. The next day the court packed up and returned to Vienna, where the musicians were able to rejoin their waiting families.

Such a gesture explains the high esteem in which Prince Esterházy's musicians held their "Papa" Haydn. To the composer, this particular work was simply the Symphony in F-sharp minor. The title of "Farewell" is a nickname. Many of Haydn's other works have been given nicknames, although it is not always easy to know which ones were approved by the composer himself.

When Haydn first met Mozart (left) in 1781, he commented: "More than a century will pass before such a talent will be found again."

Haydn's capacity for kindness, and his ability to recognize genius in others, is shown by his frienship with Mozart. Haydn praised Mozart's music on every occasion, and Mozart responded by dedicating six of his finest string quartets to Haydn. The two men met for the first time in 1790, shortly before Haydn went abroad. His symphonies had begun to be published in England in the 1780s, and in 1791 he went to London. He stayed for 18 months, writing the London symphonies and being feted wherever he went. This London visit, and another one in 1794–95, were the Indian summer of his career, when he completed his grand total of 104 symphonies. In a final burst of creativity in Vienna, between 1796 and 1801, Haydn wrote his oratorios *The Creation* and *The Seasons*.

Haydn's work displays that feeling for objective balance and poise that is usually called "classical" as opposed to the more subjective, "romantic" approach, foreshadowed by Mozart and carried further by Beethoven and his successors. Much of Haydn's music is as sunny and uncomplicated as his life. The system of princely patronage, which Mozart despised, had given Haydn near perfect working conditions for more than 40 years of his life.

Prince Miklós's palace of Esterháza (below) was among the most magnificent in Europe. It is still one of Hungary's tourist showplaces.

In the early 1800s, Haydn had this visiting card printed (left) to explain why he could not go out. The words mean: "All my strength is gone, I am old and weak."

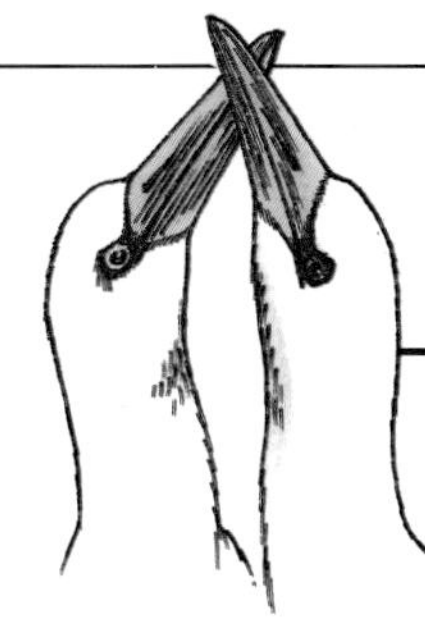

BIRD COURTSHIP

Birds need to find a suitable partner to mate with and breed. The male birds usually do the chasing, and competition among them is fierce. They have various ways of wooing females. Some show off their nest building or hunting skills, or give displays of dancing and singing. Some adopt more colorful feathers just for the breeding season. Puffins grow even more colorful beaks, which molt when the season is over.

Impressive pouch
Male frigate birds have bright red pouches of skin on their throats. To attract a female, they inflate these like giant balloons, sometimes for several hours. When a female bird chooses her mate, she rubs her head against his pouch.

Ruff

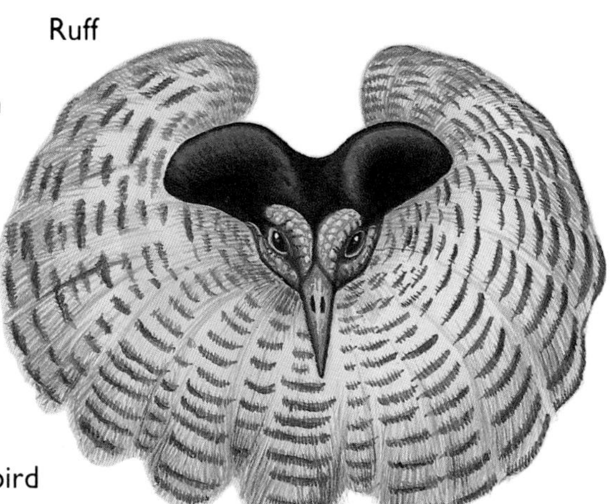

Frigate bird

Attractive feathers
Male ruffs perform their courtship display on communal grounds, called leks. Males defend a small patch, where they can show their feathers.

Good provider
Some male birds, like this British robin, bring the female a gift of food. This shows her whether the male is going to be a good provider of food.

Robin

Survival of the fittest
Male birds of different species have a wide variety of ways to attract a mate. These range from the beautiful plumage of a peacock to the elegant dance of a riflebird. The reason for courtship displays is that the males need to impress prospective mates. If a male's appearance or display is effective in attracting females, he will be able to pass on the characteristics which made him successful. In this way, traits that help an animal reproduce gradually spread to the whole species. This is one aspect of evolution.

Charles Darwin was the British naturalist who developed the theory of evolution in the 1850s.

The female riflebird (left) is wooed each year by the male's amazing dance.

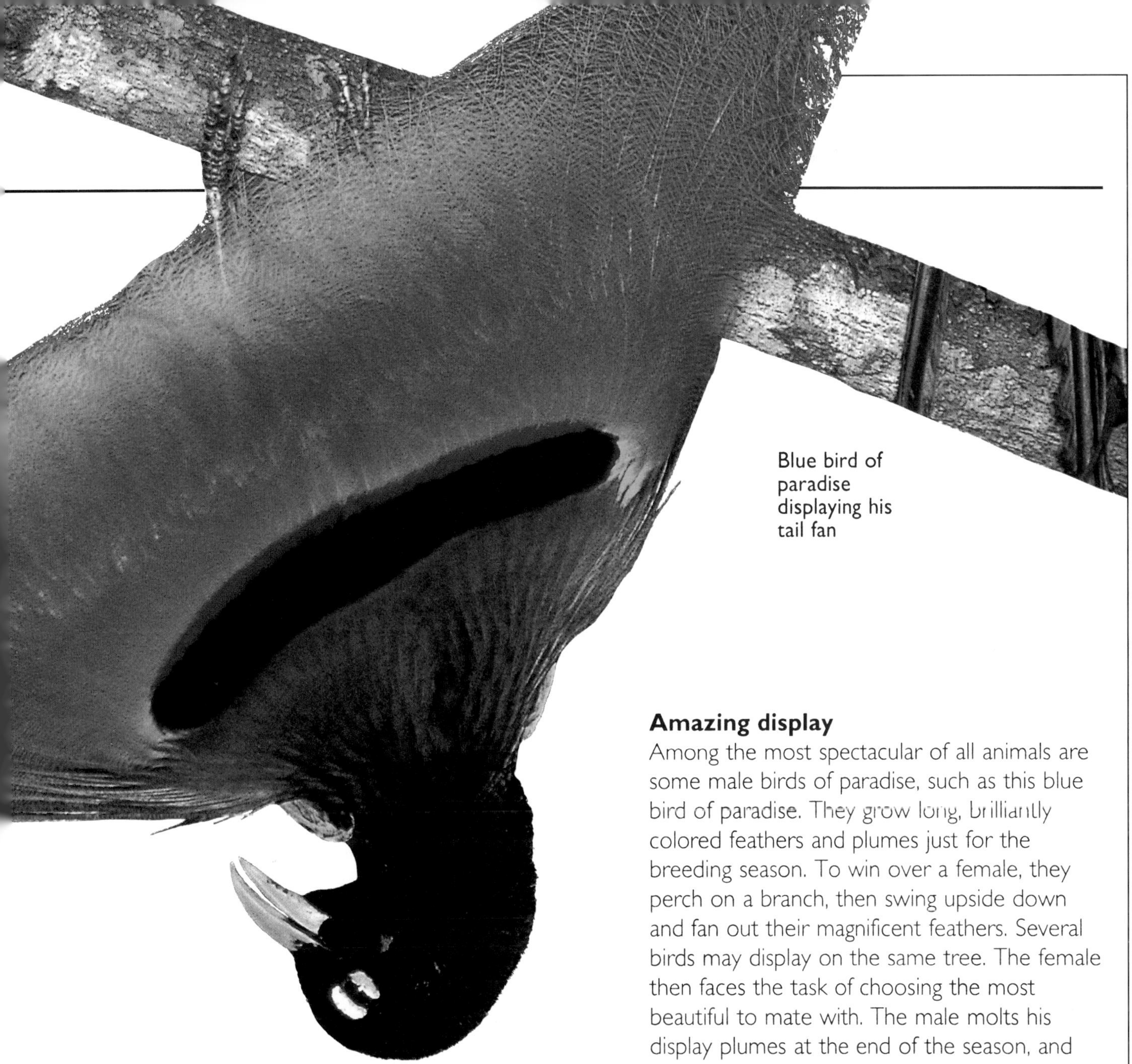

Blue bird of paradise displaying his tail fan

Amazing display

Among the most spectacular of all animals are some male birds of paradise, such as this blue bird of paradise. They grow long, brilliantly colored feathers and plumes just for the breeding season. To win over a female, they perch on a branch, then swing upside down and fan out their magnificent feathers. Several birds may display on the same tree. The female then faces the task of choosing the most beautiful to mate with. The male molts his display plumes at the end of the season, and grows them again the following year.

Attracting attention

For hundreds of years, native peoples of New Guinea have decorated themselves in the courtship display feathers of birds of paradise to make themselves more attractive. Elaborate feather headdresses are worn in tribal dances to impress members of the opposite sex. Although many birds were killed for this tradition, birds of paradise were not under serious threat until 1522, when Eiropeans caught their first glimpse of one brought back on a Spanish trading ship. By the end of the nineteenth century, bird of paradise feathers were in such demand for European fashion that the birds began to decline seriously. They are now protected and most species are slowly recovering their numbers.

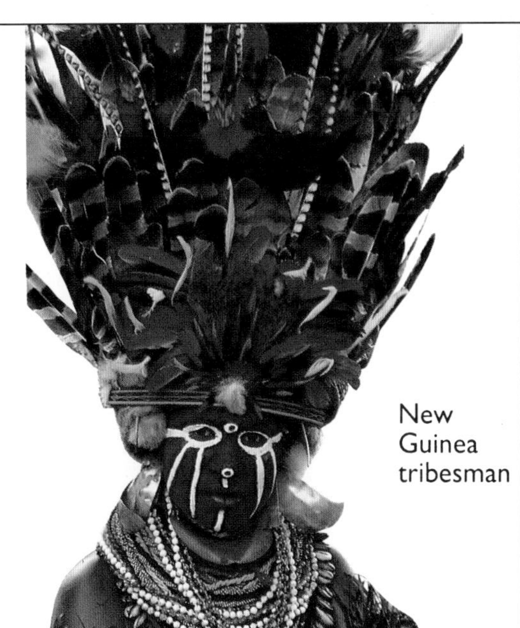

New Guinea tribesman

Reading the HIEROGLYPHS

The Egyptians had invented a picture writing that we call hieroglyphs by about 3000 B.C. Some of their signs were single letters; others had the value of two, three or more letters. These were combined to form words. Hieroglyphs take a long time to write, so the Egyptians invented a "shorthand" script which we call *hieratic*, and another, *demotic*, about 2,500 years later. These were used in daily life, and hieroglyphs were kept for religious texts only. For centuries, no one could read the hieroglyphs, but in 1822 a great breakthrough was made...

* *no translation*

*	i	y	y	*
w	*	b	p	f
m	n	r	h	
h	kh	h(soft)	s	s
sh	q	k	g(hard)	
t	tj	d	dj	

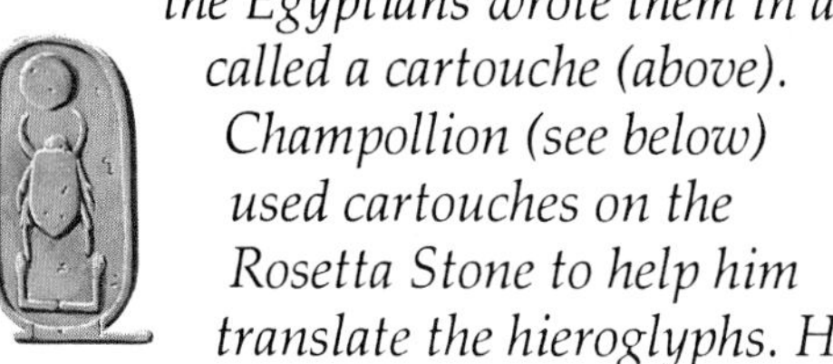

THE ROYAL CARTOUCHE
To emphasize and protect royal or holy names, the Egyptians wrote them in a frame called a cartouche (above). Champollion (see below) used cartouches on the Rosetta Stone to help him translate the hieroglyphs. He read the one below in its Greek version. It was Ptolemy, a ruler of Egypt. He then worked out which hieroglyphs spelled the name.

P T O L M Y S

FINDING THE KEY
The Rosetta Stone is carved in hieroglyphs, demotic and Greek. It was discovered in Egypt in 1799.

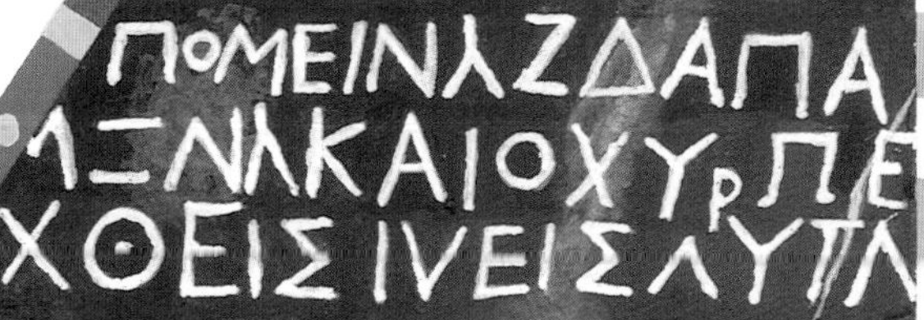

CRACKING THE CODE
In 1822, a brilliant young French scholar, named Jean François Champollion, used his knowledge of ancient Greek to read the Rosetta Stone. At last, the mysterious hieroglyphs could be translated.

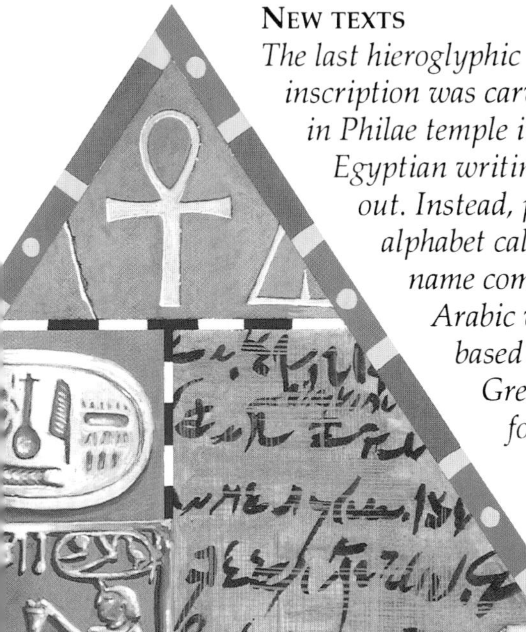

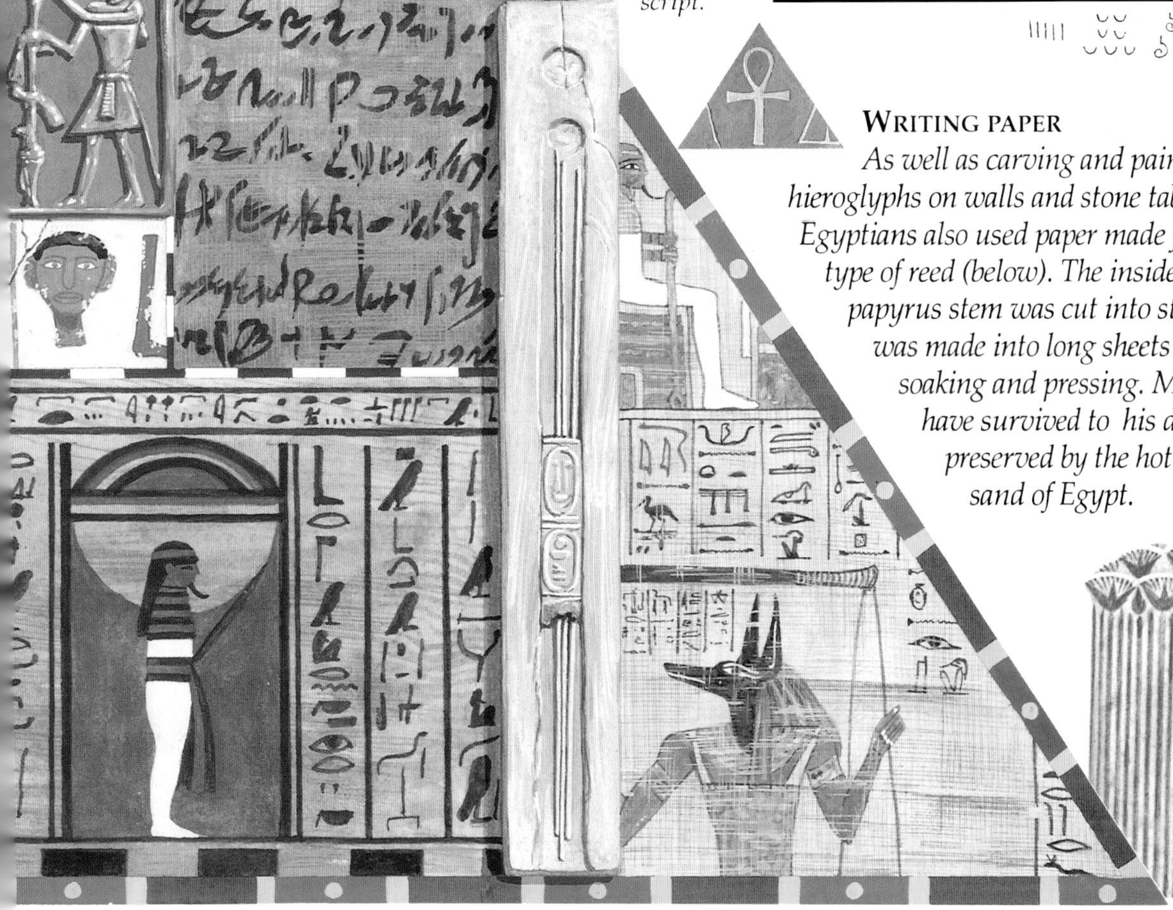

New texts

The last hieroglyphic inscription was carved in Philae temple in A.D. 394. Old Egyptian writing then died out. Instead, people used an alphabet called coptic. The name comes from an Arabic word, gubti, based on the ancient Greek name for Egypt.

A letter in demotic script.

Ancient math

The Egyptians also used symbols for their numbers. Can you write 2,375 in Egyptian numerals?

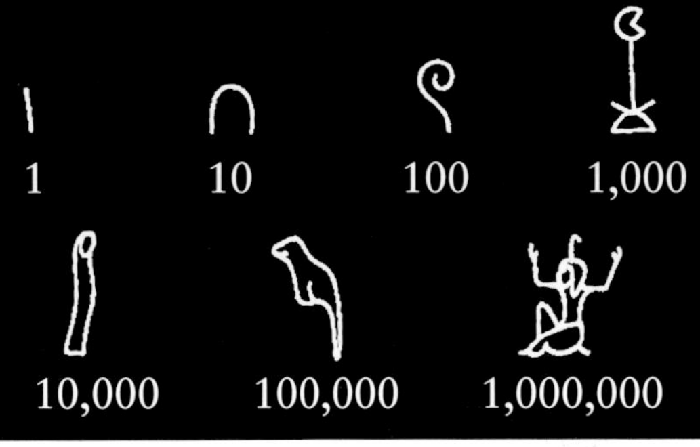

1 10 100 1,000

10,000 100,000 1,000,000

ANSWER:

Writing paper

As well as carving and painting hieroglyphs on walls and stone tablets, the Egyptians also used paper made from papyrus, a type of reed (below). The inside part of the papyrus stem was cut into strips and was made into long sheets of paper by soaking and pressing. Many papyri have survived to his day, preserved by the hot sun and sand of Egypt.

Heavenly guide books

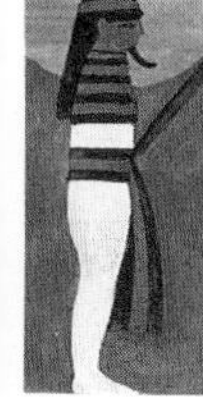

In the pyramid of the last king of Dynasty V and in all Dynasty VI pyramids, we find writings called the Pyramid Texts. These were believed to help the king move easily into the Next World (heaven).

They contained prayers, pleas, and ritual pronouncements to the gods. It was hoped that the gods, such as Anubis (left), would welcome the King and allow him to pass into the next world to live a new, happy, and everlasting life.

AIR RESISTANCE

If you open an umbrella and try to run with it on a calm day, you will find it difficult as the umbrella captures the air like a parachute, dragging you back. Whenever we move we have to push the air out of the way and we experience air resistance. Sometimes air resistance is helpful, for example in slowing down a parachute. It becomes a nuisance when it acts against a sports car. Some shapes are "streamlined" to move smoothly through the air. They experience less air resistance because the air does not rub against them too much and block their movement.

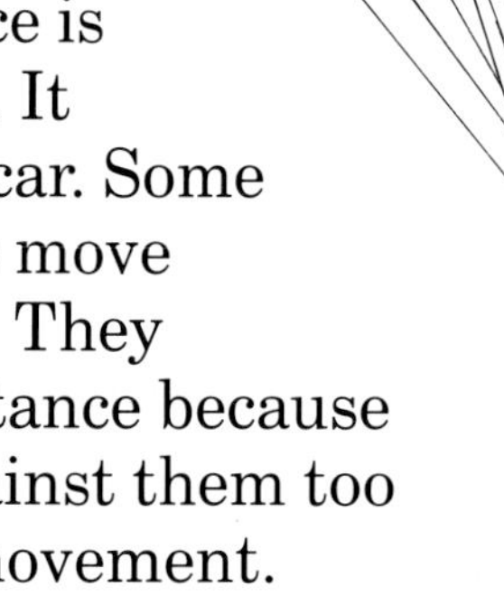

STREAMLINED SHAPES

1 You can test the force of air resistance. To make a fair test you need two of the same model cars. Make sure their wheels turn freely.

2 Cut two rectangles from a piece of cardboard. Again, to keep the test fair, make them the same size and shape.

3 Attach the rectangular cardboard to the front end of each car. Fold one smoothly over the top and bend the other one as shown. Tape them in place.

WHY IT WORKS

The shape of your cars makes them roll quickly or slowly. Air flows smoothly over the car with the rounded paper front. This streamlining allows it to roll faster than the car with the square front, which is held back by air resistance, or drag. Drag slows things down, creating ripples of air behind them. These moving ripples, or eddies, lower the air pressure behind the unstreamlined car, keeping it back as it moves.

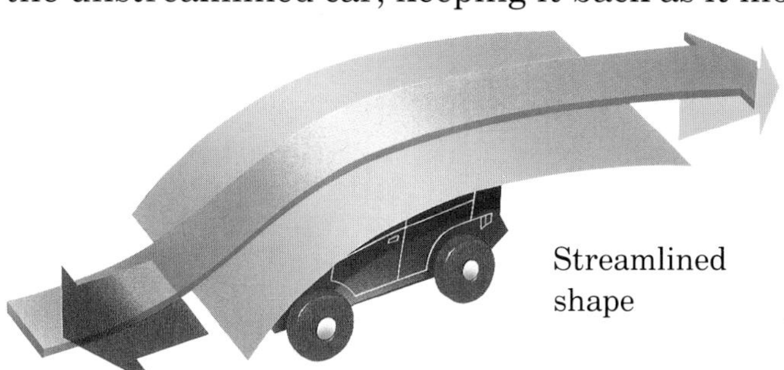

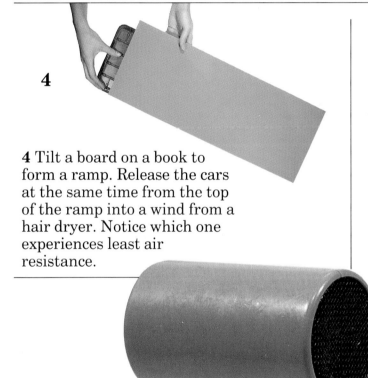

4

4 Tilt a board on a book to form a ramp. Release the cars at the same time from the top of the ramp into a wind from a hair dryer. Notice which one experiences least air resistance.

BRIGHT IDEAS

Capture air with a simple parachute. Tie four strings to the corners of a large handkerchief. Fix a blob of modeling clay to the strings. Now make a larger parachute from paper, attaching the same piece of clay. It will drop more slowly than the first one because it captures more air.

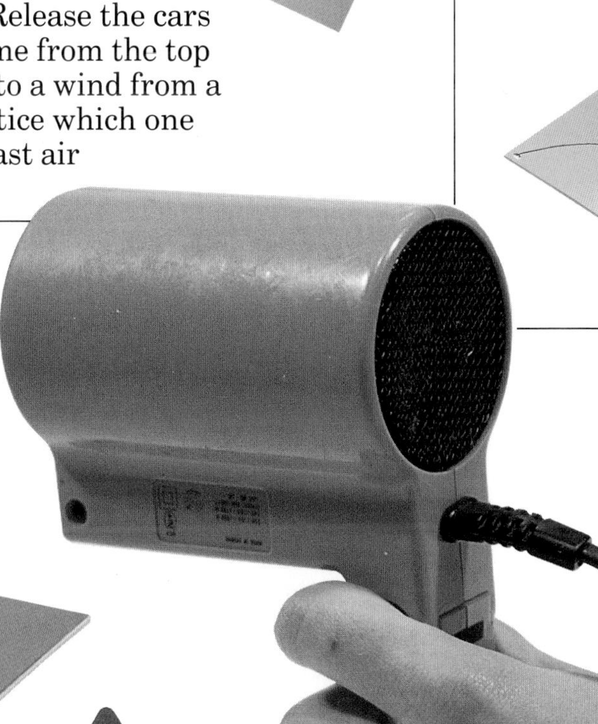

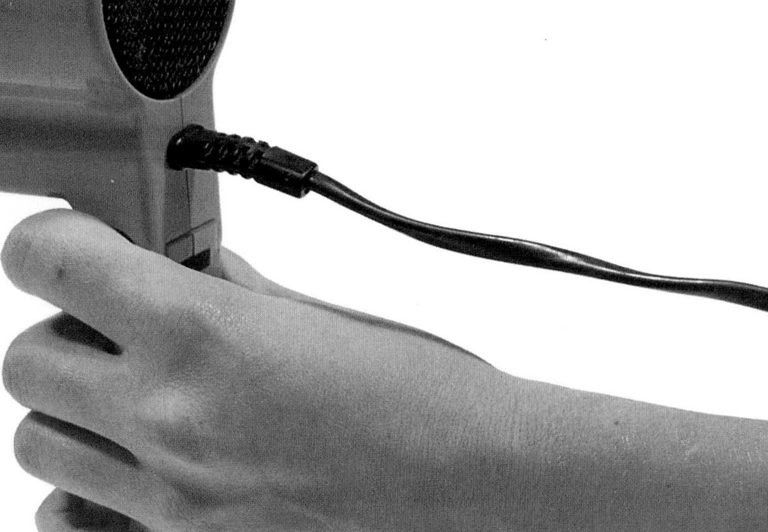

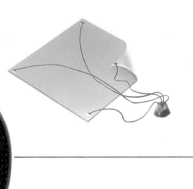

RACING TO VICTORY

Many forms of transportation are used for sport and leisure. While some people go cycling, canoeing, or ballooning for pleasure, sportspeople test their skill and stamina by competing against each other to set new records. These sports are also a test of machines. Manufacturers and designers compete to produce faster, more efficient vehicles: The racing cars of 1914 (*right*) look a bit like toys compared to today's sleek, aerodynamic cars (*below right*).

SPEED ON THE WATER

Yachting is a popular recreation as well as a sport. It started in the Netherlands (the word "yacht" comes from the Dutch "jacht" meaning small vessel). By 1900 (*above*), yachting was popular worldwide. The America's Cup (*below*) was first raced in 1851. American yachts won the trophy consistently until 1983, when an Australian boat won.

SURF'S UP!
Windsurfing (*above*) is an energetic sport with speeds of over 52 mph (84 kmh) – and it does not cause any air pollution!

DAMON HILL (1960-)
Damon Hill, who won the 1996 World Motor Racing Championship, has followed in his father's footsteps. Graham Hill twice won the championship in the 1960s.

PUSHING THE BOAT OUT

Competitive rowing began in the 1700s and was accepted as an Olympic sport in 1900. Rowing races, called regattas, are held annually in many parts of the world. Most boats have two four or eight oars, each rowed by one person, but single-person sculls (where one rower uses two oars) are also used

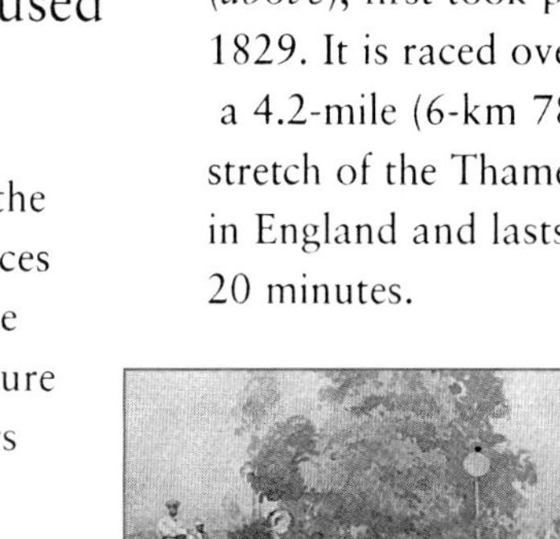

THE BOAT RACE
The most famous annual boat race, between Oxford and Cambridge universities (*above*), first took place in 1829. It is raced over a 4.2-mile (6-km 780-m) stretch of the Thames River, in England and lasts about 20 minutes.

FORMULA ONE
The most important motor races are the Formula-One Grand-Prix races which are held all over the world. These races feature the fastest racing cars driven by the most skilled drivers. Some cars (*left*) reach speeds of 213 mph (340 kmh).

*These cyclists (*right*) lead the 1930 Tour de France.*

TOUR DE FRANCE

Organized cycle racing began in France in 1868. The greatest race of all is the annual Tour de France, which was first run in 1903. For three weeks riders race for 3,105 miles (5,000 kilometers) along a grueling route that includes a climb into the French Alps. At the start of each stage the overall leader is given a yellow jersey to wear (*right*). Over ten million people follow the race on T.V.

LAND-SPEED RECORDS
The 1-mile (1.6-km) land-speed record increased from 127.659 mph (205.447 kmh) in 1906 to 763.035 mph (1220.9 kmh) in 1997. American Al Teague holds the record for the fastest wheel-driven car (*below*) – 432.692 mph (696.331 kmh).

Although the term "avalanche" can mean the fall of any material – snow, soil, rocks, ice, or volcanic lava – it generally refers to a falling mass of snow. Dry-snow avalanches can travel at speeds of up to 225 mph. The melting snow of a wet-snow avalanche moves more slowly, at about 20 mph.

Wet-snow avalanche

Wet-snow avalanches often begin in rocky areas. Here, the snow melts around rocks that have warmed up in the sunshine. The fresh, wet snow can set as hard as concrete when the avalanche finally comes to a halt.

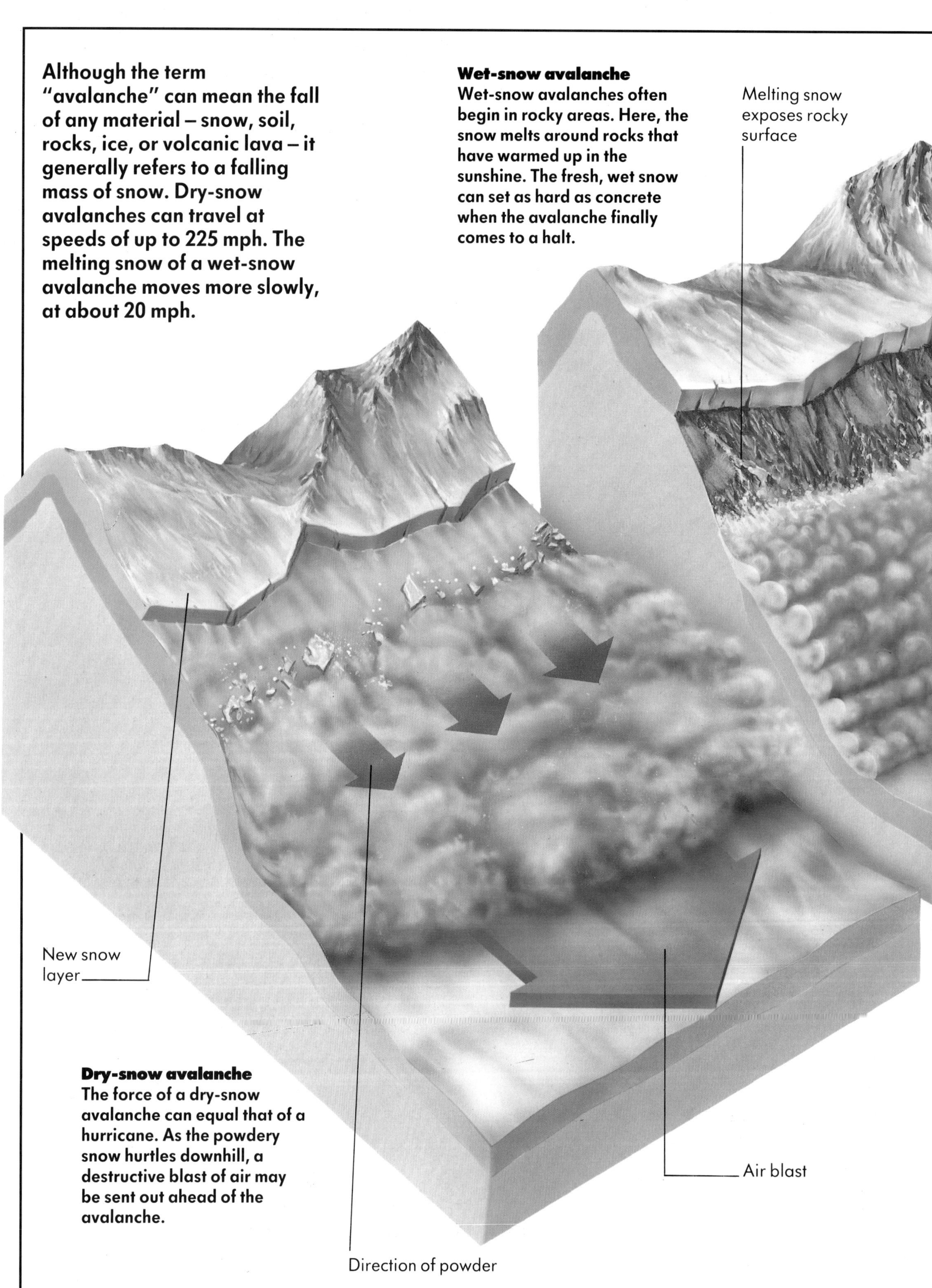

Dry-snow avalanche

The force of a dry-snow avalanche can equal that of a hurricane. As the powdery snow hurtles downhill, a destructive blast of air may be sent out ahead of the avalanche.

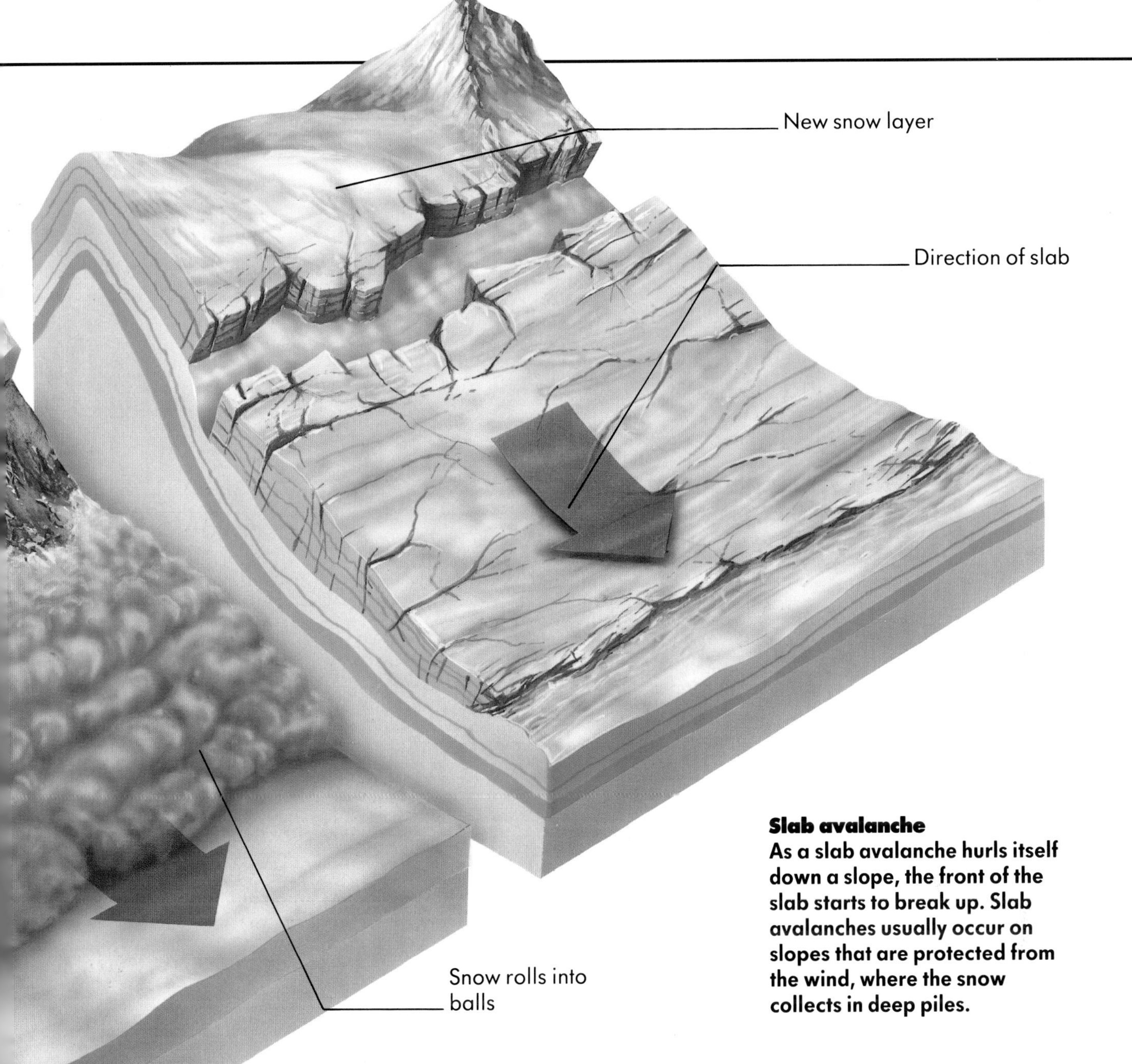

Slab avalanche
As a slab avalanche hurls itself down a slope, the front of the slab starts to break up. Slab avalanches usually occur on slopes that are protected from the wind, where the snow collects in deep piles.

WHAT IS AN AVALANCHE?

An avalanche is a huge mass of ice and snow which breaks away from the side of a mountain and surges downward at great speed. The greatest avalanches probably occur on the high peaks of the Himalayas. However, those which cause the highest death toll fall in the populated valleys of the Alps.

Scientists have grouped avalanches into three main kinds: wet-snow avalanche, dry-snow avalanche, and slab avalanche. Wet-snow avalanches usually occur in the spring, when the loose, melting snow forms into large boulders of snow as it rolls downhill. More deadly are the dry-snow avalanches, which either slide along close to the ground, or lift off the ground completely and swirl through the air, often hundreds of feet high. In a slab avalanche, a huge chunk of solid, sticky snow breaks away from a slope. It slides across a layer of loose snow crystals lying beneath the surface.

PISTOLS AND REVOLVERS

Pistols are much easier to handle than muskets and were used by officers, cavalrymen, highwaymen, and gentlemen in duels. Early pistols, called wheel locks, were replaced in the 17th century by flintlocks, which were cheaper and more reliable. During the 19th century, inventors began to design handguns that would fire several shots before the cylinder needed reloading. The first of these multi-shot weapons was the revolver, followed by the automatic pistol.

FLINTLOCKS
To fire a flintlock pistol (*above*), the spring-mounted cock was drawn back. When the trigger was pulled, the cock was released and would hit the steel striking plate (*below*), producing sparks which ignited the gunpowder.

WILD WEST WEAPONS
The expansion of the American West in the 19th century coincided with the development of many new weapons, including breech-loading rifles and revolvers, such as the Colt .45, which were used by everyone, from cowboys (*above*) to soldiers, settlers, and Native Americans.

CRACK SHOTS

In the late 18th century, flintlock pistols began to replace swords as the main dueling weapon (*above*). Dueling pistols were always made in pairs and were of the highest quality to ensure accuracy. Today, the military and police practice accurate shooting at target ranges using modern pistols (*above right*).

HISTORICAL DUELS
Many important people took part in duels, including the Duke of Wellington, who defeated Napoléon at the Battle of Waterloo in 1815, and Lord Castlereagh, who became British foreign secretary in 1812. The famous Russian writer Aleksandr Pushkin was killed in a duel in 1837.

Colt .45

REVOLVING CYLINDERS

During the 1830s and 1840s, several inventors began to develop handguns with cylinders containing five or six cartridges. The cylinder revolved so that the cartridges could be fired one at a time up the barrel. Only when the last cartridge was fired would the cylinder have to be reloaded. Colt (*left*) and Remington (*above*) were two of the most famous makes of the new handgun – called a revolver – which replaced the single-shot pistol and the slow, unreliable pepperbox pistol (*right*).

Remington

SAMUEL COLT (1814-1862)

Colt was an American inventor and gunmaker who carved an early version of a revolver out of wood. He produced the first working revolver in 1835, and introduced a system of mass production for the weapon.

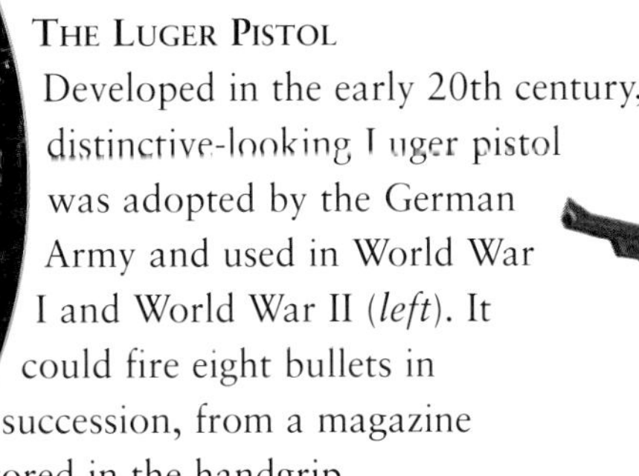

Pepperbox

THE LUGER PISTOL
Developed in the early 20th century, the distinctive-looking Luger pistol was adopted by the German Army and used in World War I and World War II (*left*). It could fire eight bullets in succession, from a magazine stored in the handgrip.

MODERN WEAPONS

The Israeli Desert Eagle (*above*) is a large, powerful, semi-automatic pistol, which uses a propellant gas to reload each time the trigger is pulled. Revolvers, too, are still widely used by armies and police forces: The highly powerful and exceptionally heavy .44in Magnum is perhaps the most famous since its use by the actor Clint Eastwood in the *Dirty Harry* movies (*right*).

WHAT IF A LION HAD NO PRIDE?

It would be very lonely. Lions are the only cats that live in groups, or prides. As with any group of animals, each of the lions has a different role. The females hunt for food and bring up the babies, or cubs. The males defend the females of the pride and the area of land where they live, called the *territory*, from rival males and other prides of lions.

Solitary cats
Apart from the lion, all 34 other kinds of cats – from tigers to wildcats – are mainly solitary. They live and hunt alone. Only during the breeding season when a male and a female are together, and when a mother is with her cubs, do these cats have any company.

Elephants on parade
When moving from place to place, elephants may walk in a long line, like soldiers on parade. The herd is led by the oldest female, or cow, the matriarch. The rest of the herd, including her sisters, daughters, and their babies, rely on her to find food and water.

Rival male
A fully grown male will leave his original pride. He will then wander alone for a while, then try to join another pride, so that he can mate with the females, and father offspring. But first he must challenge the pride's leader.

Leader of the pride
The chief male of the pride defends his females and territory fiercely. He fluffs up his mane to look large and strong, and growls loud and long. He tries to repel the rival by fright first. If this doesn't work, it may come to a real fight!

Female hunters
The older, experienced females are the pride's main hunters. They work together to chase and separate a herd of zebra and wildebeest, then they run down a young, old, or sick member. However, they will let the pride-leading male eat first.

Safety in numbers

Many large plant-eating mammals form herds with others of their kind. Sometimes they form mixed herds too, like zebra with wildebeest and gazelles. These herds can number from a handful to many thousands of animals.

There are many noses and pairs of eyes and ears that can detect any approaching danger. If one herd member spots trouble, it can warn the others. Should a predator approach too closely, the herd panics and runs. The hunter then finds it hard to single out one victim from the blur of bodies, heads, legs, and stripes that flash past very quickly.

Trooping baboons

The baboon is a type of monkey that spends much of its time on the ground. Baboons dwell in groups called *troops*, which can be subdivided into bands, clans, and family groups. The troops can number up to 250 baboons. These are based around the mothers and their children. There are a few males, and the biggest, most senior of these lead the troop from danger or defend it against predators, such as the leopard.

Lion cubs
Females with young cubs guard their offspring and feed them on mother's milk. However, danger may come with a rival male, which will kill any existing cubs if it takes over the pride so that its own can be reared.

Young males
The growing males stay with the pride, as long as they do not threaten the leading male. When they want to have any cubs of their own, then they must either challenge the leading male, or leave and take over another pride.

EXPLORING THE POLES

Norwegian Roald Amundsen left the Bay of Whales and took a new route up the Axel Heiberg Glacier. Robert Scott's English party set out from McMurdo Sound, following the path pioneered by Shackleton two years previously. The race to the South Pole was on.

Amundsen traveled on skis and dog sleds. He reached the Pole a month before Scott and swiftly returned to base. Meanwhile, Scott and his five colleagues reached their destination on foot and turned for the long trudge home. The weather worsened. Dispirited and exhausted, they made painfully slow progress. Two men died.

Finally, 150 miles from base, the four remaining Englishmen froze to death in their tent while the blizzard raged outside.

"Mine at Last"
American Robert Peary (1856–1920, left) *said he was the first explorer to lead a party to the North Pole, arriving on April 6, 1909. There are still those who dispute his claim.*

A HEROIC MESSAGE

The fame of Robert Scott (1868–1912) rests as much on what he wrote in his diary as what he achieved. A search party found the diary beside his frozen body. Its famous final entry – "For God's sake look after our people" – touched the hearts of the British public and made Scott an instant hero.

GREAT SCOTT! Supported by composer Ralph Vaughan Williams's moving music, *Scott of the Antarctic* (1949, *left*), reinforced the myth of Scott as a doomed hero rather than a stubborn

The Oddball Explorer

In ordinary life Sir Ernest Henry Shackleton (1874–1922) was an oddball. Fortunately for him, he did not lead an ordinary life.

He made his name as a brave and inspiring leader of Antarctic expeditions. None achieved their goal. On one he turned back 97 miles from the Pole.

On another, his ship the *Endurance* was crushed by ice (*left*) and he had to sail an open boat 800 miles across the icy Southern Ocean to safety.

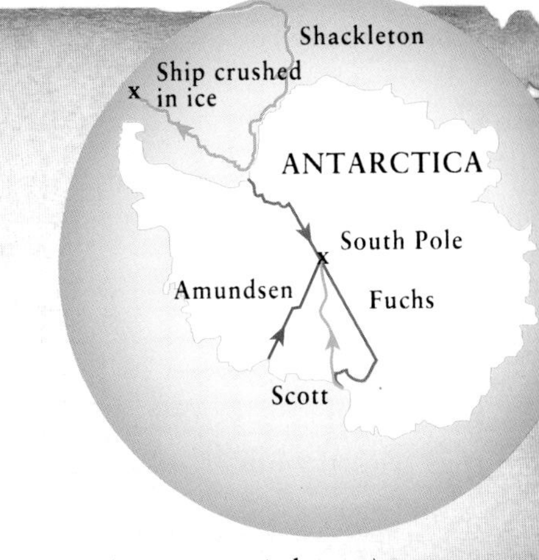

Antarctic routes (above), *including that of Vivian Fuchs, who reached the South Pole using motor sleds.*

The Pole! (main picture) *December 14, 1911. Roald Amundsen (1872–1928) arrives at the South Pole after a two-month crossing of the frozen continent by dog sled and skis. He beat Scott by 35 days.*

Wisdom of the Inuits

The traditions and practices of the Inuit people of the frozen north, originally known as Eskimos ("raw meat eaters"), were adopted by all wise Polar explorers. Peary relied heavily on Inuit assistance in his Arctic expeditions.

Amundsen's victory over Scott in the race to the South Pole owed much to his use of traditional dog sleds (*right*).

Frozen fantasy. As late as 1973, Walt Disney still saw the Arctic as a credible setting for a land stuck in a time warp. *The Island at the Top of the World* tells the story of explorers who travel to the Arctic by balloon and find a fantasy valley inhabited by Vikings. Pursued by killer whales, the party eventually escapes on an iceberg!

Until Peary's journey in 1909, there was fierce argument about what was at the North Pole. Because the sun never sets at the Pole in summer, some scientists believed it was a warm paradise like the biblical garden of Eden!

In Edgar Rice Burrough's story, *The Land That Time Forgot* (filmed in 1974, *right*), a polar island is inhabited by prehistoric monsters.

ENERGY CYCLE

Nearly all the energy we use comes originally from the Sun. It radiates through space and reaches Earth, causing plants to grow. These plants provide us with food energy in the form of crops and feed the animals which we eat as meat. They also provide fuel because plants and microscopic creatures that lived millions of years ago formed the fossil fuels – coal and oil. Rainwater, evaporated by the Sun's heat from the oceans, fills the rivers and provides hydro-electric power, while the wind is also produced by the Sun.

Sun worship

The Incas, Mayas and Aztecs, of South and Central America, worshipped the Sun with sacrificial offerings on Sun temples (left). The Incas thought the emperor was a descendant of the Sun. When he died his body was preserved and kept in his palace, where servants continued to wait on him.

an Egyptian Sun-god

In ancient Egypt, the Sun was one of many gods until king Akhenaten decreed that the Sun-god, Aten, should be the only god.

Myths and legends

In Greek mythology there were many gods. Phaeton, the son of the Sun-god Helios, was granted his wish that he should control the chariot of the Sun for a whole day. But Phaeton lost control of the horses and the Sun came too close to the Earth. He was about to burn the Earth up when Zeus, the chief god, struck him down with a thunderbolt.

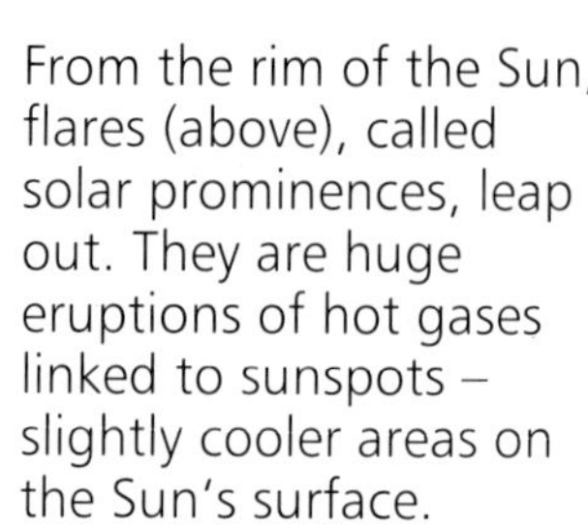

From the rim of the Sun, flares (above), called solar prominences, leap out. They are huge eruptions of hot gases linked to sunspots – slightly cooler areas on the Sun's surface.

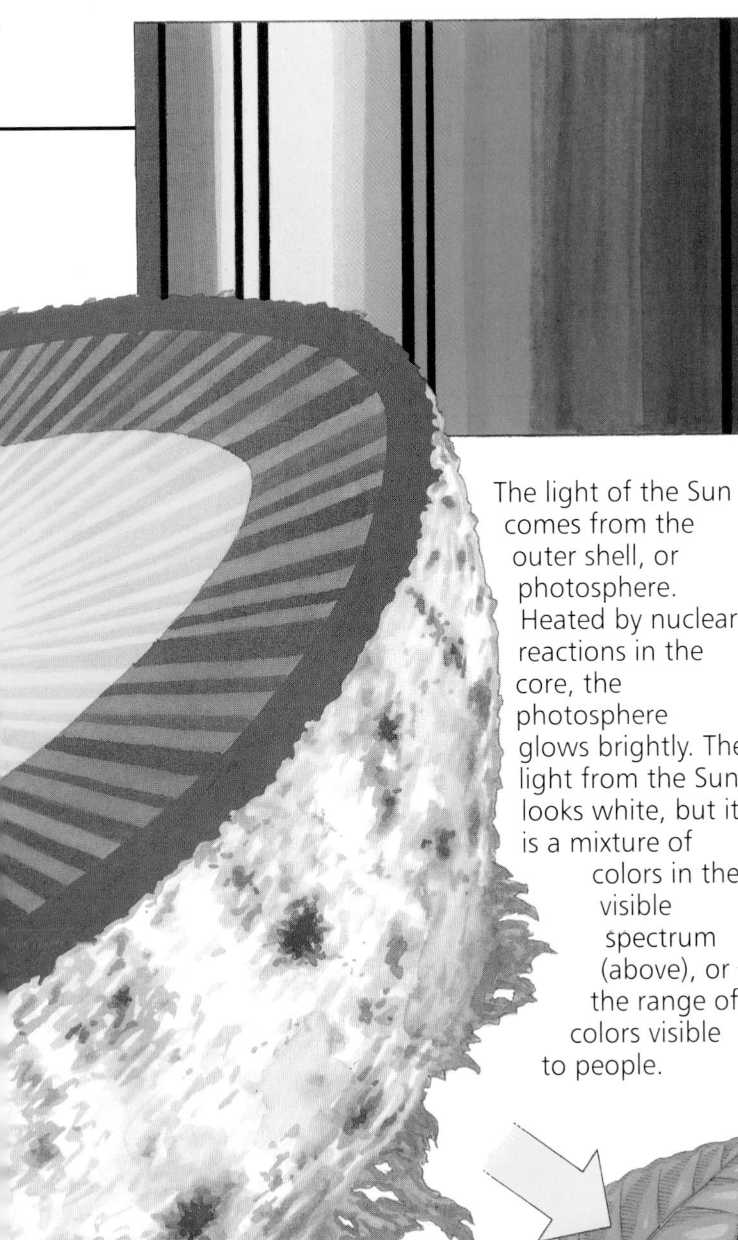

The light of the Sun comes from the outer shell, or photosphere. Heated by nuclear reactions in the core, the photosphere glows brightly. The light from the Sun looks white, but it is a mixture of colors in the visible spectrum (above), or the range of colors visible to people.

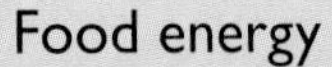

Food energy

Different foods provide different amounts of energy, measured in kilocalories (or kcals). Each day we need 2,200 - 2,900 kcals from our food. A gram of fat contains nine calories; a gram of flour or sugar just under four; a gram of fish between one and two. Just sitting still uses 1.1 kcals a minute, while walking uses 3-4 kcals a minute and running fast about 15 kcals a minute. Sportspeople have a special diet to give them enough energy to compete.

Plants capture the Sun's energy by a chemical process – photosynthesis (left). A green chemical, chlorophyll, creates sugars from water in the plant's roots and carbon dioxide gas in the air. Other chemicals – nitrogen, calcium, phosphorus and potassium – come from the soil.

a single plant cell

Wheat worldwide

Six crops – wheat, rice, maize, barley, oats and rye – provide about half of all human food energy. Wheat is used for making bread and is very efficient at converting sunlight into food energy, while for thousands of years rice has formed the basic diet of half the world's population. Wheat grows easily in cold, northern climates with low temperatures as opposed to rice, which needs warmer, wetter conditions in order to thrive and is grown on graduated terraces.

Getting started IN GYMNASTICS

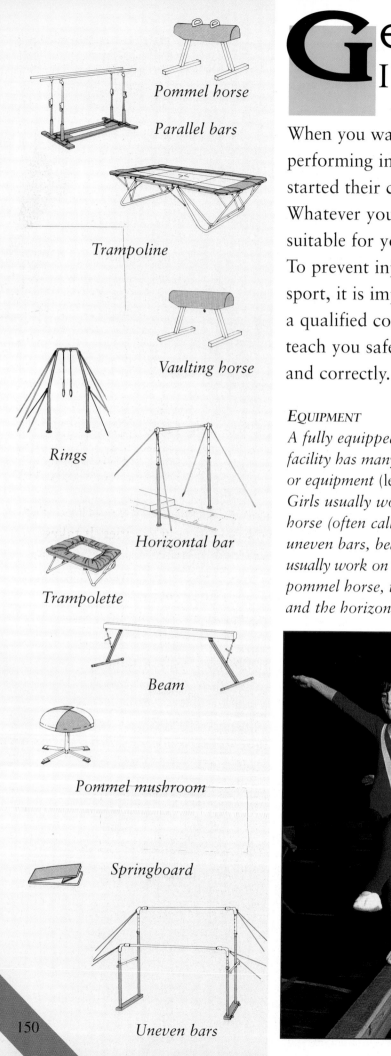

Pommel horse

Parallel bars

Trampoline

Vaulting horse

Rings

Horizontal bar

Trampolette

Beam

Pommel mushroom

Springboard

Uneven bars

When you watch television and see the top gymnasts performing incredible exercises, remember that they all started their careers with a basic gymnastics class! Whatever your ability and age, there will be a class suitable for you, either at school or in a gymnastics club. To prevent injury and to make the most of the sport, it is important that you are taught by a qualified coach or teacher who can teach you safely and correctly.

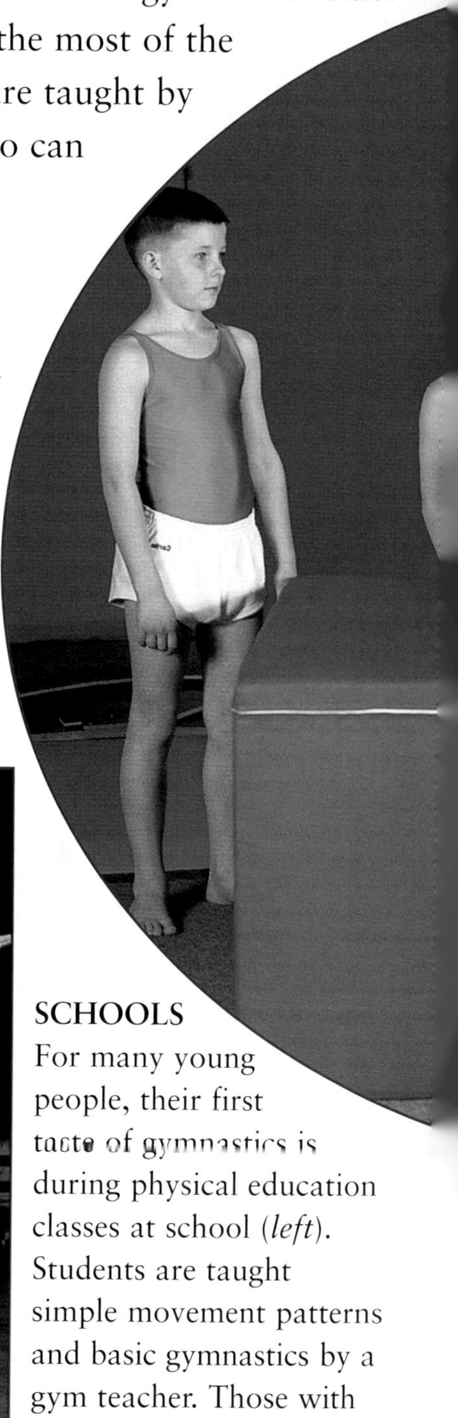

EQUIPMENT

A fully equipped gymnastics training facility has many pieces of apparatus or equipment (left) *and safety mats. Girls usually work on the vaulting horse (often called the vault), uneven bars, beam, and floor. Boys usually work on the floor, the pommel horse, the rings, the vault, and the horizontal and parallel bars.*

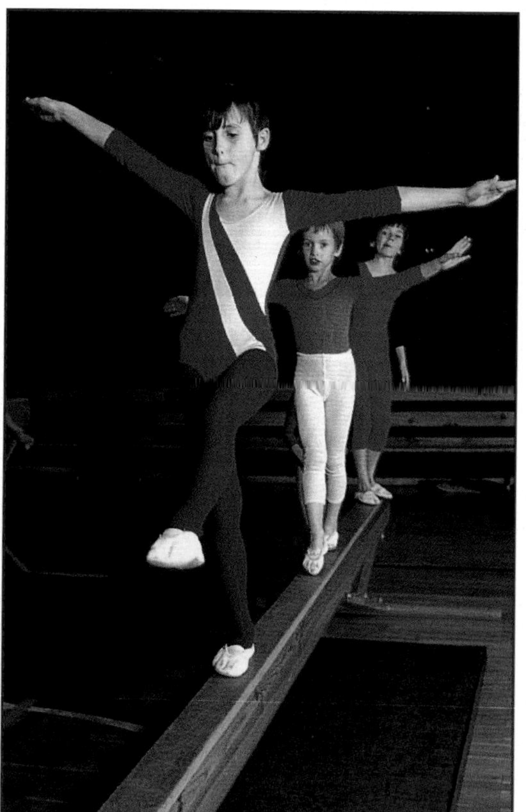

SCHOOLS

For many young people, their first taste of gymnastics is during physical education classes at school (*left*). Students are taught simple movement patterns and basic gymnastics by a gym teacher. Those with more ability or greater interest can learn more by joining an after-school gymnastics class.

JOINING A CLUB

If you enjoy gymnastics at school, why not join a local, recognized gymnastics club (below)? *Your school may have connections with a local club. Before joining, ask to look around the gym – check too that the gym is safe and well-equipped. Ask if you can watch a training session.*

INSPIRATION

Many young people (and sometimes their parents too!) are inspired to join a gymnastics club after they have seen superstars, such as Shannon Miller *(right)*, on the television.

Top gymnasts reach the peak of their careers through hard work and talent – but remember, you don't have to score a perfect 10 to enjoy gymnastics!

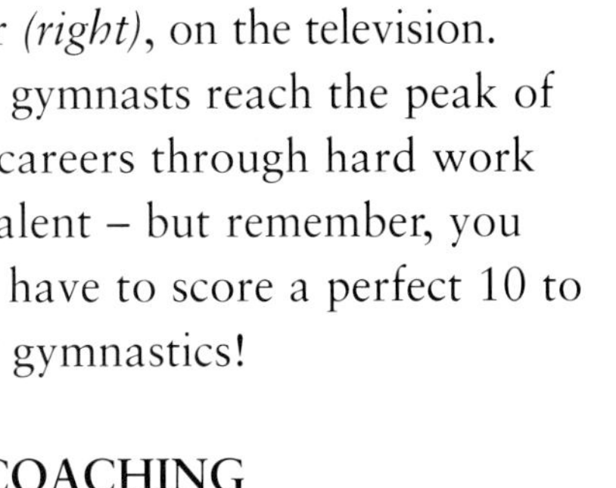

COACHING

As well as looking after your safety and well-being, your coach will identify your strengths and weaknesses. In considering these, he or she will design a program to help you learn and develop to the best of your abilities. It takes great determination and dedication to become a successful gymnast – a good coach will try to develop these characteristics, as well as supervise your physical training. Your coach will also try to motivate you by offering frequent encouragement.

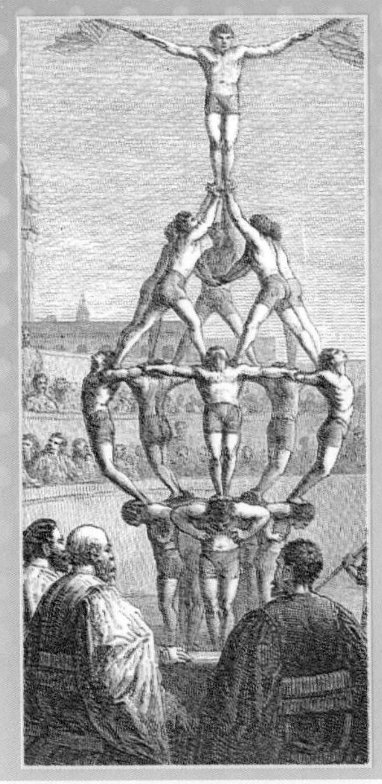

HISTORY OF GYMNASTICS

The word "gymnast" was first used to describe the naked athletes who performed gymnastics movements in the ancient Greek and Roman civilizations.

During the Middle Ages only acrobats *(left)* performed gymnastics, but in the late 18th century people began to recognize the benefits of physical activity *(right)* on the body and mind. A German schoolteacher, Friedrich Jahn (1778-1852), built the first modern gymnastics equipment. The military adopted this to help keep soldiers fit and strong.

Men's artistic gymnastics has been featured in the Olympic Games since 1896. It was only in 1928 that women were allowed to compete.

WHAT IF THERE WERE NO SPACECRAFT?

How would astronauts get back to Earth?

An astronaut could survive in a spacesuit for a short time. But coming back into Earth's atmosphere creates lots of heat, as an object pushes through the ever-thickening air molecules. A heat shield might help a rear-first re-entry!

Space exploration would be much less exciting without spacecraft that carry people. It began with the Space Race in the 1950s and 1960s. The United States and Russia raced to launch the first satellite, the first spaceman and woman, and the first Moon visit. The satellite Sputnik 1, launched in 1957, was the first man-made object in space, and the Russian Yuri Gagarin was the first man in space. But the United States was first to land on the Moon in 1969 with the spacecraft Apollo 11 carrying Neil Armstrong and Edwin "Buzz" Aldrin. Without spacecraft, none of these achievements would have happened.

What would Yuri Gagarin have done?

Yuri was the very first person in space. On April 12, 1961, he orbited Earth once in his ball-shaped spacecraft Vostok 1. Without this spacecraft, he would never have become world famous. But he could have carried on as a successful test pilot for the Russian Air Force.

What if there were no satellites?

We would have no satellite T.V. or satellite weather pictures, and mobile phones would not work very well. Ships, planes, and overland explorers could not use their satellite navigation gadgets. Without satellites, countries would have to find new ways to spy on each other. They could go back to the high-flying spyplanes used just after World War II, or use high-flying balloons carrying surveillance equipment.

How much money would we save?

Space programs run throughout the world by different countries, like the Apollo Moon missions, have cost billions of dollars. Manned space flights are the most expensive type of missions. It has been estimated that NASA has spent over $80 billion on its manned space flights up to 1994, with nearly $45 billion spent on the space shuttle program alone! Even a single spacesuit worn outside the space shuttle costs $3.4 million!

Nonstick earthlings

Our everyday lives have been affected by the enormous technological leaps made during the age of space exploration. These "leaps" include nonstick coatings, used for lubrication in spacecraft. Also, the microtechnology needed in satellites has led to smaller and faster computers, some found in household appliances.

The King of Beasts

The year was 1900. The plan was to build a 700-mile railroad from Kampala, capital of Uganda, to the port of Mombasa on the Indian Ocean. It was a massive task, but the engineers said it could be done. Building the track soon proved the least of their worries.

At Tsavo, near the foothills of Mount Kilimanjaro, the line had to cross lion territory. The beasts objected. The man-eaters of the Tsavo killed 28 railroad workers and work stopped for weeks (*main picture*). Finally, the lions were hunted down and shot. But the local people knew exactly what had been happening: An ancient king and queen had returned as beasts to defend their territory.

Beware the Lioness
Although smaller than the male, the lioness (above) *can run faster (at 32 mph) and is more dangerous, especially if her cubs are threatened. It is she who teaches the young to hunt. A lion can kill an animal three times its own weight.*

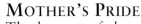

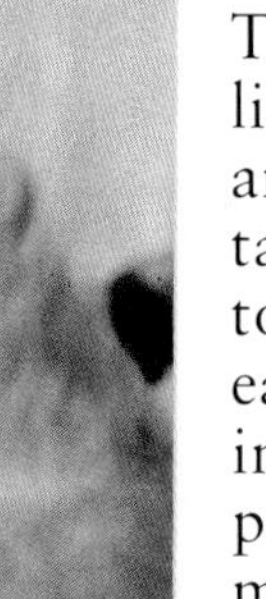

Mother's Pride

The largest of the cat family, a lion can weigh over 400 pounds and measure 10 feet from nose to tail. Once found from Greece to India, most lions now live in east and southern Africa, usually in family groups (called prides) of one or more adult males and several females.

Using their sharp claws and teeth (*left*), lions will eat almost any available creature, from 8,000-pound hippopotami and giraffes to grass mice and tortoises.

KING OF BEASTS. The lion, widely regarded as the King of Beasts, is often seen as the symbol of might and power. It is celebrated by the Bapende people of Kongo (*left*), is the destroyer of demons in Hinduism, the defender of the law in Buddhism, and is featured in many coats of arms, particularly that of British kings and queens.

Sacred Cats

To the people of South and Central America the jaguar is the Master of Animals. Mayan rulers were said to be descended from jaguars, and the elite Aztec jaguar warriors were dressed as them (above right). *Today the jaguar symbol is used by a car manufacturer* (right).

Traditional African priests wear leopard skins. Peoples who believe the beast is holy may not eat its flesh because it helps the spirits of dead.

TEAM HUNTERS

Healthy lions feed off grazing animals, such as gazelles. They hunt together, stalking their prey downwind and striking with sudden speed and ferocity. However, even working in packs, only one in five hunts ends in a kill.

Lions' eyes are designed for seeing at night, and most hunts occur just after dark or before sunrise. Older beasts, with failing teeth and strength, may acquire a taste for human flesh, but attacks on people are not common.

Spot the Leopard?

Though the leopard (left) *weighs just 154 lb, it is a far more cunning predator than the lion. It hunts alone at night, and has been known to drag away human victims without waking up other people living in the same house.*

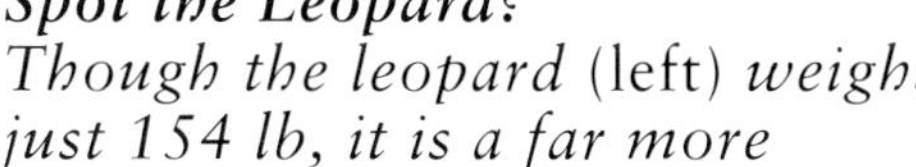

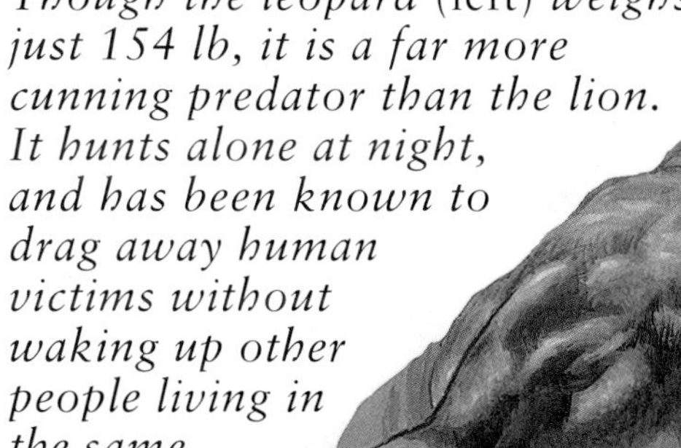

The Printing Press

If printing had never been invented, then

...Exactly!!

The year: 1455. The place: Mainz, Germany. The person: Johann Gutenberg. The result: about 300 copies of what we now call the Gutenberg Bible, the first full-length book made on a proper mechanical printing press. It had 1,284 pages, two columns on each page, 42 lines in each column. Fewer than 50 copies survive.

Johann Gutenberg

We see printed words and drawings and photographs not only in books. They are in newspapers and magazines, on containers and labels, on billboards, even on T-shirts, almost everywhere! Printing is central to the way we learn. Imagine life without school textbooks! (Then again, don't.)

One copy at a time
There was printing five centuries before Gutenberg. In China, shapes of pictures and writing were cut onto wood or stone blocks. Printers spread ink on the block, pressed paper on it, and the ink on the raised bits stuck to the paper. They could make many prints from one block.

Early printing block

But each new work needed a new block. So a system was developed with small metal blocks, which could be moved and arranged in different orders. However, the complicated Chinese writing system, with thousands of symbols, meant slow progress.

Early Chinese

There were also hand-made books before Gutenberg. Monks, especially, spent years writing and decorating the letters by hand, with pens, one beautiful book at a time.

Moveable type
Gutenberg and his helpers produced hundreds of small metal blocks, each with a raised part of one letter or symbol, in reverse. The letters could be chosen and arranged in a frame, to print copies of a page from the book. Then a new set of letters was put into the frame for the next page. And so on, one page at a time.

Gutenberg Ink Inc

Another Gutenberg advance was new ink that stuck to the metal type, rather than to the usual carved woodblocks. And another was a powerful pressing machine that squeezed the paper against the inked type. It was adapted from a winepress, for squashing grapes!

Because the raised, inked letters were pressed onto paper, the method was called letterpress.

The letters and symbols were called type, and setting them up correctly was typesetting. For a long time they were placed by hand. In 1884 the Linotype machine made a line of type from molten metal that quickly went solid.

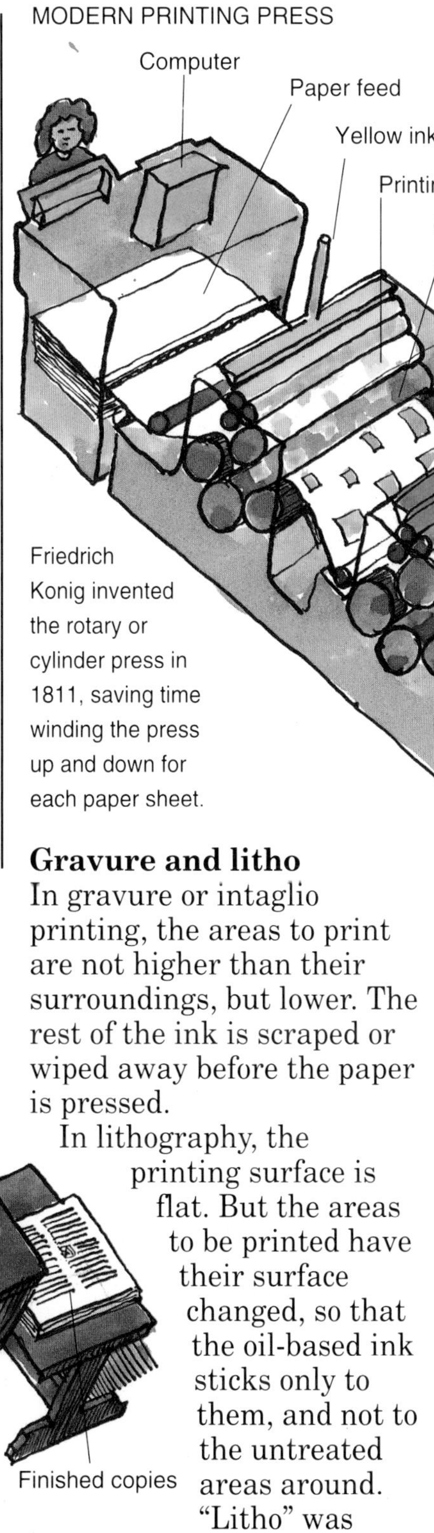

Color pictures are printed from tiny dots of four ink colors: yellow, cyan (greeny-blue), magenta (reddy-purple) and black. Look at this one under a magnifying lens.

Friedrich Konig invented the rotary or cylinder press in 1811, saving time winding the press up and down for each paper sheet.

Gravure and litho

In gravure or intaglio printing, the areas to print are not higher than their surroundings, but lower. The rest of the ink is scraped or wiped away before the paper is pressed.

In lithography, the printing surface is flat. But the areas to be printed have their surface changed, so that the oil-based ink sticks only to them, and not to the untreated areas around. "Litho" was invented about 1796 by Aloys Senefelder. It is now the most popular kind of printing – this book was printed using litho.

The Age of Learning

Within 50 years of Gutenberg, there were printers in 200 towns around Europe, producing over 15,000 works. The main result was cheaper books. Many more people could buy them, and learn to read and write. Then they bought more books, read them, and learned even more. Schools and education changed forever.

Well I never!

- A printing system at the Lawrence Radiation Laboratory, California, can print the entire Bible in 65 seconds. That's 773,700 words!

ANIMAL SHAPES

DESPITE THE GREAT variety of animal shapes in nature, all creatures need to have some way of keeping their bodies from collapsing or falling apart.

Some, called vertebrates, have an internal skeleton, made out of bone or cartilage. The skeleton is centered around a backbone. It supports the body's shape and protects the internal parts. Vertebrates include mammals, such as humans and horses, fish, such as sharks, and birds.

Others have no internal skeleton and need different ways of keeping their body shape, such as a hard outer skeleton. These animals are collectively known as invertebrates, and they include crustaceans, such as lobsters, mollusks, such as slugs, and jellyfish.

JELLYFISH
This beautiful creature has no solid skeleton to support its body. Instead, its shape is maintained by soft, water-filled inner tissues, over which its outer layers are stretched. Take a jellyfish out of water, and its body will collapse.

SLUG
As with the jellyfish, a slug keeps its body shape by stretching its skin over fluid-filled body parts. The slug, however, is not supported by water, like the jellyfish. The pressure from inside keeps its body from collapsing.

LOBSTER
The lobster is surrounded by a rigid skeleton, like a suit of armor. Although it protects the lobster, it prevents growth and is shed each time the animal grows. It is also very heavy, and makes the lobster clumsy when placed out of water.

HORSE
Like you, the horse has an internal skeleton of bone to support its body. Instead of walking on two legs, its skeleton is one of a powerful, four-legged runner, with long leg bones and large neck bones to support a heavy head.

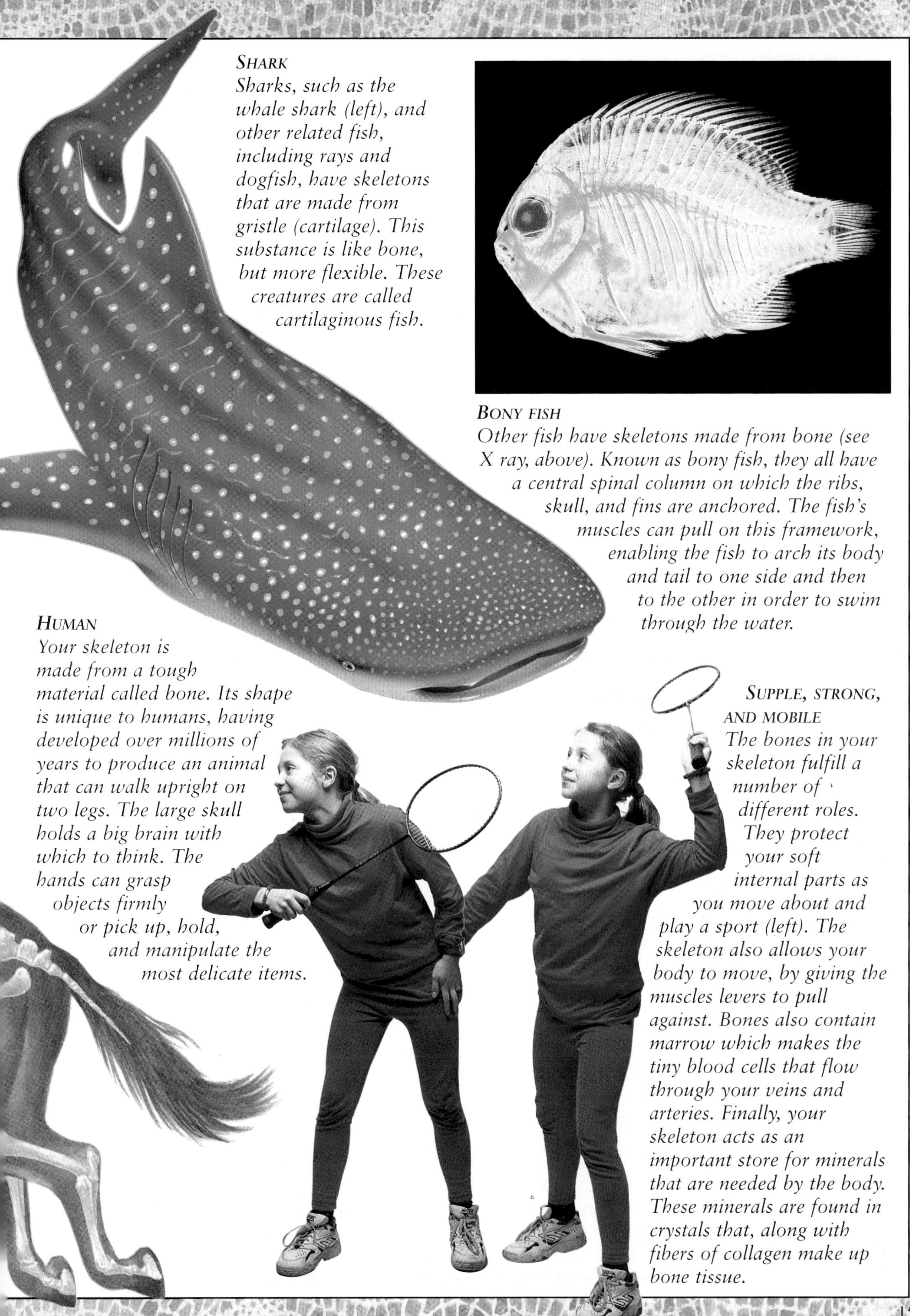

SHARK

Sharks, such as the whale shark (left), and other related fish, including rays and dogfish, have skeletons that are made from gristle (cartilage). This substance is like bone, but more flexible. These creatures are called cartilaginous fish.

BONY FISH

Other fish have skeletons made from bone (see X ray, above). Known as bony fish, they all have a central spinal column on which the ribs, skull, and fins are anchored. The fish's muscles can pull on this framework, enabling the fish to arch its body and tail to one side and then to the other in order to swim through the water.

HUMAN

Your skeleton is made from a tough material called bone. Its shape is unique to humans, having developed over millions of years to produce an animal that can walk upright on two legs. The large skull holds a big brain with which to think. The hands can grasp objects firmly or pick up, hold, and manipulate the most delicate items.

SUPPLE, STRONG, AND MOBILE

The bones in your skeleton fulfill a number of different roles. They protect your soft internal parts as you move about and play a sport (left). The skeleton also allows your body to move, by giving the muscles levers to pull against. Bones also contain marrow which makes the tiny blood cells that flow through your veins and arteries. Finally, your skeleton acts as an important store for minerals that are needed by the body. These minerals are found in crystals that, along with fibers of collagen make up bone tissue.

SWARMING SETTLERS

With the arrival of swarms of Europeans and Africans, America buzzed with activity. By about 1800, only in the remotest regions were Native Americans left alone: the Inuits enjoyed an icy isolation in the refrigerated North, while a barrier of snakes, swamp, and illness protected the peoples of the South American jungles.

Inuits
Plains Tribes
First American Colonies
South America

By 1650, the Europeans were shoving Native Americans off their land and their god down their throats. When the Americans objected, European gunslingers beat Native axeswingers every time.

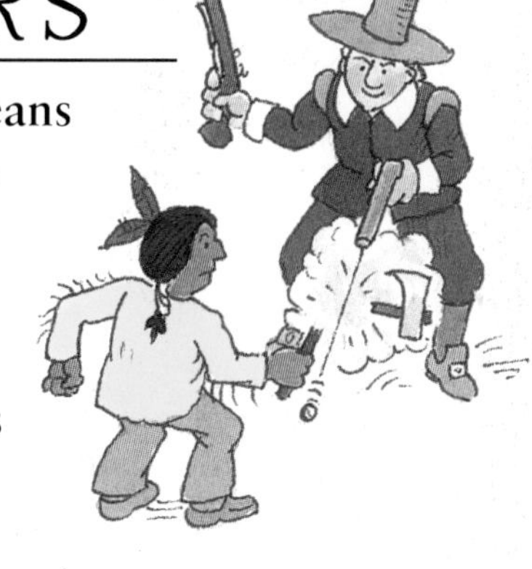

NONSENSE NAME

When Columbus landed in what is now the West Indies, he did not realize he had come to America. He thought he was in the East Indies, so he called the people he met "Indians."

British and French settlers also squabbled among themselves (*above*). The British bagged 13 coastal colonies. The French, helped by their Native American pals, slipped around behind and began waving their flag over Canada and the Mississippi River. By 1750, they were ready to heave the British into the sea.

In the early 17th century, European visitors and the North Americans got along quite well. The residents taught the visitors useful tricks, such as corn growing and how to walk on snow. In return, the residents learned what a horse was and how to ride it.

This was such fun that they swapped farming for buffalo hunting and galloped around the prairies to see who their other neighbors were. The fun ended when the visitors began to call themselves residents.

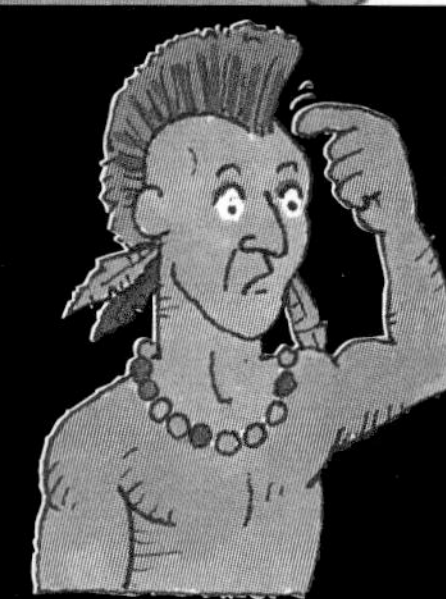

But the advancing French and company fell foul of British Prime Minister Pitt. He paid his European friends Prussia and Austria to keep the French busy at home in a Seven Years' War (1756–1763), while British General Wolfe ate up Canada and everywhere east of the Mississippi.

Signing Up

As many different languages were spoken on the Plains, American tribes developed a special sign language to keep in touch (left).

The Caribbean is one of the Earth's most pleasant spots. It is not surprising, therefore, that the happy-go-lucky residents (Caribs and Arawaks) were forced to share their island paradises with others.

By about 1800, ravaged by pistols and pox, the unfortunate Caribs and Arawaks existed in name only. The new Caribbeans (*top*) were a colorful mixture of sugar planters, pirates, and slaves (escaped and otherwise).

Since the British filled their colonies with people they didn't really care for, they didn't pay much attention to what they were up to.

The Spanish and Portuguese didn't care much for their colonists, either. But they did mind what they mined. The groans of the slaves digging silver, gold, and diamonds in the New World kept the merchants of the Old World grinning all the way to the bank.

The Spanish court sent out a string of hoity-toity sub-kings (viceroys) to keep colonials and their slaves humble, grateful, hard-working, etc.

By 1782, the ex-Spaniards and ex-Incas, led by Tupac Amaru, were so fed up with all this long-range snooping that they rebelled (*below*). The revolt failed. Nevertheless, it forced the Spanish to watch their step in the future.

BITTERSWEET

Medieval Europe was a bitter place – a lick of honey was the sweetest treat most people ever tasted. So when cheap sugar came pouring over from New World sugar cane plantations (from 1650 onward), they went sugar crazy. They boiled it into candy, piled it in puddings, stirred it into tea, coffee, and chocolate – and brought smiles to the lips of tooth-pullers.

The Starry SKIES

Like human beings, stars are born, grow old, and die. If we look hard enough, we can find stars of every age in the sky. Stars are formed from clouds of hydrogen gas collapsing under the force of gravity and turning into helium gas, in a process that produces huge amounts of energy. Near the end of the lives of giant stars, the helium changes into even heavier substances. Eventually these giant stars blow up in huge explosions called supernovae, scattering elements like carbon, silicon, iron, and oxygen into space. New stars and planets form from this debris. The Earth and everything in it, including ourselves, is in fact made of recycled material from a long-dead star.

GIANTS AND DWARFS
The biggest stars, or "red giants," have a lot of pressure in their core, burn quickly and brightly and die earliest, leaving the core as a "white dwarf." Tiny, dim stars, or "brown dwarfs," never become true stars. They get gradually fainter, and finally fade into "black dwarfs."

Into the void
After a huge star explodes, the core is left behind and collapses into a tiny point – a black hole. The pull of gravity from a black hole is so strong that not even light can escape from it.

THE LIFE OF A STAR
A star like the Sun begins as a cloud of gas and dust, which is gradually squashed by the force of gravity to make the star. At the end of its life it swells up into a "red giant" star, then puffs off its outer layers of gas into space. Even our Sun will finally end its life as a tiny "white dwarf" star.

A SCIENTIFIC BREAKTHROUGH
Sir Arthur Eddington (1882–1944) was the first person to realize that the mysterious spiral shapes seen in the sky were galaxies. He also proved that Einstein's theory of gravity was correct, by watching light being bent during an eclipse in 1919. Eddington wrote several famous books that explained the nature of the universe in a simple, understandable way.

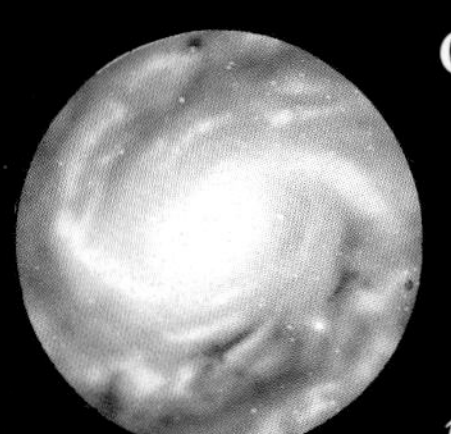

Our own galaxy

The Milky Way is a spiral-shaped galaxy. Our solar system is on one of the "arms" of the galaxy, about two-thirds of the way out.

Star pulses

Super-dense stars called neutron stars, which measure about 20 miles across, spin quickly and send out radio signals. The regular pulses picked up from these stars by large radio receivers on Earth give them the name pulsars.

Patterns in space

Galaxies form in four different shapes. Spiral galaxies are like pinwheels, and the oldest stars are contained in elliptical (oval-shaped) galaxies. Barred spiral galaxies have a thick line running through the middle. Other galaxies have irregular shapes, depending on the number of stars and their position in space.

What would happen if I fell feet first into a black hole?

You would be stretched out like a piece of spaghetti, because the force at your feet would be stronger than that at your head. Then you would disappear beyond the "event horizon." Nothing, not even light, can escape from the black hole once it has passed this point.

The brightest star

Eta Carinae is the most luminous known star of all. It is 150 times bigger than the Sun, and six million times brighter.

The constellations

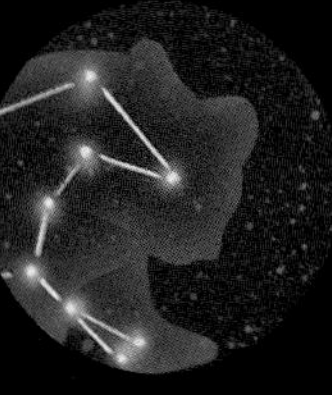

There are 88 identified constellations in the universe. Each has its own area of the sky, decided in 1930. The constellations are useful for finding your way around the sky.

HYDROELECTRIC DAMS

*Dams control the flow of rivers in order to prevent flooding or drought, and to generate electricity (*above, *Glen Canyon Dam). A huge lake, or reservoir, forms behind the dam, and this water turns turbines to create electricity known as hydroelectric power. The reservoir also provides a water supply for irrigation and drinking. In some cases, old villages lie beneath the water (*below*) — they were evacuated first!*

Glen Canyon Dam, at the Grand Canyon in Arizona, controls the raging waters of the Colorado River.

DUTCH DIKES

In 1953, hurricane-force winds of over 100 mph (160 km/h) blew huge waves over Holland's sea walls. Most of this northwest European country lies below sea level, and, at high tide, 40 percent of the land would flood if it was not protected by hundreds of miles of dikes and dams. Many people were caught off guard by the flood. One man lay on his kitchen table as his house flooded: He was found alive the next day, floating just beneath the ceiling.

Holland's dikes also broke after heavy storms in 1775 (left).

National guardsmen and volunteers are busy at work shoring up this river with sandbags to protect surrounding lands against flooding.

Dam busters

"The gates slowly opened, and an enormous wall of water came toward us." ***Eyewitness, Florence, Italy, 1966***

Dams hold back such vast amounts of water that a failure can cause terrible floods. Failure usually results from neglect, poor design, or earthquake damage. When a dam bursts, an overpowering surge of water is released downstream that destroys everything in its path.

At exactly 7:26 a.m. on November 4th 1966, every electric clock in the city of Florence, Italy stopped. There was no power for the next 24 hours, and all communication with the outside world was severed. The worst storms in Italy for 1,000 years had caused the Arno River in Florence to flood (*above*).

The operators of a hydroelectric dam 29 miles (46 km) upstream should have gradually released rainwater as it built up. Instead they waited until the strain on the dam gates was so immense that they were forced to open them at once. Within minutes, the city was under 6 ft (2 m) of water. The ancient sewer system broke up and waste was forced out of manholes all over the city. Helicopters were drafted in to airlift survivors from rooftops and rescue workers were brought in from other countries to assist. The extent of the disaster caused 5,000 people to lose their homes and inflicted severe damage on many of Florence's priceless works of art.

PHOTOMONTAGE

A collage made up of a number of photographs is called a photomontage. Photomontages can often look more like pictures of dreams than of everyday life. In dreams, familiar objects or people are often transformed into the unfamiliar, and sometimes the same thing happens repeatedly. In photomontage, too, shapes can be repeated, and familiar images can be transformed into strange and bizarre ones.

This photomontage project is about exploring the patterns you can make with repeated shapes. You will need a craft knife and magazines.

Repeating shapes
Look through the magazines and find an image that appeals to you. Choose a figure or a simple form that is easy to recognize from its outline or silhouette alone. Cut around the outline, pressing down hard on the magazine and cutting through several other pages as you do so. When you've cut out your outline, you will be left with a series of identical shapes (see the illustration below).

Positive and negative
You will also have a number of holes in backgrounds – negative shapes –

Front and back
On the left below, the figure has been cut out and moved from its original setting, leaving the negative shape.

On the right, both figures and backgrounds have been turned over, to produce a series of shapes which mirror those on the left.

as well as the positive ones of the figure itself. The idea is to use these shapes as well in your collage.

Magazines are printed on both sides of the paper, so your positive and negative images will have parts of other pictures printed on the back of them. These, too, can become part of your picture.

Once you have a series of images and backgrounds, start to experiment with them. Turn some over and see how they mirror the others. Put them all together in your own collage. The montage below is based on this mirroring technique, and also on the dreamlike transformation of one thing into another.

▽ ***"In my photomontage, single leaves have transformed themselves into whole trees. A cat's face has become a butterfly; its shape echoes the floating features of the face on the opposite side."***

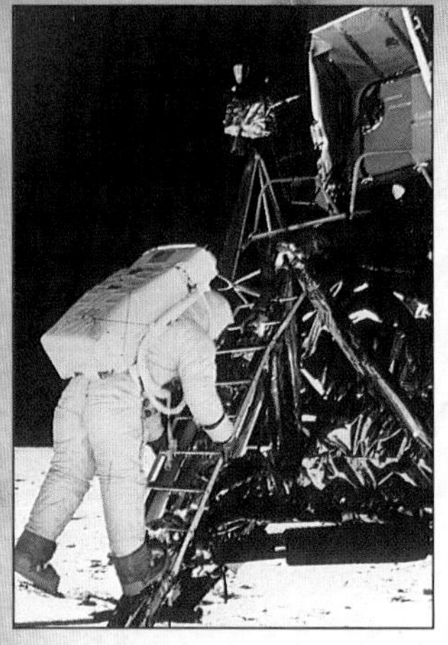

"To Boldly Go..."

Space is the final frontier, the explorer's ultimate and infinite goal. Even before exploration of our own planet was complete, people started to investigate other worlds. *Sputnik I*, the first man-made satellite, orbited the Earth in 1957. Three years later the Soviets launched Yuri Gagarin into orbit. In 1966 *Venera 3* crash-landed on Venus. When astronauts Neil Armstrong and Buzz Aldrin (*left*) became the first humans to walk on the moon in 1969, they achieved a thousand-year-old human dream.

Space stations and unmanned voyages of discovery to distant planets followed. At great expense, we are gradually beginning to piece together a picture of our larger environment. The last and greatest age of exploration has begun.

Moon dreams. In 165 A.D. Lucian of Samos said moon travelers would find a huge mirror suspended over a well! H.G. Wells's novel *The First Men in the Moon* (1901) described explorers finding small humanoid moon-creatures (*right*).

Fifty-eight years later the Soviet probe *Luna 2* hit the moon. Finally, ten years later, American astronauts confirmed that there were no moon-men or mirrors – only dust and rocks!

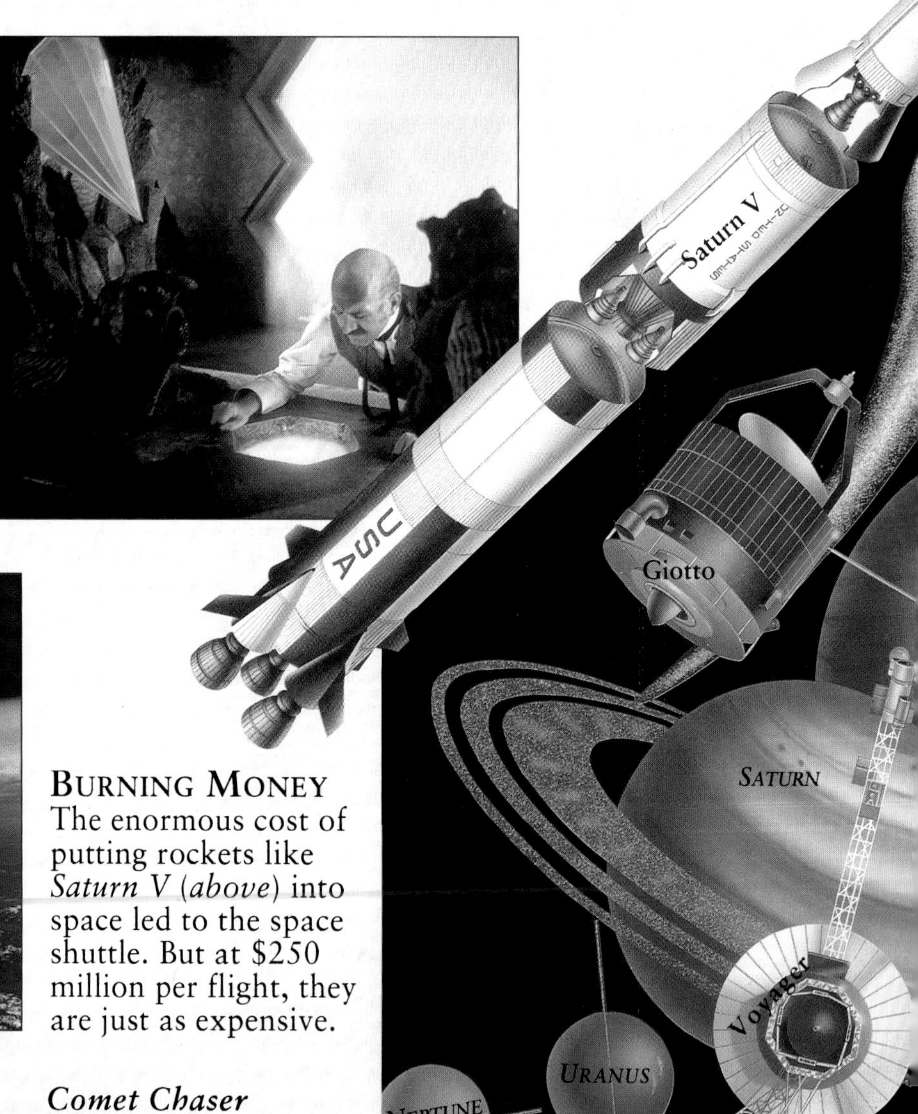

Burning Money
The enormous cost of putting rockets like *Saturn V* (*above*) into space led to the space shuttle. But at $250 million per flight, they are just as expensive.

Living in Space
Space Station Alpha (*above*) will be the first continuously occupied space station, a vital stepping stone toward future crewed missions.

Comet Chaser
Giotto (right) *was one of many probes that studied Halley's Comet in 1986.*

Robot Explorers
For centuries, humans had dreamed up strange creatures from Mars, but when the Pathfinder *probe* (below) *touched down on the surface of the red planet in 1997, no signs of life were found. However, such probes have proved that exploration is possible without the huge risk and expense of putting humans into space.*

Hello Universe
Pioneer *probes have now left the solar system, carrying a welcome message from humankind into outer space.*

Solar Navigators
Two Voyager *satellites saw volcanoes on Jupiter's moon, Io, storms racing around Neptune, and found new moons around Saturn.*

Small, Green, and Slimy?

Past generations inhabited unknown regions with mermaids, sea monsters, and giants.

They also wondered what strange creatures inhabited the heavens, like this creature from Sirius (the Dog Star), drawn in the 18th century (*right*).

Today, we fill the distant universe with creatures of our own imagination.

Friend or Foe?
If we do meet other intelligent lifeforms, will they be friendly, like E.T. (left)*? And will we conquer or wipe them out like so many species and peoples on our own planet?*

BEAM ME UP SCOTTY. As a T.V. series and films, *Star Trek* (*below*) remains the most popular modern exploration fantasy. Are the heroics of explorers on the edge of the universe so different from those of their 15th-century counterparts on the edge of the Atlantic?

We have come a long way from our prehistoric ancestors trekking across the Earth, but we still wonder – what is out there – and can we beat it?

RUNNING DINOSAURS

A lot of people imagine that dinosaurs plodded along at an extraordinarily slow pace. It is probably true that the giant plant-eating sauropods could only walk fairly slowly; if one of them had broken into a run, it would have fallen over or broken its bones. The medium-sized plant-eating ceratopsians however, may have trotted quite fast, just like modern rhinos. Some of the smaller meat-eaters could even have run as fast as a racehorse, especially *Ornithomimus* and the vicious *Deinonychus*. But how do paleontologists know how dinosaurs could run and swim when they all died out so long ago? And how can they work out how fast they could run?

Modern animals use different ways of moving at different speeds. A horse can walk, trot, canter, and then gallop, as it moves faster and faster. Normally, the four legs move in pairs on opposite corners of the horse, but when galloping, both front legs and both hind legs move as pairs together. Some smaller dinosaurs may have been able to gallop, but most could only walk and trot, and the biggest could only walk.

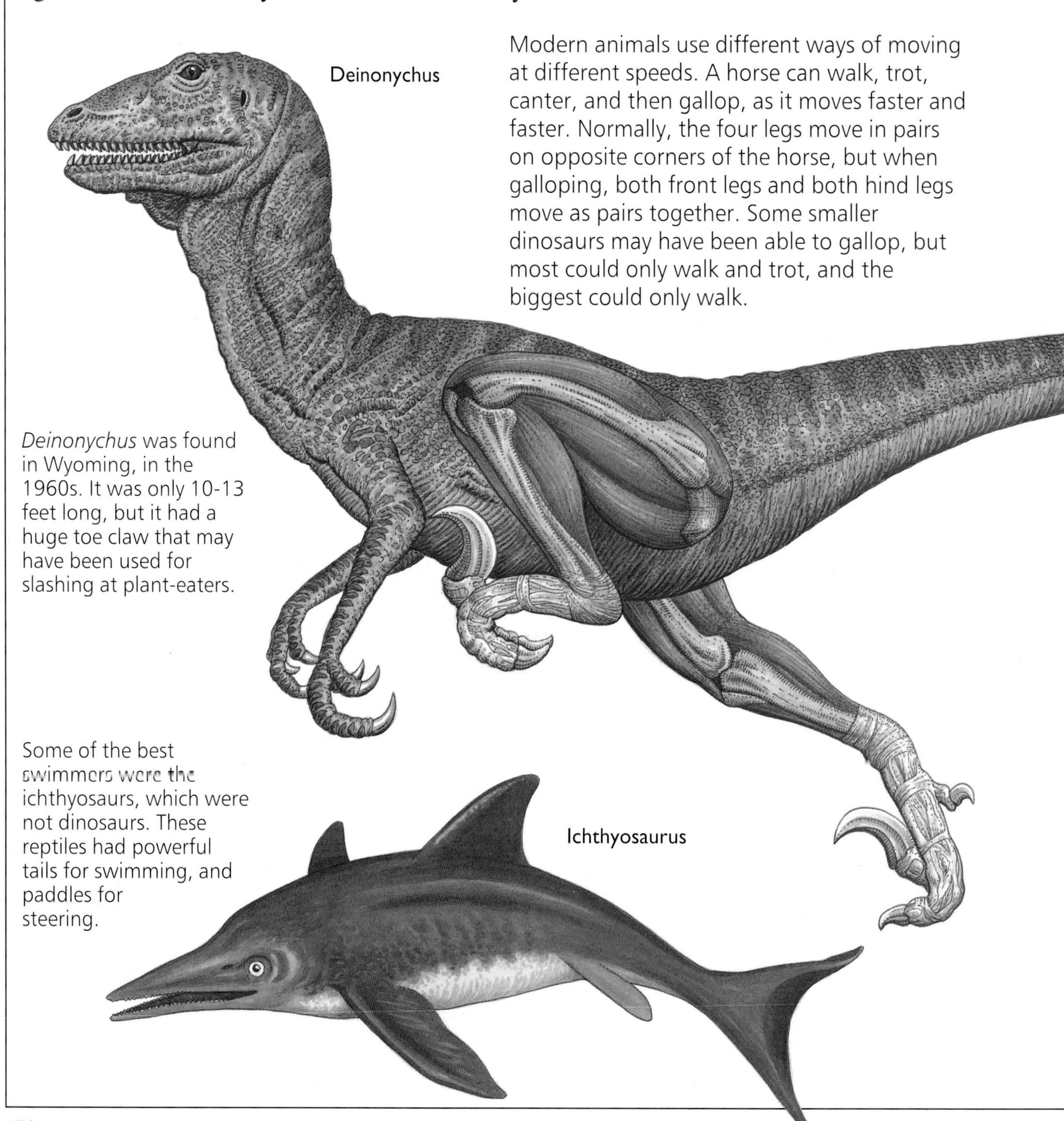

Deinonychus was found in Wyoming, in the 1960s. It was only 10-13 feet long, but it had a huge toe claw that may have been used for slashing at plant-eaters.

Some of the best swimmers were the ichthyosaurs, which were not dinosaurs. These reptiles had powerful tails for swimming, and paddles for steering.

Evidence

When a dinosaur moved over damp mud or sand, it left footprints. These could then be covered with more sand which preserved the tracks. Fossil dinosaur footprints have been found all over the world. These can show which dinosaur made the track, where it was going, and how fast it was moving.

Migration

Recently, paleontologists have found some dinosaur footprint sites where there are thousands of separate trackways. In some cases, the tracks all head in the same direction, and appear to have been made by small and large animals of the same species. These trackways seem to be evidence that there were great herds of dinosaurs marching over long distances. Perhaps they were migrating in search of food or to find warmer winter climates.

These footprints show how the animals walked and how their legs were held. The mammal-like reptile (1) was a sprawler; a dinosaur ancestor (2) walked partly upright; the theropods (3) walked upright on two legs; and the ornithopod (4) could use all fours or walk upright.

1

2

3

4

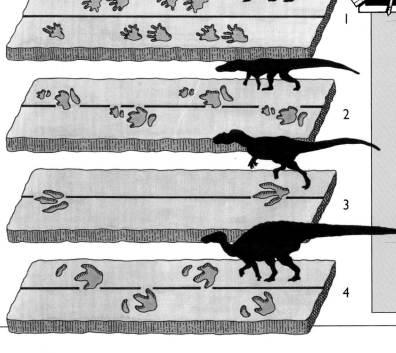

Calculating dinosaur speeds

The faster you run, the longer your strides become. You can test this by walking slowly, walking fast, and then running across some sand. Cover the same distance each time and figure out your various speeds by using a stopwatch. Now measure the distance between each footprint and plot your speed against your stride length. Scientists can calculate dinosaur speeds in the same way by looking at the spacing of their footprints. The wider apart the dinosaur tracks appear, the faster they must have been traveling. If the footprints are very close together, it's likely that they were walking along quite slowly.

Samurai Warriors

The samurai were the knights of Japan. They emerged as mounted peacekeepers in the 9th century, fighting with swords and bows and arrows. Like European knights, they were bound by a code of honor, known as *bushido*.

By the 12th century, two samurai families, the Taira and the Minamoto, were among the most powerful in Japan. In 1185, Minamoto Yoritomo set up his own government in the emperor's name.

When he was appointed *shogun* (commander-in-chief) in 1192, he sent out samurai warriors to govern the provinces.

For 650 years after Yoritomo's death, the Samurai dominated many aspects of Japan's social, artistic, economic, and religious life. Even when feudal Japan collapsed, *bushido* remained a powerful moral code.

Samurai Armor
The samurai did not wear plate armor until the arrival of firearms in the 16th century.

Before that, they wore highly decorated, flexible armor made of leather, mail, and metal scales (below).

Toyotomi Hideyoshi *(1539-1598,* above), *the first person to unify all of Japan, began his career as a foot soldier.*

The Warrior's Way

"The Way of the Warrior" or *bushido*, was similar to chivalry. Both began as warrior codes, praising loyalty and bravery, even to death.

As chivalry drew from Christianity, so *bushido* drew from Confucianism. When not fighting, the samurai *shih* (gentleman) was expected to be courteous, artistic, and noble.

KNOWN BY YOUR POEM. The samurai equivalent of heraldry was *sashimono*. Each warrior was identified by the small flag that was attached to his back (*right*). On one side of the flag he sometimes wrote a poem. One tribe shared the same poem. Only when they were all gathered together could it be read:

Colors smell sweetly, but they will fade.
Nothing in the world lasts forever...

Sashimono
Three examples of the personal flags worn by samurai (below).

SLAVES TO THE SAMURAI

In medieval Japan, women were even less well regarded than in medieval Europe. They were expected to be totally subservient to their husbands, dying for them if necessary. They were often forced into arranged marriages to increase the power of their families.

Kabuki *plays often retold tales of heroic samurai* (below). *Like Shakespearean theater, all women's roles were played by men or boys.*

A Female Warrior (main picture)
Tomoe Gozen, the heroic wife of Minamoto Yoshinaka, is one of the few samurai women whose reputation as a fighter matched that of her husband.

A QUESTION OF TASTE

BOTH NOSE AND TONGUE detect dissolved chemicals. In the mouth, these usually arrive in the form of flavor molecules from foods and drinks. In fact, it is believed that the multitude of flavors you experience when you eat and drink are based on various combinations of only four basic flavors – sweet, sour, salty, and bitter (see opposite).

Originally our sense of taste probably evolved to warn us about foods that were bad, rotten, or poisonous in some way. Then people learned what was good to eat, and how to recognize, cook, and flavor foods with a huge variety of sauces, herbs, spices, and other substances. Along with progress in agriculture and food storage, this turned eating from a necessity for survival into an enjoyable taste experience.

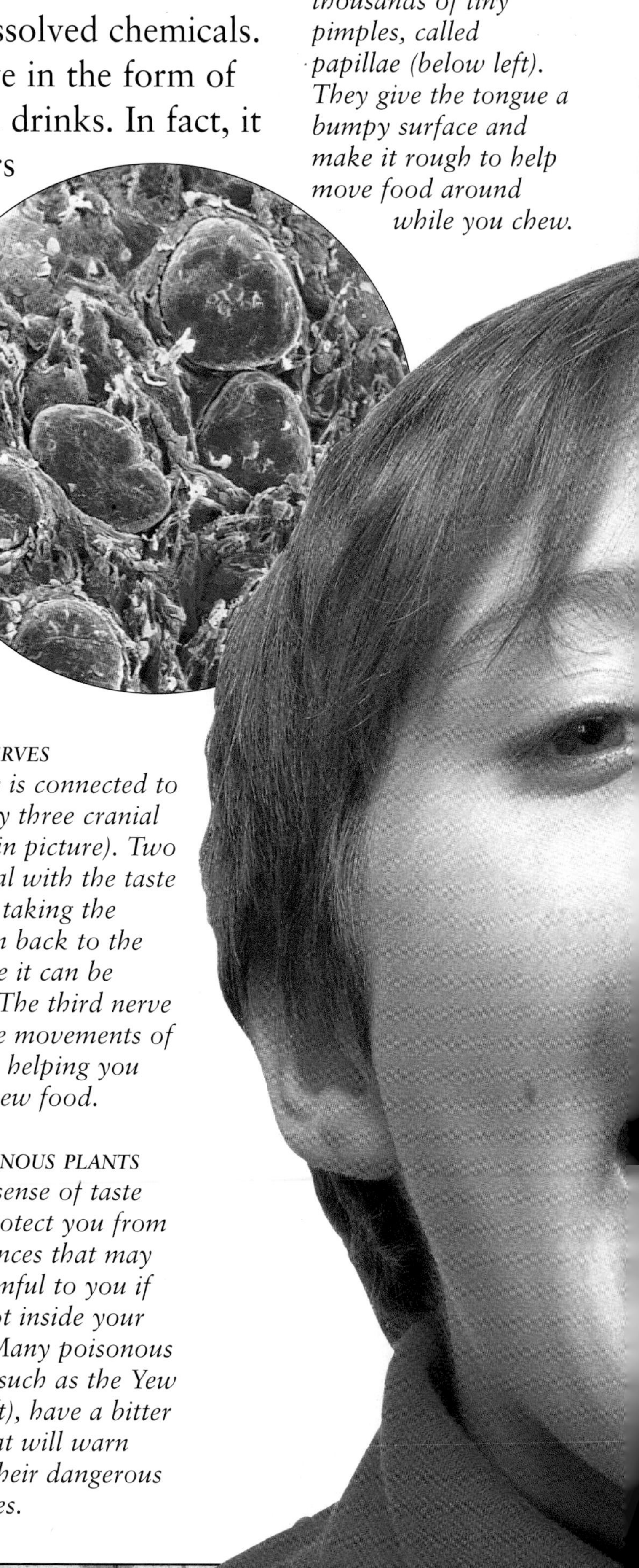

PAPILLAE
The surface of the tongue is covered with thousands of tiny pimples, called papillae (below left). They give the tongue a bumpy surface and make it rough to help move food around while you chew.

TONGUE NERVES
The tongue is connected to the brain by three cranial nerves (main picture). Two of these deal with the taste sensations, taking the information back to the brain where it can be processed. The third nerve controls the movements of the tongue, helping you talk and chew food.

POISONOUS PLANTS
Your sense of taste can protect you from substances that may be harmful to you if they got inside your body. Many poisonous plants, such as the Yew tree (left), have a bitter taste that will warn you of their dangerous properties.

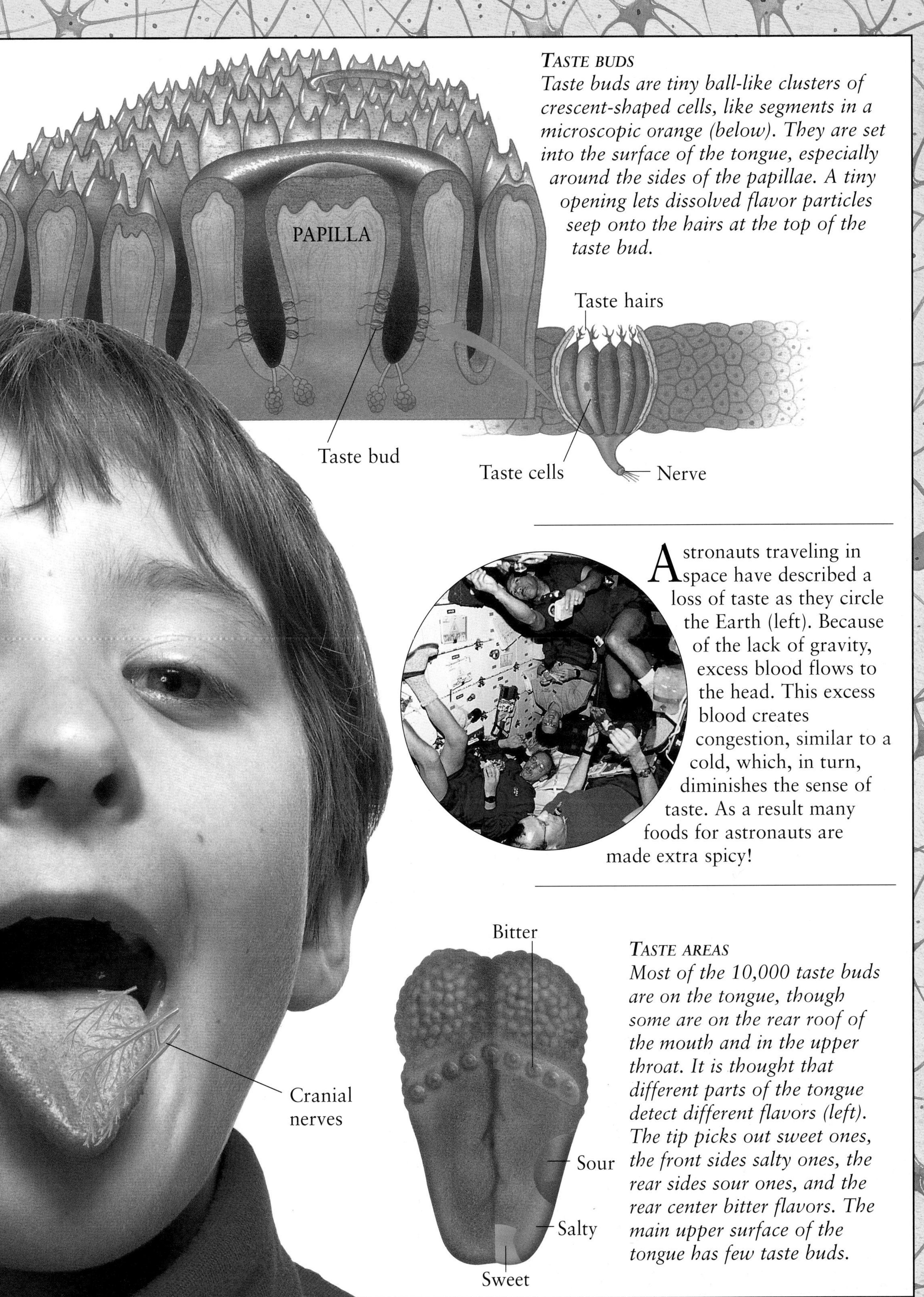

TASTE BUDS
Taste buds are tiny ball-like clusters of crescent-shaped cells, like segments in a microscopic orange (below). They are set into the surface of the tongue, especially around the sides of the papillae. A tiny opening lets dissolved flavor particles seep onto the hairs at the top of the taste bud.

Astronauts traveling in space have described a loss of taste as they circle the Earth (left). Because of the lack of gravity, excess blood flows to the head. This excess blood creates congestion, similar to a cold, which, in turn, diminishes the sense of taste. As a result many foods for astronauts are made extra spicy!

TASTE AREAS
Most of the 10,000 taste buds are on the tongue, though some are on the rear roof of the mouth and in the upper throat. It is thought that different parts of the tongue detect different flavors (left). The tip picks out sweet ones, the front sides salty ones, the rear sides sour ones, and the rear center bitter flavors. The main upper surface of the tongue has few taste buds.

Mighty Wagner

WAGNER
(1813-1883)

OPERAS

Rienzi

The Flying Dutchman

Tannhaüser

Lohengrin

Tristan and Isolde

The Mastersingers

The Ring of the Nibelungs cycle:
The Rhinegold
The Valkyrie
Siegfried
The Twilight of the Gods

Parsifal

For over a century musical pilgrims have walked up the hill outside the little Bavarian town of Bayreuth, to soak themselves in the operas of the most dynamic and single-minded of all composers. Wagner's music, Wagner's words, and Wagner's opera house still form a unique lure. They are a monument to an extraordinary man, whose colossal willpower dominated his friends and enemies alike. Wagner can still, through the sheer force of his genius, compel an audience to sit for four evenings through the 16 hours of his *Ring of the Nibelungs* – probably the greatest single-handed creative effort in the history of Western art.

Richard Wagner's life was a long succession of adventures and misadventures. Born in Leipzig in 1813, he grew up at a time when the tide of nationalism was rising over Europe. Apart from a few minor compositions, the whole of his artistic energy went into the creation and establishment of German opera – serious and uplifting in style, as opposed to the frivolities of Italian opera. After a few early works, Wagner wrote the first of his masterpieces, *The Flying Dutchman*, during 1840 and 1841. It tells the story of a sea captain, doomed to sail the world forever unless he can find a woman to give up her life for him, and it unites two of Wagner's constant themes: the use of an ancient legend, and the idea of salvation reached through self-sacrificing love.

The opera's magnificently descriptive sea music was inspired by a voyage Wagner made in 1839. At the time he was working in Riga, on the Baltic. To escape his creditors, he boarded a ship sailing for England. It was blown off course and the journey took three weeks instead of the expected eight days. In his autobiography Wagner described the origins of the boisterous sailors' chorus in the *Dutchman*. The ship took refuge in a Norwegian fjord and, says Wagner, "a feeling of indescribable content came over me when the enormous granite walls echoed the hail of the crew as they cast anchor and furled the sails. The sharp rhythm of this call clung to me like an omen of good cheer, and shaped itself presently into the theme of the seamen's song."

This journey was the first of many. Under threat of arrest for his support of the 1848 Revolution, he fled from Dresden to Switzerland.

LUDWIG OF BAVARIA

In April 1864, Wagner wrote to a friend: "You know that the young King of Bavaria sought me out ... He wants me to stay with him always, to work, to rest, to produce." The king was Ludwig II (above), who succeeded his father at the age of 18. Obsessed with Wagner's early operas, especially *Lohengrin*, he summoned the composer to him and promised him all the money he needed to carry out his projects. This impetuous behavior was typical of Ludwig, who, although not mad at this stage, was certainly unstable. His infatuation with Wagner lasted until the end of 1865 when Wagner, under political pressure and heavily in debt, was forced to leave Bavaria. Ludwig, however, remained passionately devoted to the composer. He put up a large sum of money to help build the opera house at Bayreuth (below), completed in 1876. In August the whole cycle of the *Ring* was first performed. Less than seven years later, Ludwig heard that Wagner had died in Venice, and insisted that the body be brought to Bayreuth for burial. Ludwig is also remembered for his "dream palaces," especially the fabulous castle of Neuschwanstein, which contains murals of scenes from *Tannhaüser* and *Parsifal* – like a stage set for a Wagner opera.

Wagner wrote the most passionate of his operas, *Tristan and Isolde*, in the intervals of producing his gigantic *Ring* cycle of four operas. The costumes (below) for the first performance in 1865 were designed by Franz Seitz.

Tristan (above) is the nephew of King Mark of Cornwall. Sent to bring Isolde (below), who is to marry King Mark, Tristan falls in love with her. The drawing shows Isolde holding a cup containing a love potion that both she and Tristan drink. The opera tells the story of their tragic passion, which ends when they die together in the *Liebestod* ("Love in Death") scene, a supreme operatic moment.

In Switzerland, he began work in earnest on his *Ring* cycle of four vast operas. This gigantic undertaking was to last for the best part of 25 years – with a gap between 1857 and 1865, when Wagner abandoned the third of the sequence, *Siegfried*, and turned to the tragic love story of *Tristan and Isolde* and the earthy good humor of *The Mastersingers of Nuremberg*.

The *Ring* is set in the mist-filled past of German mythology – a twilight world of gods and heroes, dwarfs, and giants. The gods' downfall stems from a struggle to possess a hoard of gold hidden in the depths of Rhine. Like the gods and goddesses of the ancient Greeks, Wagner's characters are both timeless mythical beings and recognizable people, quarreling, eager for power, falling in love, and dying. In the *Ring* operas Wagner made the fullest use of his musical innovation, the *leitmotiv* or "leading motive" – a short theme, symbolizing a character, a feeling, or an inanimate object, from the gold in the Rhine to the spear of the god Wotan. Wagner's use of these motives means, for example, that a character can be singing about one thing while the orchestral accompaniment reveals some contrasting thought or event.

Wagner was able to finish the *Ring* and to build his own opera house at Bayreuth through the generosity of Ludwig II, the "Mad King" of Bavaria. But Ludwig was only one of the many friends exploited by Wagner. The conductor and pianist Hans von Bülow, who was married to Cosima, Liszt's daughter, was a champion of Wagner's works, but this did not prevent Wagner from making Cosima his mistress. He finally married her in 1870, and they remained together until his death in 1883.

In his last opera, the massively slow and stately *Parsifal*, Wagner returned to the world of medieval knighthood and Christianity, which had inspired two of his earlier operas, *Tannhaüser* and *Lohengrin*. *Parsifal* deals with the quest for the Holy Grail. It would be hard to imagine a less operatic subject, in the normal sense of the word, and its intense seriousness and solemnity make it a work for convinced Wagnerians only. But it ended Wagner's career on a lofty note, summing up his ideas of a work of art in which words, music, costumes, and sets combine in perfect unity.

TOKAMAK

POWER FROM THE ATOM

Scientists in Britain and the United States are close to finding a way of controlling nuclear fusion reactions, like those that power the sun and the hydrogen bomb. If they succeed, nuclear fusion could provide an inexhaustible source of energy that would be far less polluting than either fossil fuels or conventional nuclear plants. The reaction they are trying to control takes place at high temperatures, between atoms of deuterium and tritium (both forms of hydrogen). Heated sufficiently, they combine to produce helium and a huge amount of energy. Just 10 grams of deuterium and 15 grams of tritium can, in theory, supply enough electricity to last the lifetime of an average person in a developed country.

Another way of taming *fusion is to make a tiny pellet of deuterium and tritium the target of a number of powerful lasers (left). When the lasers are fired together they are capable of reaching the very high temperatures needed to create fusion. The heating is so rapid that the atoms have no time to fly apart before they have fused together. American scientists have already had some success with this method, but there is still a long way to go.*

Lasers used to create fusion.

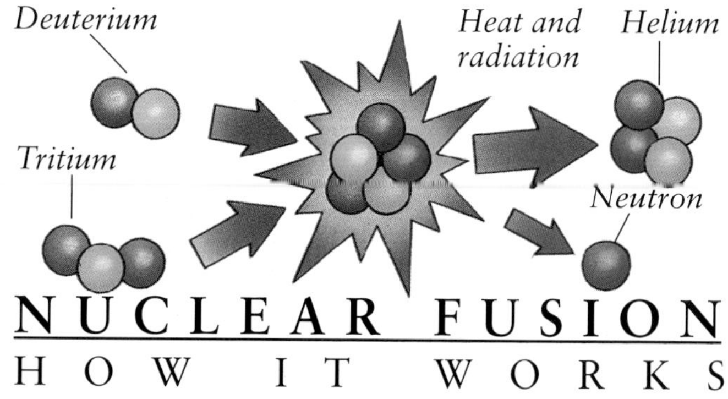

NUCLEAR FUSION

HOW IT WORKS

The diagram above shows how a fusion reactor causes the nuclei of deuterium and tritium to combine forming helium and a neutron, as well as heat. Nuclei usually repel one another, but if heated enough they will fuse together.

Scientists check the interior of the Tokamak Fusion Test Reactor *at Princeton, New Jersey (above). The fusion reaction takes place at about 180 million degrees Fahrenheit.*

Because no container could survive this temperature, a magnetic field keeps the atoms away from the walls. The by-products of the reaction are helium and high-energy protons.

Scientists have created nuclear fusion in a tubular reactor that has been curved to form a continuous ring, known as a torus. The Russians were the first to try this shape, which they call a *Tokamak*. The atoms are injected into the ring and heated to about 180 million degrees Fahrenheit. The atoms try to escape, but a magnetic field holds them there long enough for them to start fusing together. So far, the most successful experiment, in the *Tokamak* at Princeton, has produced a short burst of energy. This was enough to prove to scientists that fusion will work. The European-funded Joint European Torus (JET), at Culham in Oxfordshire, England, has also produced brief, intense bursts of power. A practical power station will have to be much bigger than the *Tokamak*, and ways of removing the heat to generate electricity have to be found. The next stage will be an international project called ITER – International Thermonuclear Experimental Reactor – involving the United States, Europe, and Russia. If that succeeds, we could see the first fusion power stations in the first half of next century, perhaps by about 2020.

The Princeton Tokamak *(right) holds the record for fusion output. In 1993 it produced a burst of power peaking at four megawatts and lasting seven seconds. So far the* Tokamak *experiments have consumed more energy than they created. There is still a long way to go before fusion becomes a viable energy source. Scientists have yet to find a way to release the energy slowly rather than explosively.*

The outside of the Princeton Tokamak.

WHAT IF THERE WERE A LOT MORE VOLCANOES?

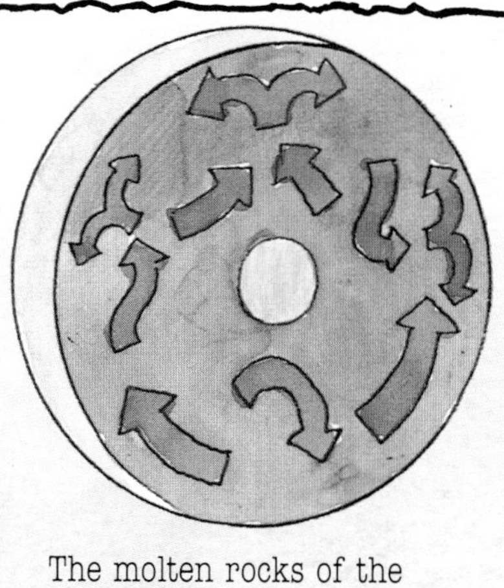

The molten rocks of the Earth's middle layer, or mantle, flow around slowly like thick jello or soft plastic.

You'd have to be careful where you went because a volcano could erupt anywhere, at anytime! Below the Earth's hard outer surface (crust), the rocks are so hot that they are melted. Sometimes the pressure builds up so much that these melted rocks burst through a crack in the crust. This is a volcanic eruption, and the red-hot rock that comes out is known as *lava*.

From volcano to paradise island

Volcanoes that erupt under the sea build up layers of hardened lava, and poke above the water as islands. Coral reefs develop around their shores. Earth movements make the island sink. The coral continues to grow, leaving a ring-shaped reef called an *atoll*.

Undersea volcano erupts

Hardened lava builds up and coral forms

Island sinks, more coral forms atoll

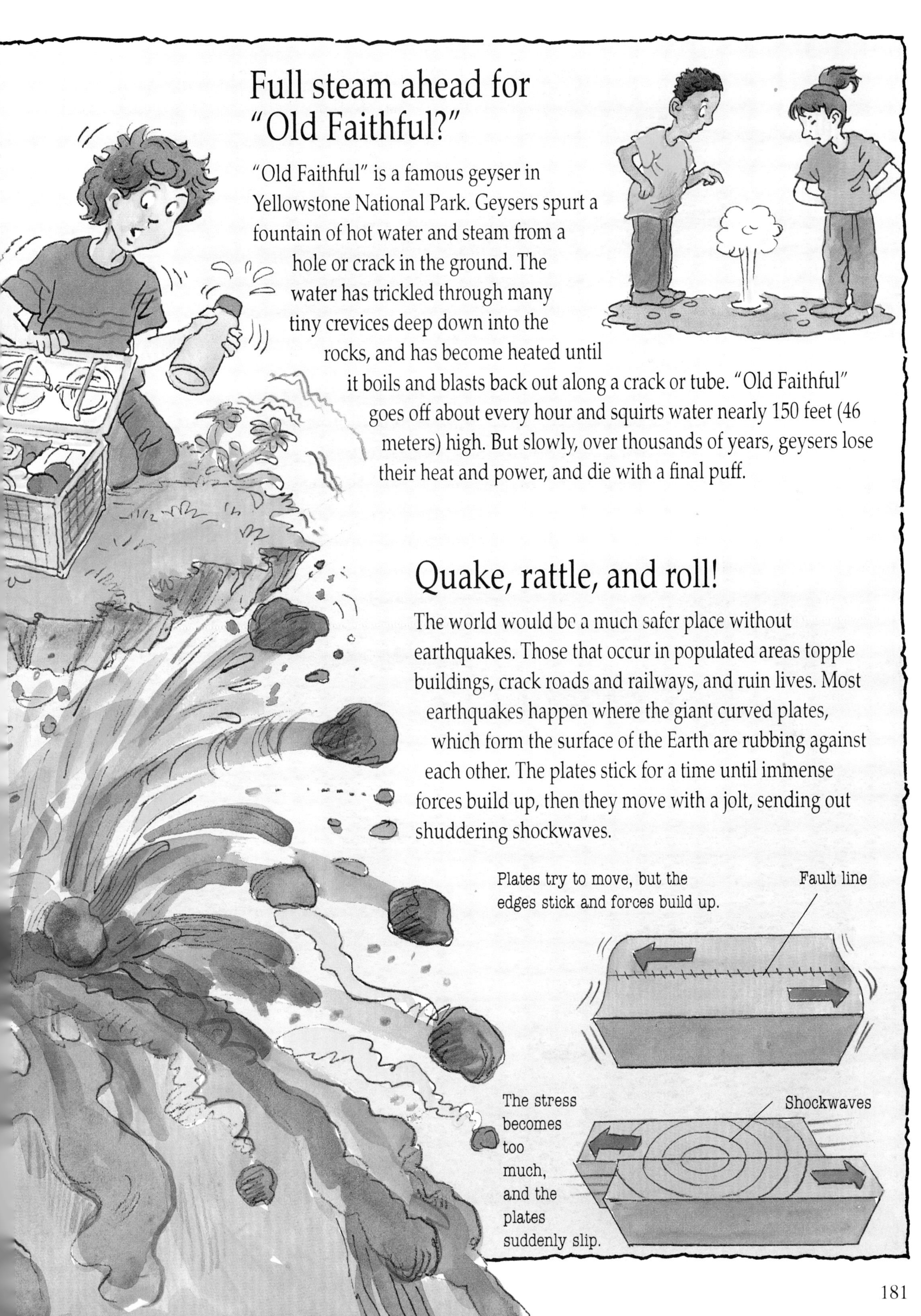
Plates try to move, but the edges stick and forces build up.
Fault line
The stress becomes too much, and the plates suddenly slip.
Shockwaves

Full steam ahead for "Old Faithful?"

"Old Faithful" is a famous geyser in Yellowstone National Park. Geysers spurt a fountain of hot water and steam from a hole or crack in the ground. The water has trickled through many tiny crevices deep down into the rocks, and has become heated until it boils and blasts back out along a crack or tube. "Old Faithful" goes off about every hour and squirts water nearly 150 feet (46 meters) high. But slowly, over thousands of years, geysers lose their heat and power, and die with a final puff.

Quake, rattle, and roll!

The world would be a much safer place without earthquakes. Those that occur in populated areas topple buildings, crack roads and railways, and ruin lives. Most earthquakes happen where the giant curved plates, which form the surface of the Earth are rubbing against each other. The plates stick for a time until immense forces build up, then they move with a jolt, sending out shuddering shockwaves.

FRUITS AND NUTS

Once fertilization has taken place, the ovule develops into a seed. The ovary around it grows into a protective covering, called the fruit. There are many different forms of fruit – berries, nuts, pods, fleshy fruits, or, in the case of conifers, cones. The fruit protects the seeds and its shape helps them get carried to a suitable place to grow. Fruits and nuts are often tasty and nutritious – they have evolved this way to attract animals, which will eat them and disperse the seeds.

3

A bee pollinates an apple blossom and fertilization takes place (1). The flower dies, its job done (2). The ovary and base of the flower develop into a fleshy fruit around the apple seeds, or pits (3).

A VARIETY OF FRUITS AND NUTS FROM TREES

Coconut

Grapefruit

Plum

Lemon

Pear

Walnut

Apple

Cob nut

The first foods

Fruits and nuts were among humankind's first foods. Our early ancestors would gather these foods from the trees near them. However, depending on wild trees for food can be risky, so thousands of years ago, people began to cultivate fruit-bearing trees from seeds. These small orchards supplied a more stable source of food than gathering could provide.

Ancient Egyptian orchard

Nuts to music

Nuts are large, dry, edible seeds with a strong husk (the fruit) protecting the flesh. This shell is usually discarded after the nut itself has been eaten. But some nutshells can make percussion instruments. On old radio shows, the two halves of a coconut shell were clapped together to make the sound of horse's hooves. You can use them as a rhythm instrument. Smaller nuts, like pine kernels, can be enclosed in a plastic cup to make a shaker, or *maraca*.

Dispersal

Fruits are designed for various methods of dispersal. Trees cannot move, so seeds must be carried away from them, where there will not be as much competition for light and water.

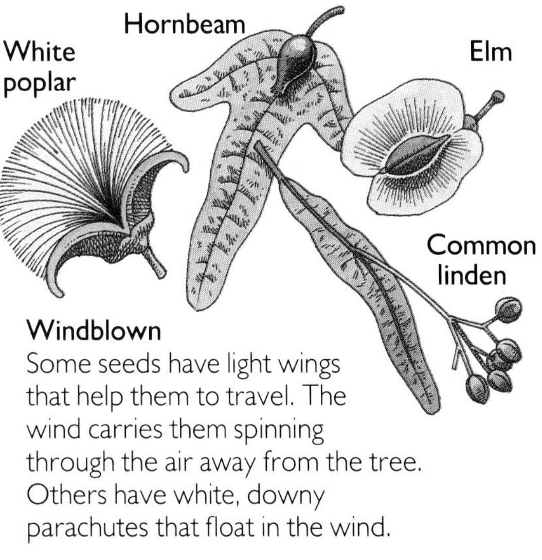

Windblown
Some seeds have light wings that help them to travel. The wind carries them spinning through the air away from the tree. Others have white, downy parachutes that float in the wind.

Carried by animals
Mammals and birds eat the soft fruits, berries, and nuts of trees and drop the seeds to the ground. Some seeds can also pass through animals' digestive systems unharmed.

Bursting forth
The seeds of some trees are protected by pods until they ripen and the pods break open to release the seeds. The pods of different tree species vary in shape.

Laburnum

Waterborne
The white flesh of a coconut is actually a large seed. Its shell, covered with coarse fibers, acts as a float and carries the seed across the seas. When it reaches a beach, it can take root and grow.

Questions and Answers about...

What is prehistory?

People first started to write about 5,500 years ago. Time before this is known as prehistory. So prehistory is not the time before history (if there could be such a time!), but the time before there was any written history.

What were the Stone, Bronze, and Iron ages?

Archaeologists use these terms to classify early periods of human history. The terms refer to the main material used to make tools in the periods. The materials reflect the development of culture at the time. The Stone Age began about 2 million years ago and lasted until the Bronze Age, which started about 3,000 B.C. The Iron Age began between 1,500 and 1,000 B.C.

FALL OF ROME (A.D. 400-500)

MIDDLE AGES

ITALIAN RENAISSANCE (BEGAN A.D. 1400s)

What were the Middle Ages in the middle of?

The Middle Ages were the period in Europe between the end of ancient times and beginning of modern times. Historians generally consider the end of ancient times to be the fall of the Roman Empire between A.D. 400 and A.D. 500. The beginning of modern times is regarded as the start of the Italian Renaissance, the great flourishing of arts and sciences in the 1400s.

Why were the Dark Ages dark?

The period in the history of Europe known as the Dark Ages lasted roughly from A.D. 500 to A.D. 1000 (the first half of the Middle Ages). The word "dark" refers to a lack of learning and knowledge during this time. Many of the technical and artistic skills from the ancient civilizations were lost, as was much other knowledge. Modern historians, however, have realized that the Dark Ages were not as dark and dreary as everyone used to think they were.

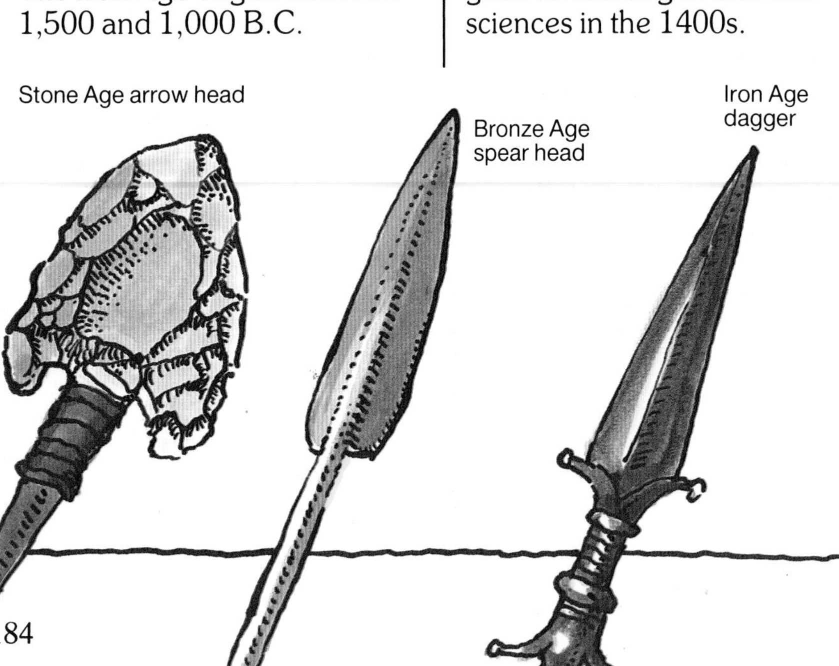

Stone Age arrow head

Bronze Age spear head

Iron Age dagger

Where did the first people come from?
It is difficult to say who the first humans really were. There were originally a number of humanlike species. Most scientists regard *Homo habilis* as the first true group of humans. They lived in Africa about 2 million years ago, and used stone tools. Fossils have been discovered in Kenya and other parts of East Africa.

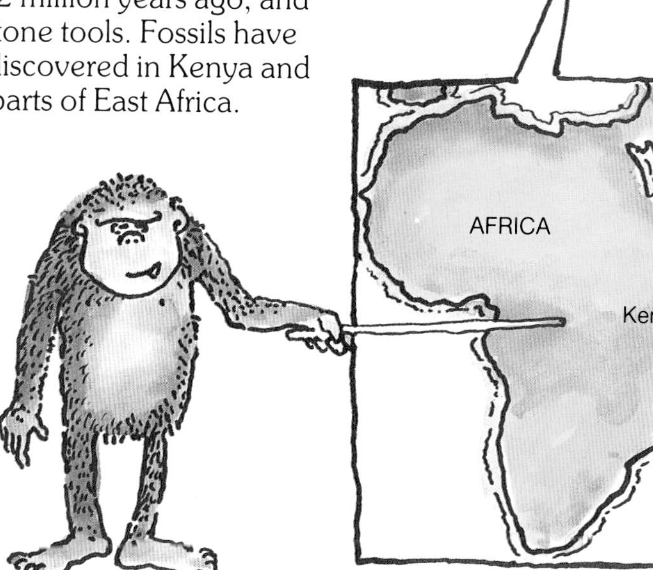

Did cavemen live in caves?
A few of them did. Most Stone Age people lived in shelters built from branches, animal hides, and other natural materials. There simply would not have been enough caves to go around for all of them! However, caves do not fall down easily, so they are the only "cavemen" houses we still can see.

When was money first used?
Before money was used, people would always barter goods. As time went by, certain goods (such as shells or metals) became standard items that everyone would accept in exchange. Coins were first made as a convenient form of precious metal with a known weight, and so a known value. The earliest coin discovered was made between 600 and 700 B.C. in Lydia (now part of western Turkey).

Where did the dollar and pound signs come from?
The dollar sign is a stylized figure 8. This originates from the old Spanish coin called a piece of eight, which was worth eight reals. The pound sign is a stylized letter L. This originates from the ancient Roman coin, the librum. The sign is also sometimes used for Italian lira.

Piece of eight

Roman Librum

How did people pay taxes before money was invented?
People paid with goods. For example, a farmer might pay taxes to a local landowner with a part of the harvest from his land. A common tax was known as a tithe; this was a tenth of what a person had produced a year.

Magnetic Attraction

Archaeologists and beachcombers often make use of metal detectors to locate buried objects or treasure. Materials are either magnetic or nonmagnetic. Most, but not all, metals are magnetic. Iron has the strongest magnetic attraction. Nickel and cobalt are also magnetic, as are the alloys, or mixtures, of these metals. Aluminum, copper, and gold are nonmagnetic. Magnetic ferrites (metals containing iron) can be used to make hard magnets, like the refrigerator magnets pictured here. These are known as permanent magnets. Soft magnets are temporary and are easy to magnetize and demagnetize. Magnetic materials can be easily separated from other materials. When aluminum cans are recycled, they are sorted from other metals by using a magnet. You can make your own metal detector with an ordinary magnet. See if you can find any buried treasure!

Secrets In The Sand

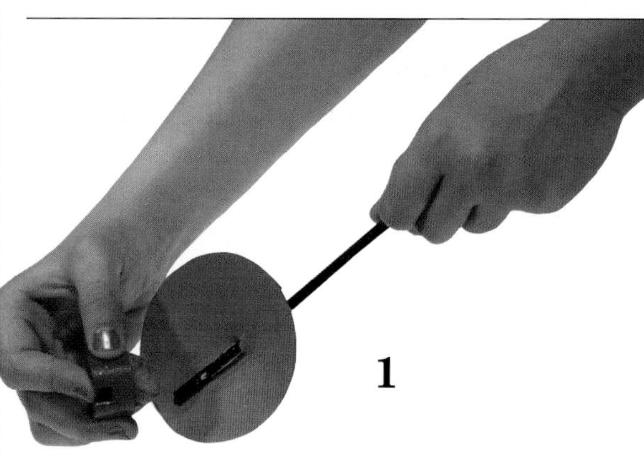

1

1 Make a circle, 4 inches across out of colored cardboard and cut a slit from the edge to the center. Overlap the two ends and glue, to create a flat cone. Push one end of a stick through the center and attach a button magnet to the stick with clay.

2 Hold the cone in place by attaching small strips of paper to it and winding them tightly around the stick. Now decorate the cone with paint or colored paper.

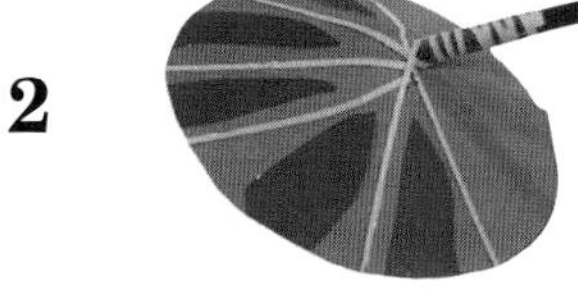

2

3 Half fill a shallow container with clean sand. Bury a variety of objects in the sand, metals and nonmetals.

3

4 Move your metal detector slowly above the surface of the sand. Try it at various heights. You will soon discover how low you must hold it to attract objects.

Why It Works

A magnet exerts a force on a nearby piece of magnetic material by turning it into a weak magnet – this is magnetic induction. A magnet is made up of many tiny parts called domains. Each one is like a mini-magnet, and they all point in the same direction. The domains in a metal are jumbled up. When a magnet comes into contact with the metal, the domains line up and the metal becomes magnetized. A strong magnet can act over quite a distance. Each object picked up from the sand is a temporary magnet because the domains inside become aligned.

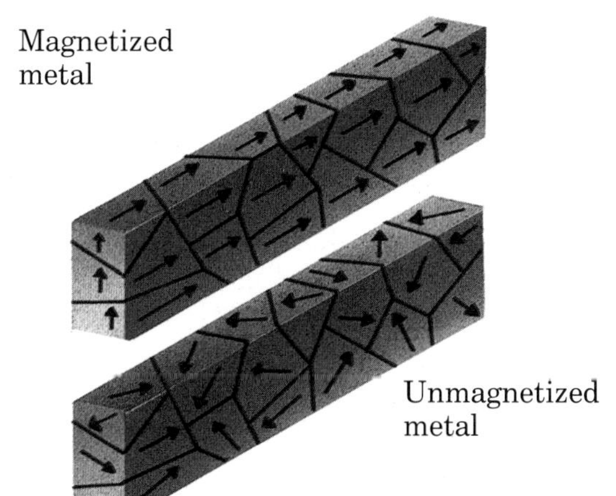

Bright Ideas

Predict which objects you expect your magnet to pick up - you may be surprised! See how near to the sand the magnet must be held before it picks anything up. At what height does it fail to attract any of the hidden objects? Keep a record of your results.

Which objects does your magnet pick up? Which are left buried in the sand? What does this tell you about them? (Hint: the answer is on this page.) Notice whether any of the magnetic objects keep their magnetism and attract other objects.

Try a different kind of magnet. See if you can pick up any more objects with it. See what happens if you add more sand to the container.

Find out which other metals are non-magnetic. Collect some empty drink cans and sort them with a magnet. Remember, aluminum is nonmagnetic. Save the cans for recycling.

4

BASKETBALL

One thousand years ago, the Maya and Aztecs of Central America played a ball game called *Pot-ta-Pok* (Mayan, *below*) or *tlatchi* (Aztec) as part of a religious ceremony. The object of the game was to shoot a solid rubber ball through a ring high on a wall. The winners received gifts from the spectators, but the losing captain was often beheaded. Basketball is a little like this grisly game – but no one loses their head! It is one of the major sports in the United States and is played all over the world, but it is only just over 100 years old.

THE BASKET
In 1906, hoops with open bottoms were introduced, to make it easier to retrieve the ball after a goal was scored. Modern hoops stand at 10 feet (3.05 m) high.

HUMBLE ORIGINS

James Naismith, a priest in Springfield, Massachusetts, invented basketball in 1891. He worked for the Young Men's Christian Association (YMCA), who wanted an indoor game to play during the cold winter months. Naismith nailed a peach basket high up at each end of the gym. Teams scored by throwing a soccer ball into their basket. Nowadays, lightweight balls are used. Players "dribble" (bounce) them as they run.

"MAGIC" JOHNSON (b. 1959)

Earvin "Magic" Johnson had a huge following as the Los Angeles Lakers' star player and the most valuable basketball player ever. But in 1991, he retired from the game after discovering he was HIV positive. Since then, he has led campaigns about HIV and AIDS, and has encouraged young people to become involved in sports.

Johnson

A TALL ORDER
The taller you are, the closer you can get to the basketball hoop – so tall players are in great demand! Most players are over 6 feet (1.8 m) tall; some have been as tall as 7 ft 7 in(2.3 m)!

INSTANT SUCCESS

The first real basketball game was played in January 1892, with seven men on each team. Team sizes later went up to nine, then decreased to eight. Eventually it was decided that a team of five was best. Basketball caught on right away. Colleges and schools began to organize competitions and soon it was the most widely played team game in the United States. Exciting modern players, like the great Michael Jordan, have made sure that basketball has continued to be a popular game around the world.

VOLLEYBALL
Volleyball is another indoor sport invented by a YMCA teacher. In 1895, William Morgan devised the game, in which two teams of six players hit the ball over a high net with their raised hands. Today, over 150 countries are members of the International Volleyball Federation and it is an Olympic sport.

NETBALL

This seven-per-side game, based on basketball, was invented in the 1890s. It is played only by women. The method of scoring and goal height are similar to basketball, but the players are not allowed to run with the ball. Netball courts are slightly larger than basketball courts.

THAT'S ENTERTAINMENT!
The world's best-known basketball team is the Harlem Globetrotters, a professional team founded in 1927. The Globetrotters tour the world, playing exhibition games (rather than official contests) in front of huge crowds.

PLAYING ZONES
Netball players wear colored vests showing their positions. The letters mean: K-keeper *(pictured)*; G–goal; W–wing; D–defense; C–center; A–attack; S-shooter.

SUSPENDED STRUCTURES

The first bridge was probably a fallen tree laid across a stream and early bridge-builders may have observed the strength of rock arches, carved by natural forces. There are 3 types of bridge – arch, girder and suspension. Each one displaces its weight differently. The Golden Gate Bridge, in San Francisco (left), completed in 1937, is a suspension bridge with a main span of 4,200 feet. The Humber Bridge, in England, is the world's longest single span suspension bridge. It has a span of 4626 feet. The newest type of bridge is the cable-stayed, a design related to the suspension bridge but the cables are connected directly to

CROSS THE RIVER

1. For this project you will need a large board as a base. On the board, paint a river scene like the one shown here. Use a craft board and carefully cut 6 polystyrene sections for the roadway of the bridge. You will need a large ball of strong string because the 'cables' carry the weight of the roadway.

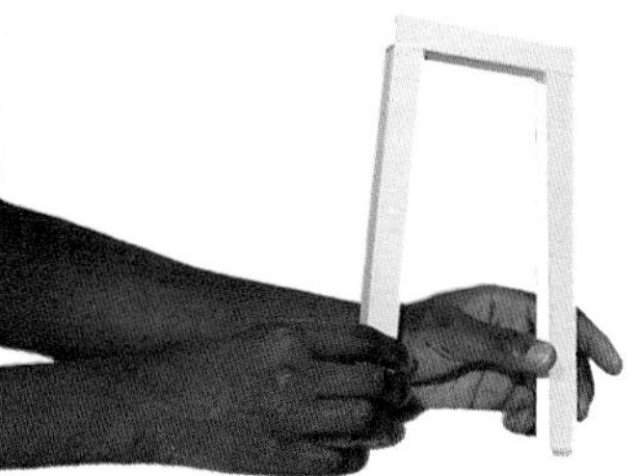

2. Cut 10 of the smaller shapes out of stiff card. Measure and mark the scoring lines. Score and fold along the lines to make the tower sections. Glue two sections together to form the sides of each tower and use one section as a cross beam. Glue the finished towers firmly to the board. Make sure that they are directly opposite each other, on either side of the river.

3. Use card and plasticine to make the anchorage points that hold the bridge 'cables' in place. Suspend two parallel lengths of string between the anchorage points as shown. Make the supports for the roadway by knotting loops of string between the cables.

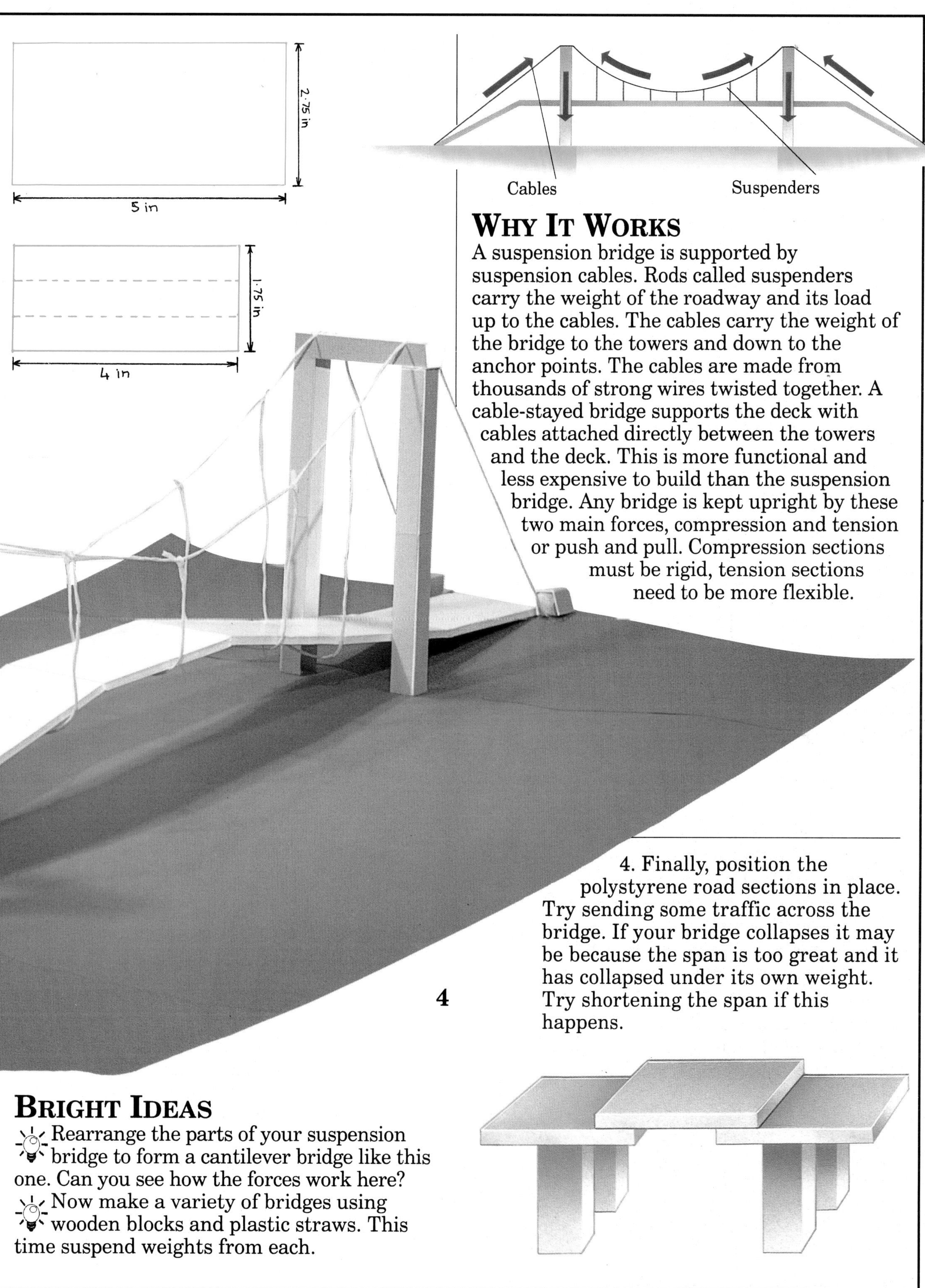

Why It Works

A suspension bridge is supported by suspension cables. Rods called suspenders carry the weight of the roadway and its load up to the cables. The cables carry the weight of the bridge to the towers and down to the anchor points. The cables are made from thousands of strong wires twisted together. A cable-stayed bridge supports the deck with cables attached directly between the towers and the deck. This is more functional and less expensive to build than the suspension bridge. Any bridge is kept upright by these two main forces, compression and tension or push and pull. Compression sections must be rigid, tension sections need to be more flexible.

4. Finally, position the polystyrene road sections in place. Try sending some traffic across the bridge. If your bridge collapses it may be because the span is too great and it has collapsed under its own weight. Try shortening the span if this happens.

Bright Ideas

Rearrange the parts of your suspension bridge to form a cantilever bridge like this one. Can you see how the forces work here?

Now make a variety of bridges using wooden blocks and plastic straws. This time suspend weights from each.

REACH FOR THE STARS

Scientists have not only set their sights on exploring the solar system — the nine planets, including Earth, that orbit our star, the Sun. One day they hope to reach other stars that lie far beyond. Interstellar travel is no mean feat. The nearest star, *Proxima Centauri*, is a staggering 25 million million miles away. Light, the fastest thing in the universe, takes over four years to travel that far, so scientists say this star is over four "light years" away.

FUEL PARADOX

If scientists want a crew to reach another star within a single lifetime, they will need to make a very fast spacecraft. This means they will have to build an engine that can rapidly accelerate it (speed it up). Spacecraft can be accelerated by rockets. The faster a rocket burns fuel, the more it will accelerate. Unfortunately though, a rocket that burns fuel quickly will need to carry lots of fuel to get to its destination. This will make it very heavy, so it will be hard to accelerate out of Earth's atmosphere.

BUILT FOR SPEED

Scientists designing tomorrow's rockets have taken their inspiration from the stars themselves. Ordinary rockets burn fuels like liquid hydrogen to make heat — but stars make heat in a process called nuclear fusion (see box, *above*). This releases huge amounts of energy from even the smallest quantity of fuel.

NUCLEAR FUSION

Nuclear fusion occurs when certain kinds of atoms are squeezed together at extremely high temperatures. The atoms fuse (join), releasing a huge burst of energy (and a few stray particles). Unfortunately, scientists think they will need more energy to run a fusion reactor than they will get out of it.

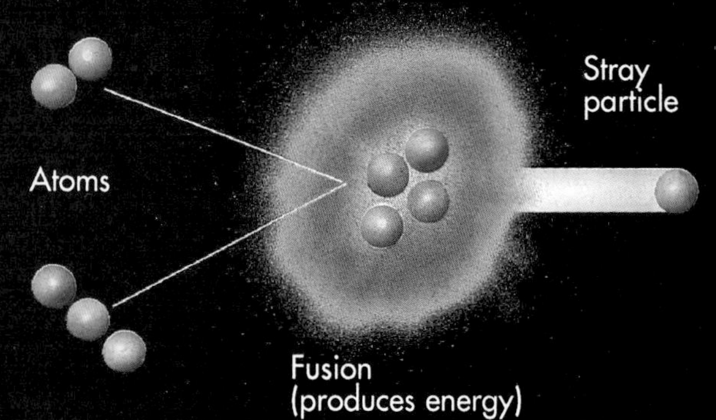

Left *Taking a year to travel to Mars,* Viking 1 *was powered by a small nuclear generator. The* Viking Lander, *carried by this craft, sent back the first-ever images of rocks on the Martian surface.*

NUCLEAR STARSHIP

FEASIBLE TECHNOLOGY	○○○●●
SCIENCE IS SOUND	○○○○○
AFFORDABLE	○●●●●
HOW SOON?	○○○○○

ON THE DRAWING BOARD

Designed for interstellar travel, this theoretical spaceship, Daedalus, *would have a top speed of 60 million miles (100 million km) per hour, a tenth of the speed of light. Driven by 250 nuclear explosions per second,* Daedalus *would take four years to reach this speed. Although it has no room for passengers, it could travel to* Barnard's Star, *six light years away, and send information back to Earth within 50 years.*

NUCLEAR FISSION

Some materials, such as one form of the metal uranium, are unstable — they break down, releasing energy and forming other materials. This is nuclear fission. At the heart of a nuclear power station, particles are fired at materials like this to release energy.

LIZARDS

The lizard group is by far the biggest group of reptiles living today, and the most widespread around the world. In many regions, especially the tropics, lizards are a familiar sight. They hunt mainly by day, in the open, so people see them more often than other reptiles. Lizards do not have poisonous bites, except for two North American species, the gila monster and the Mexican beaded lizard. Some species, such as the Australian frilled lizard, have evolved elaborate crests or frills, to make themselves look fiercer to enemies, or to impress their mates.

Shape and form

Most lizards have a large head with prominent eyes, a slim body, four legs of equal length, and a long tail. However, this basic body shape has become adapted in many different ways, to suit various lifestyles. Some lizards that burrow rapidly in soft soil have lost their limbs, and look more like snakes. Some lizards have strong, agile limbs and grasping fingers, for moving through branches.

The Komodo dragon from Southeast Asia is the largest lizard.

Flap-necked chameleon

The Australian frilled lizard can erect a ruff of skin.

Impressing a mate

The anole lizard from South and Central America is one of many species in which the male is larger and more brightly colored than the female. He can display a flap of skin on his throat, known as the dewlap, by moving his throat bone forward to hold the flap out like a fan. The dewlap is vivid red or yellow, and its flash of color tells the female that he is courting her and wishes to mate. Flying lizards have a similar dewlap.

Disposable tail

A lizard's tail is useful as a counterbalance, when climbing over rocks or branches. But it is not vital for survival. If a predator grabs the tail, the lizard tightens its tail muscles at a special point, so that the tail snaps off. The lizard escapes, the muscles spasm to prevent too much bleeding, and a new tail gradually grows.

Spiny-tailed lizard from Africa and Southern Asia

Animal distribution

Like many other land animals, lizards show distinct patterns of distribution. In other words, the group of animal species found in one area is different from that found in another. In the 1850s the English naturalist Alfred Russel Wallace studied animal distribution. Wallace proposed an imaginary line separating the animal life of Australasia from that of Southeast Asia, as shown below.

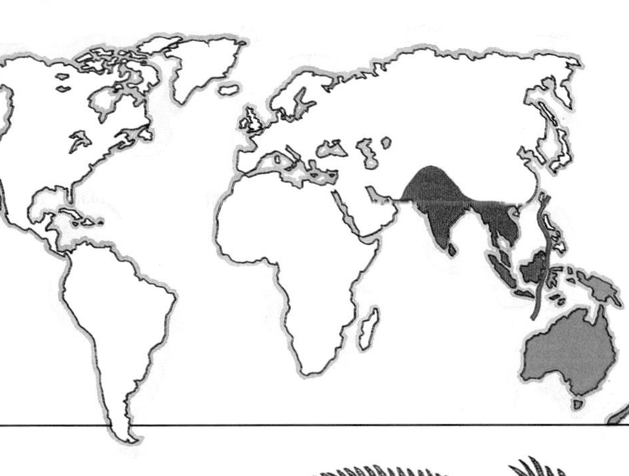

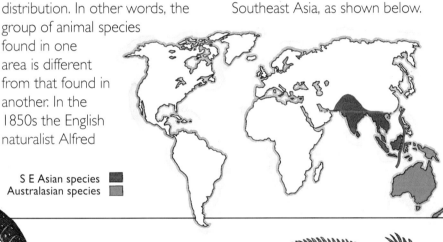

S E Asian species

Australasian species

Tegu lizard from South America

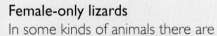

Galapagos marine iguana

Female-only lizards

In some kinds of animals there are no males at all, only females. This is fairly common among insects and worms, and also occurs in lizards. The females are able to lay eggs which hatch into young without first mating with a male. This method of reproduction is called parthenogenesis. The New Mexico whiptail lizard is parthenogenetic. It has been bred in captivity for many generations, with no males at all.

Pirate Life

Pirates led two, or sometimes three, different lives. Many who went to sea to seek their fortune left wives and families at home. When they returned they lived as ordinary citizens. But once on board, they were seamen, keeping an eye open for likely victims and busying themselves with the ship's maintenance.

This meant cleaning weapons (rust was a continual problem with firearms), mending torn sails, swabbing the decks of salt and dirt, pumping out the bilges, and repairing broken ropes and spars. After a patrol, the pirates led yet another type of life (*above*). If they had been successful and had money in their pockets, they spent it on frantic sprees with wine and women. Drunken pirates were known to gamble away a fortune in a single evening!

***Everyday items** found in the sunken city of Port Royal*

Clay pipe

Drinking bottle ***Pewter mug***

Food and Health

At sea life was very harsh. There was no way of preserving fresh food on board ship, so seamen either had to take live animals with them, or made do with dried food preserved with spices. Once they had been at sea for a week or so, they ate little but crackers and salt meat. For drink they had stale, slimy water and large swigs of rum or wine.

One of the major problems at sea was scurvy. This disease is caused by a lack of vitamin C (found in fresh fruit and vegetables). A scurvy victim's skin dried up, his gums swelled, his hair and teeth fell out, and eventually he died. Citrus fruit prevents scurvy, but this was not widely recognized until the 18th century.

Lime juice helped prevent scurvy.

Who's for Captain? *Discipline on board a pirate ship was hard to maintain. Each captain had to run his ship as best he could. If he was successful, his crew might desert to return home with their loot, if not, he faced mutiny!* (Left) *Despite the job's danger, fights for the captaincy were common.*

Below the Water Line

A ship's hull soon became encrusted with barnacles and other marine life. This slowed the ship and made her difficult to handle. The only way to deal with the problem was to beach the vessel so she tipped over on her side, and scrape off the growth with sharp tools (*above*). This was known as "careening."

The rough underside of a ship gave rise to "keel hauling." A rope was attached to a victim's feet and hands, and unable to breathe, he was dragged around the sharp bottom of the boat. This torture was in fact used more by the British Navy than by pirates!

TREASURE ISLAND. Robert Louis Stevenson's *Treasure Island* is probably the best known of all pirate tales. Stevenson did his research well, which is why the book seems so realistic – he even used the names of real pirates. He drew on his experience of traveling by sea to make the voyage of the ship *Hispaniola* appear authentic. But above all it is the character of Long John Silver that has caught the popular imagination (*left*). As soon as we hear the word "pirate" we think of the one-legged rascal with a parrot on his shoulder!

WHAT IS AIR?

Air is everywhere on Earth, even inside our own bodies. We cannot see, smell, or hear air but our lives would be very different without it. Air causes changes in the weather, keeps things warm or cool, lets fires burn, and allows sounds to travel. Air consists of a mixture of gases, mainly nitrogen and oxygen, and can be squashed or compressed into small spaces. The air is constantly recycled by nature – so the air we breathe today is the same air that helped plants to grow millions of years ago (above left).

Gases in the air

Most of the air, about 78 percent, is nitrogen gas. About 21 percent is oxygen gas. All living things need oxygen to release energy from their food. The remaining 1 percent of the air consists of gases such as carbon dioxide, argon, neon, helium, krypton, hydrogen, xenon, and ozone.
The carbon dioxide in the air helps to keep the Earth warm. The air also contains dust, and moisture in the form of water vapor.

Early morning dew

Humidity

The amount of water vapor in the air is called its humidity. As air cools down, some of the water vapor turns into liquid water, called condensation. This happens because cool air holds less water vapor than warm air. Condensation may cause clouds, fog, or dew to form.

Pressure

Barometers (see above) measure air pressure, which is caused by the force of gravity pulling the air down towards the Earth's surface. Changes in air pressure signal changes in the weather. High pressure usually indicates fine, settled weather, while low pressure usually means cloudy, rainy weather.

Air studies

Before the 1700s, air was thought to be a pure substance. However, in 1754, Joseph Black discovered carbon dioxide in air. Oxygen was found by Carl Scheele in the early 1770s and by Joseph Priestly (shown right) in 1774. Nitrogen was discovered in 1772 by Daniel Rutherford, but inert gases such as argon were not detected until the 1890s.

Air particles
In a shaft of sunlight, you can often see dust floating in the air. Air always contains many tiny solid particles, from car exhausts, factory smoke, and forest fires. Other sources include pollen from plants and salt from the sea. Polluted air over a large city, may contain billions of particles.

Useful gases
The gases in the air can be collected separately by a process called fractional distillation. Air is made into a liquid by being cooled to very low temperatures. When it warms up, the gases boil off the liquid at different times because they have different boiling

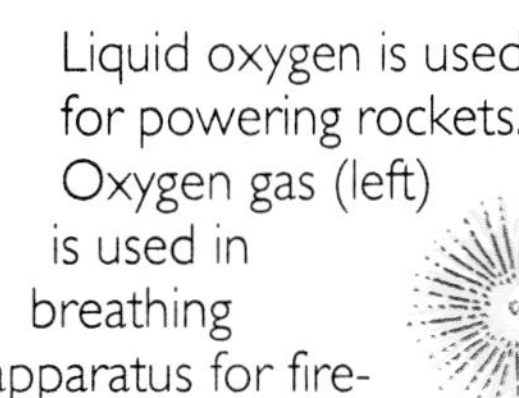

Liquid oxygen is used for powering rockets. Oxygen gas (left) is used in breathing apparatus for fire-

Nitrogen gas is used to make fertilizers (above right), while nitric acid (a compound of nitrogen and sulfate dissolved in water) is a key ingredient in explosives.

Feeding a fire
Fires need the oxygen in the air to burn. People sometimes blow on a fire to give it more oxygen. To put out a fire, they cut off the supply of oxygen by spraying it with water, foam, or carbon dioxide.

Argon is used to fill the space in most light bulbs as it is an extremely unreactive (or inert) gas.

Rusty pipes
If iron or steel are exposed to air and moisture, they usually rust and the metal is eaten away. Rust happens when iron joins up with oxygen in the air to form iron oxide.
Protective paint can stop oxygen from reaching iron or steel and therefore stops rusting taking place.

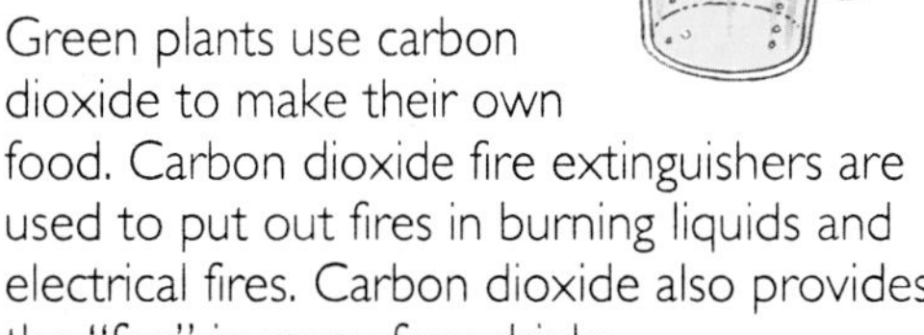

Green plants use carbon dioxide to make their own food. Carbon dioxide fire extinguishers are used to put out fires in burning liquids and electrical fires. Carbon dioxide also provides the "fizz" in many fizzy drinks.

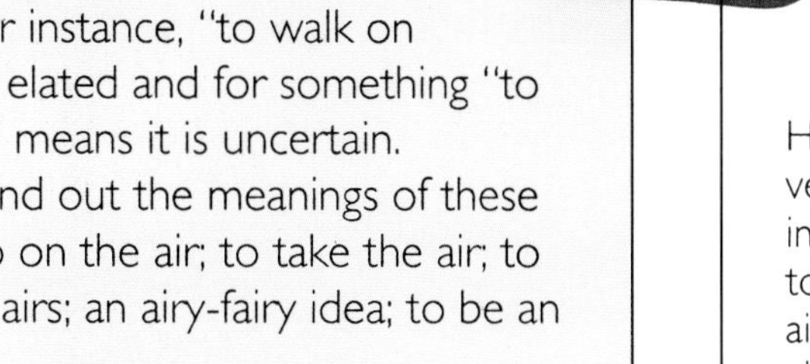

Air sayings
The word air is often used in sayings to convey different meanings. For instance, "to walk on air" is to feel elated and for something "to be in the air" means it is uncertain.

Can you find out the meanings of these sayings: to go on the air; to take the air; to give yourself airs; an airy-fairy idea; to be an airhead?

See if you can compose a poem or a song using some common air sayings.

Neon, another colorless, odorless inert gas, is used in fluorescent signs and strip lighting.

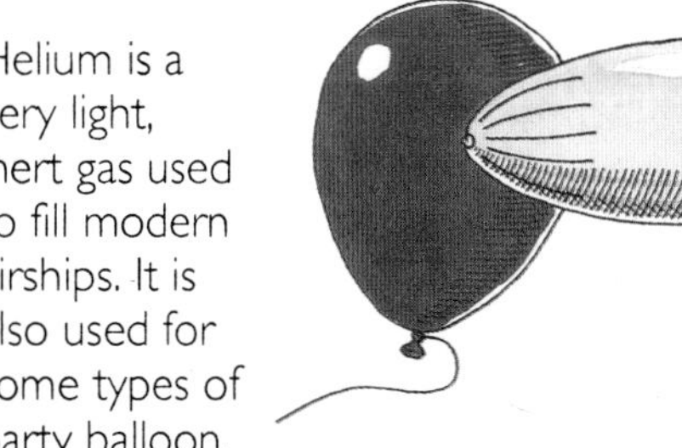

Helium is a very light, inert gas used to fill modern airships. It is also used for some types of party balloon.

SQUID

WHAT DO THE FOLLOWING animals have in common? Land snails, pond snails, sea snails like whelks and periwinkles, cone shells, slugs, oysters, clams, scallops, and mussels. They're all mollusks! They're also called "shellfish" because their fleshy, flexible bodies are protected by a hard shell. Except, that is, for this one – the squid.

SHELL

The squid's need for speed means a heavy shell would just hold it back. Instead, there's a thin, light shell (called a pen) inside the body. Washed up on the shore after death, it looks like clear plastic.

INK SAC

If a predator comes near, the squid can squirt a dark-colored liquid from its ink sac, out of its anus. This clouds the water and hides the squid – with luck, just long enough to make a quick getaway.

STOMACH

LIVER

HEARTS

GILLS

BRAIN

EYES

Big enough to see you with! The squid and its close relations, octopus and cuttlefish, rarely bump into things. They have large eyes and excellent sight, for spotting prey, enemies, or a breeding partner.

BEAKLIKE MOUTH

SUCKERS

ARMS

There are two long arms and eight shorter ones, with suckers for grabbing prey. This is torn up by the beaklike mouth in the middle of the arm bases.

ANATOMY *AT WORK*
SQUIRT POWER

A mollusk's body is wrapped in a cloaklike, fleshy part, called the mantle. Between this and the main body is a mantle space. A squid sucks water slowly through a large opening into the mantle space, then squirts it out through a small funnel opening, and water streams away – backward.

LOBSTER

LIMBS ARE VERY IMPORTANT. They can help some animals, walk, run, flap, kick, grab, push, pull, even breathe! The huge animal group called arthropods get their name from their "jointed legs." They include lobsters and other crustaceans, shown here, as well as insects, spiders, and centipedes.

ANATOMY *AT WORK*
SHEDDING THE SHELL

Arthropods have a hard outer body casing or "shell," the exoskeleton. This can't expand as the creature grows. So it's shed, or molted. The old casing splits along the back, and the animal crawls out and quickly enlarges in its soft new casing, before this hardens.

CRUSTACEAN COUSINS
The big and varied crustacean group includes crabs, prawns, shrimps, crayfish, krill, barnacles, water fleas, and sand hoppers. The only ones that live on land are wood lice (sow bugs). Even they need damp places, to keep their breathing gills moist. A dry crustacean is a dead crustacean!

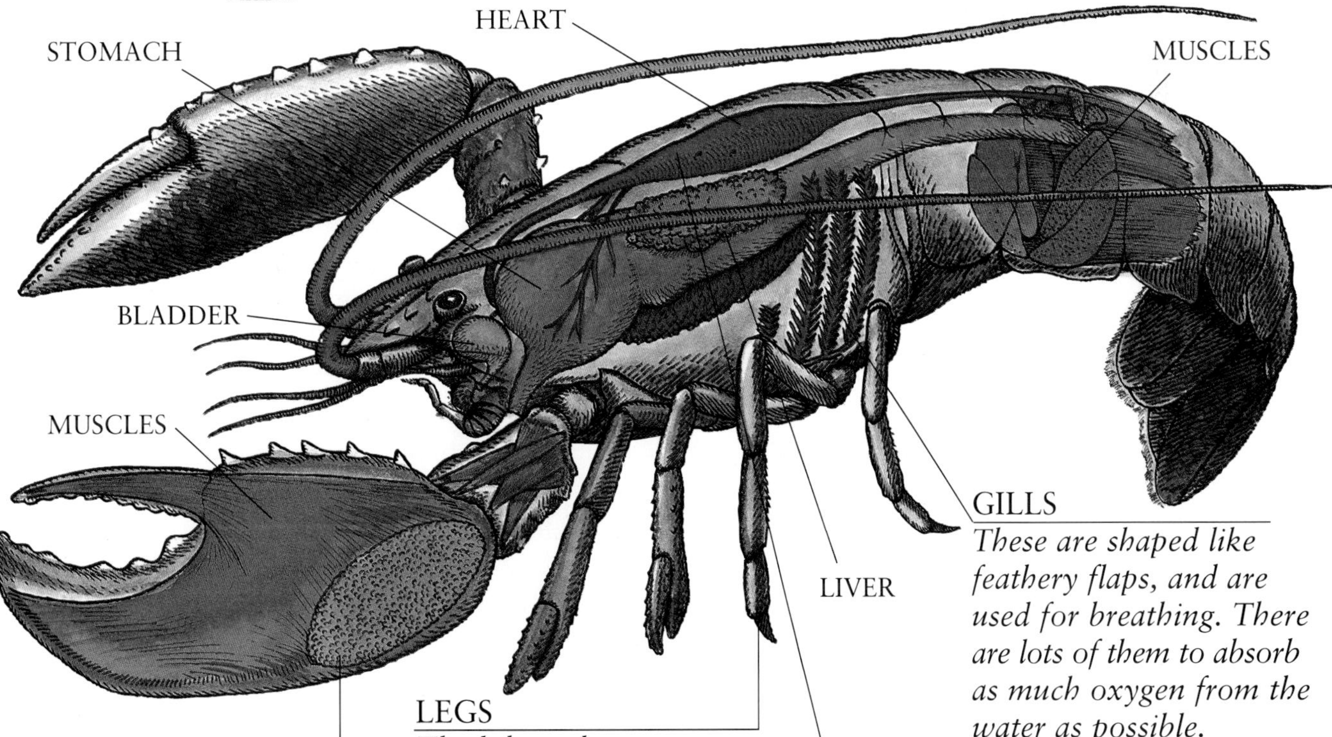

GILLS
These are shaped like feathery flaps, and are used for breathing. There are lots of them to absorb as much oxygen from the water as possible.

PINCERS
The big pincer is mainly for crushing food, while the smaller, sharper one is for cutting.

LEGS
The lobster has ten proper jointed legs. But the first two are its big pincers. The other eight have claws on the end, to grip slippery seabed rocks.

BLOOD
The lobster's well-developed blood system has a powerful heart and lots of vessels. And its blood is blue!

ON YOUR BIKE!

You can ride a mountain bike on city streets, or you can go "off-road," riding in the open countryside.

When you have practiced the basic riding techniques, and you feel safe and confident on your bike, try out some of the different types of mountain bike riding, from riding trails (routes through the countryside, *below*) to tricks.

COMPETITION TIME

As a mountain biker you can simply hit the trail with a friend and just enjoy the ride, or you can take the sport more seriously (*above*) by entering different competitive events. From cross-country racing to downhill racing, there are events for everyone. Check out mountain biking magazines or specialized stores for up-to-date information on events that you can enter.

Whatever your level of riding and whatever the type of riding you are involved in, stay safe. Only attempt moves or ride distances for which you have the necessary skills and strength.

TIME FOR TRICKERY

*Many riders enjoy the thrill of stunt riding. This involves tricks such as the "wheelie" (*right*). Wait until you are an experienced and skilled rider before you attempt a stunt.*

Taking up MOUNTAIN BIKING

Mountain biking is one of the most exciting sports you can enjoy. A mountain bike is often easier to ride than a regular road bike — its chunky tires, wide range of gears, and powerful brakes make it easy to cross even the roughest terrain. A mountain bike reaches the places that other bikes cannot reach, from woody tracks to steep hills.

ON THE TRAIL
When you are on a trail ride, make sure that you carry tools and spares for your bike.

REASONS TO RIDE
"You can just put on your helmet, get on your bike, and be out in the fresh air in no time. It's a great sport for girls and boys... It's excellent to go out on a ride with your friends... There are so many tricks to learn... It doesn't matter if you're a beginner — you can always have a good time."

HOT ROCKS

POWER FROM THE EARTH

The Earth's core is very hot – between 7,000° F and 8,000° F.
The heat is caused mostly by the breakdown of radioactive elements and, to a lesser extent, by heat left over from the earth's fiery beginnings. Tapping only a tiny fraction of this heat could produce large amounts of energy. In many places, where heat reaches the surface naturally in the form of hot water, geothermal power stations have been established. In the past decade, engineers have been trying to find ways to tap the Earth's heat where it remains beneath the surface. This involves either drilling into underground sources of hot water, or creating them. To achieve this, holes are drilled into hot dry rocks, water is pumped down, then allowed to return to the surface hot enough to generate power.

Pipes (below) carry steam from the wellhead at *Nesjavellir in Iceland. The hot water produced heats the capital, Reykjavik. The steam is also used to heat greenhouses where fruit and vegetables are grown.*

People suffering from skin diseases bathe in hot *water at the power station in Svartsengi, Iceland (below). Salt, clay, and algae in the water are said to be good for skin conditions.*

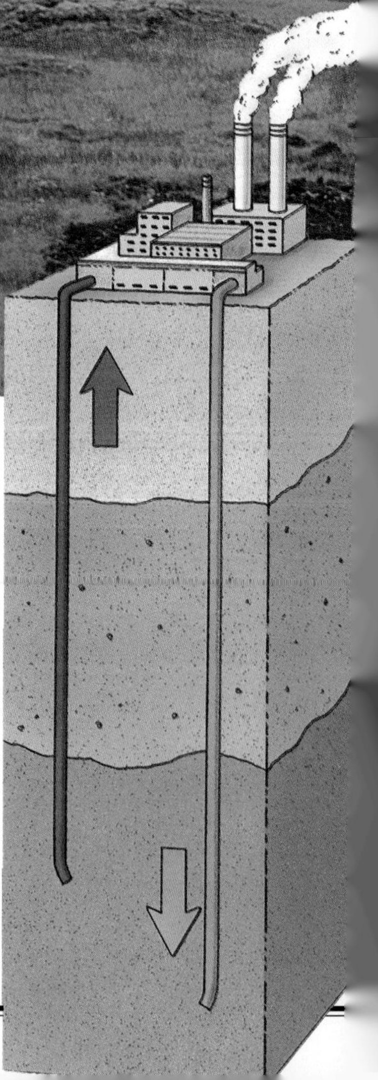

Hot-rock projects in the *United States and Britain have produced some hot water, but less than was hoped. The British project, at a granite mine in Cornwall, lost a lot of water, and recovered less than one tenth of the heat expected. The American experiments in New Mexico, found that the granite deep in the earth could not be easily broken open.*

In some places, hot water reaches the surface *unaided. A geyser (right) erupts at Cerro Prieto geothermal plant in Mexico. Geothermal power plants create no pollution.*

HOT ROCK PROJECT

HOW IT WORKS

Hot rock projects (left), involve drilling two holes four to six miles down into rock that is up to 400°F hotter than the earth's surface. Granite is the best rock for this. A special drill bit is used to make the holes curve at the bottom like a "J." Water is pumped at high pressure into the deeper hole, causing the rock to crack. The water passes through the cracks to reach the shorter hole, and is heated as it travels through the hot rock. It emerges from the second hole heated to a temperature high enough to raise steam and generate electricity.

POISONS AND STINGS

Animals use poisons for two reasons: to defend themselves against predators, and to overcome their own prey. Insects are no exception to this. Some have poisonous stings in their tails, some bite with poisonous jaws. Others are just poisonous all over. Insects that use poisons to catch prey are often masters of disguise. Those that use poisons for defense usually advertise the fact by having bright warning colors on their bodies, usually red- or yellow-and-black. Other insects are not poisonous, but mimic those that are.

Bee stings

Worker honeybees will defend the hive quite literally with their lives. The sting at the end of the worker bee's abdomen is a sac full of poison connected by a tube to a sharp, barbed spine. When the bee stings, the barbs make sure the sting stays in the victim while the venom is pumped into the wound. But they also mean that when the bee flies off, the end of its abdomen is torn away and it then dies.

Plates pump venom.

Bulb full of venom

Venom sac

Worker bee

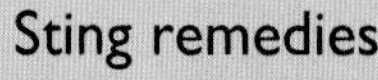

Sting remedies

Bees and wasps only sting when they feel threatened, so you are more likely to get stung if you shout or wave your arms to drive one away. If you are stung by a bee, remove the sting with tweezers, taking care not to squeeze the poison sac. Wasps will not leave their sting in your skin if you allow them to remove it.

Wash the wound thoroughly with antiseptic, and put a cold, damp cloth on it to relieve the pain. Bee and wasp stings are not dangerous unless the swelling blocks the throat, or unless the victim who has been stung has an allergy to insect stings.

Lethal weapon

The bodies of some kinds of insects are poisonous, and taste disgusting. This provides a good defense against predators who recognize the species, and do not attack it. Some squirt stinging liquids, others have irritating hairs that get stuck in an attacker's skin. The grubs of a South African leaf beetle are so poisonous that Kalahari bushmen (right) use them to tip the ends of their arrows.

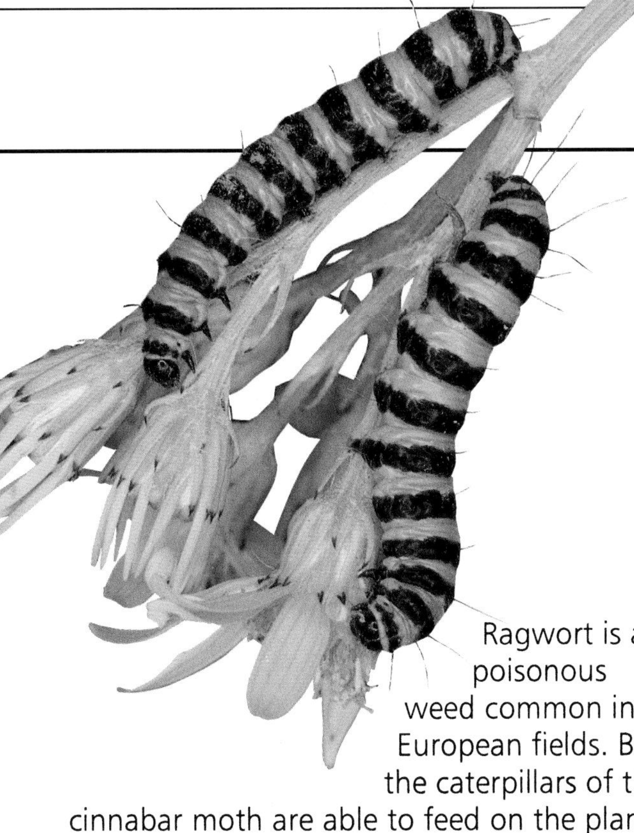

Ragwort is a poisonous weed common in European fields. But the caterpillars of the cinnabar moth are able to feed on the plant, and store the poisons in their body tissues. A bird who eats one will become very sick. These caterpillars have yellow-and-black warning stripes on their bodies to advertise their identity. Birds learn after only one experience to leave them alone.

Insects in folklore medicine

The bodies of blister beetles contain an irritating fluid called cantharidin which these insects use to defend themselves against predators. Before modern medicines were developed, doctors used to apply this substance to their patients' skin as a treatment for warts. The blisters caused by the fluid were also thought to allow the escape of poisons that built up inside the body. Bee stings were thought to cure rheumatism, so bees were allowed to sting the inflamed joints of rheumatic patients.

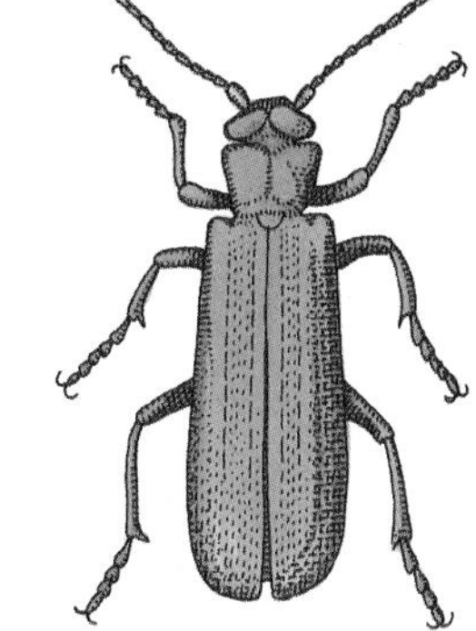

Proverbial insects

Traditional sayings or proverbs often refer to the familiar characteristics of common insects to help describe people's behavior. A group of people working very hard at a joint task are sometimes called "busy bees." If someone has a particular concern which others may not share, they are said to have a "bee in their bonnet." Children who will not sit still and concentrate at school are said to have "ants in their pants." Can you describe someone who has a "butterfly mind?"

Bee in your bonnet

Beetle chemists

Bombardier beetles use a spectacular chemical reaction as a powerful weapon against attackers. The beetle has special chambers in its abdomen where it stores two chemicals, each fairly harmless on its own. When the beetle is alarmed it mixes the chemicals in another chamber, together with an enzyme, which aids the reaction. A rocket-like jet of hot, poisonous spray shoots from the end of the abdomen. The beetle can direct the spray by twisting its abdomen towards a victim. The boiling chemicals produced cause painful blisters.

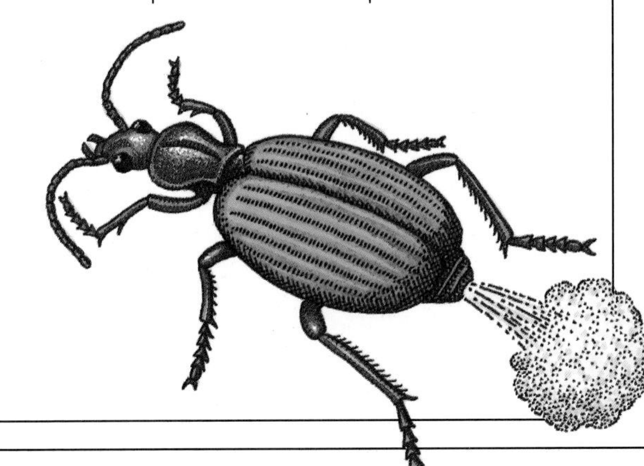

VIKING LONGBOATS

The Vikings are famous for their shipbuilding skills and for their longships which carried them far and wide. Their ships were among the finest built in Europe. There were various kinds of ship, each developed for different uses. One of the best known was the longship, a canoe-shaped warship. Longships were tough enough to withstand the stormiest seas, shallow enough to sail up rivers and yet light enough to be carried overland. They were about 65-100 feet long. Each had a woolen sail, which was often striped red and white or blue and white. The ships could also be rowed when the wind dropped.

Evolution of boats

The Viking ships were the product of a long process of development and refinement. The earliest evidence of Scandinavian ships comes from the Bronze Age. Rock carvings at Kalnes in Norway depict ships with pronged prows and stems. They were made from wooden frames and, it is thought, covered with ox hides. These early vessels were the forerunners of the plank-built boats of the Iron Age. The long, narrow shape of the Viking longships first appeared in the Nydam ship of the A.D. 400s, and the strong keel used in the Viking ships was introduced in the Kvalsund Boat in the A.D. 700s.

Each oarsman packed his belongings into a chest which he then used as a seat while he was rowing.

Steering oar

Boat building

Viking longships were "clinker-built." This means that they were built from overlapping planks of 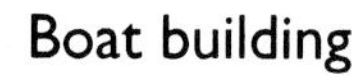 oak, nailed together. Pine was used for the masts. The joints were stuffed with ropes, moss or animal hair to make them both watertight and flexible in stormy seas.

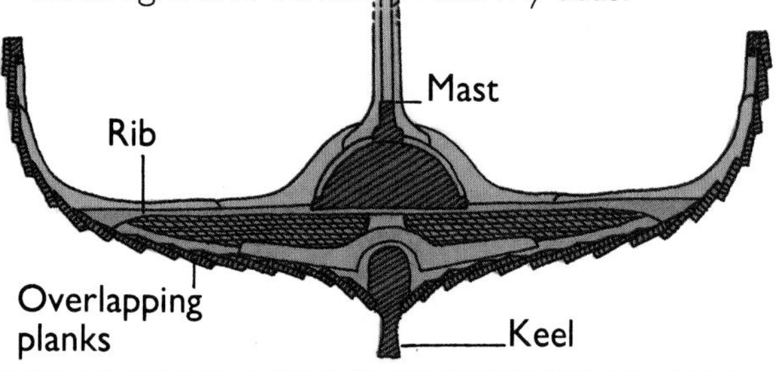

A solid oak keel formed the backbone of the ship. The keel supported a sturdy mast and a single full sail to propel it forward at great speed when it was windy. Oars could be used in calmer weather.

Natural navigation

With no instruments or maps to guide them, the Vikings depended on sightings of the stars and the Sun to determine direction. They also relied on landmarks and the presence of seaweed or seagulls. By the A.D. 900s, the Vikings had developed a way of working out the latitude (how far north) in which they were sailing. They used a table of figures, in which the Sun's midday height for each week was recorded, and a measuring stick.

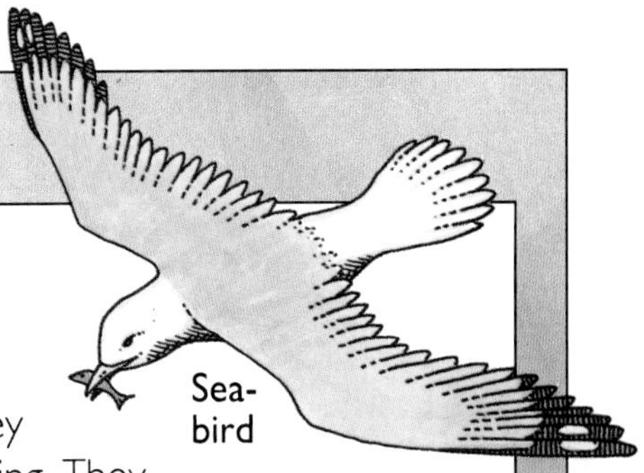

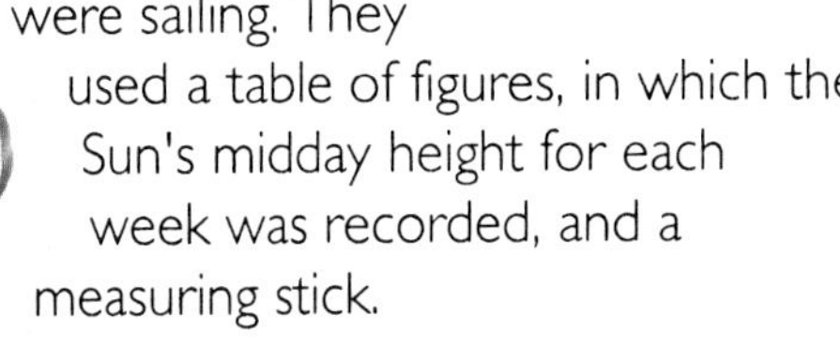
Sea-bird

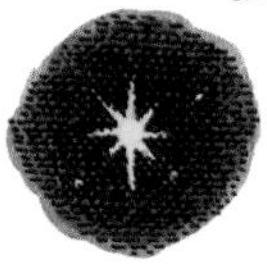

Polar star

Seaweed

Viking longships were often called "Serpents of the Sea" because they had figureheads at the front carved in the shape of fierce dragon or snake heads. The rest of the ship looked like the body of the sea serpent.

PROFESSOR PROTEIN'S HINTS AND TIPS ON *personal hygiene*

WHEN YOU NEED A BEST FRIEND

YOU SMELL - IT'S NATURAL Each human body has its own distinctive odor. But exactly how much it smells is up to its owner. Too much of the wrong smell can make a person unpopular, because others avoid their nasty odor. This is where washing and hygiene triumph. Wash your body properly, regularly, and in all the right places, and you can avoid the dreaded B.O. Otherwise your best friend might not stick around for too long.

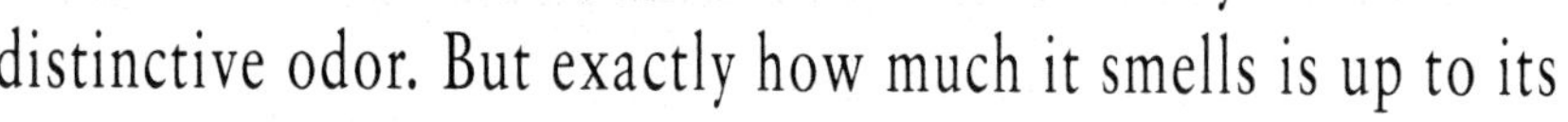

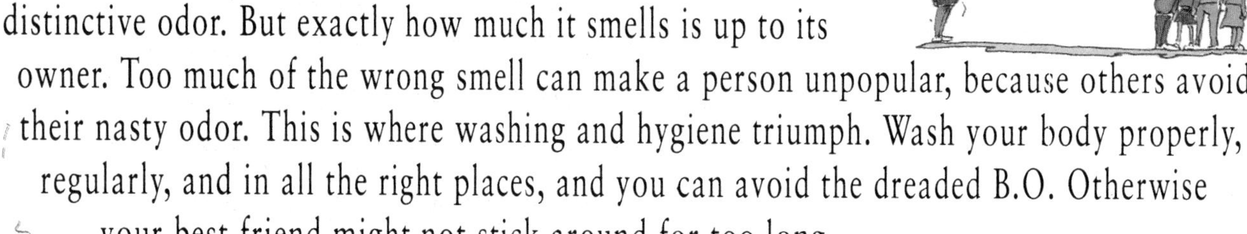

PROFESSOR'S FACT WHAT IS B.O.?

• Body odor is a mixture of smells:

• Old sweat still on skin – not so much the sweat itself, but the bacteria

that feed on it and then rot.

• Natural scents of sebum and skin oils, as they collect and become stale.

• Dirt, dust, grime, smears, and substances picked up by the skin.

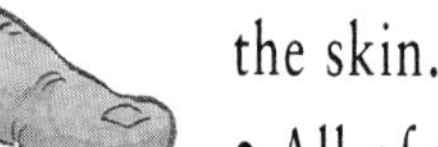

• All of the above rubbed into clothes that aren't washed. Sometimes it's not B.O. at all, it's C.O. – clothes odor.

INSENSIBLE SWEAT

Skin sweat glands make perspiration or sweat, to cool the body. The hotter you get, the more you sweat. But there's also "background sweating" that happens all the time, even in cold conditions. It's called insensible perspiration and it produces 1 pint (a half liter) daily. So even when you're cool, you're sweaty!

WHERE SWEATS MOST?

Sweat glands are more common in some parts of the skin, compared to others. So these areas sweat most, like the forehead, temples, armpits, palms, groin, backs of the knees, and soles of the feet.

Sweat cannot dry or evaporate from some parts, like the armpits, groin, and feet, since these are usually covered. Instead, it builds up in these areas – so they're the ones you should wash really well.

BIG TIP NO COVER-UP

Perfumes, scents, and deodorants can help to cover up natural body smells, for a while. But they soon wear off, and they aren't the sole answer. There's no substitute for a good wash with water and soap. Put on the scent afterward, if you want.

PROFESSOR PROTEIN'S HINTS AND TIPS ON *personal hygiene*

PICKING UP PETTY PESTS

THE WALKING ZOO You are covered in thousands of tiny animals, including fleas, lice, mites, ticks, worms, and other mini-beasts who are just trying to survive. They look for a meal of blood and fluids – and you might be the main course. These mini-monsters can get picked up from pets or farm animals, or a walk in the country or town. Most times, you know about them from an itchy bite or spot, where they bite to suck. Get rid of them quickly and easily, with a suitable soap or shampoo.

FLEAS

Most flea bites come from pet fleas. Not fleas that are pets, but fleas from pets, like cats and dogs. These long-jumping insects stray to human skin and suck a meal occasionally, but they usually soon move on. To solve the problem at the source, treat your pets and their bedding with anti-flea powders or sprays.

~~MICE~~ LICE

Mice are tiny and pale. They live in hair and suck blood ... No, hang on, mice are small furry rodents. LICE are tiny and pale, live in hair, and suck blood. These insects lay eggs called nits, which are glued strongly to hairs. An anti-louse shampoo should get rid of them.

~~MICE~~ MITES

These are arachnids, micro-cousins of spiders. There are hundreds of kinds. The scabies mite burrows into skin, lays its eggs, and causes REALLY ANNOYING ITCHING. These can be treated with a special soap to kill the poor little mites.

BIG TIP FAMILY MATTERS

Sometimes people seem to catch skin pests again and again. It may be that other family members or close friends also have them, and the pests just get passed around. Ask the doctor or pharmacist, who'll advise the proper treatment. Then make sure other people in close contact get treated, too.

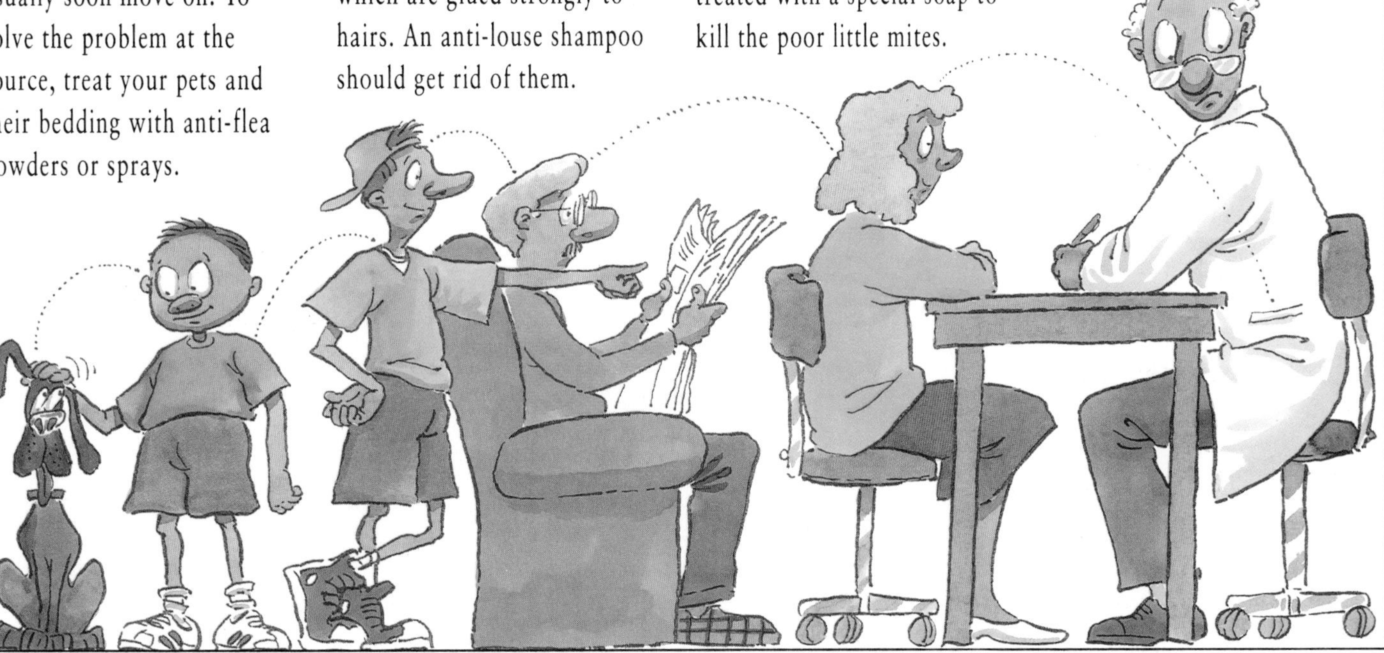

SPACE PLANES

TRAVELING AT MACH 18

Beyond the supersonic transport lies a new kind of plane altogether, one that combines flight and space technology to reach speeds of more than 10,000 mph.

The German space-plane design, Sanger, consists of a rocket piggy-backing on a hypersonic aircraft. The mother craft would carry the second stage rocket high into the atmosphere and up to a speed of Mach 16, where it would separate and go into orbit. The British version, called Hotol, has been developed by British Aerospace and Rolls-Royce.

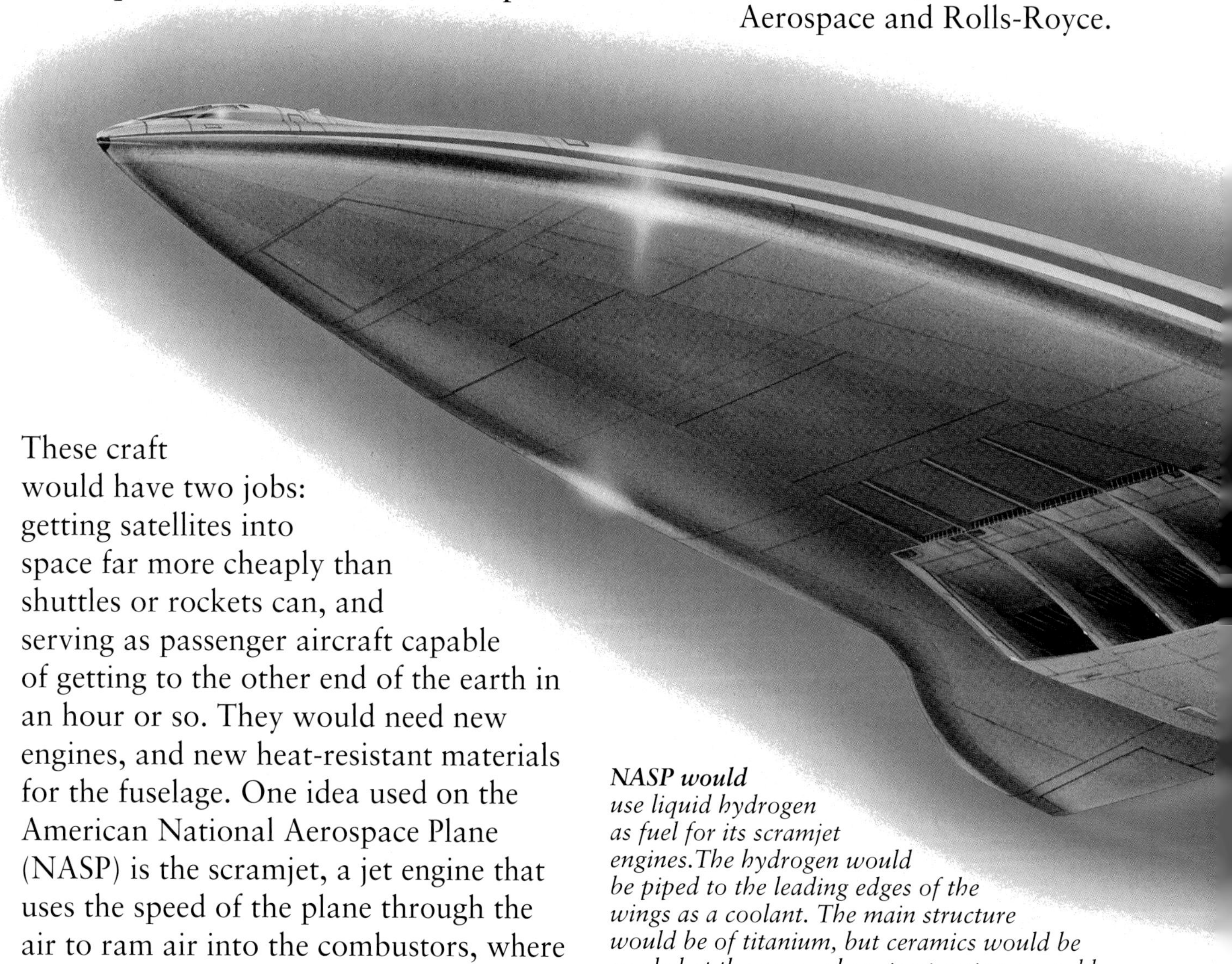

These craft would have two jobs: getting satellites into space far more cheaply than shuttles or rockets can, and serving as passenger aircraft capable of getting to the other end of the earth in an hour or so. They would need new engines, and new heat-resistant materials for the fuselage. One idea used on the American National Aerospace Plane (NASP) is the scramjet, a jet engine that uses the speed of the plane through the air to ram air into the combustors, where it mixes with fuel and burns.

NASP would *use liquid hydrogen as fuel for its scramjet engines.The hydrogen would be piped to the leading edges of the wings as a coolant. The main structure would be of titanium, but ceramics would be needed at the nose, where temperatures would reach 4,900 degrees F.*

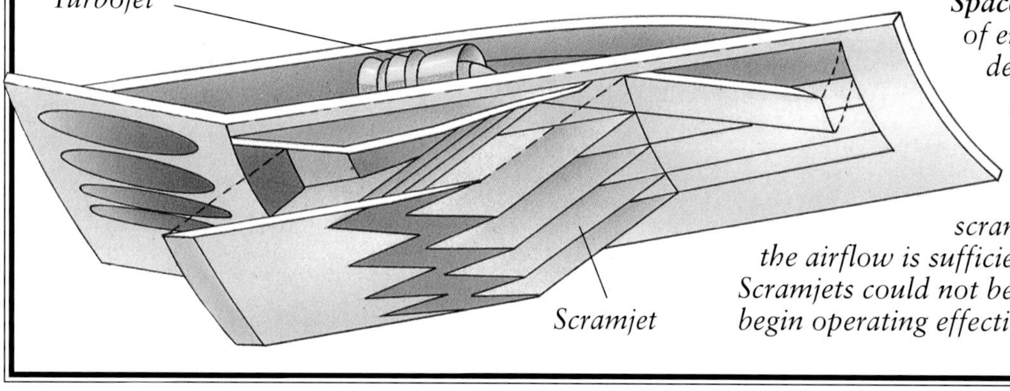

Space planes will need two types *of engines. In this early NASA design (left), an ordinary turbojet engine is used for takeoff from the runway and acceleration to 2,000 mph. At this speed, scramjets can take over because the airflow is sufficiently fast for them to work. Scramjets could not be used alone, because they only begin operating effectively at high speeds.*

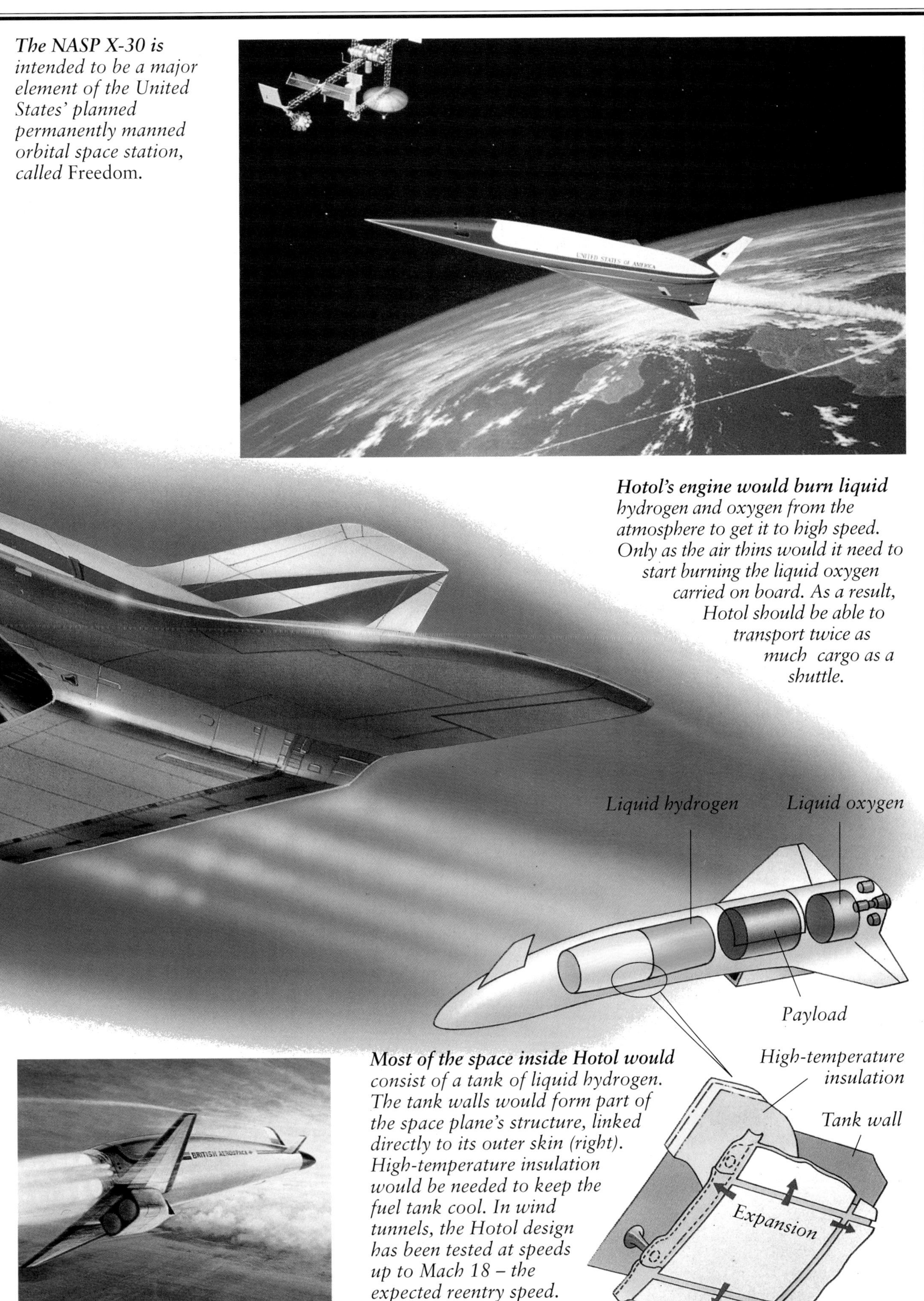

***The NASP X-30 is** intended to be a major element of the United States' planned permanently manned orbital space station, called* Freedom.

***Hotol's engine would burn liquid** hydrogen and oxygen from the atmosphere to get it to high speed. Only as the air thins would it need to start burning the liquid oxygen carried on board. As a result, Hotol should be able to transport twice as much cargo as a shuttle.*

***Most of the space inside Hotol would** consist of a tank of liquid hydrogen. The tank walls would form part of the space plane's structure, linked directly to its outer skin (right). High-temperature insulation would be needed to keep the fuel tank cool. In wind tunnels, the Hotol design has been tested at speeds up to Mach 18 – the expected reentry speed.*

Monkey Business

The earliest written reports said the gorilla was a ferocious beast. It was reported to kill people and even attack elephants that disturbed it. The friendly-looking chimpanzee, on the other hand, was popular from the start. The first specimen to reach the London Zoo traveled by bus, sitting inside beside its keeper! Rarely have we been more deceived by appearances.

The gorilla is a peaceful creature that lives on plants, while the chimp is one of the world's most aggressive animals. Chimps roam through the forest, leaving a trail of destruction. And it is not just the vegetation that suffers. Gangs of chimps actively hunt down monkeys and even other chimps using ruthless tactics that give their prey no chance of escape.

Monkey Spite
A baby baboon that has lost its way is viciously attacked by a troop of aggressive chimpanzees (right).

All in the Family

Humans are members of the primate family, which includes bush babies and lemurs. Apes (gibbons, chimps, gorillas, and orangutans) are our nearest relatives.

Monkeys are distant, largely tree-dwelling cousins, though baboons (*top* and *right*) spend much of their time on the ground. Several African and Asian varieties have spectacularly unattractive bottoms. Many American species have tails that can grasp objects like a hand.

Ape power. Cartoon monkeys are usually mischievous beings, inferior to humans. This idea was turned on its head in the famous 1967 movie *Planet of the Apes*. Astronaut Charlton Heston (*above*) travels in time to find Earth run by talking apes who decide that humans like Heston are the "missing link" between them and an earlier, primitive species!

Idols or Idiots?
The ancient Chinese considered the monkey to be one of the Three Senseless Creatures. The Hindus of India, on the other hand, thought their monkey god Hanuman was clever, skillful, and loyal (right).

GENTLE GIANTS. Once called "pongos," gorillas are the giants of the ape family. The huge vegetarians, standing almost 7 feet tall and weighing 550 pounds, are famous for beating their chests. This is a sign of excitement, not anger.

Movies like *King Kong* (*below*) made many people think that gorillas were ferocious. But *Gorillas in the Mist* (1988), which told the story of Dian Fossey's study of mountain gorillas, highlighted their gentle nature.

Mystic Monkey Trio
Mythology's most famous monkeys are The Three Mystic Monkeys of Japan. *With paws covering eyes, ears, and mouth, they stand for: "Speak no evil," "See no evil," and "Hear no evil"* (below).

Inhabiting the OCEANS

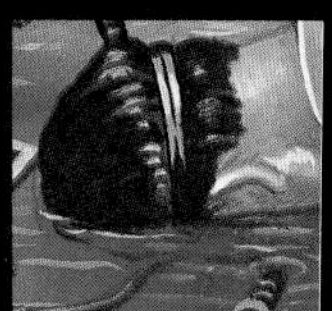

BREATHING UNDER THE SEA
In the 1960s, scientist Waldemar Ayres used a special membrane to take oxygen from sea water through artificial "gills." He breathed underwater for over an hour. No one has yet used his system for diving.

People have always dreamed of living underwater. Many fantastic stories have been written about "human fish" and underwater cities. The first steps have been taken toward making this dream come true. Scientists have developed a membrane that keeps water out but allows oxygen to pass in. It has been tried successfully on rabbits. Could it one day allow humans to breathe freely underwater? Divers are already able to live for some time in "underwater homes," or saturation habitats. These are small and cramped but, one day, larger underwater homes may be created, in which people can live and work for many months or even several years.

WATERY HOUSES
The first "underwater home" for divers was the Conshelf I, *invented by Jacques Cousteau. In 1962, two divers spent a week in it at a depth of 33 feet (10 m).* Sealab *(right) and* Tektite *are habitats in which people have lived for up to 30 days at depths of nearly 660 feet (200 m).*

AN ICY ENVIRONMENT
Even the cold waters of the Arctic and Antarctic are being explored by diving scientists. They have discovered giant sea spiders, anemones, and fish with antifreeze in their blood.

FARMING THE OCEANS
Many countries have sea farms where fish, shrimps, shellfish, (right), and seaweeds are cultivated for food. At present, these are mostly established in shallow water where they can be looked after easily. One day, it may be possible to farm deep-sea fish with diver-farmers living in underwater farmhouses.

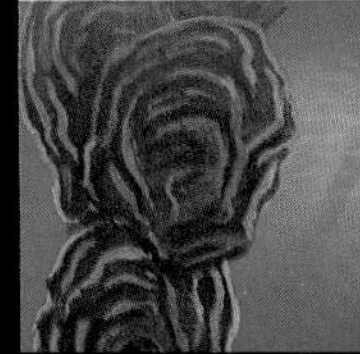

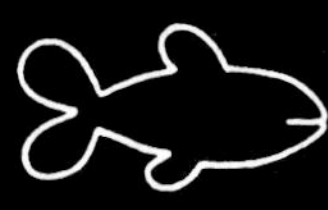

How long can people hold their breath underwater?
Most people can hold their breath for about 30 seconds. In December 1994, Francesco "Pipin" Ferreras became the world breath-holding champion when he dived to 420 feet (127 m). He held his breath for 2 minutes, 26 seconds. **WARNING: THIS IS A VERY DANGEROUS THING TO DO AND SHOULD NOT BE TRIED.**

TAKING THE PLUNGE
Scuba gear means that almost anyone can learn to dive and explore the deep. But compressed air, used by most divers, is unsafe below about 165 feet (50 m).

Special mixtures of the gases nitrogen or helium and oxygen allow trained divers (left) to reach 330 feet (100 m). Below that, divers use a diving bell as a base, to work down to about 1,320 feet (400 m).

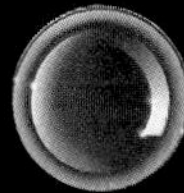

Cities of the future

Many books and films have explored the possibilities of humans living underwater in specially designed towns and cities. Already, a few travel agencies are experimenting with submerged hotels (right) from which guests can watch fish, snorkel, and scuba dive. But as the Earth's population increases, will underwater buildings have more serious uses? Will human colonies be able to live in the depths of the oceans?

BIRD FEET

Apart from walking and running, birds also use their feet for gripping and tearing food, climbing, swimming, and preening their feathers. Most birds have three or four toes on each foot, but the exact size and shape of their feet depends on their life-style. The partridge spends most of its time on the ground, so it needs strong feet that are good for running and scratching for food. When perching birds roost on branches at night, their toes lock around the branch so they do not fall off.

For running
Ostriches have only two toes on each foot. These are highly specialized for fast running. Ostriches cannot fly, but they can run at up to 45 mph (70 km/h) for short distances.

Ostrich foot

For balance
The African jacana, or lily trotter, has toes about 3 inches (8 cm) long – the longest of any bird. These enable it to spread its weight over its feet so it can walk across water lily leaves without sinking.

Coot foot

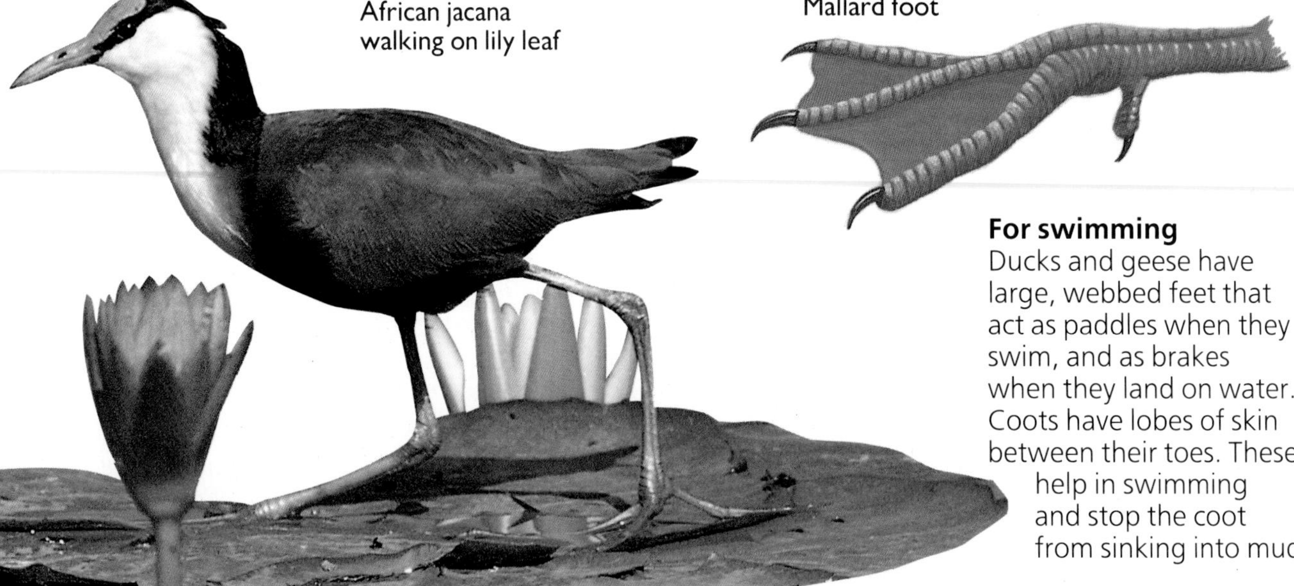

African jacana walking on lily leaf

Mallard foot

For swimming
Ducks and geese have large, webbed feet that act as paddles when they swim, and as brakes when they land on water. Coots have lobes of skin between their toes. These help in swimming and stop the coot from sinking into mud.

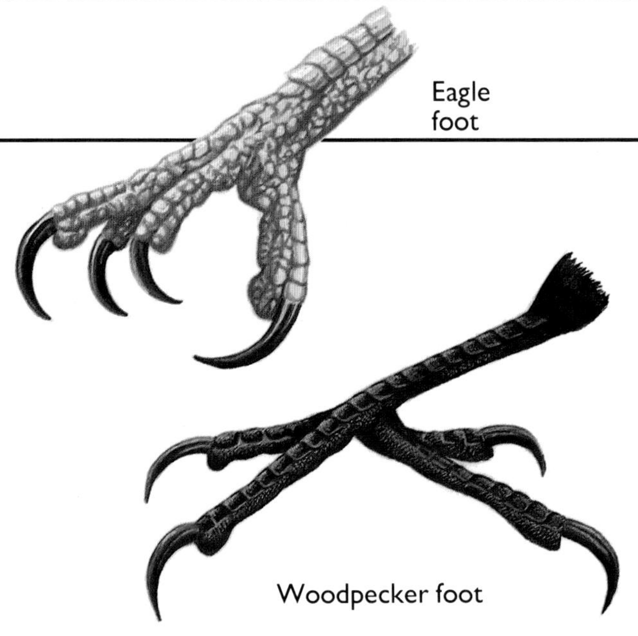

Eagle foot

Woodpecker foot

For gripping

Eagles and other birds of prey have sharp, curved talons on their feet for holding and tearing meat. Their legs and feet are very strong, but these birds find walking difficult because their talons are so long. The long-clawed feet of woodpeckers are designed for climbing tree trunks. They have two toes pointing forward and two backward.

Claws for combing

To keep their feathers clean and neat, birds preen them with their beaks and feet. Herons and bitterns specialize in using their feet to preen. They feed on eels, which makes their feathers slimy. To remove the slime, some of the feathers on the breast disintegrate into a powder which they rub into their dirty feathers. The heron then "combs" off the slime with tiny teeth on the middle claws of its feet. Nightjars are nocturnal birds which feed on a diet of moths and other insects. They also have comblike central claws to clean moth scales off their feathers.

Heron claw

Bittern claw

Great blue heron preening

Plaster casting bird prints

Before you set out to find a footprint of a bird to plaster cast, first collect the following materials: a small can, a stick, oak tag, paper clips, plaster of paris, water, clear varnish, and a knife. When you select a bird print, stand a 1 in (3 cm) wide strip of oak tag in a circle around the footprint (1). Fasten it together with a paper clip. Mix the plaster of paris in a can with water, stirring with your stick. Add water until the mixture is thick but can still be poured. Then pour the mixture into the oak tag ring, until the area is evenly covered (2). Let the plaster dry for 10 – 15 minutes. Then pry the cast loose with a knife and clean off the mud and grass. In 24 hours when the cast is completely solid, carefully clean and varnish it (3). Compare the print with a bird identification book to see if you can find out what kind of bird made it.

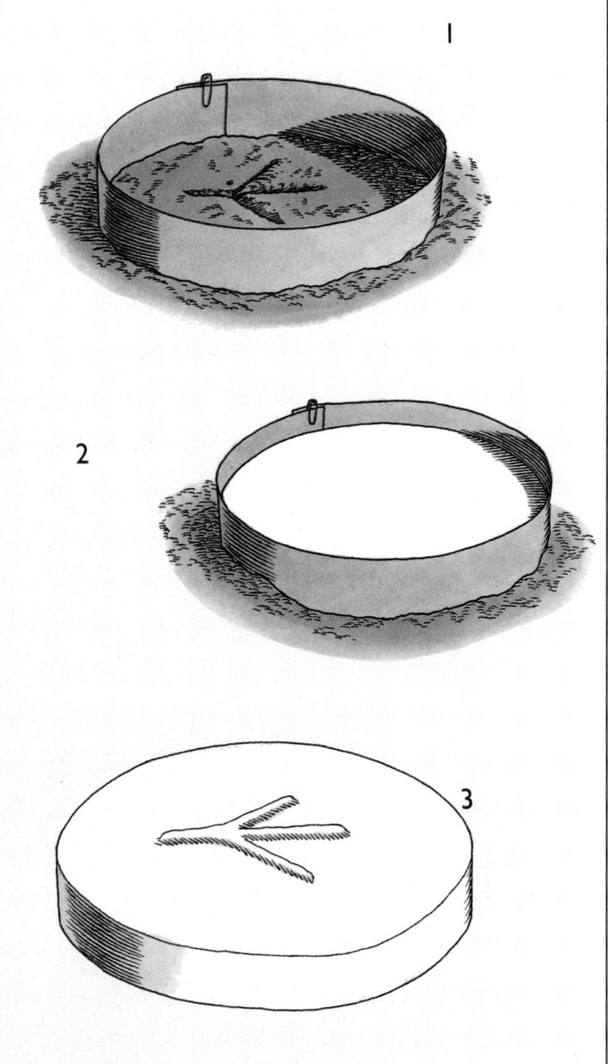

IDEAS AND INVENTIONS

For thousands of years really good ideas – such as wheels or decimals – didn't come along very often. They fell in slow drips, about one every 500 years, plopping mostly onto China or the Middle East, then trickling out to other places. Around 1400, this changed: Europeans took over as the "no.1 ideas people;" the drip of new ideas and inventions became a stream, which ran quickly around the world.

Like everyone else, the Pole Nicolaus Copernicus (*left*) thought the sun, stars, and planets went around the Earth. But when he tried to discover exactly how this happened, he got nowhere. So he tried pretending the Earth went around the sun. He did his math again... and bingo – everything worked out just right. The Earth really did spin around the sun! Nicolaus felt dizzy and sick, and kept his discovery a secret until his death in 1543.

In 1609, Italian Galileo Galilei proved Nicolaus right by looking up at heavenly bodies through his new telescope. Dutchman Anton van Leeuwenhoek preferred to gaze at tiny earthly bodies, through his microscope (1674). Europeans also looked into human bodies – in England, William Harvey found that blood went around and around, like water in a radiator (1628).

Key Men

For most of history, learning was rare and quite secret. The German Johannes Gutenberg invented the modern printing press (about 1440), and a flood of cheap books gave everyone the key to knowledge.

Sir Francis Bacon (1561–1626) unlocked science: Instead of doing experiments to back up an idea, he said we should start with experiments, then come up with theories to fit the facts.

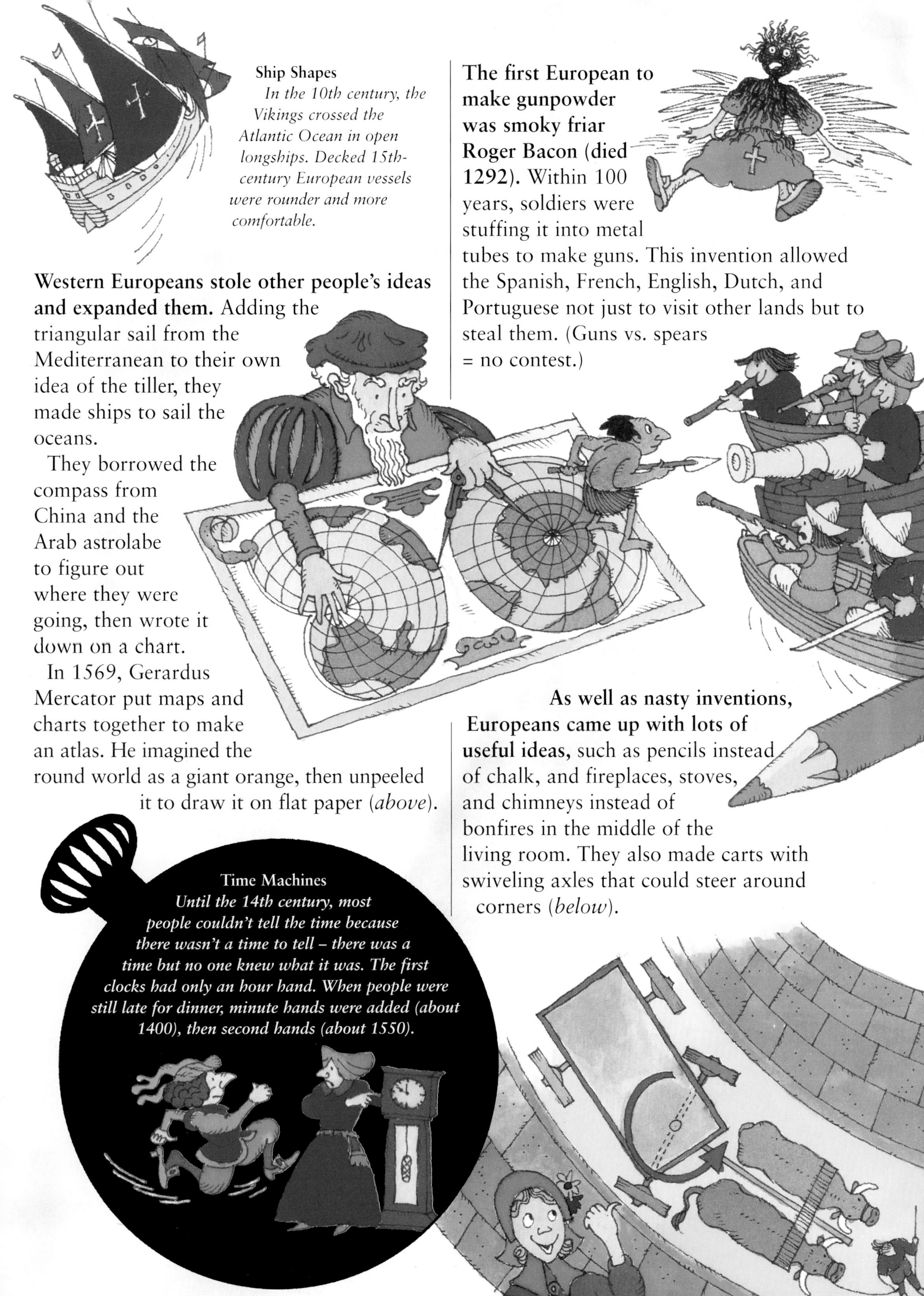

Ship Shapes

In the 10th century, the Vikings crossed the Atlantic Ocean in open longships. Decked 15th-century European vessels were rounder and more comfortable.

Western Europeans stole other people's ideas and expanded them. Adding the triangular sail from the Mediterranean to their own idea of the tiller, they made ships to sail the oceans.

They borrowed the compass from China and the Arab astrolabe to figure out where they were going, then wrote it down on a chart.

In 1569, Gerardus Mercator put maps and charts together to make an atlas. He imagined the round world as a giant orange, then unpeeled it to draw it on flat paper (*above*).

The first European to make gunpowder was smoky friar Roger Bacon (died 1292). Within 100 years, soldiers were stuffing it into metal tubes to make guns. This invention allowed the Spanish, French, English, Dutch, and Portuguese not just to visit other lands but to steal them. (Guns vs. spears = no contest.)

As well as nasty inventions, Europeans came up with lots of useful ideas, such as pencils instead of chalk, and fireplaces, stoves, and chimneys instead of bonfires in the middle of the living room. They also made carts with swiveling axles that could steer around corners (*below*).

Time Machines

Until the 14th century, most people couldn't tell the time because there wasn't a time to tell – there was a time but no one knew what it was. The first clocks had only an hour hand. When people were still late for dinner, minute hands were added (about 1400), then second hands (about 1550).

WATER'S CYCLE

Whether falling from a storm cloud or spurting from a kitchen sink, water moves in an endless cycle between Earth and sky. Year after year, the sun performs a fantastic feat, its energy evaporating 95,000 cubic miles of water from oceans, rivers, lakes, and streams. Rain and snow deliver this water back to Earth. The water cycle is this chain of evaporation and condensation, where water turns to vapor and back to liquid again. Heat accelerates evaporation; cooling leads to condensation. You can illustrate this cycle using hot water and ice.

CLOUDBURST

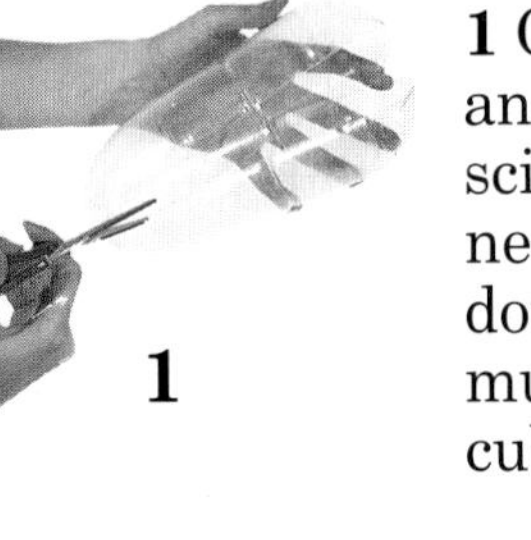

1 Clean a plastic soda bottle and remove the label. With scissors, carefully cut off the neck and make a wide opening down one side. The opening must be big enough for ice cubes. (Put these in last.)

2 From an empty cereal box cut out the forested mountain slope shown here. Make the front tree section lower than the rear sky section. Paint the scene to look like a real mountainside.

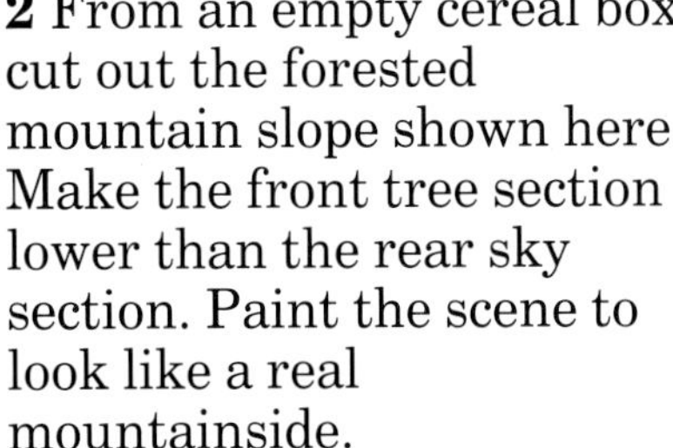

3 Make sure that the bottle fits inside the box as shown. It will be your cloud.

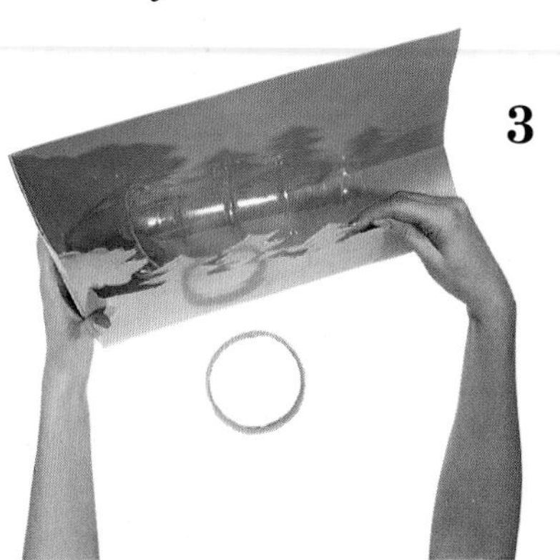

6 Place an aluminum foil dish inside the bottom of the cereal box as shown. Fill the dish with hot water from a kettle. Be careful!

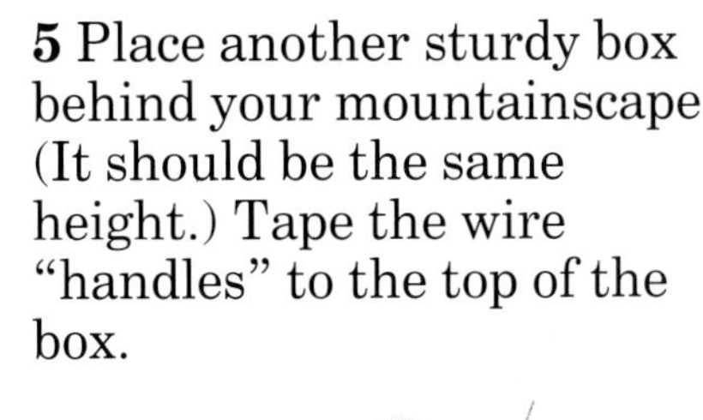

5 Place another sturdy box behind your mountainscape. (It should be the same height.) Tape the wire "handles" to the top of the box.

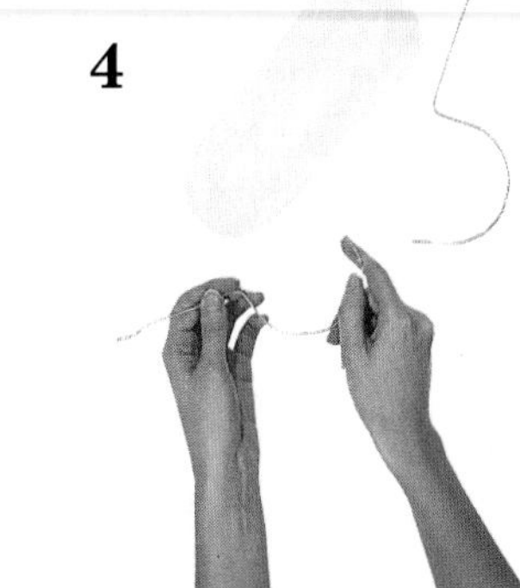

4 Ask a grown-up to cut a wire coat hanger into two lengths. Curve each piece of wire to fit around the plastic bottle. These metal loops will support the ice-filled bottle.

WHY IT WORKS

The sun's heat (1) fills molecules, or tiny particles, of surface water with energy, causing them to rise from the mass of water and escape into the air as water vapor (2). Trapped in the cool air, they condense around dust particles as droplets of water. These droplets join as the air cools, forming clouds (3). When the drops become too big and heavy to stay in the air, rain falls (4). The rainwater runs off the land back into the sea in rivers and streams (5).

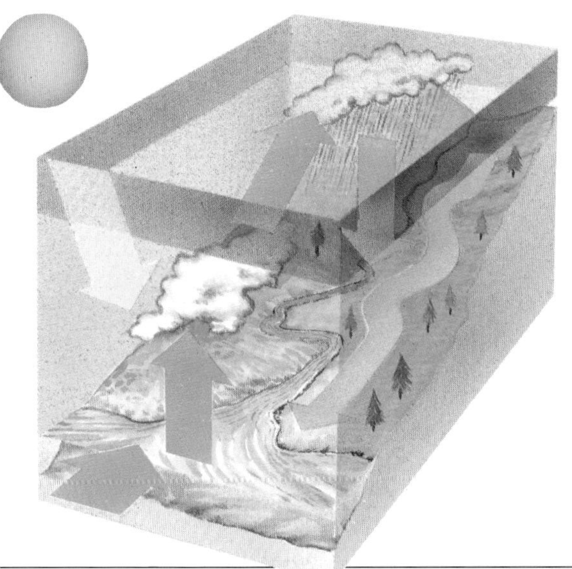

BRIGHT IDEAS

Measure rainfall with a rain gauge.

Carefully cut the top off a dishwashing liquid bottle and set it upside down inside the bottom half like a funnel. Mark 1/8- or 1/16-inch divisions from the bottom of the container. Stand it outside in an exposed place. Keep a daily record – remember to empty the gauge every time.

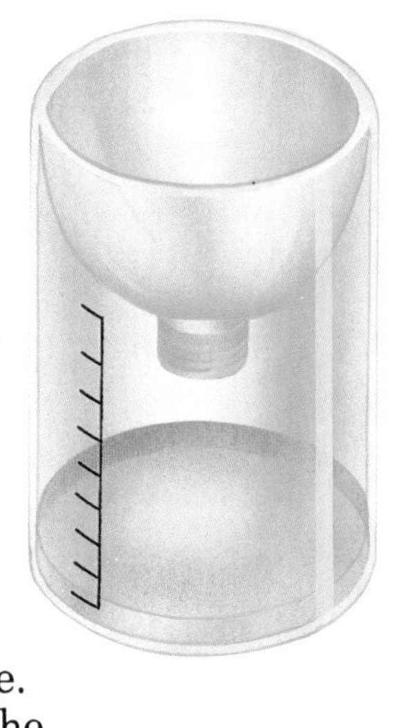

Take two bowls filled to the brim with water. Stand one in a sunny place, the other in the shade. Compare the water levels at the end of each day to measure evaporation.

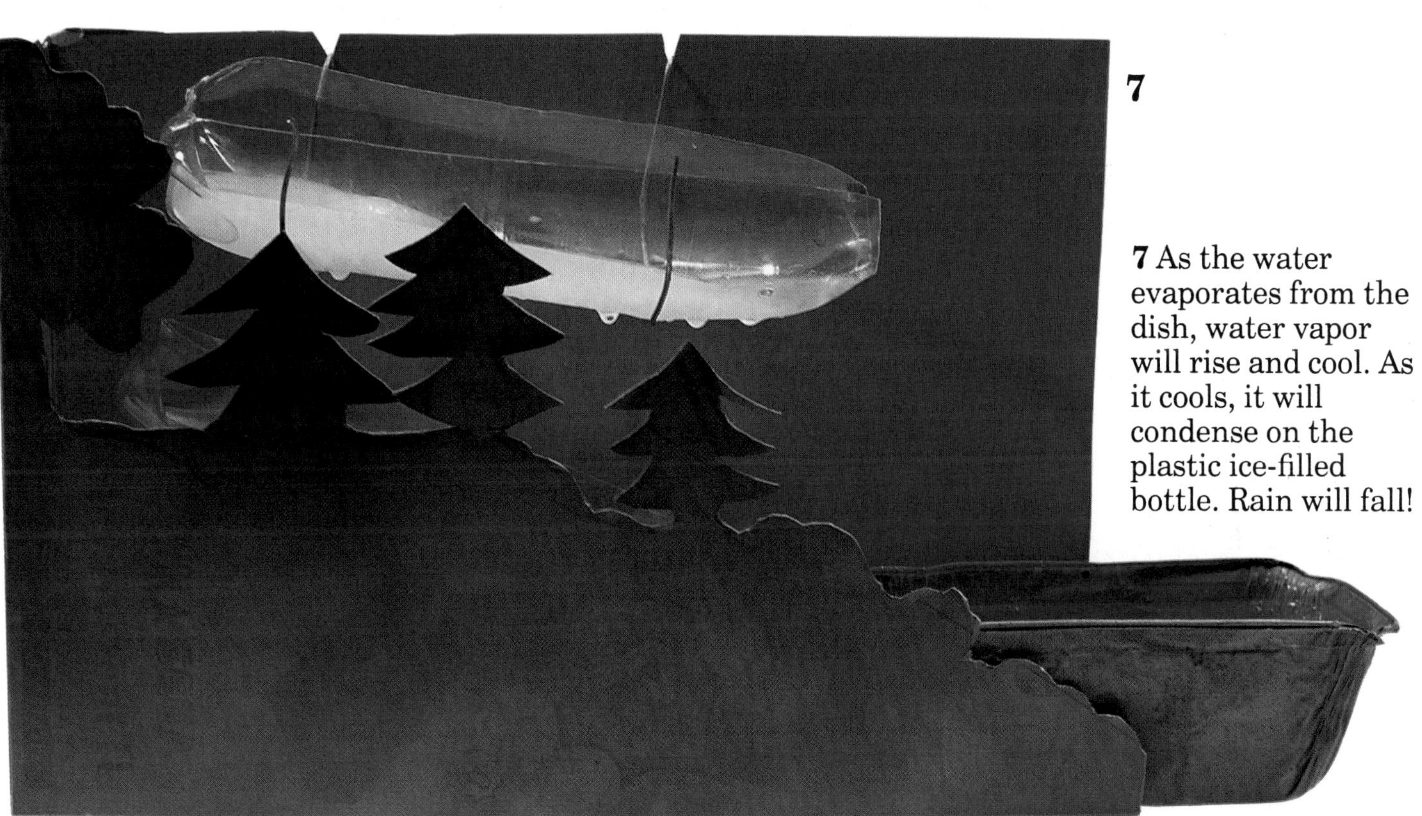

7

7 As the water evaporates from the dish, water vapor will rise and cool. As it cools, it will condense on the plastic ice-filled bottle. Rain will fall!

WHAT IS AN EARTHQUAKE?

An earthquake is the sudden, and often violent, trembling of part of the earth's surface. It sends shock waves racing through the earth's crust, which is the name given to the rocky outer layer surrounding the earth. Earthquakes are generated in the huge tilelike sections, called plates, which make up this crust.

A plate boundary is the area where two of these plates meet. Continual movement at plate boundaries creates a buildup of pressure beneath the surface. Rocks are elastic up to a point and can absorb the strain from this pressure for hundreds, even thousands, of years. Eventually, however, they snap, or rupture, at their weakest point, relieving the enormous strain. Huge amounts of energy are released as shock waves, called seismic waves, radiate outward from the point where the rocks fractured. The area within the earth's crust where the shock waves begin is called the earthquake's focus. The place on the surface directly above the focus is the epicenter.

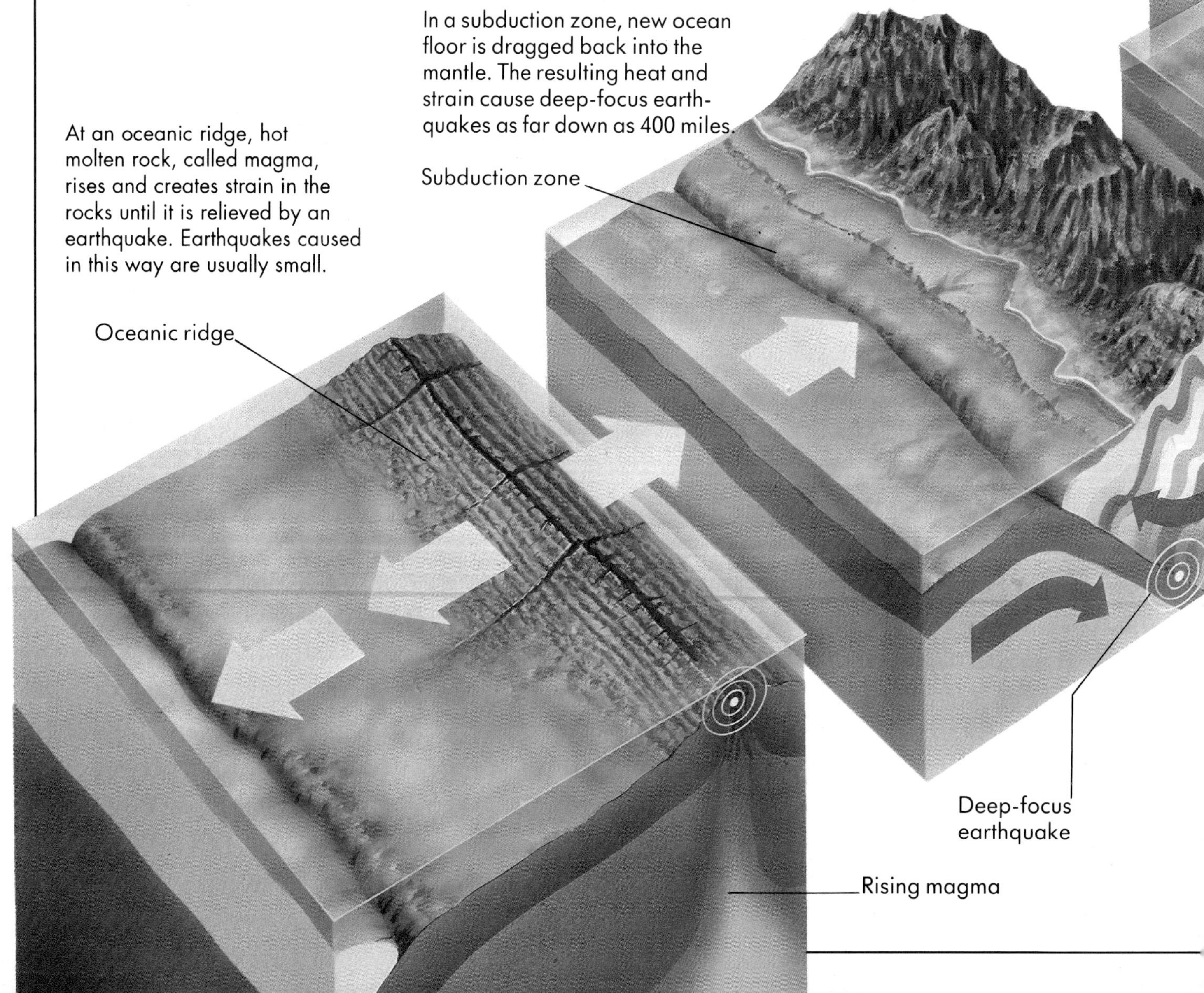

In a subduction zone, new ocean floor is dragged back into the mantle. The resulting heat and strain cause deep-focus earthquakes as far down as 400 miles.
At an oceanic ridge, hot molten rock, called magma, rises and creates strain in the rocks until it is relieved by an earthquake. Earthquakes caused in this way are usually small.
Subduction zone
Oceanic ridge
Deep-focus earthquake
Rising magma

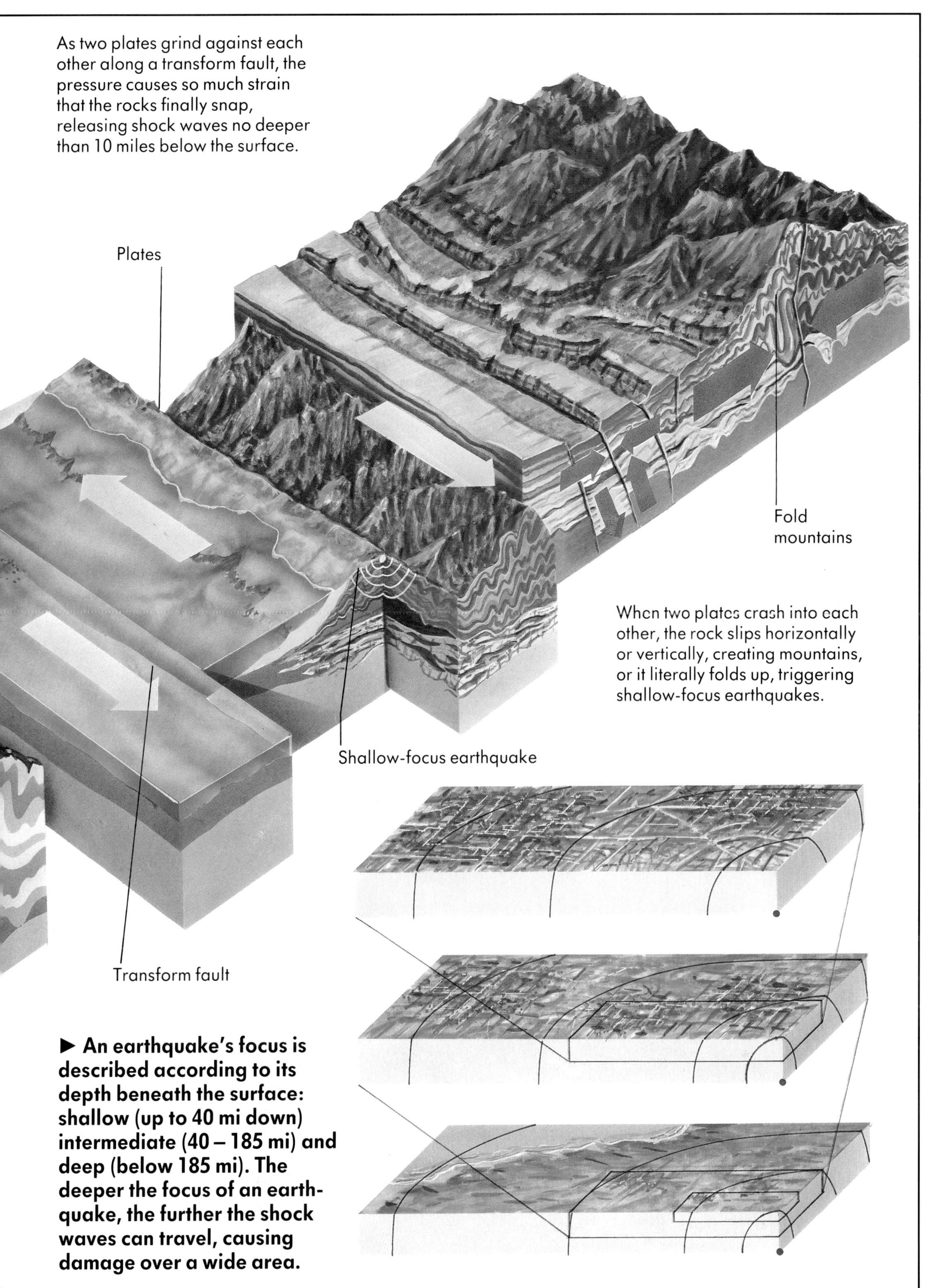

As two plates grind against each other along a transform fault, the pressure causes so much strain that the rocks finally snap, releasing shock waves no deeper than 10 miles below the surface.
Plates
Fold mountains
When two plates crash into each other, the rock slips horizontally or vertically, creating mountains, or it literally folds up, triggering shallow-focus earthquakes.
Shallow-focus earthquake
Transform fault

► An earthquake's focus is described according to its depth beneath the surface: shallow (up to 40 mi down) intermediate (40 – 185 mi) and deep (below 185 mi). The deeper the focus of an earthquake, the further the shock waves can travel, causing damage over a wide area.

CARS

U.S.-built Touring Stanley (1904)

STEAM CARS
Before the invention of the motor engine, some cars ran on steam (*above*). Such machines were restricted at first to a speed limit of 4 mph (6.5 kmh), later raised to 14 mph (22.5 kmh).

The first gas-driven cars were made possible by the invention of the internal-combustion engine in 1863. One hundred years later there are more than 95 million cars in the world. The internal-combustion engine, powered by coal-gas and air, was more compact and powerful than the steam engines that had been used previously. The first cars, produced during the 1880s by a German engineer, Karl Benz, were known as "horseless carriages" (*left*). Some were little more than gas-driven tricycles!

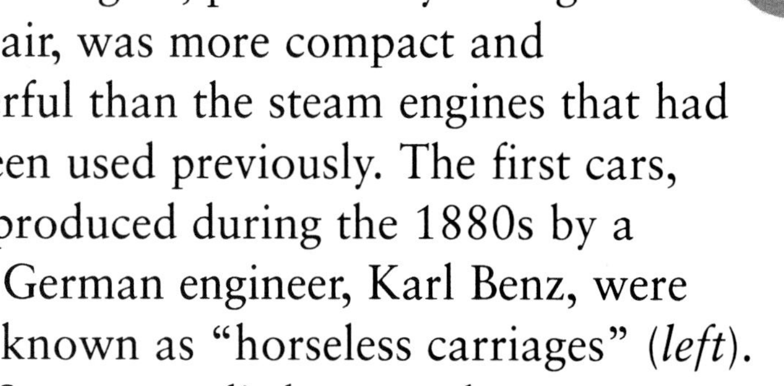

U.S.-built "horseless carriage" (1906)

Delahaye type-135 (1936)

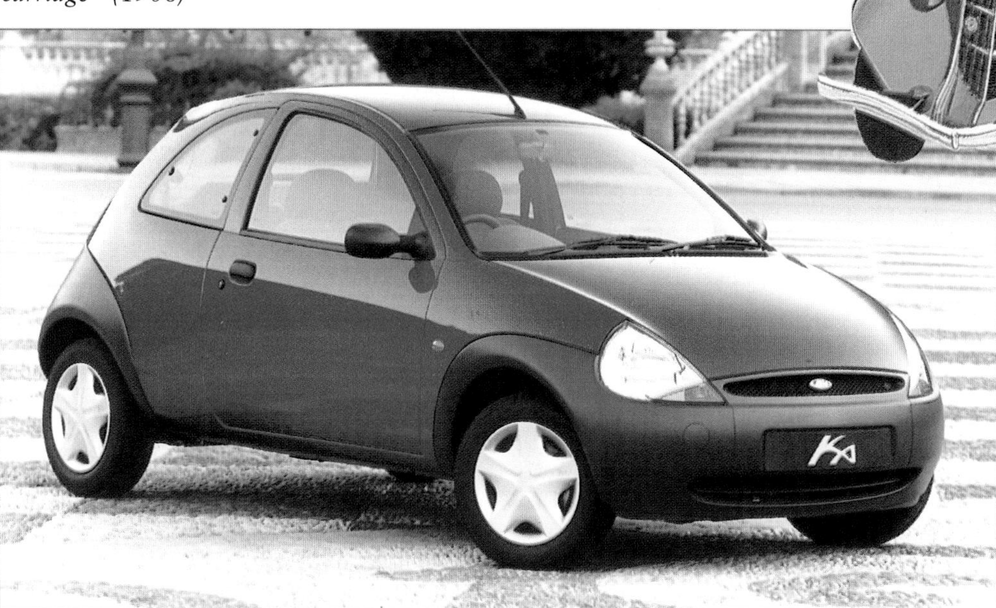

CARS FOR EVERYONE
In the 1930s, cars – such as the Delahaye type-135 (*above*) – were handmade by skilled craftsmen, and cost more than $1,500, then a huge sum of money. Cheaper, mass-produced cars were first made in the United States by Henry Ford. German Volkswagen Beetles (*below*), designed in the 1930s and first built in 1945, were marketed as "people's cars." They paved the way for the small cars of today (*above left*).

HENRY FORD (1863-1947)
In 1896, Henry Ford built his first car, the Quadricycle, mostly out of bicycle parts. His ambition was to build cars that everyone could afford. He set up an assembly line to build his famous "Model T." The firm he founded remains one of the world's most important companies.

HUMAN OR ROBOT HANDS

In 1913, Henry Ford introduced the moving assembly line (*below*), in which workers add parts to the cars as they pass. Many parts of modern mass-production cars are assembled by robots (*right*). The exact specifications of new models are fed into computers to enable engineers to accurately program the assembly-line robots.

Robotic arms "spot-welding" a body shell.

JAPANESE SUCCESS

In the 1980s, Japan overtook Britain, Germany, and the United States in car production. Japan's success is partly due to the efficient working methods in its factories and its investment in robotic welders, assemblers, and painters. As fuel became more expensive after the 1973 Arab-Israeli War, the Japanese sold millions of small cars that had the advantage of being cheap to run.

This is the EDSEL
"It acts the way it looks, but it doesn't cost that much"
The Edsel's eighteen elegantly styled models are priced through the range where most people buy
EDSEL
New member of the Ford family of fine cars

DRIVING INTO THE FUTURE

Cars in the future may be made from lightweight materials such as aluminum and carbon-fiber, which would make them more economical on fuel. Electric cars, which run off rechargeable batteries, are another alternative (although power stations would still be used to make electricity). Solar-powered cars (*right*) have also been road-tested – but they need plenty of sunlight in order to work.

THE GAS GUZZLERS

During the 1950s large, sleek American cars with tail fins, chrome, and bright colors became popular (*above*). They were a sign of wealth. Although they used a great deal of gasoline, fuel was inexpensive in the 1950s.

WHAT IF MAMMALS LAID EGGS?

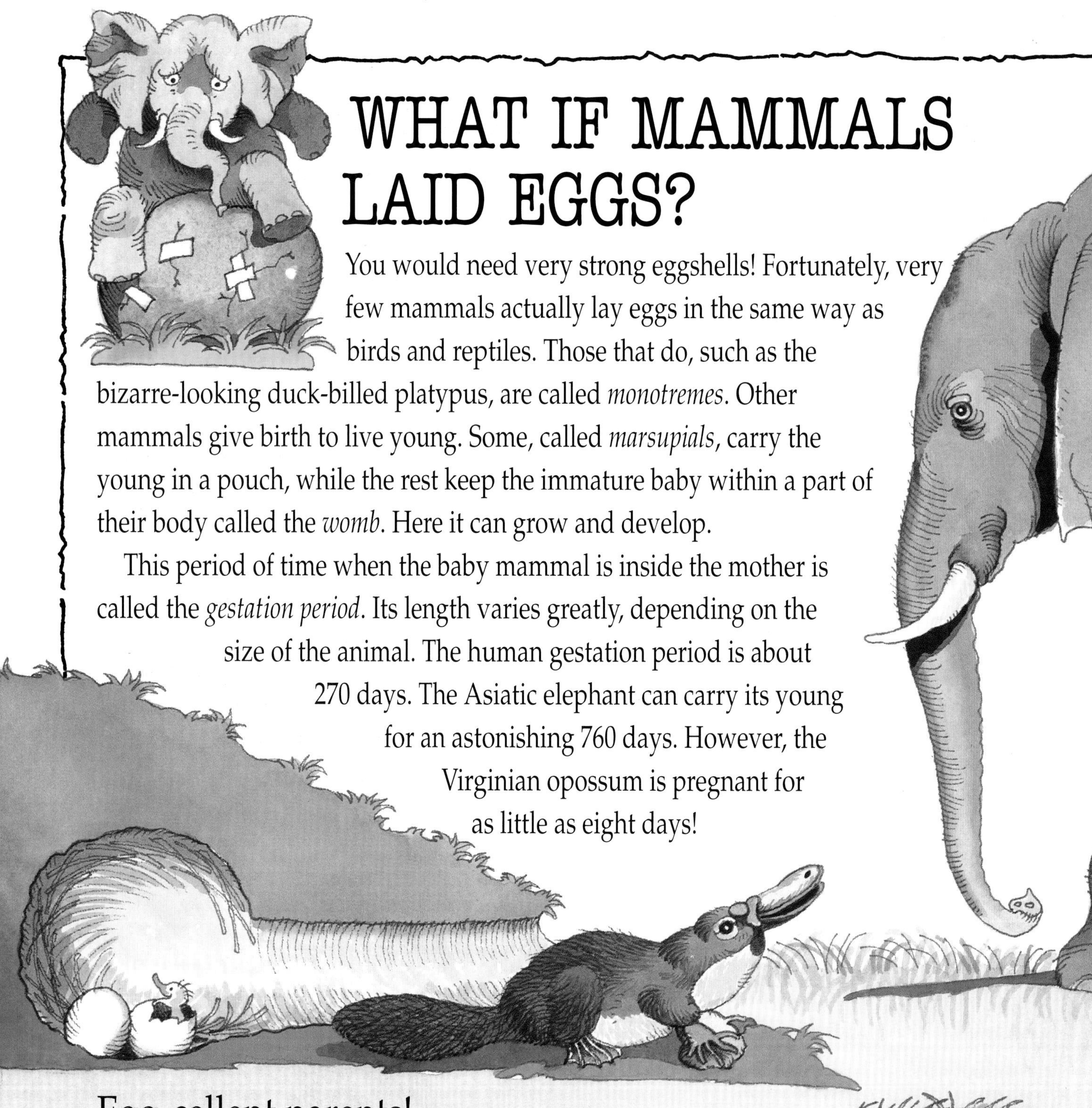

You would need very strong eggshells! Fortunately, very few mammals actually lay eggs in the same way as birds and reptiles. Those that do, such as the bizarre-looking duck-billed platypus, are called *monotremes*. Other mammals give birth to live young. Some, called *marsupials*, carry the young in a pouch, while the rest keep the immature baby within a part of their body called the *womb*. Here it can grow and develop.

This period of time when the baby mammal is inside the mother is called the *gestation period*. Its length varies greatly, depending on the size of the animal. The human gestation period is about 270 days. The Asiatic elephant can carry its young for an astonishing 760 days. However, the Virginian opossum is pregnant for as little as eight days!

Egg-cellent parents!

There are only three species of mammal that actually lay eggs. These are the duck-billed platypus (above), the long-beaked echidna (right), and the short-beaked echidna, which all live in Australasia. The duck-billed platypus usually lays two eggs in an underground den. These eggs are covered in a tough leathery shell to protect them.

After about ten to twelve days in the den, the babies hatch from their eggs and feed on milk. This is produced by special glands on the mother.

Eggs without shells

Although most mammals don't lay eggs like birds or reptiles, they all (including humans) produce tiny, microscopic eggs from organs inside the female, called *ovaries*. After mating, these eggs may be fertilized with sperm from the male, they embed themselves into an area of the mother's womb. The baby grows here, protected from the outside world and fed by nutrients that pass from the mother's blood. These nutrients are passed from the mother to the baby through an organ called the *placenta*, and along the umbilical cord. Once the baby has developed enough, it is born. It passes from the womb, through the birth canal, and out into the world.

What if a kangaroo didn't have a pouch on its belly?

It would have to find some other way of carrying around its young. Kangaroos give birth to very immature, furless babies. The tiny creature has to crawl through its mother's fur, into the pouch, where it attaches itself to one of four milk teats.

The pouch is called a *marsupium*, and mammals that have this are referred to as marsupials. These include possums, opossums, koalas, and wombats.

THE EXPLORATION OF AFRICA

A flotilla of small boats, including a dismantled 80-foot steamboat (*left*), were being carried hundreds of miles across the high plains between the Congo and the White Nile. The sight was one of the most extraordinary Africa had ever seen.

The purpose of Jean-Baptiste Marchand's bizarre expedition was to claim the upper Nile for France and prevent British expansion from Egypt. Marchand duly hoisted the French flag at Fashoda in 1898 and waited to see what would happen. A few months later, General Kitchener arrived with a large British force. Only skillful diplomacy prevented war and the two European powers divided large tracts of northeast Africa between them.

Within 20 years, small groups of explorers had led two full-scale military expeditions to back up territorial claims.

KING SOLOMON'S MINES. In 1885, novelist Sir Henry Rider Haggard wrote the ultimate novel about African exploration. *King Solomon's Mines*, set in southern Africa, tells how a trio of Englishmen overcome numerous perils to restore an African king to his rightful inheritance. Finally, they discover the long-lost treasure of King Solomon and return home as wealthy men. The book was made into a film, starring Richard Chamberlain (*above*), in 1985.

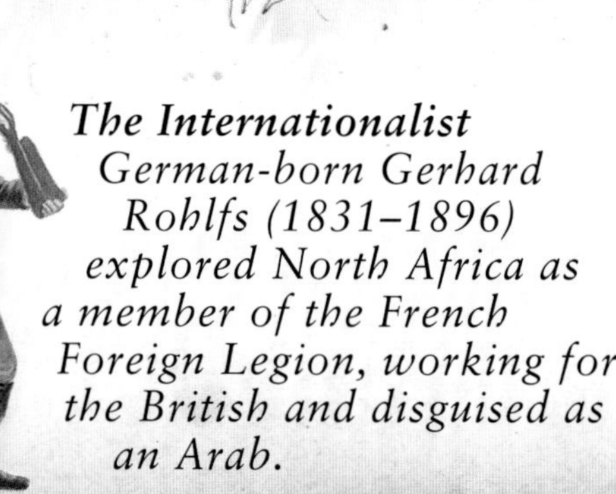

The Internationalist
German-born Gerhard Rohlfs (1831–1896) explored North Africa as a member of the French Foreign Legion, working for the British and disguised as an Arab.

The British and the Boers

Dutch farmers (known as "Boers") were the first Europeans to settle in Africa. Shortly after the British bought South Africa in 1814, the Boers left on a "Great Trek" north to establish their own republics. However, envious of the Boers' gold fields, the British were drawn into the long and costly Boer War (1899–1901, *far right*).

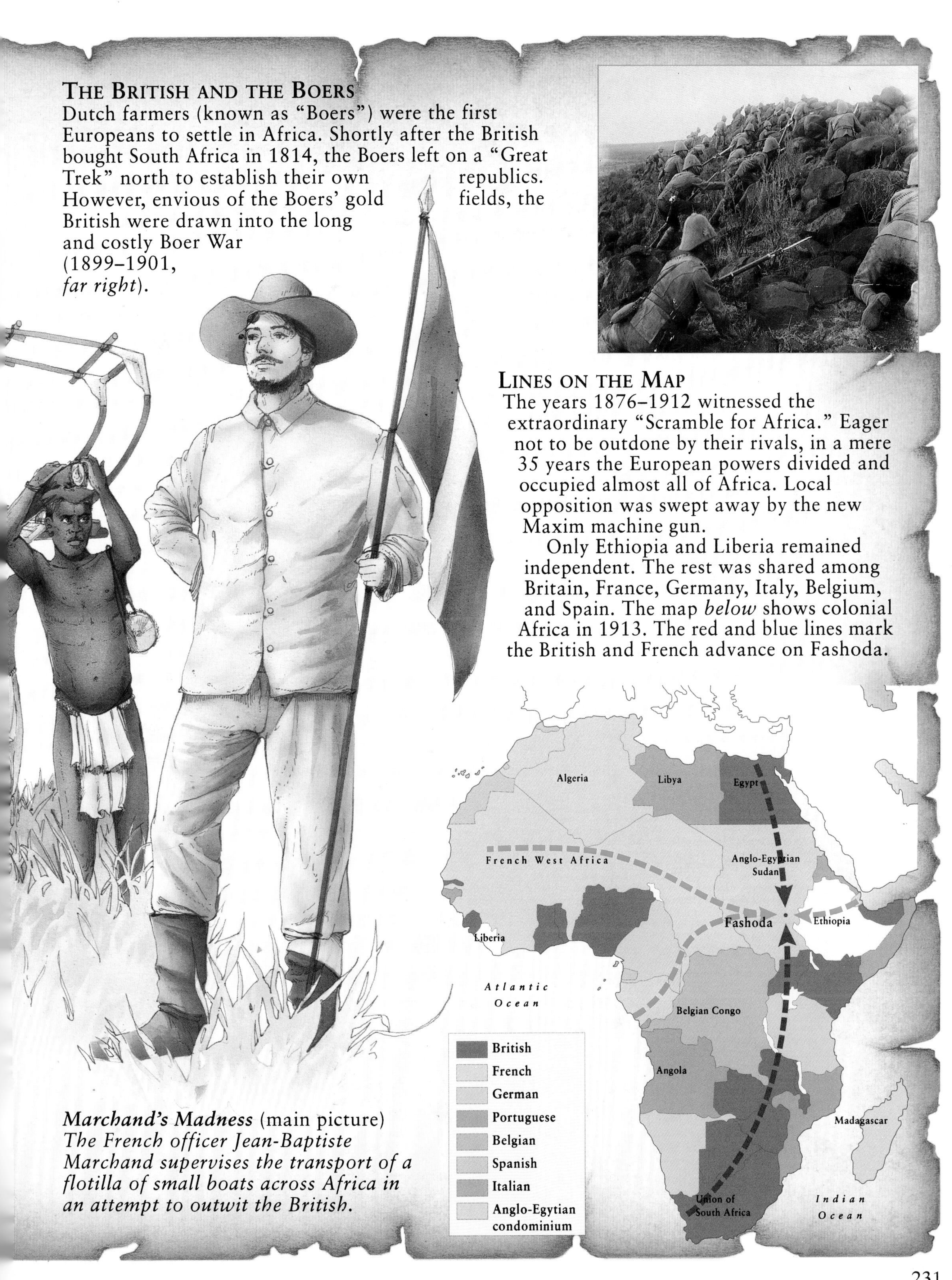

Lines on the Map

The years 1876–1912 witnessed the extraordinary "Scramble for Africa." Eager not to be outdone by their rivals, in a mere 35 years the European powers divided and occupied almost all of Africa. Local opposition was swept away by the new Maxim machine gun.

Only Ethiopia and Liberia remained independent. The rest was shared among Britain, France, Germany, Italy, Belgium, and Spain. The map *below* shows colonial Africa in 1913. The red and blue lines mark the British and French advance on Fashoda.

Marchand's Madness (main picture) *The French officer Jean-Baptiste Marchand supervises the transport of a flotilla of small boats across Africa in an attempt to outwit the British.*

FOSSIL FUELS

Coal, oil, and natural gas are known as fossil fuels. They were formed from plants and the tiny creatures that lived on them, which were buried and subjected to the heat and pressure of the Earth over many millions of years. As energy from the Sun is stored in plant leaves as potential chemical energy (by photosynthesis), fossil fuels are a form of stored solar energy. The amounts available are large, but one day they will run out. Until then, we can use them as fuel and as raw materials for plastics, fertilizers, and chemicals.

Vincent Van Gogh

The painter Vincent Van Gogh (1853-1890) knew a lot about coal-mining communities, as he spent some time working as a missionary among the miners before becoming a painter in 1880. His early paintings were mainly of people in their work places, such as *The Return of the Miners* (below).

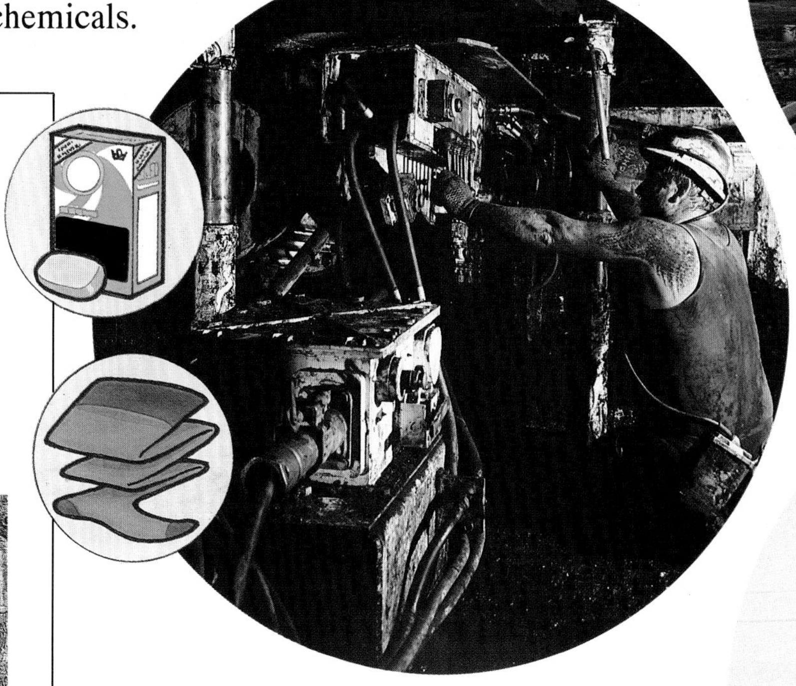

Coal deposits vary in location as well as quality. Coal can be extracted from near the surface by opencast mining. Often, however, the seam is deep underground and vertical shafts must be dug down to the seam. Tunnels or galleries are then cut into the seam as the coal is extracted.

SWOPS

When oil is found under the oceans, huge production platforms can be built to extract it. But if the well is small the cost may not be justified. Then a wellhead can be placed on the seabed, and oil pumped up to a tanker above, in a system called SWOPS – the Single Well Oil Production System. A single tanker, with room for 300,000 barrels, can serve up to three small fields.

seismic truck

the SWOPS system

The study of sound, or seismic, waves in the solid earth can help companies to locate oil and gas. Trucks can be fitted with equipment which sends controlled sounds into the earth.

Coal gas has now been replaced by cleaner natural gas, found in reservoirs in the Earth's crust, often with oil. It consists mainly of methane. The cheapest fuel available, gas is ideal for heating.

Gas lighting

In 1792 a Scottish engineer, William Murdoch, produced gas by heating coal in a closed container. By 1814 the first streets were lit by gas in London. However, really good lights were not available until 1885.

Swampland

Plants and animals flourished on Earth 300 million years ago. At that time, large areas of the Earth were swampy forests. These waterlogged conditions preserved the vegetation as part of its slow change to coal.

Crude oil is a heavy liquid that must be broken down, or refined, before being used. The process used to refine oil is distillation, and is based on the fact that different parts (fractions) of oil boil at different temperatures. The lightest fractions make petrol, with heavier fractions being used for heavy fuel oil and tar.

Oil is less plentiful than coal, and is found where rocks prevent it escaping. Exploration rigs all over the world drill through ice and sea in the hope of striking oil. When they do, pipelines and tankers take it away. It is so valuable that its discovery can make a country very wealthy.

D.H. Lawrence

Coal mining was a major industry in the 19th century and produced mining communities around pits. It was a dangerous job which bred a strong community spirit. The novelist D.H. Lawrence (1885-1935), the son of a miner, wrote novels centered in these communities from his own life and experience.

MARBLING AND RUBBING

Marbling paper is fun, and can produce the most amazing results for you to use in collage. You will need oil paint, linseed oil, turpentine, a bowl and some jelly jars. Cover your working area with newspaper, and follow the instructions below.

Rubbings

Rubbings are impressions of textures in color. Look around you for objects with interesting textures. Place a sheet of thin paper over each, and rub the paper with colored crayon, pencil, or chalk.

▷ ***"When you've produced a number of rubbings and marbled papers in different colors, study them and see what the different textures remind you of. Use them to make a collage, perhaps a landscape like the one on the right."***

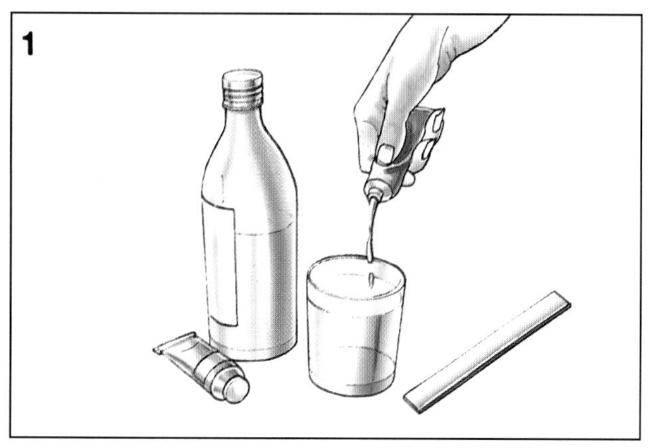

△ ***"In a jelly jar, mix up one teaspoonful of linseed oil with two of turpentine. Add six inches of paint squeezed from a tube, and stir the mixture with a stick."***

△ ***"Make up several jelly jars with different colors. Fill a bowl with water. Pour in a jar of paint. The mixture will float on the surface of the water. Stir it again."***

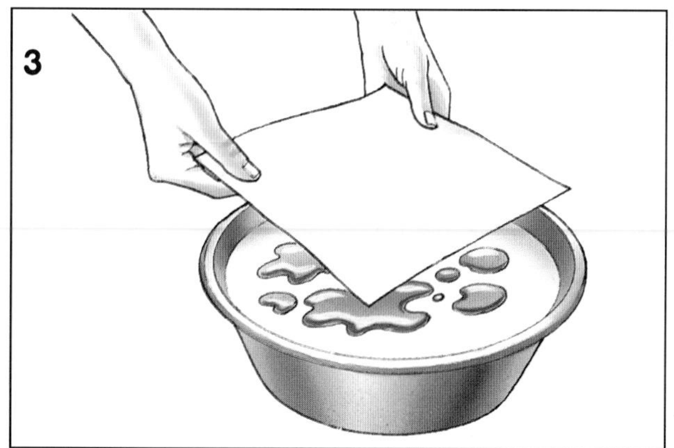

△ ***"Take a piece of plain paper and gently lay it on the surface of the water. Lift it off again almost immediately, and let the excess water drain off. Lie it flat to dry."***

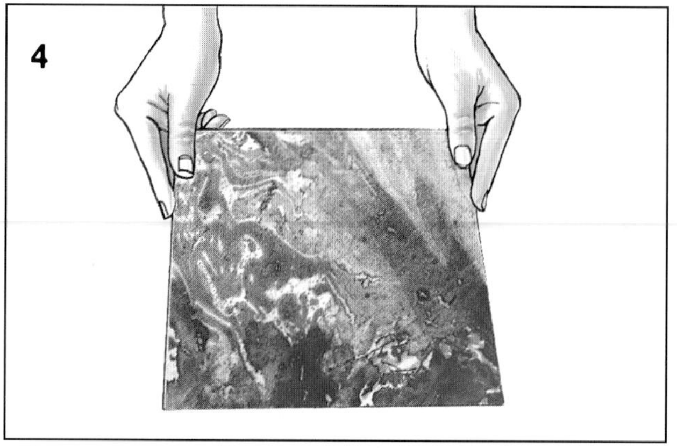

△ ***"Your paper will now be marbled. You could immerse it again in a different color, or add a new color to the water and try again with a fresh sheet."***

Making a good impression
Below are some examples of different textures obtained by rubbing. Try rubbings of coins and the grain of wood.

Many kitchen utensils also have interesting textures – try a cheese grater, a sieve, and a straw place mat. You'll discover a new world at your fingertips!

THE STEAM ENGINE

Ah, the Golden Age of Steam. Locomotives puffing across the countryside, and steam-powered machines clanking away on farms and in factories. Watt happened to steam engines? They were noisy, dirty, and inefficient, that's watt! So they aren't used much today. But for a time, steam power was the invention of the Industrial Revolution – which changed our world forever.

Hero, of Ancient Greece, made a simple engine using steam. But the modern Age of Steam began with Thomas Savery, an English military engineer, in about 1698.

Tin was a valuable metal. But the tin mines in Cornwall were often flooded by water seeping through the rocks. Savery's engine pumped out the water.

A fire heated water in a boiler, to give off steam. This passed into a large iron vessel, the condenser. Water sprayed over the outside, and the steam inside cooled and condensed into water. This left a vacuum, which sucked water up a pipe from the mine. More steam pushed the water away along another pipe.

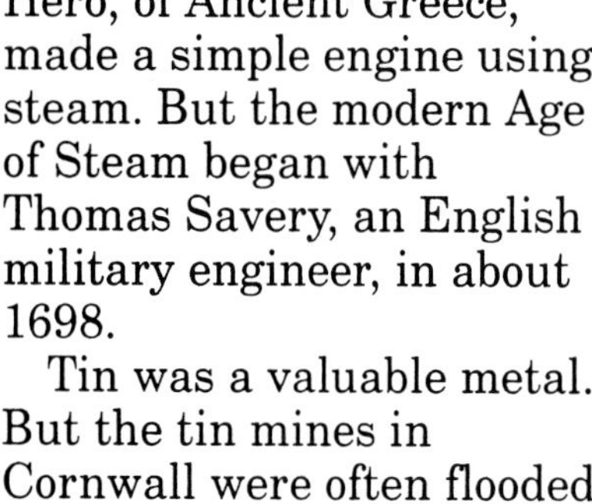

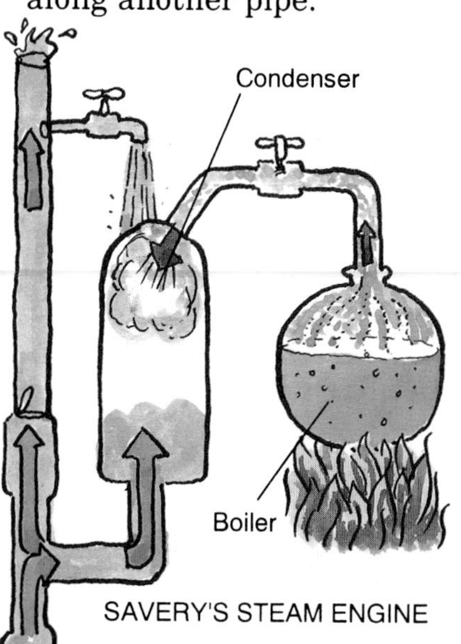

SAVERY'S STEAM ENGINE

Another Thomas
An English ironmonger, Thomas Newcomen, made the next advance in 1712. His engines pumped water from coal mines near Birmingham.

Newcomen's steam engine

The Newcomen version had a piston inside a cylinder. Steam was let into the bottom of the cylinder as the piston moved up. Then water sprayed onto the cylinder and condensed the steam, making a vacuum which sucked the piston down. The piston's up-and-down movements rocked a crossbeam that worked a water pump.

Guess Watt's next . . .

The father of steam
Yes, it's famous Scottish engineer, James Watt. He did not invent the steam engine. But by the 1780s he had made several great improvements.

One was a separate condenser, to change the steam back into water. This meant the main cylinder did not have to heat up and cool down all the time, which wasted energy. Another improvement was squirting steam into one side of the cylinder, to push the piston one way, then squirting it into the other side, to push the piston back. Yet another Watt advance was to change the up-and-down motion of a piston into the round-and-round motion of a wheel, using a connecting rod. Steam power had arrived!

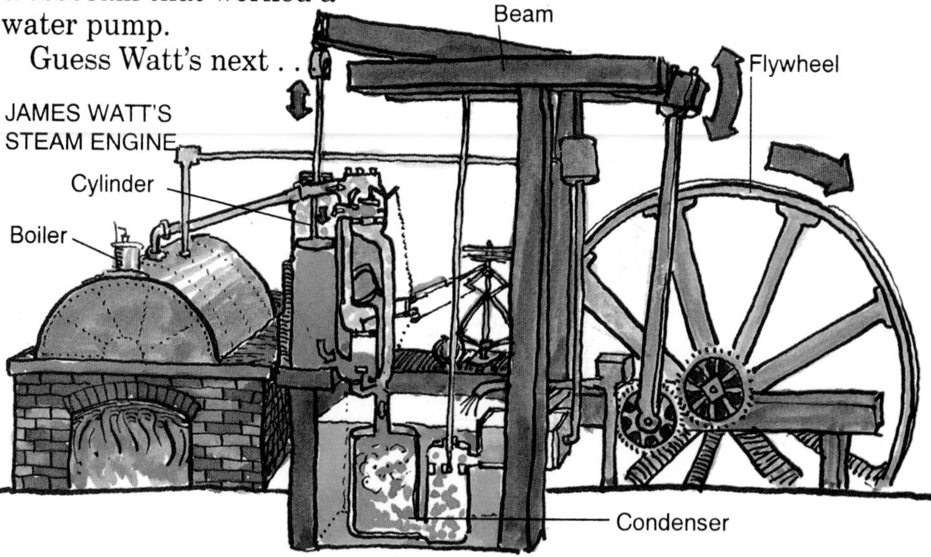

JAMES WATT'S STEAM ENGINE

The coming of the railroads

Richard Trevithick was a mine engineer in Cornwall, England. Many mines at the time had iron rails, for hauling wagons. Trevithick put railroad wheels on a Watt-type steam engine and made the first locomotive, for mine work, in 1804.

Steam locomotives were soon chugging along the surface. The first steam passenger railroad opened in 1825 between Stockton and Darlington, in northern England. Its locomotive Locomotion was designed by George Stephenson. In 1829, Stephenson's better locomotive Rocket pulled railroad wagons weighing 20 tons at 25 mph.

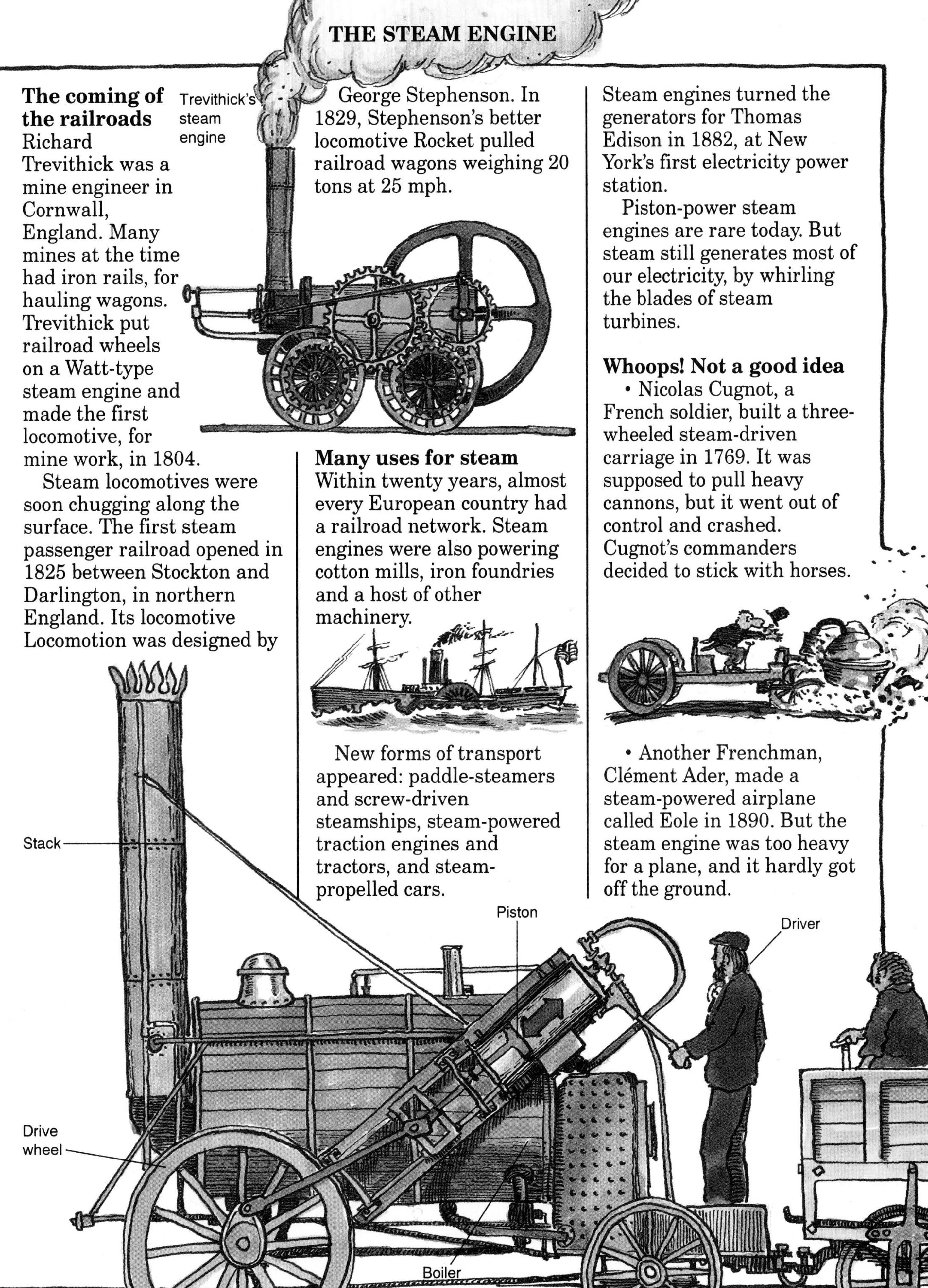

Many uses for steam

Within twenty years, almost every European country had a railroad network. Steam engines were also powering cotton mills, iron foundries and a host of other machinery.

New forms of transport appeared: paddle-steamers and screw-driven steamships, steam-powered traction engines and tractors, and steam-propelled cars.

Steam engines turned the generators for Thomas Edison in 1882, at New York's first electricity power station.

Piston-power steam engines are rare today. But steam still generates most of our electricity, by whirling the blades of steam turbines.

Whoops! Not a good idea

- Nicolas Cugnot, a French soldier, built a three-wheeled steam-driven carriage in 1769. It was supposed to pull heavy cannons, but it went out of control and crashed. Cugnot's commanders decided to stick with horses.

- Another Frenchman, Clément Ader, made a steam-powered airplane called Eole in 1890. But the steam engine was too heavy for a plane, and it hardly got off the ground.

The Stuff of LEGENDS

When something really exciting happens, people like to tell the story over and over again. Unless it is written down immediately, it changes as time passes. Details get left out; others are added; the deeds of two or more people can be credited to one "super-hero." Over time, people even forget what some things were or what they meant, so they invent explanations – which are often wrong! A story might be given a new meaning so that it fits in with the politics and religion of the time. But somewhere, buried in every story, there remains a kernel of truth.

CONQUISTADORES!
The early Spanish conquerors of America were driven by a desire to serve God (by converting people to Christianity) and their king (by winning him an empire). But they were also ruthless and greedy, out to make their own fortunes from the gold and silver of the "New World." In Colombia, they heard the fantastic but true story of El Dorado – the "Gilded Man."

THE ULTIMATE QUEST
People have searched all over the world for Atlantis, but many now believe that the story was inspired by Minoan Crete . The memory of the great island kingdom with its powerful navy, the importance of bulls in its religion, and its sudden decline had become mixed up with natural disasters and myths. The stories were muddled and misunderstood as time passed, but some accounts do seem to contain an echo of the great Minoan civilization.

The golden ruler

When a king came to the throne in the region of Lake Guatavita, Colombia, he was covered in gold dust then sailed to the middle of the lake, where he threw in gold offerings to the gods. Imagination and greed embroidered the story, and tales spread, of a city and a land made of gold. For two centuries, people searched for "El Dorado" and it cost many lives. Others tried to drain the lake, but failed.

Eruption and devastation

Thera (now Santorini), 72 miles (120 km) north of Crete, was an outpost of Minoan culture. In about 1450 B.C.*, there was a huge volcanic eruption which blew away most of the island. It also caused a tidal wave that wrecked Minoan settlements in northern Crete.*

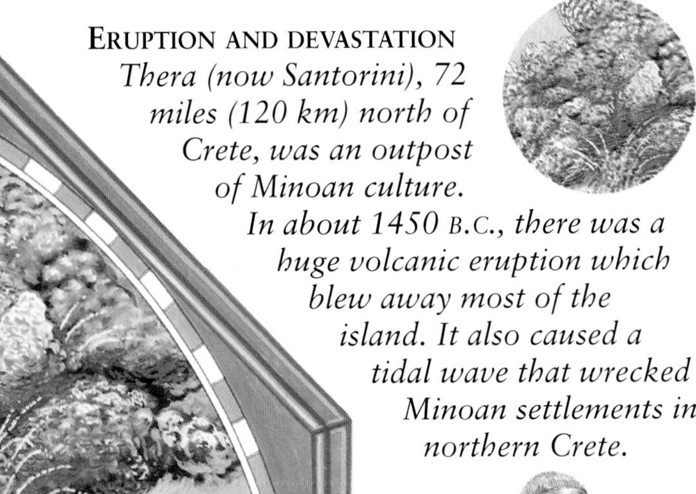

The stuff of legends

The Greek writer Plato (above) wrote about Atlantis, a lost island kingdom which sank below the waves in a terrible disaster. Debates have raged ever since. Did Plato invent it? Was it based on Thera and Crete? Or was it another lost place? The tale had been passed on by word of mouth for almost 200 years before Plato heard it – plenty of time for errors to creep in!

King Solomon's mines

Some people have embarked on quests for things mentioned in the Bible – the Ark of the Covenant, the treasure from the temple of Jerusalem, Noah's Ark, and many others. Others have looked for places. The fabulous mines of King Solomon caught people's imagination and inspired films and novels. When the ruins of Great Zimbabwe (below) were found in Africa, some suggested that these were the famous mines. But Zimbabwe belongs to a much later African empire. Solomon's mines remain out of our grasp.

Can texts really lead us to lost places? Ancient Mesopotamian texts refer to a place called Dilmun, describing it as so wonderful that, until recently, scholars dismissed it as fantasy. Studies of earlier texts and ruins have shown that it was a staging post in the trade between Sumer and the Indus Valley. When the trade ceased, Dilmun was forgotten – in fact, it was the island of Bahrain!

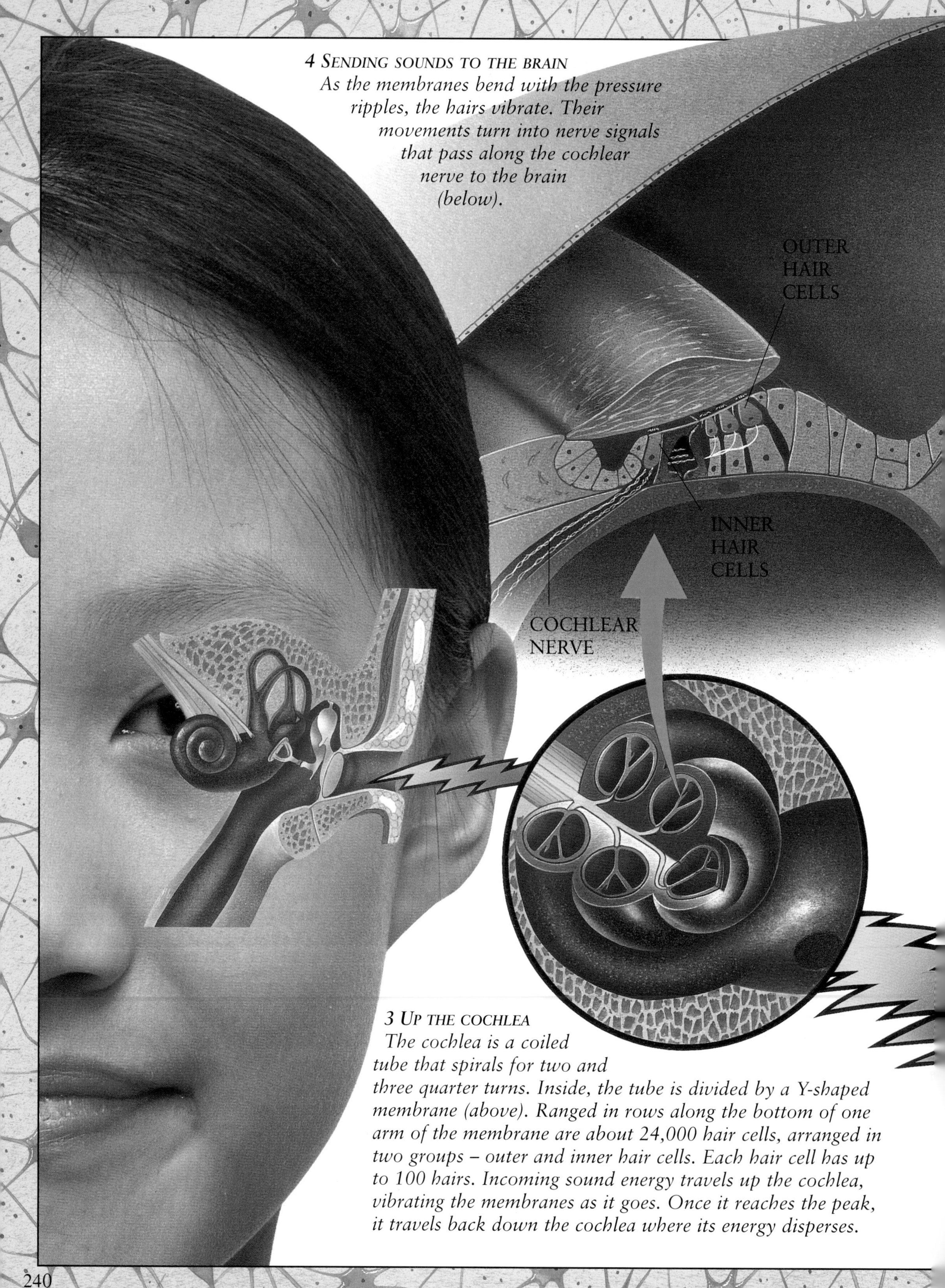

4 Sending sounds to the brain

As the membranes bend with the pressure ripples, the hairs vibrate. Their movements turn into nerve signals that pass along the cochlear nerve to the brain (below).

3 Up the cochlea

The cochlea is a coiled tube that spirals for two and three quarter turns. Inside, the tube is divided by a Y-shaped membrane (above). Ranged in rows along the bottom of one arm of the membrane are about 24,000 hair cells, arranged in two groups – outer and inner hair cells. Each hair cell has up to 100 hairs. Incoming sound energy travels up the cochlea, vibrating the membranes as it goes. Once it reaches the peak, it travels back down the cochlea where its energy disperses.

INSIDE THE EAR

LIKE ALL OTHER SENSE ORGANS, the ear converts one type of energy – in this case, the energy of sound waves – into tiny electrical nerve signals. This transformation happens deep inside the ear, in the snail-shaped organ of hearing called the cochlea. This grape-sized part is embedded and protected inside the skull, just behind and below your eye.

The whole of the ear is divided into three main parts – the inner, middle, and outer ear. The outer ear is made up of the funnel-shaped piece of flesh that sits on the side of your head and the ear canal. The middle ear consists of the eardrum and the three ear bones. Finally, the inner ear is made up of the cochlea and the cochlear nerve.

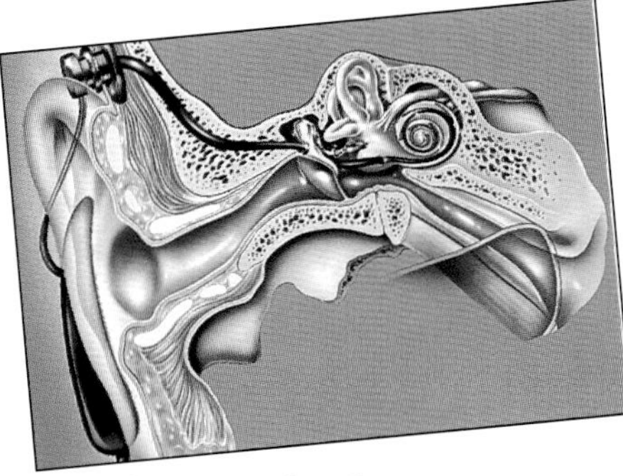

Should the cochlea or ear bones become damaged, hearing may be lost. Doctors can restore hearing by using an artificial implant (above). This has a microphone that converts sounds into electronic pulses. These are sent down a wire into the cochlea, where they stimulate the cochlear nerve.

2 INTO THE COCHLEA
The base or foot of the stapes is attached to a thin, flexible part of the cochlear wall. As the stapes tilts and pushes in and out like a piston, it transfers waves or ripples of pressure along the fluid inside the cochlea.

STAPES
INCUS
MALLEUS
EARDRUM

COCHLEA

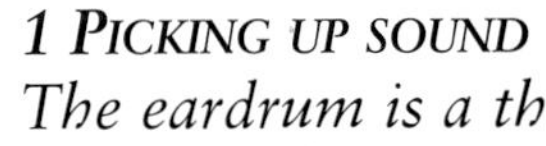

1 PICKING UP SOUND
The eardrum is a thin, tight sheet of skin-like material. Sound waves bounce off it, making it vibrate. These vibrations are passed along the three ear bones, or ossicles: malleus, incus, and stapes. The bones pass the vibrations to the cochlea.

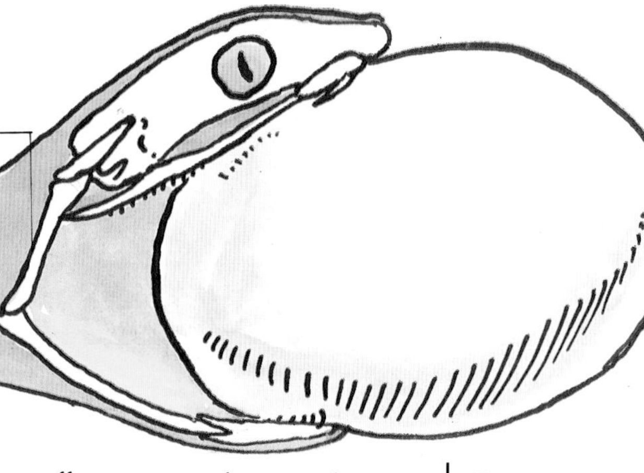
Jaw bones dislocate themselves when swallowing huge objects

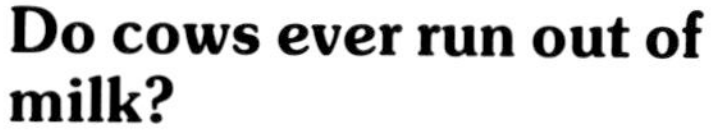
Egg-eating snake

How does a snake swallow something bigger than its head?
Some snakes, such as pythons and egg-eating snakes, can swallow things that are many times bigger than their heads. For example, a large python with a head less than a foot (30 centimeters) across can swallow an antelope with a body over a yard wide. The main secret to this is that their jaws can dislocate themselves and come apart. Also, the skin at the side of the mouth can stretch enormously. This means that the snake can make its mouth, and so its head, many times larger.

Do cows ever run out of milk?
A cow can carry on producing milk for most of its life. But only as long as it is milked regularly. When a cow has a calf, it starts to produce milk. It will continue to provide milk as long as the calf needs it. A cow's udders, therefore, produce milk for as long as milk is taken from them. But illness or a bad shock can stop a cow from producing milk. A milking cow normally has a calf each year.

How do homing pigeons find their way home?
They use many different clues, including the magnetic field of the Earth, the position of the Sun, and familiar landmarks. Pigeons have found their way home when they were released halfway across the continent.

Do fish sleep?
When fish sleep, their bodies slow down, but their brain wave patterns don't change. They have no eyelids so they can't close their eyes, but they do become rather less aware of their surroundings. So fish do sleep, but not quite in the way that most animals do.

Why do I find spiders in the bathtub?

The main reason is that they get stuck there. There are more spiders than you realize walking around in houses. Once a spider has walked into a bathtub, the sides are too slippery for it to climb out again. The bathtub acts like a kind of spider trap.

Why do cats purr?

Like all animal noises, a cat's purr is a form of communication. It shows pleasure, comfort, and friendship. Cats are unusual because they have two sets of vocal cords, one above the other. Many scientists think that they use the lower set for meows and high-pitched noises, and the higher set for growls, purring, and low-pitched noises.

Why don't fish living in the Arctic sea freeze?

The temperature of the water in the Arctic sea can be below the normal freezing temperature of water. This is because salt reduces the freezing point. Most fish do not have nearly as much salt in them as there is in the sea, so there is a real risk of the fish freezing. To avoid this, they have special substances (glycoproteins) in their bodies. These substances work just like the antifreeze you put in car radiators in winter.

Why do zebras have black and white stripes?

The stripes are for camouflage. This may seem surprising, because the stripes seem to make zebras very visible. But the stripes break up the outline of the zebra. At a distance, anything with a broken outline is more difficult to see. Stripes also help if a herd of zebras is being attacked. Many striped zebras all running together can confuse the attacker. Battleships in World War I had large striped patterns in black and white painted on them to prevent the enemy from finding the correct range.

Why do bats hang upside down?

Many species of bat roost in caves. They also live in other dark, sheltered places. It is much safer for bats to roost off the ground if they can. In caves, however, there is not much to hold on to except the roof. This means that bats have to hang upside down. Bats that live in caves have specially adapted claws to hold on to hard rock surfaces.

THE HORROR OF TAMBORA

The global weather changes caused by Tambora's eruption in 1815 inspired one of the great modern horror stories! Writers Percy and Mary Shelley and Lord Byron were staying at Lake Geneva, when the weather became oddly cold and dark for the time of year. Forced to stay indoors, they told ghost stories to suit the eerie mood and this inspired Mary Shelley to write her book Frankenstein *(*right*). Volcanoes erupt in different ways; Tambora was the most violent kind, in which clouds of hot gas, steam, and rock blast out from the volcano's crater (*left*).*

MOUNT PELÉE: NUCLEAR-FORCE EXPLOSION

*In 1902, Mount Pelée in Martinique exploded with the force of a nuclear bomb. A super-heated cloud of gas and ash burst out of the side of the mountain, engulfing the town of St. Pierre in fire. Three minutes later, the town ceased to exist. Of its 30,000 inhabitants, only a handful survived (*below*). The ships in the harbor sank; their passengers and crews boiled alive in the water.*

When Krakatoa erupted in 1883 (*right*), it was heard nearly 3,100 miles (5,000 km) away in Australia.

Active volcanoes almost seem to breathe... Observers of Sakura-Jima, in Japan, noticed how the volcano appeared to expand and contract as it filled up with magma (hot, melted rock).

PETRIFIED PEOPLE AT POMPEII

The ancient Roman city of Pompeii was overshadowed by a huge volcano, Vesuvius. When this erupted in 79 A.D., the whole city and its inhabitants were covered by 25 ft (8 m) of pumice and ash, which hardened around the bodies like wet cement, and created statuelike casts. These show the people at the moment of death, trying to protect themselves.

Historic volcanoes

"The whole mountain appeared like a body of liquid fire." *Eyewitness, Tambora, 1815*

The eruption of the volcano Tambora on an island in Indonesia (*right*) was the greatest in history, and caused worldwide destruction. Light ash fell over a 400-mile (640-km) area, followed by red-hot boulders that crushed hundreds of homes. Next, red-hot volcanic ash shot high into the atmosphere and blotted out the sun, reducing temperatures worldwide. Weather conditions changed dramatically. Cold and rain ruined harvests in Europe and, in New England, snow fell in the summer, freezing laundry on the line — farmers called the year "eighteen hundred and froze to death."

Around 90,000 people died as a result of the eruption. From the start, rescue operations were ineffectual. Early explosions were mistaken for cannon fire, so the local people were not warned. The later explosions ripped the island apart, and so the governor of Java was not able to send shiploads of rice to feed starving survivors until the volcano had blown itself out over three months later. People were left to forage the few remaining edible plants.

1 The loudest explosion ever was in 1883, when the small Indonesian island of Krakatoa violently erupted.

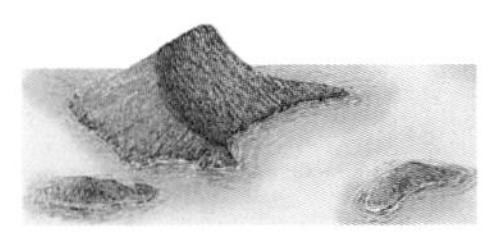

2 As Krakatoa erupted, the island collapsed, forming a wide 40-mile (6.5-km) underwater caldera (crater) and creating giant waves called *tsunamis*.

WIND ENERGY

POWER FROM THE WIND

One of the most promising renewable sources of energy is wind power. By the end of 1993, Britain's 19 wind farms supplied electricity to about 37,000 households. The world leaders are Denmark where wind farms supply 120,000 households, and the U.S. where 600,000 households are supplied. Wind energy is free, but to capture it requires sophisticated wind turbines, so the electricity it generates is no cheaper than that from a conventional power plant. The best sites for wind turbines are where the wind blows continuously.

The world's most powerful wind generator is on the Isle of Orkney, off Scotland's coast. It stands 145 feet high, with rotors measuring 195 feet across. It can operate in winds of between 15 and 60 mph, and produces its maximum output at 37 mph. The rotors turn at 34 rpm (revolutions per minute), about the same speed as a long-playing record.

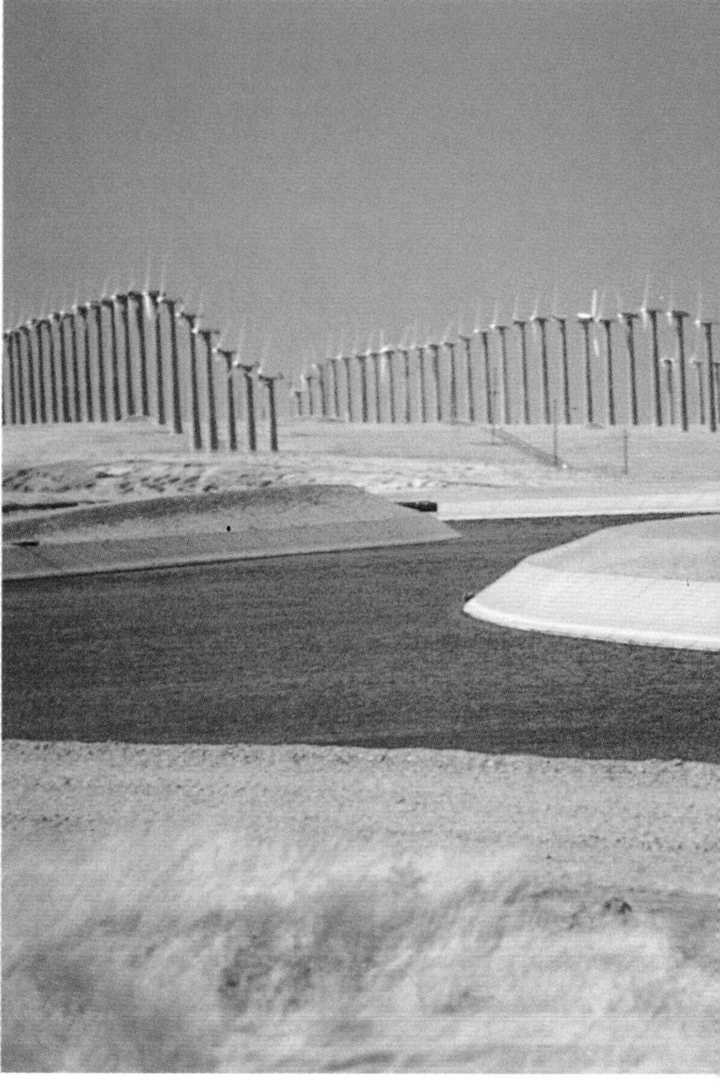

Wind turbines can *disfigure the landscape, and be noisy. These problems might be solved by building the turbines out at sea, where the wind is stronger. But this would add to the cost and make maintenance difficult.*

Most wind energy projects have been financed by government. If the technology proves economical, the British Department of Energy estimates wind energy should be able to supply about a tenth of Britain's electricity. But problems remain: wind turbines must first demonstrate efficiency, low maintenance costs, and long life.

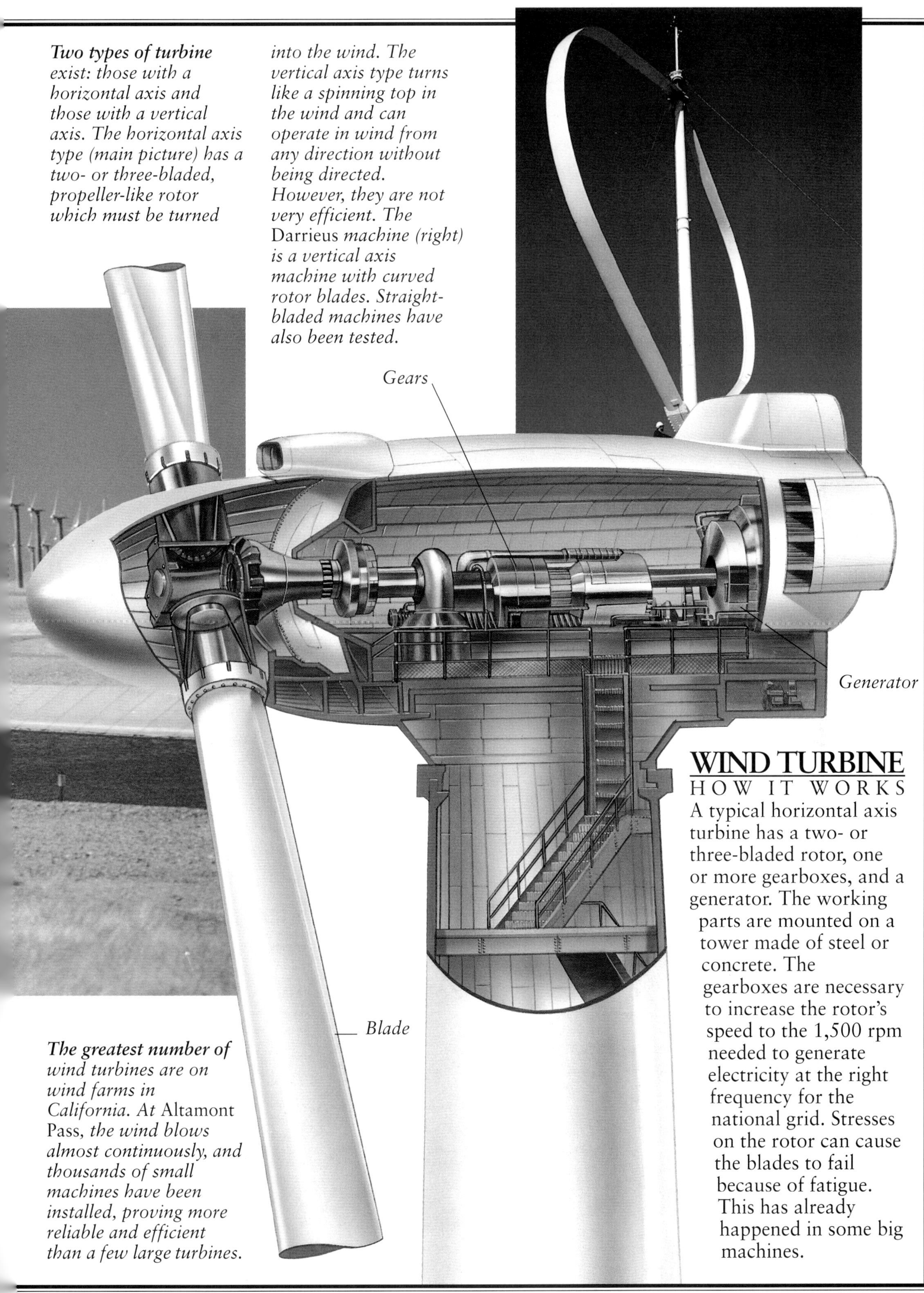

Two types of turbine *exist: those with a horizontal axis and those with a vertical axis. The horizontal axis type (main picture) has a two- or three-bladed, propeller-like rotor which must be turned into the wind. The vertical axis type turns like a spinning top in the wind and can operate in wind from any direction without being directed. However, they are not very efficient. The* Darrieus *machine (right) is a vertical axis machine with curved rotor blades. Straight-bladed machines have also been tested.*

The greatest number of *wind turbines are on wind farms in California. At* Altamont Pass, *the wind blows almost continuously, and thousands of small machines have been installed, proving more reliable and efficient than a few large turbines.*

WIND TURBINE

HOW IT WORKS

A typical horizontal axis turbine has a two- or three-bladed rotor, one or more gearboxes, and a generator. The working parts are mounted on a tower made of steel or concrete. The gearboxes are necessary to increase the rotor's speed to the 1,500 rpm needed to generate electricity at the right frequency for the national grid. Stresses on the rotor can cause the blades to fail because of fatigue. This has already happened in some big machines.

TEMPERATURE CONTROL

One of the great debates in recent years has been whether the dinosaurs were cold-blooded or warm-blooded. Were they really just cold-blooded animals like modern fish and reptiles, whose body temperatures are the same as the surrounding air or water? Or could they keep a constant warm body temperature, like modern birds and mammals? The answer remains unclear. All that can be said is that the dinosaurs were probably somewhere in between. If this is the case, it could explain why dinosaurs were so successful. A constant body temperature would have allowed them to be active all of the time, not just when the air was warm. However, they would not have had to eat as much as true warm-blooded animals do; nine-tenths of what we eat is for body-heat control.

Polar dinosaurs

It was once thought that dinosaurs lived only in the warmer parts of the world, and this fit the idea that they were simply cold-blooded reptiles. However, recently, dinosaurs have been found in Alaska, in the Arctic Circle, and in southern Australia, which used to lie within the Antarctic Circle. The dinosaurs from Australia include *Hypsilophodon,* medium-sized plant-eaters known also from Europe and North America.

Hypsilophodon skeleton

Dimetrodon, an early mammal-like reptile, had a "fin" that took up the morning heat quickly and acted as a cooling radiator when the body was too hot.

Stegosaurus had blood vessels in the skin over its bony plates. Heat was taken in and given off.

Dimetrodon

Warming up

In the morning, reptiles stand out in the sun and soak up the heat. This is called basking. Some fossil reptiles had special devices to help them do this faster. Some mammal-like reptiles had fins made from bony spines and skin, and the plant-eating dinosaur *Stegosaurus* had skin-covered bony plates.

Cooling down

Modern reptiles take shelter when they become too hot. In the midday heat, they hide behind rocks. Dinosaurs may have used their fins, spines, and skin to give off heat, or they may have curled up on the ground in some shade and stopped moving altogether until they cooled down.

Mathematical dinosaurs

Experiments with living alligators have shown that small ones have the same body temperature as the air around them. Large alligators, weighing 100kg, have more constant body temperatures, even when the days are hot and the nights are cold. So, a dinosaur weighing 10 tons or more is likely to have kept the same body temperature day or night, simply because it was so big.

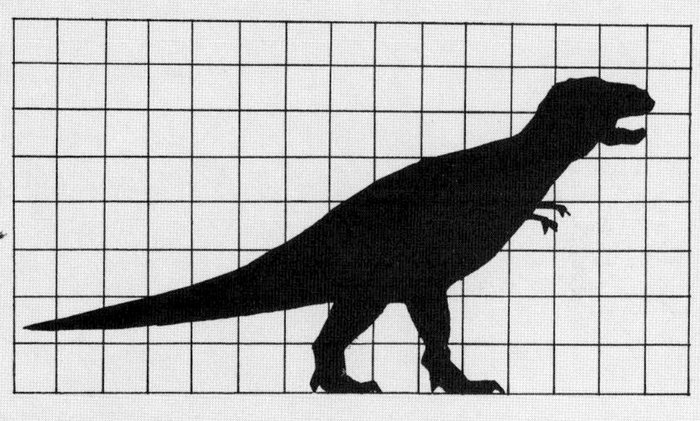

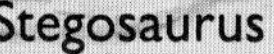

Stegosaurus

The new dinosaur artists

Early pictures of dinosaurs made them look like rhinoceroses. Since 1850, however, dozens of artists have used all their skills to illustrate what scientists have found out about the life of the dinosaurs. In 1968, some exciting drawings by a new dinosaur artist, Robert Bakker, were published in the United States. These showed dinosaurs as active, lively animals, running with their backs level, and not standing up like kangaroos.

Dinosaurs were probably cold-blooded, just like modern reptiles. But most of them were so big that they were as good as warm-blooded. In other words, they took so long to warm up in the morning and to cool down at night, that their body temperatures were nearly constant.

Punishment And Law

A rare sight – highwaymen repairing the roads. Most were hung once caught.

Medieval society was divided between peasants and a comparatively small number of landowners and wealthy merchants. The privileged few feared banditry because it threatened to overturn the established order.

Rulers made laws that protected their interests. Methods of trial were crude, and torture was widespread. Horrific punishments, such as boiling and lashing alive (slicing off the skin), were designed to deter criminals. But they could never deter those bandits who made a living by crime – or died of starvation. Yet up to the 19th century, the penalty for robbery remained death.

Confess – or Die

Suspects were tortured to get information about other criminals, or to make them confess. Victims in extreme pain often confessed to crimes they had not done, just to stop the torture!

Tortures included gouging out eyes, and stretching on the rack, which slowly dislocated arms and legs. Victims were also dropped into water (*above*). They were forced under until they confessed to their crimes.

A 17th-century thumbscrew

Trial by Fire

In the triple ordeal by fire (below), *suspects walked nine feet carrying a 3-pound lump of red-hot iron. The wound was bound and left for three days. If burn marks remained when it was unwrapped, the accused was declared guilty.*

Fingers and Toes

Hands and feet were a torturer's favorite targets. Thumbscrews crushed fingers, so they could never be used again.

The "boot" was a large metal shoe. The victim's foot was placed inside and the boot was tightened with screws, grinding the foot to a pulp. Many prisoners told their captors what they wanted to hear before the tightening began.

I've Got a Crush on You

Today, suspects can plead "Not Guilty." But in the 17th century the accused had to plead guilty before a trial went ahead. Those refusing to plead were crushed by weights (peine forte et dure) *until admitting guilt – or dying.*

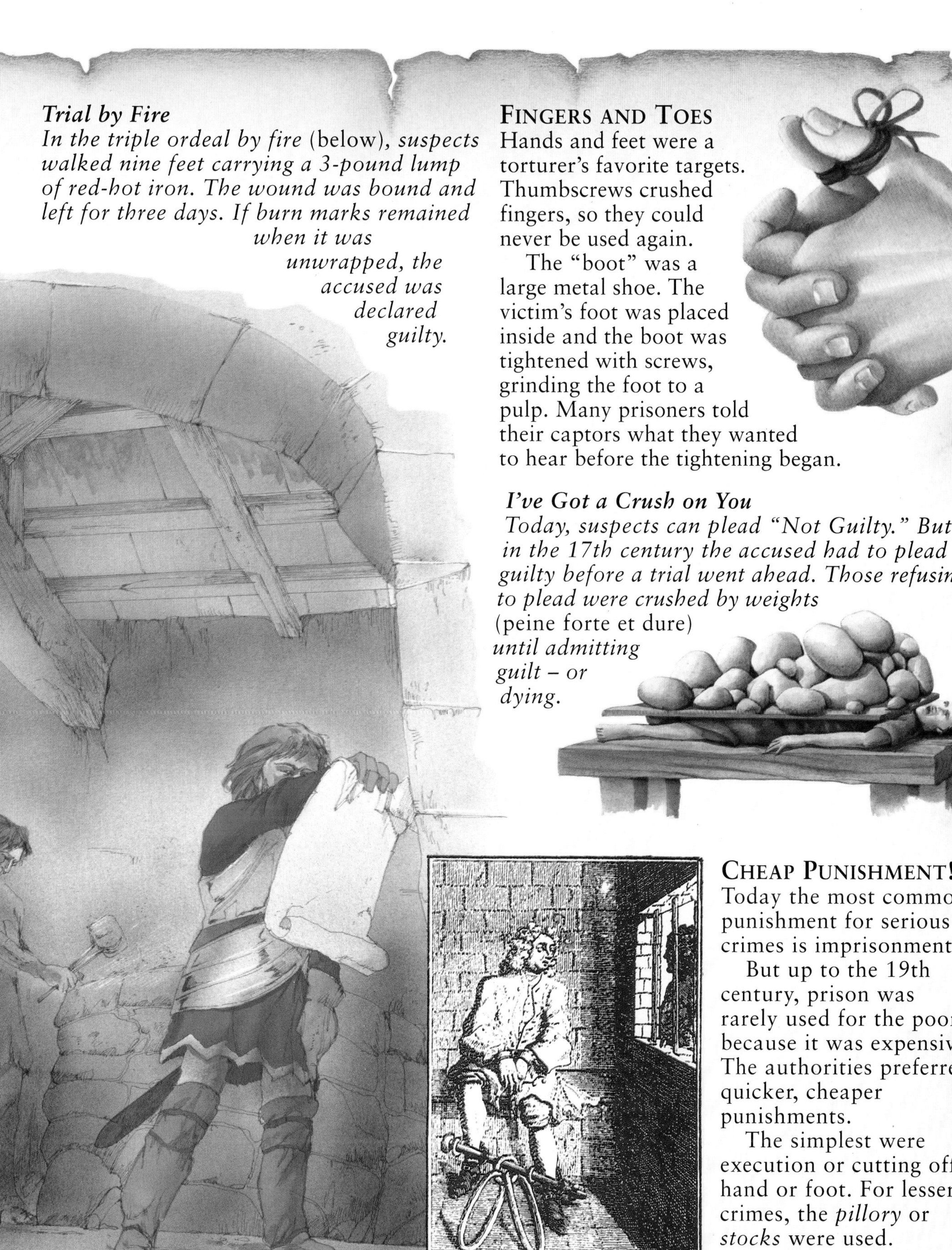

An 18th-Century Prison
No place for the weak!

Cheap Punishment!

Today the most common punishment for serious crimes is imprisonment.

But up to the 19th century, prison was rarely used for the poor, because it was expensive. The authorities preferred quicker, cheaper punishments.

The simplest were execution or cutting off a hand or foot. For lesser crimes, the *pillory* or *stocks* were used.

Torture was officially abolished in the 1620s, but terrible prison conditions may have made prisoners wonder if it was true (*left*)!

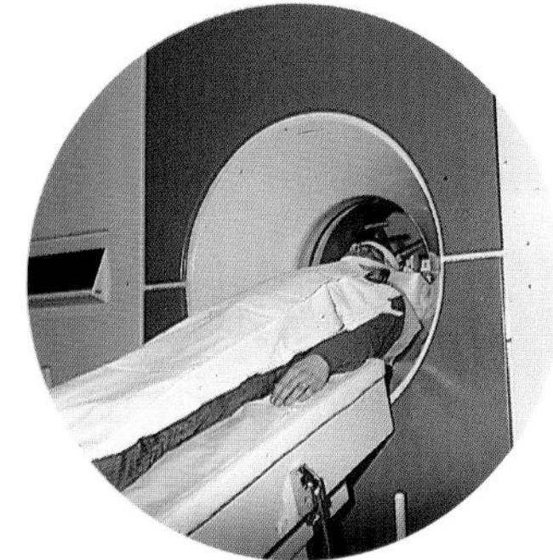

Electromagnetism

The English physicist, Michael Faraday, discovered that electrical energy could be turned into mechanical energy (movement) by using magnetism. He used a cylindrical coil of wire, called a solenoid, to create a simple electric motor. He went on to discover that mechanical energy can be converted into electrical energy – the reverse of the principle of the electric motor. His work led to the development of the dynamo, or generator. You can make a powerful electromagnet by passing electricity through a coil of wire wrapped many times around a nail. Electromagnets are found in many everyday machines and gadgets. An MRI scanner (Magnetic Resonance Imaging), like the one pictured here, contains many ring-shaped electromagnets. With a solenoid and a current of electricity, you can close the cage.

Caged!

1. Take a piece of polystyrene and edge it with cardboard. Stick plastic straws upright around three sides as the bars of the cage.

1

2. Cut out another piece of polystyrene of the same size for the roof of the cage. Attach a piece of plastic straw to the side above the door. Wind a piece of wire around a nail 50 times leaving two ends. Affix the nail to the roof, as shown.

2

3. Insert a needle into the straw so that it almost touches the nail. Cut out a rectangle of plastic for the door. Make a hole at the bottom of the door for the needle to fit through.

3

4

4. Stick a piece of cardboard across the door to help hold it open, and make sure the end of the needle just pokes through the hole. Now attach one of the wires to one terminal on the battery. Leave the other free. Make sure it will reach the other terminal. Put the animal into the cage.

WHY IT WORKS

When the current is switched on, the nail becomes magnetized as the current flows through the wire. The needle in the door of the cage is attracted to the electromagnet. As the needle is pulled toward the nail, the door closes to trap the tiger.

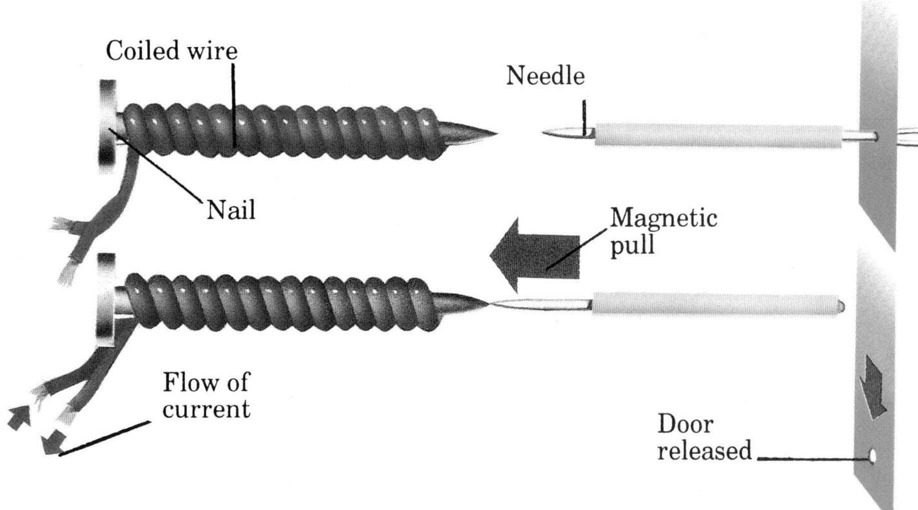

BRIGHT IDEAS

Wind more turns of wire onto the electromagnet. The magnetic effect will increase. What happens if you use a more powerful battery? (Do not let it get too hot.)

Make another electro-magnet using a shorter nail. This will also make the magnetic pull stronger.

Make an electromagnetic pickup by winding wire around a nail. What objects can you pick up? What happens when the current is turned off?

Use an electromagnet to make a carousel spin. Attach paper clips around the edge of a circular cardboard lid to be the roof. Make sure it is free to spin, and place an electromagnet close to the paper clips. The carousel should turn as you switch the current on and off quickly.

5. Now pick up the free wire. Allow the free wire to come into contact with the unconnected battery terminal. The needle should be pulled back toward the nail. The door will fall down, trapping the animal in its cage.

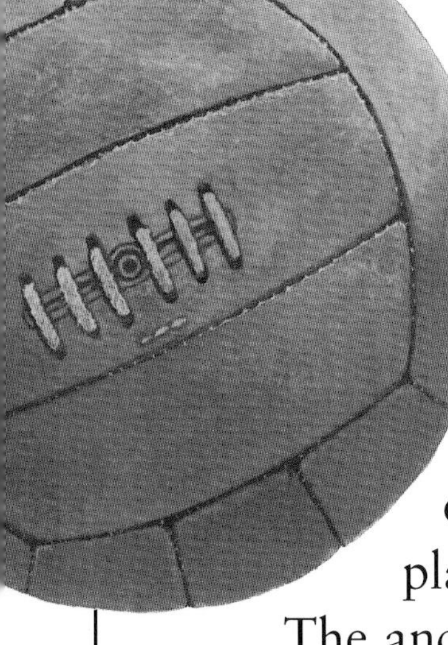

SOCCER

Soccer, or Association Football, is the most popular sport in the world. Kicking a ball has been a leisure activity for centuries; today, millions of soccer fans follow their favorite teams and top players are highly paid sports heroes.

The ancient Chinese played football with a stuffed leather ball, over 2,500 years ago. They called the game *Tsu-Chu-Tsu*, or "to kick the leather ball with the feet." At about the same time, the Romans also played several football-type games. *Paganica* was a free-for-all competition, in which two teams rushed for the ball. In another game, *Harpastum*, the ball was simply grabbed and carried over the goal line.

The Greatest Goal of All
Since 1930, the world's top soccer teams have battled with each other to win the ultimate soccer trophy, the World Cup *(above)*. The championship is played every four years, each time hosted by a different country. The first competition was won by Uruguay.

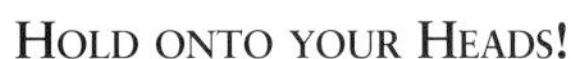

Hold onto your Heads!
Various forms of soccer were found among ancient peoples. Victories on the battlefield were celebrated in some cultures by kicking around the heads of enemy warriors! This grisly practice is thought to have been started among the Danish invaders of England, but it was most widely recorded by the ancient Chinese.

FROM MOBS TO MONEYMAKERS

Soccer in medieval England was a violent sport with no rules. "Mob football" *(right)* was played by big groups of people, often in busy streets. In 1314, it was banned, but it was still played in many towns.

During the late 1800s, soccer developed into the game as we know it today. Rules were drawn up at English schools and universities and soccer clubs were formed over the years. Soccer soon became an organized sport and players began to be paid.

Aluminum cleats

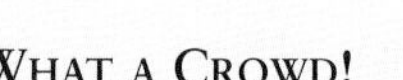

What a Crowd!
Important soccer matches have always attracted enormous crowds... but none has beaten the Brazil versus Uruguay game in the 1950 World Cup. An amazing 199,589 people packed into the Maracaña Municipal Stadium in Rio de Janeiro, Brazil, to cheer on the two teams!

THE MODERN GAME

Today, soccer for both men and women has a massive following worldwide, and huge amounts of money are poured into the game. Clubs pay vast sums to buy top players – in 1995, a transfer fee for England's Andy Cole cost $12 million; Alf Common, in 1902, was sold for just $700! Sponsorship of contests is a huge money-spinner, especially as televised matches offer worldwide advertising. Twenty-four countries now compete in the World Cup finals, with many more taking part in the qualifying matches beforehand.

Fancy Footwork
Nineteenth-century leather shoes weighed three times as much as modern ones. Today's shoes *(below)* weigh only 8 oz. Players can control the ball much more easily than before.

Pelé

PELÉ
(b. 1940) *Pelé (Edson Arantes do Nascimento) is one of soccer's greatest players. During his career (1955-1977), he scored 1,281 goals and helped Brazil to win the World Cup 3 times. He is now involved in Brazilian sports policy and training.*

Dressing Up
Early players wore tight trousers or breeches. Baggy, knee-length shorts were later introduced for freer movement.

1950s

These shorts became shorter and shorter over the years. Modern players wear close-fitting shirts and shorts, which display a sponsor's name.

PLAYING BY THE RULES

The first referees were students from upper-class English families. They helped the team captains at Oxford and Cambridge Universities to establish the rules of modern soccer in the 19th century. Today, referees make sure that the players act fairly and stick to the rules. A yellow card is shown as a warning to anyone who breaks the rules; a red card is shown for a serious offense and the player is sent from the field.

Speed and Safety
Cleats prevent slipping and are changed to suit the field.

Rubber cleats

Whatever the Weather
Some matches are played on fields of artificial grass. Astro Turf was developed in the 1960s for the Houston Astrodome, an indoor stadium. It is made of plastic and fibers, and players need to wear special shoes *(right)* to play on it.

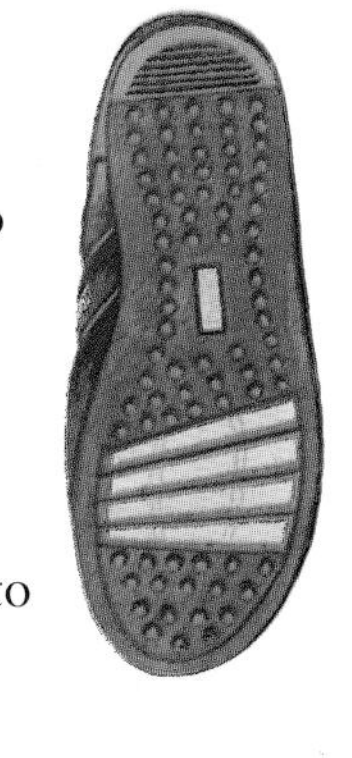

BOWS AND ARROWS

Bows were first used for hunting during the Stone Age, 250,000 years ago. The ancient Egyptians were the first people to use bows and arrows in warfare, in about 5000 B.C. Until the introduction of firearms in the 16th century, archers played a crucial role in combat. Bows were made from tough, flexible wood like yew. The equipment used in modern archery is derived from the shapes and qualities of medieval long bows.

EARLY ARCHERS
Stone Age people used arrows with flint arrowheads *(above)* to hunt large or fast-moving animals. The arrowheads, carved from pieces of solid rock, were deadly sharp.

ANCIENT WARFARE
The ancient Egyptians fought many battles against neighboring peoples, including the fierce Assyrians (*left*), in which both sides were armed with bows and arrows. The Assyrian Army, which was well-organized and its soldiers well-trained, eventually conquered the mighty Egyptian Empire.

MEDIEVAL ARCHERS

In the Middle Ages, bows were used by archers in the Norman army to help defeat the English at the Battle of Hastings in 1066 (*right*). During the late Middle Ages (14th and 15th centuries A.D.), English archers used a more effective bow, the longbow (*left*), to win several battles against the French – including Agincourt in 1415. Arrows from longbows could pierce plate armor at over 109 yards (300 feet), but using one took years of practice.

ROBIN HOOD

According to legend, Robin Hood was an outlaw who lived in Sherwood Forest, England, during the 12th century. He used his great skill with a bow and arrow to defend the poor against a corrupt sheriff.

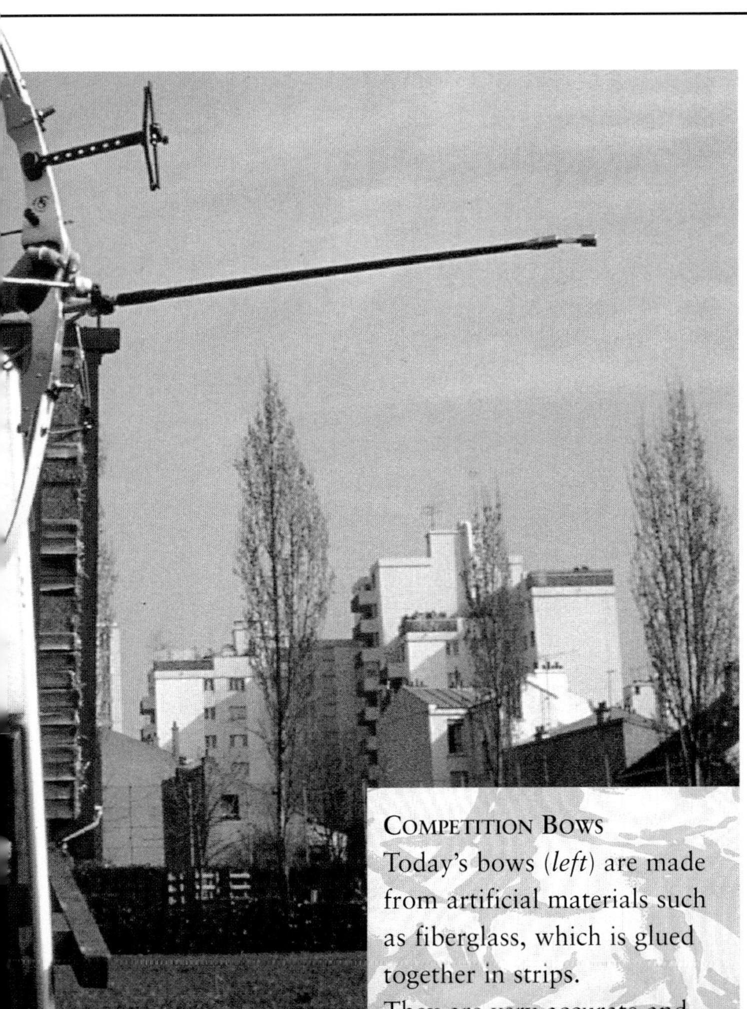

COMPETITION BOWS
Today's bows (*left*) are made from artificial materials such as fiberglass, which is glued together in strips. They are very accurate and are used in sporting competitions, including the Olympic Games.

ARROWHEADS

An arrow is made up of a wooden or steel shaft, with feathers or flights at one end (to make it fly straight) and an arrowhead (*right*) at the other. Hunting arrowheads often have barbs along the side, which catch in the animal. Bodkins are arrows designed to pierce steel plate.

General-purpose

Bodkin

Japanese

African (with barbs)

Indian

CROSSBOWS

The crossbow is a powerful and accurate bow, first used in the Middle Ages. Often the archer had to use a mechanical winding device to pull back the string (*above*). Crossbows are still used by troops today. This soldier (*below*) practices using one while wearing night-vision glasses.

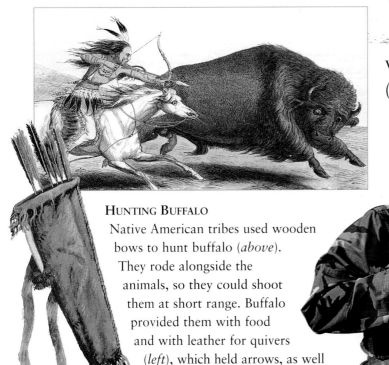

HUNTING BUFFALO
Native American tribes used wooden bows to hunt buffalo (*above*). They rode alongside the animals, so they could shoot them at short range. Buffalo provided them with food and with leather for quivers (*left*), which held arrows, as well as clothes and tents.

TREES AS HABITATS

Trees grow all over the world, even in the harshest of conditions. They live in deserts, on mountains, in jungles, and in the icy cold. Since trees can make their own food, they are not restricted to places where food can be found, as animals are. They do, however, need sunlight and water wherever they live. Many species have developed special features which help them to survive in a particular habitat.

Desert and scrubland
Desert trees face the problem of getting enough water to live on. Baobab trees store water in their swollen trunks for use in times of drought. As they use up the water their trunks shrink.

Northern pine forest
A huge band of pine forest stretches across the top of North America, Siberia, and Scandanavia. Conifers form crowded and shady forests. They can survive even where sunlight is weak.

Mountain
Some mountain trees, such as dwarf willows and dwarf conifers, grow very close to the ground. This keeps them out of the biting winds that howl down the mountainside. They may be short enough to step over – only a few inches high. These trees are given the nickname *krummholz*, or "elfin wood."

Mangrove swamps
Bands of mangrove trees grow in tropical estuaries, where rivers meet the sea. They have to cope with large amounts of salt which would normally kill most trees. Mangrove roots have special adaptations that filter the salt out of the water they take in

Tropical rain forests

Rain forest trees grow in dense groups. They have to compete for sunlight, and grow up to 165 feet tall to catch the sun. Rain forest trees absorb all the nutrients from the soil. When they are felled, the soil is left with so few nutrients that it is difficult for other vegetation to grow back.

The dying forests

Acid rain is killing trees worlwide. It is caused by pollution from burning gasoline in cars and coal or oil in power plants. When acid rain falls on trees it damages their leaves and releases toxic substances in the soil. Test the acid level of rain by collectingit in a clean pail. Get a strip of pH paper from your sceince teacher and leave it in the water for 15 minutes.Compare the strip with a pH chart to find the acid level of your sample.

The world's biomes

The earth can be divided into regions based on the kinds of trees they support. These areas, called biomes, are largely determined by climate: temperature and rainfall are the main influences on what kinds of trees and plants grow in an area. Soil type also affects vegetation, because it is the soil that supplies nutrients for plants. The map below shows the world's major biomes.

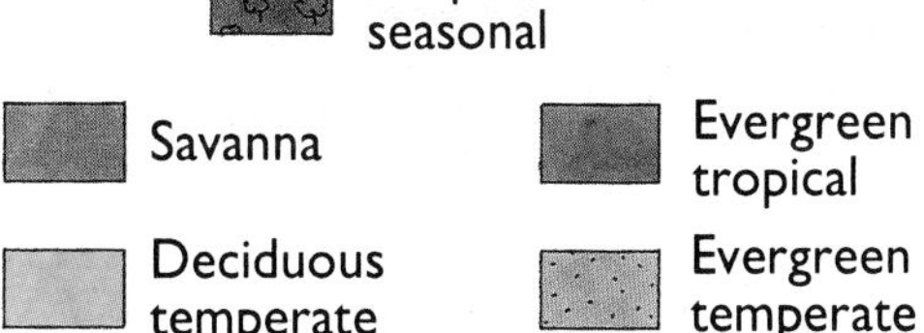

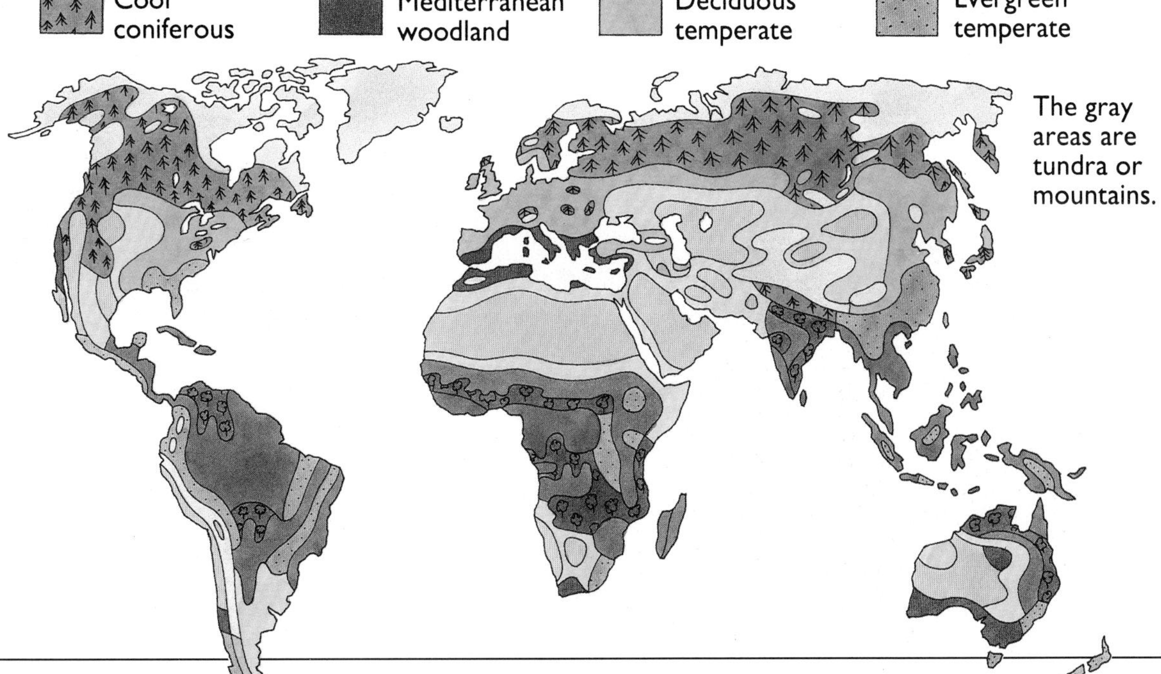

VIKING BURIALS

When a Viking died, he or she might be buried or cremated, in a ship or in the ground. This depended on the individual's position in society and on his or her wealth. Viking funerals were times of great ceremony. The Vikings believed in life after death, so dead people were buried with some of their personal possessions to ease their journey into the next world. Huge Viking cemeteries and burial mounds have been found at towns such as Jelling in Denmark. Some of the graves were marked by stones placed in the shape of ships.

A middle-class burial
Middle-class Vikings were buried in wooden chambers, with food and drink for their journey, and other personal belongings. Items such as combs and spindles have also been found in Viking graves. Warriors were buried in full battle dress, with their swords and shields.

Site evidence
Most of the evidence about the Vikings and their ships comes from the grave mounds. Ships were used for the burial of wealthy people only. Although the tradition was carried out before the Viking Age, it was also very popular among the Vikings. Two of the finest Viking ships, from Gokstad and Oseberg, were uncovered as ship burials. If the burial site was far from the sea, or if the family could not afford a ship, stones in the shape of a ship were placed around the burial site.

Ship burial
Kings, queens, and great chieftains were sometimes buried in ships which were then buried under huge mounds or burned. The mourners believed that the ship would carry the dead person safely to the next world. Their belongings were buried or burned with them, including their horses, dogs, and even slaves.

Modern day festivals

Every year, on the last Tuesday of January, the people of Lerwick in Shetland relive their Viking history. They celebrate Up-Helly-Aa, a modern version of a Viking fire festival. A model of a Viking longboat is pulled through the town by a torchlit procession which includes a "jarl" and his band of Viking warriors. Many of the participants actually dress up as Vikings. The ship is set alight to represent the funeral pyre of a Viking chieftain. This is followed by all-night feasting and singing.

During Up-Helly-Aa, the Viking galley burns furiously as the festival reaches its climax.

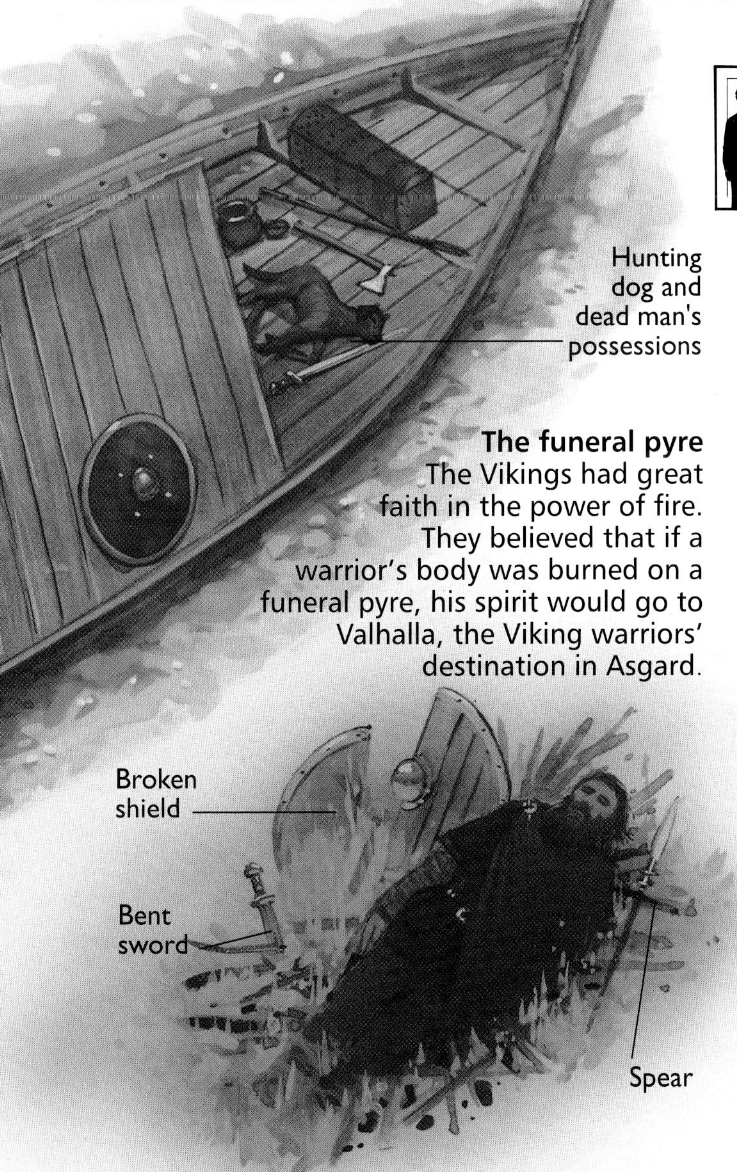

The funeral pyre

The Vikings had great faith in the power of fire. They believed that if a warrior's body was burned on a funeral pyre, his spirit would go to Valhalla, the Viking warriors' destination in Asgard.

Sacrifices

One of the most fascinating accounts of the sacrifices and rituals that accompanied Viking burials comes from an Arab trader called Ibn Fadlan. He described the ship cremation of a rich and important Viking chieftain. A young slave woman from the chieftain's household was chosen to die with her master. A ship was drawn up onto the land and surrounded with firewood. It was then filled with the chieftain's most prized possessions and his body was placed on a couch. The young servant girl lay at her master's side and was sacrificed by an old woman called the Angel of Death. She was "a stout and grim figure" who was in charge of such rituals. A relative of the dead man then stepped from the crowd, and set the boat ablaze with a torch.

Angel of Death

IN THE LUNGS

Deep in the lungs, something stirs. It is air, gently wafting in and out with each breath. The lungs' main air pipes, the bronchi, branch many times until they form hair-thin tubes, terminal bronchioles. These end in grapelike bunches of air bubbles, called alveoli. There are over 300 million alveoli in each lung. It is here that oxygen passes into the blood.

Terminal bronchiole

SLOW AND FAST

The brain constantly adjusts the breathing rate, according to the body's activity and oxygen needs. When we rest or sleep, the breathing rate is 15-20 breaths each minute. After running a race, it goes up to over 60 breaths each minute.

BLUE TO RED

Each alveolus air-bubble is surrounded by a network of microscopic blood vessels known as capillaries. Blue oxygen-poor blood flows into the capillaries. Here it picks up oxygen from the air inside the alveolus (as shown opposite), and turns into bright red, oxygen-rich blood.

CHANGED AIR

Breathed-in air is about one-fifth oxygen, O_2. Coming back out, this proportion has changed to one-sixth. The difference is made up by carbon dioxide, CO_2, one of the body's waste products. Nitrogen, which makes up four-fifths of air, stays unchanged.

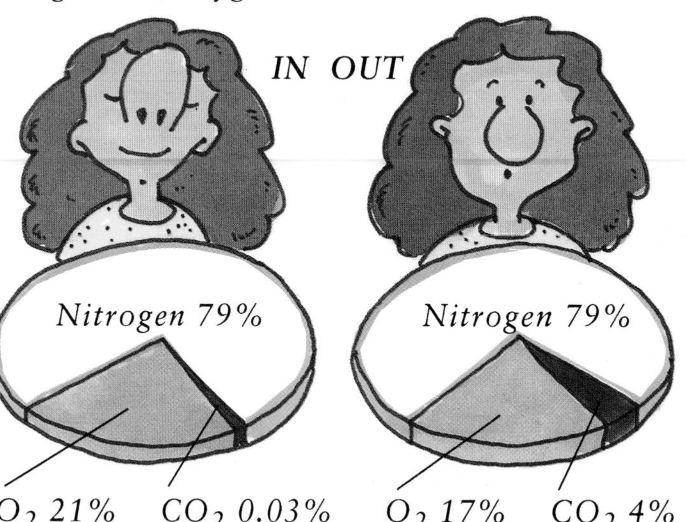

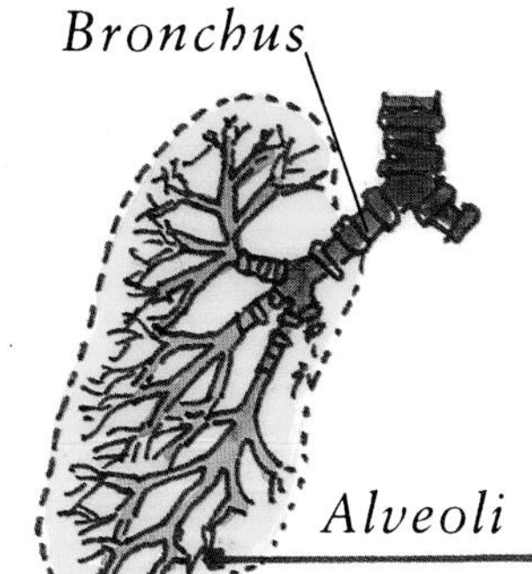

AIRWAY TREE

The bronchi branch 15 or 20 times to form the tiny bronchioles, with alveoli at their tips.

DEEP-DIVING MOUSE

Deep-sea divers must breathe a special mixture of gases, including helium, due to the great water pressure. But breathing helium makes their voices sound like Mickey Mouse!

INSIDE AN ALVEOLUS

The wall of an alveolus is only one cell thick – which is extremely thin! The wall of the blood capillary is only one cell thin, too. So oxygen in the air inside the alveolus has hardly any distance to go, to get into the blood.

THE NON-STOP SWOP

Swopping the oxygen coming from the air to the blood, for the carbon dioxide going from the blood to the air, is gas exchange.

LARGE AS OUR LUNGS

If a surgeon could iron all the alveoli flat, they would cover a huge surface, as large as a tennis court. That's a big area for gas exchange!

FIRE AND BURNING

A fire is a chemical reaction, in which a burning object combines with oxygen, producing an energy change. Most of the energy from fire is heat energy, but fire also releases energy in the form of light and sound. This is why fire can be seen, felt and heard. Fires need high temperatures and a supply of oxygen to keep them burning, so removing either of these can put out a fire. Substances such as water, sand, or foam can also be used to smother a fire and dampen the flames.

Prometheus

In Greek myths, Prometheus (right) was a god who created people and gave them reason. He stole fire from heaven and gave it to humans. Zeus chained him to a rock and sent an eagle each day to eat his liver, which grew back at night. After many years, Prometheus was rescued.

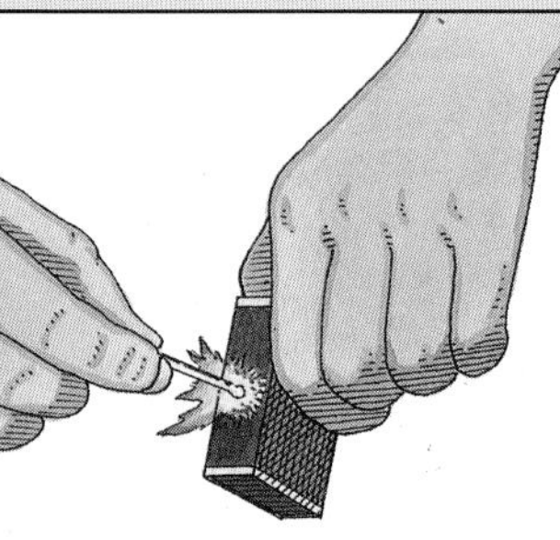

Matches have heads made of a substance that is easily ignited by rubbing. The heat generated by rubbing them on a rough surface is sufficient to ignite the match.

The Great Fire of London

The Great Fire of London, in 1666, destroyed much of the city. It spread swiftly through the narrow streets filled with wooden houses. As there was no proper fire service in England at that time, people had to wait for the fire to burn itself out, which took days. When the citizens returned, they found their homes and their city in ashes.

Modern fire fighters do not always use water to douse flames, because if fuel is burning, water may spread it and make the fire worse. Foam is used in airports, swamping the fire and cutting off the supply of air that it needs to keep burning.

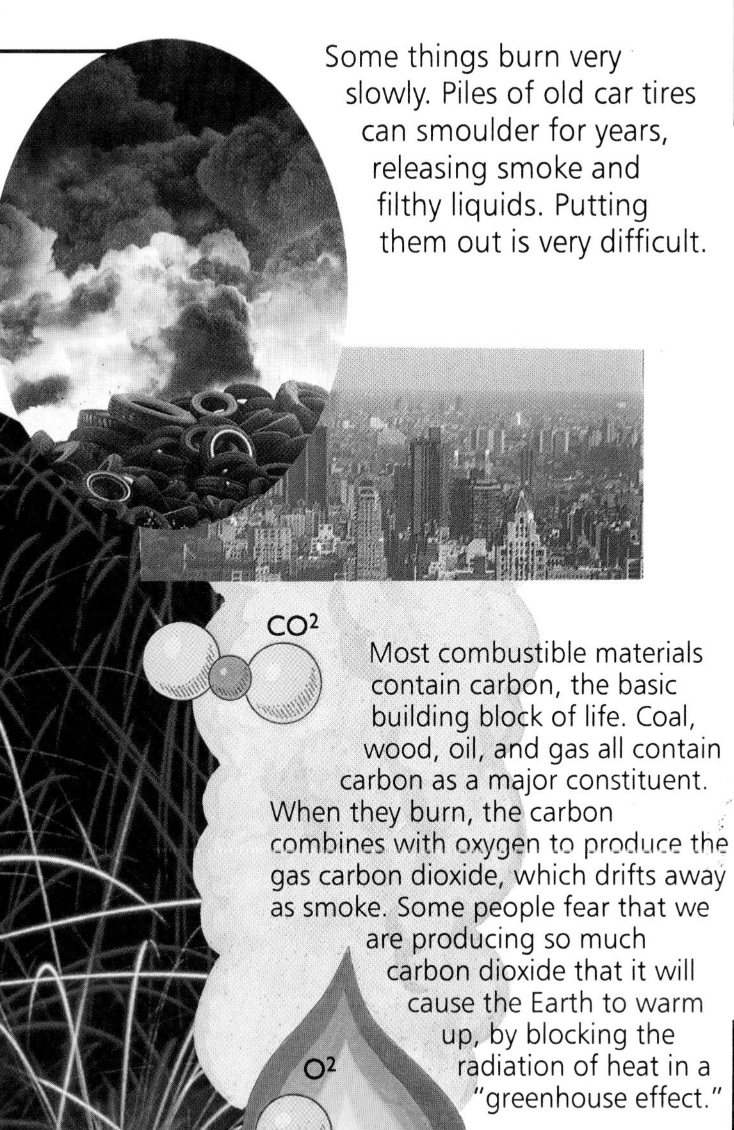

Some things burn very slowly. Piles of old car tires can smoulder for years, releasing smoke and filthy liquids. Putting them out is very difficult.

Most combustible materials contain carbon, the basic building block of life. Coal, wood, oil, and gas all contain carbon as a major constituent. When they burn, the carbon combines with oxygen to produce the gas carbon dioxide, which drifts away as smoke. Some people fear that we are producing so much carbon dioxide that it will cause the Earth to warm up, by blocking the radiation of heat in a "greenhouse effect."

Hell fires

Hell is supposed to be a place where evil people burn for ever. The theme was often used by religious artists of the Middle Ages, such as the Dutch painter Hieronymus Bosch (1450-1516). His teeming Hell is full of people regretting that they didn't lead better lives.

The internal combustion engine

The internal combustion engine emerged during the late 19th century as an alternative to steam power. The engine burns a mixture of petrol and air inside the cylinders, driving a piston with little power. Steam engines burn fuel outside the cylinders and use it to produce steam, which drives the pistons. Modern Grand Prix engines in Formula One racing cars have 8 or even 12 cylinders. For extra power, fuel can be blown into the cylinders using turbo-chargers.

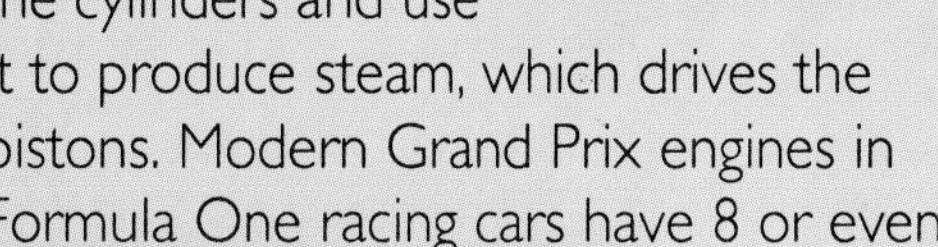

Candle combustion

Burning or combustion needs a supply of oxygen for it to continue. In order to prove that this is true, try this experiment. Light a candle in a saucer containing water, then put a Pyrex glass over it, with its rim in the water to seal it. Ask an adult to help you with this experiment, taking care with matches.

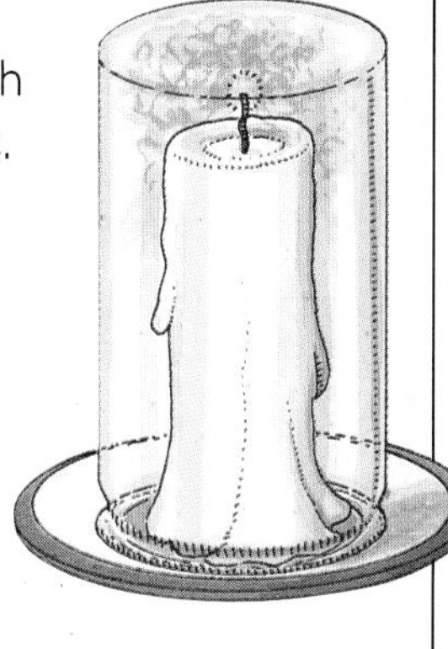

As the candle burns, it uses up the oxygen, and goes out when there is none left.

Finding the Way

Knowing exactly where you are is a matter of life or death to an explorer. The amazing adventures of English aviator Amy Johnson (1903–1941) were a triumph of solo navigation, and carried the daredevil spirit of exploration into the 20th century. In 1930, with only 100 hours' flying experience, Johnson bought a secondhand Gypsy Moth for $900 (*main picture*) and set out to become the first woman to fly solo from England to Australia. She completed the incredible journey in 19 days. On the way she flew blind through sandstorms, repaired her plane with plaster, and used judo to fight off amorous Arabs!

Drake's Compass
Sir Francis Drake used this all-in-one compass, tide tables, and solar and star tables (above).

THE LAST LOCKUP. In sailor's slang, Davy Jones was the evil spirit of the deep, sometimes associated with the Devil himself. "Davy Jones' Locker" is the bottom of the ocean, the final resting place of sunken ships and sailors who have drowned or been buried at sea. Once a ship got caught in a storm (*left*), there was little a captain could do except batten down the hatches and pray for fair weather.

Sextant (left)
The sextant, which came into use in the mid-18th century, is one of the most accurate instruments for finding a vessel's latitude.

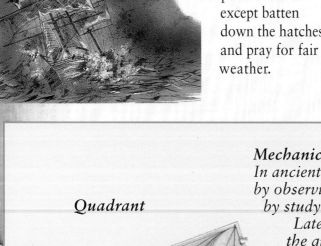

Mechanical Aids
In ancient times, sailors navigated by observing the night sky and by studying tides and winds. Later, instruments such as the quadrant (left) *and the astrolabe* (right), *were used for fixing a ship's latitude (distance above or below the equator), by measuring the angle of the sun or stars above the horizon.*

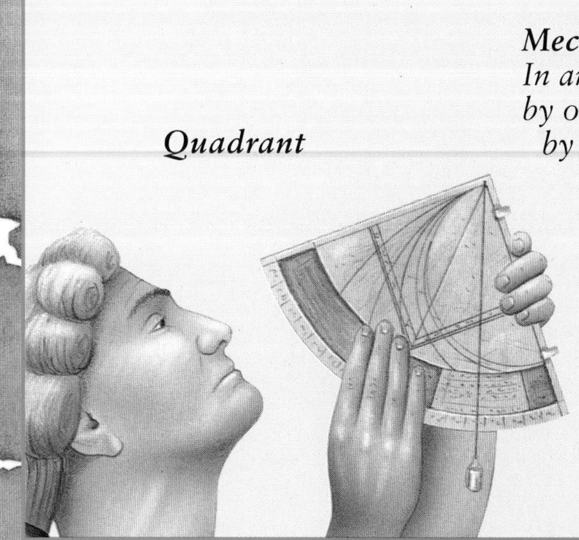

Quadrant

Astrolabe

Vanishing Brits

More than any other nation, England specializes in heroic failure. John Cabot was swallowed up by the Atlantic Ocean (1498), and Mungo Park by the Niger River (1806). Henry Hudson vanished in the bay that bears his name (1611). Cold undid Sir Henry Franklin (1847), and Robert Scott in the Antarctic (1912, *right*).

Himalayan Paradise

Not often does a film add a new world to the language. But this was the case with *The Lost Horizon* (1936, remade in 1972, *below*), written by James Hilton.

Shangri-La, the movie's heavenly valley in the Himalayas, nowadays means any earthly paradise.

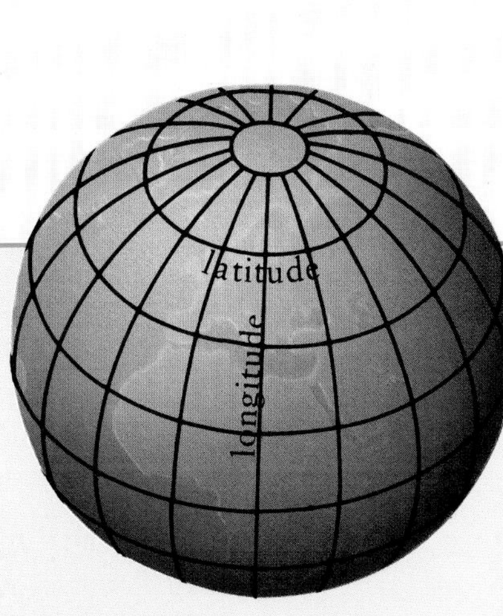

Navigators *plot their position using lines of longitude (east-west) and latitude (north-south).*

Clocking the Miles

Longitude is an east-west position on the surface of the Earth. As the Earth spins once every 24 hours, distance can be measured in time difference. One hour is 15° longitude.

However, longitude could not be accurately measured until the invention of the chronometer (a very accurate clock) in the mid-18th century. A 19th-century chronometer is shown on the *right*.

REPTILE CAMOUFLAGE

Throughout the animal world, creatures use body colors and patterns to blend in with their surroundings and merge with the background. This is called camouflage. It helps animals to hide if they are prey, being hunted by sight. It also helps them to creep up unseen on a victim, if they are hunters. The bodies of many reptiles are dull brown or green in color, to match the soils and vegetation where they live. A few are very brightly colored, to warn other animals that they are dangerous, or to advertise for mates at breeding time.

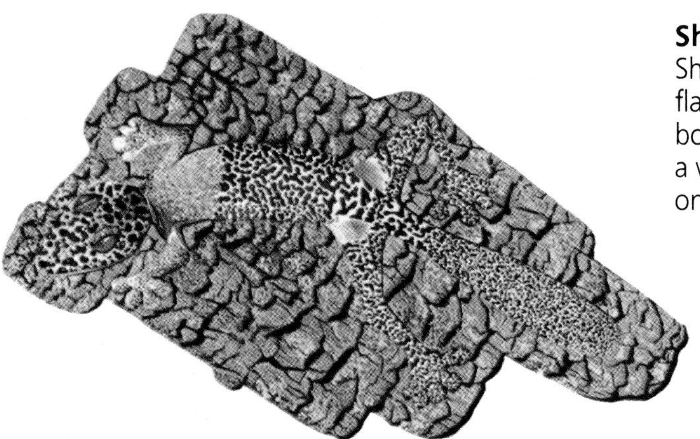

Shape
Shape is important in camouflage. The vine snake has a slim body. It resembles a vine or creeper on a tree.

Pattern
The spade-tailed gecko has a mottled pattern that blends in well with the patchy bark of trees.

Unseen in the shadows
Rudyard Kipling's exciting story *The Jungle Book* (1894) tells of how a boy, the "man-cub" Mowgli, is reared by a family of wolves in the jungles of India. One of the main characters is Kaa, a cunning and untrustworthy python. A troop of wild monkeys capture Mowgli. But Kaa arrives to help rescue him, and the monkeys are terrified. They know the stories of the great python who "could slip along the branches as quietly as the moss grows – and who could make himself look so like a dead branch or a rotten stump that the wisest were deceived, till the branch caught them." Such camouflage is even more effective at twilight and during the night, when many snakes go hunting.

Startle colors

The bright colors of many reptiles warn predators that they are venomous or that their flesh tastes horrible. This is called warning coloration. Bright colors are also used to startle an enemy. The blue-tongued skink (right) is a lizard. When threatened, it opens its mouth wide to reveal a bright blue tongue. The frilled lizard (top left) also flashes startle colors.

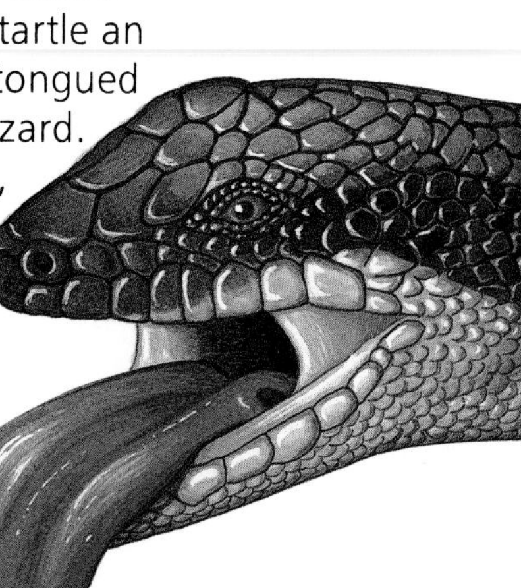

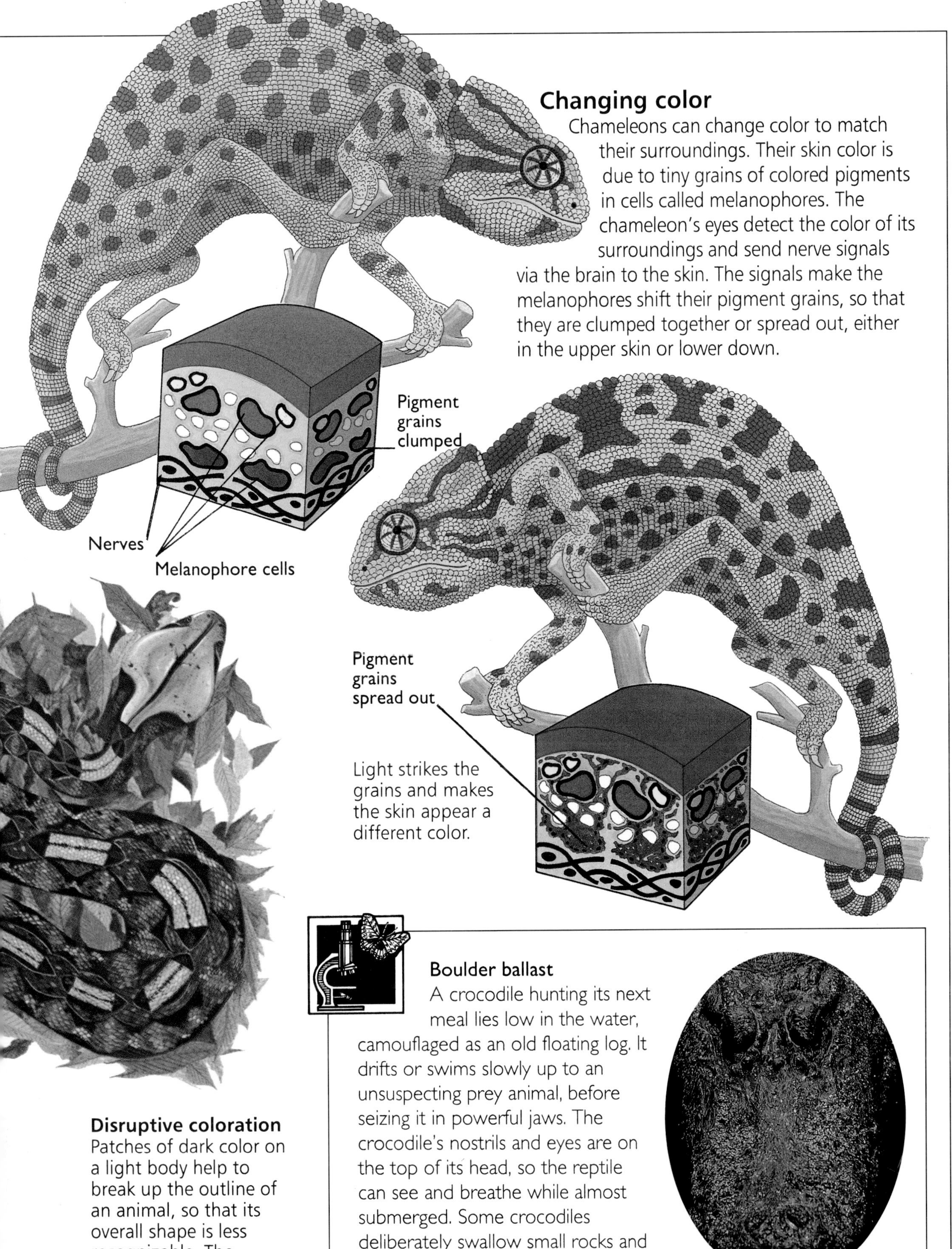

Changing color

Chameleons can change color to match their surroundings. Their skin color is due to tiny grains of colored pigments in cells called melanophores. The chameleon's eyes detect the color of its surroundings and send nerve signals via the brain to the skin. The signals make the melanophores shift their pigment grains, so that they are clumped together or spread out, either in the upper skin or lower down.

Disruptive coloration
Patches of dark color on a light body help to break up the outline of an animal, so that its overall shape is less recognizable. The Gaboon viper's coiled body is difficult to see among the fallen leaves.

Boulder ballast
A crocodile hunting its next meal lies low in the water, camouflaged as an old floating log. It drifts or swims slowly up to an unsuspecting prey animal, before seizing it in powerful jaws. The crocodile's nostrils and eyes are on the top of its head, so the reptile can see and breathe while almost submerged. Some crocodiles deliberately swallow small rocks and boulders. The extra weight of the stones in the stomach helps them to float lower in the water, and be even less noticeable.

FINDING A NEW WORLD

For the past 32 days, no land had been sighted. Mermaids (probably manatees) had even been seen swimming around the boat, and the crew was close to mutiny. The captain was worried – according to his charts, they should have reached Japan (*left*).

Then, just in time, signs of land appeared – floating branches with fresh leaves, and birds flying overhead. In the early hours of October 12, the look-out spotted a faint shape ahead. Land! It was tiny Watling Island (part of the Bahamas). Just after noon the next day, the Italian captain – Cristóbal Colón (Christopher Columbus) – stepped onto the white coral beach, and thanked God for the safe passage of his crew.

The Wrong Name

In 1507, German mapmaker Martin Waldseemäller (left) *coined the name "America" to honor the Italian navigator Amerigo Vespucci (1454–1512). He had read Vespucci's boastful accounts of his explorations. Later, Waldseemäller tried to change the name "America" but it was too late!*

A SMALL WORLD

Christopher Columbus (1451–1506) made four voyages of transatlantic exploration, but died believing his discoveries lay only a short distance from China. Meanwhile, John Cabot (c.1450–1499, *below*) had found a landmass to the north.

By 1513, when Vasco Balboa (c.1475–1519) crossed the Isthmus of Panama and gazed upon the mighty Pacific Ocean, Europeans were coming to realize that Columbus had stumbled across an entirely "New World."

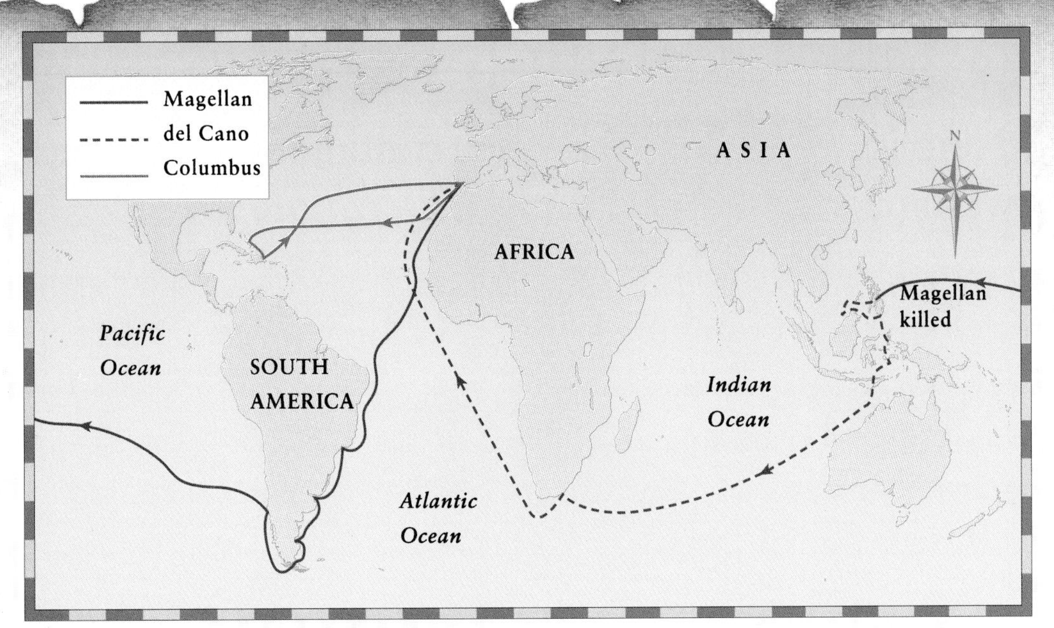

Two of the Greatest (left) *The routes of Columbus' first Atlantic crossing (1492–1493) and Magellan/del Cano's voyage around the globe (1519–1522).*

These two epic voyages changed our understanding of the world forever. One brought America into contact with Europe, the other finally proved that the Earth was round.

Beach Party (main picture) *When local Caribs met him on the beach, Columbus thought at first they were inhabitants from the fabled island of Cipangu, off the coast of China, just 4,000 miles from Europe!*

The First Time Around

In 1519 Portuguese Ferdinand Magellan (c.1480–1521) left Spain with five ships and 241 men. They found a passage around South America and crossed the Pacific to the Philippines, where Magellan was killed in a local war. One of his officers, Sebastian del Cano, took command. In 1522, with a single vessel and 18 other survivors he made it back to Spain. They had sailed around the world.

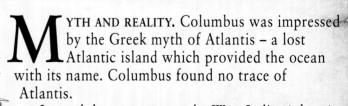

Myth and Reality. Columbus was impressed by the Greek myth of Atlantis – a lost Atlantic island which provided the ocean with its name. Columbus found no trace of Atlantis.

Instead, he came across the West Indies (*above*), inhabited by friendly Caribs who came out to greet him. Tragically, these gentle people were almost wiped out by European cruelty and

Droughts

"El Niño is continuing to evolve, continuing to be a very awesome event." ***Nick Green, Oceanologist, 1997***

Too little water can be as disastrous as too much. A lack of water is called a drought. In times of drought (*right*), people and animals die of thirst and crops wither, causing famines that can kill millions of people even in areas far away from the affected region. Wars and deforestation can make droughts worse — without trees, the soil cannot retain nearly as much moisture.

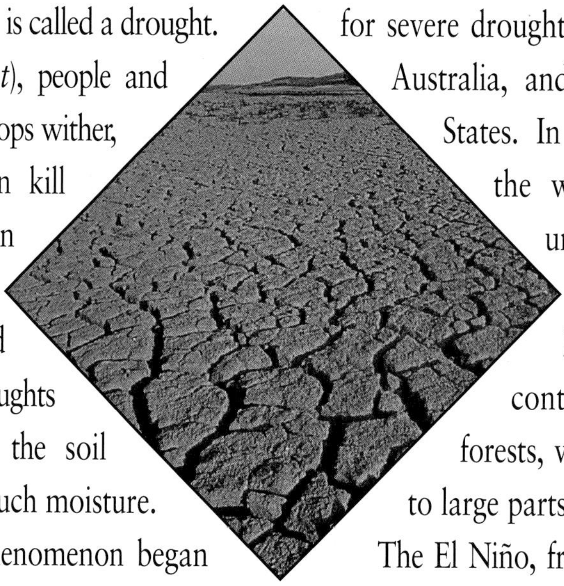

In 1997, a weather phenomenon began brewing in the Pacific Ocean. Called "El Niño," it is a warming of the equatorial Pacific off South America that causes unusual changes in the climate around the world. This may well be the largest climatic event of the century, responsible for severe droughts in Brazil, Africa, Australia, and even the United States. In Indonesia, where the weather had been unusually dry, local farmers and logging companies continued to clear forests, virtually setting fire to large parts of the country.

The El Niño, from 1993 to 1994, was not too severe. But, in August 1983, it caused global damage estimated at $24 billion. High winds and heavy rains in the Arizona desert turned streets into rivers and toppled power lines.

The worst drought related famine occurred in China from 1876 to 1878, when 13 million people died. As people starved, roving bands of human skeletons searched for food (*above*). Travelers were killed and desperate parents sold their children as food (*above*).

Water falls over mountains
Warm, moist air rises and cools
Dry air (rain-shadow zone)

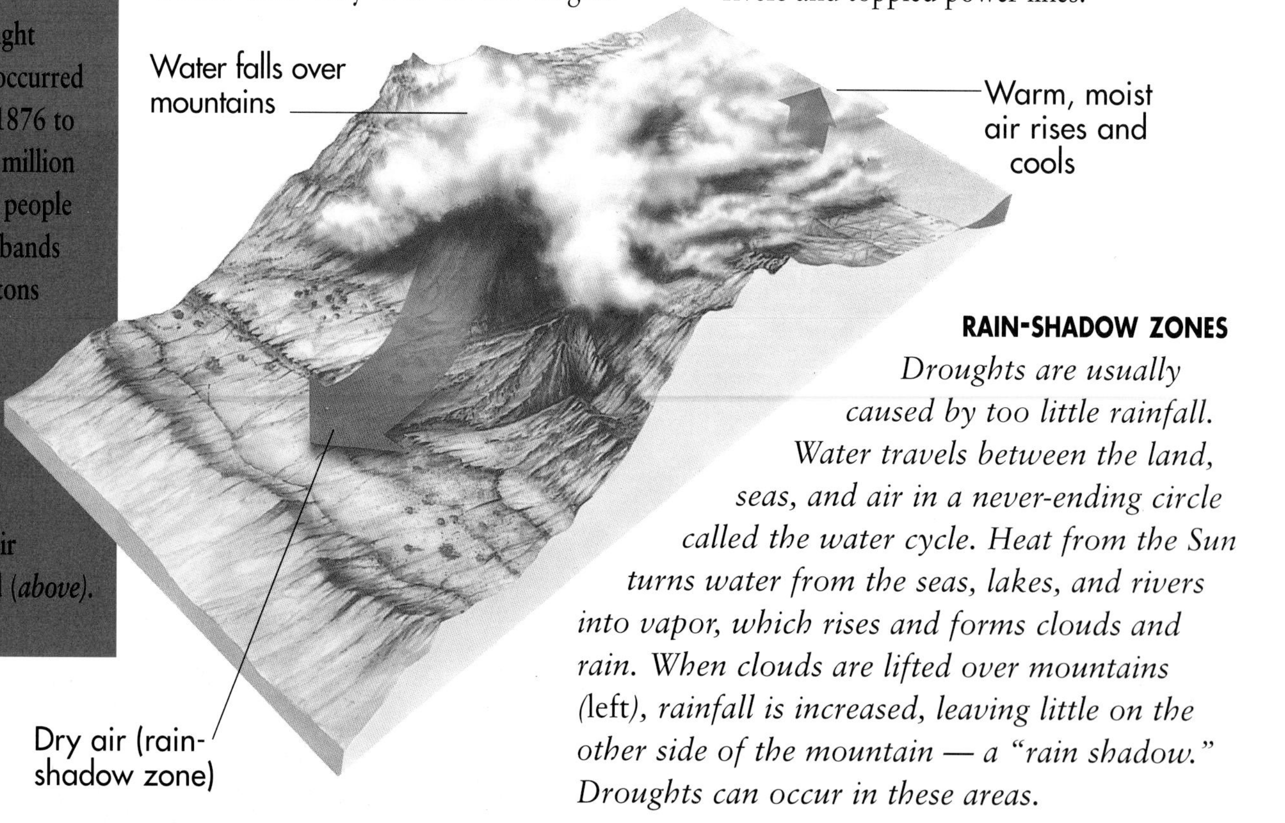

RAIN-SHADOW ZONES

*Droughts are usually caused by too little rainfall. Water travels between the land, seas, and air in a never-ending circle called the water cycle. Heat from the Sun turns water from the seas, lakes, and rivers into vapor, which rises and forms clouds and rain. When clouds are lifted over mountains (*left*), rainfall is increased, leaving little on the other side of the mountain — a "rain shadow." Droughts can occur in these areas.*

LIFE-GIVING WATER

The water in this pipe is usually reserved for watering crops. Here, in a time of drought, it provides a much-needed drink for a farmer. This is Mauritania, a country in western Africa, mostly covered by the Sahara desert. Intensive farming and clearing of scrubland causes desert areas to spread. Droughts get worse, and people flee from the drought-stricken countryside into overcrowded urban areas.

A farmer in Mauritania, where water is scarce.

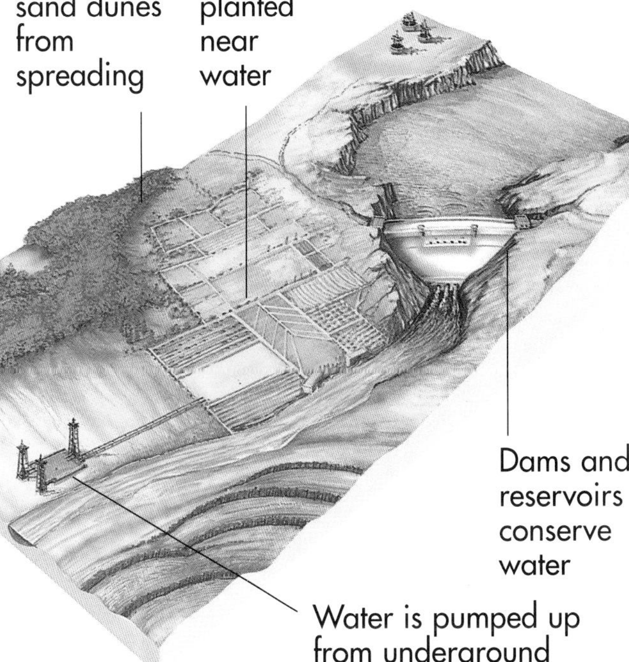
Trees stop sand dunes from spreading
Crops are planted near water
Dams and reservoirs conserve water
Water is pumped up from underground

WHAT CAN BE DONE?

*There are a number of ways of reducing the effects of droughts (*right*). Dams can be built across rivers, providing reservoirs of water for irrigation and drinking. Trees are grown to hold the soil together and bring up water from deep in the ground. Terracing prevents the runoff of rainwater and soil from hilly areas. The ancient system of building ditches and canals (*left*) is still used in many areas.*

KEEPING WATER IN

These dry stone walls in Mauritania are not to keep animals from wandering. They are built by laborers to function as dams around fields to prevent soil from wearing away (erosion) and to trap in much-needed rainwater.

CUDDLY KILLERS

In the still of the early morning, a group of Inuit hunters in northern Canada heard a scuffling noise outside their tent. Suspecting a thief, one of the men went to investigate. It was indeed a thief – not a human one, but a massive polar bear! Terrified, the hunter edged toward the tent.

The great white beast followed, rearing up on its hind legs (*main picture*). Seconds later, a blow from the bear's powerful paw snapped his neck. Polar bears, the world's largest carnivores, are said to be the only bears that deliberately hunt humans for food. One explanation is that the weak-eyed creatures mistake Inuits dressed in sealskin clothing for their favorite food – seals!

Grizzly Swipes
The grizzly bear (Ursus horribilis, below right) *is an aggressive cousin of the brown bear. It does not hug its enemies to death, as once believed, but swipes at them with deadly 6-inch claws. Despite being 7 feet tall and weighing 1,100-pounds, it can run faster than an Olympic sprinter!*

UN–BEAR–ABLE?

The intelligent brown bear (*above*) was once common in many parts of Europe. It is now found in north and central Asia and North America. In colder habitats the beasts hibernate during the winter.

Bears generally prefer to avoid people. Although vicious if threatened (especially if guarding cubs), the brown bear is not normally dangerous. But stay clear of the Asian black bear – although small, it is unpredictably vicious!

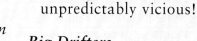

Big Drifters
Polar bears, distinguished by their white fur, long necks, and small heads, inhabit the Arctic Ice Cap, Greenland, Canada, and Russia.

Drifting on ice floes, they have traveled as far south as Iceland. Thick fur (which covers the pads of the feet to help grip the ice) and layers of fat enable them to survive the freezing conditions. They supplement their usual diet of fish and seals (and the occasional person!) with berries and grass.

Furry Ancestors

Humans have always thought that bears were very special creatures. This has not always been to their advantage – prehistoric peoples sacrificed them to the gods. Celtic goddesses, such as Artio (*left*), were also shown as bears, while early Christians thought they carried the devil (*right*)! Some primitive peoples believed humans were descended from a bear, the "Animal Master."

Hey, Good Licking!

The saying "licked into shape" comes from the belief that this is what mother bears did to their cubs, who were born without shape! "Teddy" bears are named after big game-hunting president Theodore Roosevelt, who in 1902 refused to shoot a bear cub.

Starry Bears

In Greek myth, bears were sacred to Artemis, goddess of hunting. When the nymph Callisto had a son by the god Zeus, his jealous wife changed her into a bear. The nymph and her son eventually became stars – the Great (*above*) and Little Bear constellations are still named after them.

THOR'S BEARS. In Northern Europe the bear, rather than the lion, was the King of Animals. The Viking god Thor (*right*) kept two bears: Alta (the mother of all things female) and Alti (the father of all things male).

SWOPS

OIL PRODUCTION SYSTEM

When oil companies began extracting oil from beneath the world's oceans, they started with the biggest oil deposits, building huge platforms to drill from. But there are a large number of smaller deposits, containing under 100 million barrels of oil. Although the total amount of oil they contain is large, individually they are too small to justify a production platform. In the North Sea, the problem has been solved by introducing SWOPS – the Single Well Oil Production System. Two small oil fields, *Cyrus* and *Donan*, are now in production using the system which was developed by the oil company, British Petroleum.

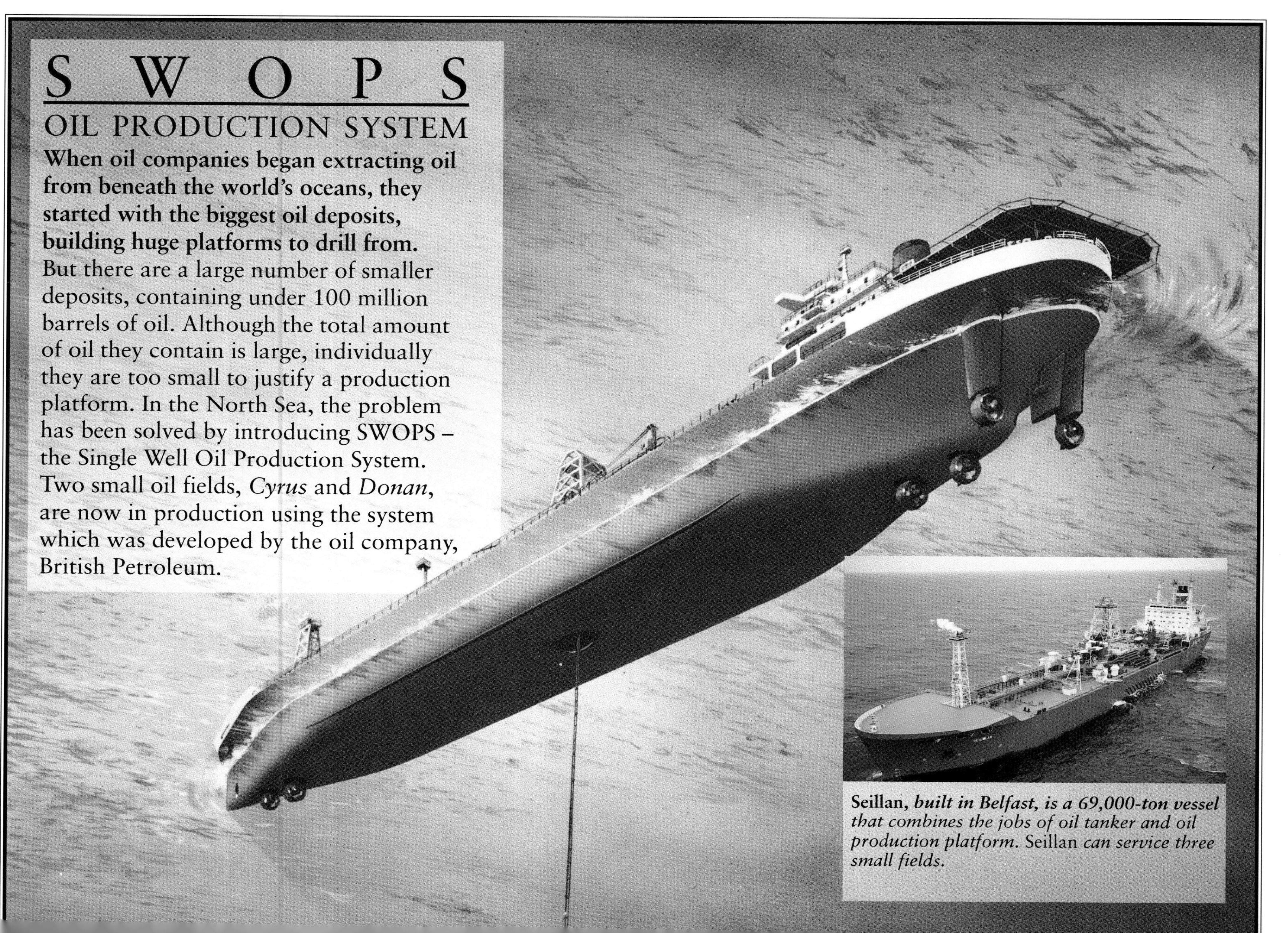

Seillan, ***built in Belfast, is a 69,000-ton vessel*** *that combines the jobs of oil tanker and oil production platform.* Seillan *can service three small fields.*

SWOPS involves drilling into the oil reservoir, and attaching a wellhead (which acts like a tap, or faucet) to the seabed. *Seillan,* a specially built production vessel, visits the wellhead, links up to it, and fills up with oil. When the oil emerges from the well, it is mixed with water and gas. *Seillan* is equipped with separators that can process the mixture into 15,000 barrels of oil a day. *Seillan* is kept exactly in position by seven stabilizing thrusters, powered by the separated gas. When its 300,000-barrel tanks are full, *Seillan* takes the oil to an onshore refinery. One ship can serve three small fields. Between visits, well pressure has a chance to build up again.

THE MOVING PLATFORM

HOW THE SWOPS WORK

Seillan positions itself over the wellhead and lowers a pipe, known as a riser, to the seabed. Seven thrusters on the ship keep it exactly in position. A T.V. camera guides the riser into position. The riser and the wellhead mechanically lock together, and *Seillan* fills up with oil, like a car at a gas station pump.

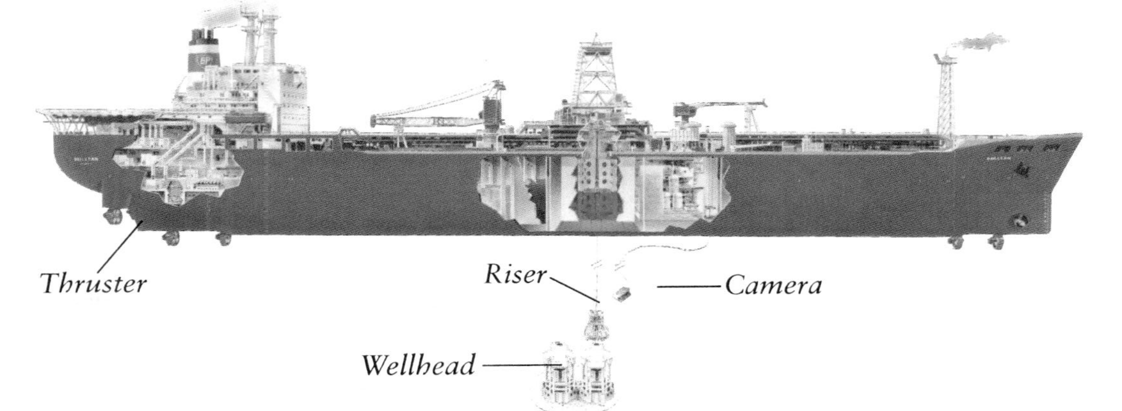

FISH COURTSHIP

Animals use courtship behavior to make sure that they are pairing up with a mate of the same species, and one who is fit and healthy. In this way, the mating is likely to produce healthy offspring. Fish courtship is not usually so spectacular as it is in many birds and mammals. Most fish come together only fleetingly to mate, and then go their own way again. However, some pond and coral reef fish use visual displays and courtship behavior in the brightly lit waters of their habitats.

Courting and caring

In most species of fish, the female lays her eggs (roe), the male adds his milky sperm (milt) to fertilize them, and then the eggs are left on their own. However, some fish have complex courtships, and care for their babies. The male stickleback (below) entices a female to his nest by showing off his bright breeding colors. He also cares for his young as they develop in the nest. So does the male seahorse, in a "pocket" on his belly.

Father gives birth

The seahorse is a strangely-shaped fish related to the stickleback. After the female lays her eggs, the male gathers them into the brood pouch on his front. The babies develop in this protected place. A few weeks later their father "gives birth" through the small opening of the pouch.

The mating dance

In spring, the male stickleback's underside goes bright red and his eyes turn bright blue. He builds a nest of plant debris on the bottom. Then he swims around a female in a zig-zag courting dance, attracting her with his bright colors. He encourages her to the nest. She lays her eggs and he adds his sperm – the process known as spawning.

Prized eggs

Sturgeons are massive fish ten to thirteen feet long, with large back scales and pointed snouts. The salted, unlaid eggs of the female sturgeon form the delicacy called caviar. At one time sturgeons were common, and even poor people ate caviar. But centuries of overfishing have made sturgeons very rare, and caviar very expensive.

Bred for beauty

For centuries, people have selected and bred together certain specimens of fish. This has been done to enhance their natural shapes and colors, or in the hope of producing new features such as frilly fins or goggle eyes. Koi and other carp have been bred in China and Japan for over 4,000 years. The goldfish was produced by selective breeding about 1,600 years ago.

Places for protection

Some fish lay their eggs in a protected place, such as under a rock or among weeds, where they are less likely to be noticed and eaten by other fish. Many cichlids, freshwater fish from warm climates, keep their eggs in their mouths! Usually the female does this, a process known as mouth-brooding. Other fish, like sharks and rays, lay eggs with tough, leathery cases (below) that protect the developing young inside.

Baby cichlids swim in a cloud around the mother's head. But they are ready to dash back into her mouth if danger threatens.

Hanger-on

In the vast, inky depths of the sea, it is difficult to find a suitable partner. So when a male deep-sea anglerfish meets a female, he joins himself to her body. He becomes more and more firmly attached until his body is fused to hers. The female has a male at hand ready to fertilize her eggs. But she also has one or several hangers-on, or "parasites," who she carries everywhere, and who she has to supply with food.

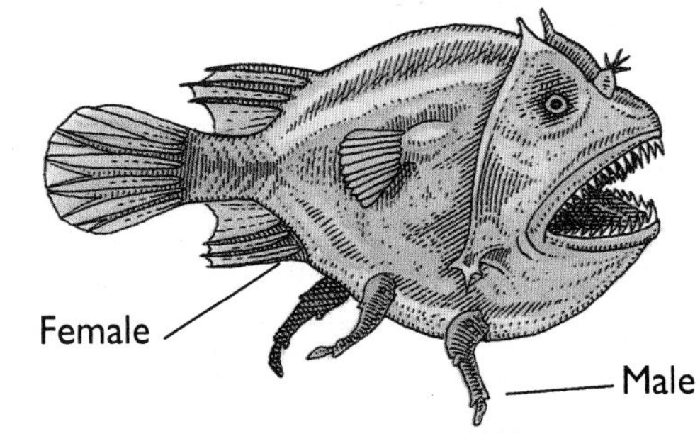

Life cycle of the salmon

Salmon spawn (lay eggs and sperm) in the shallow waters of small inland streams. The eggs hatch and the young salmon spend several years in the river, before migrating to sea where they become mature. To breed, the adults battle from the sea and make their way upriver. Surveys on tagged fish show that each salmon returns to the very stream where it hatched. It probably finds its way by its chemosenses.

PACIFIC PEOPLES

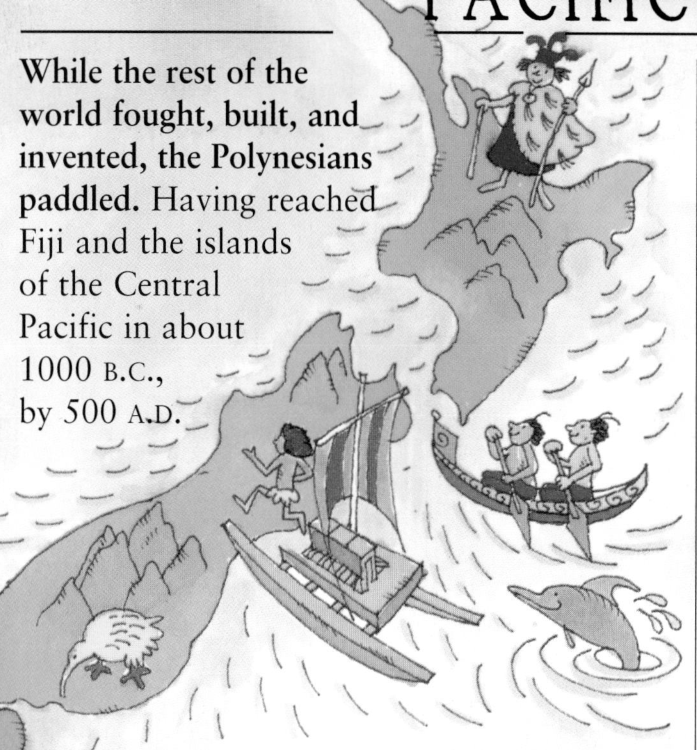

While the rest of the world fought, built, and invented, the Polynesians paddled. Having reached Fiji and the islands of the Central Pacific in about 1000 B.C., by 500 A.D. they had splashed over to Hawaii and Easter Island. Around 900, the Maoris doubled back and landed in New Zealand.

The Pacific people were happy fishing and chasing after moas (*left*) **and dodos,** so it was some time before they felt the need to build anything other than huts. In about 700, they set up some fancy stone shelves on Easter Island. By 1100, deciding they looked a bit bare, they livened them up with gigantic stone statues.

Back in Southeast Asia, the Polynesians' home base, the civilization habit was spreading. There was a wide range of options to choose from: Indian (Hindu or Muslim), Arab, Chinese, or a pick-and-mix culture of one's own.

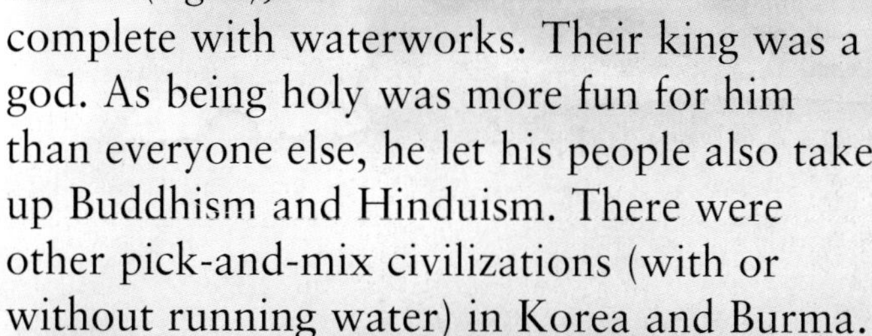

In about 900, the Khmer people of Cambodia built a big stone headquarters at Ankor (*right*), complete with waterworks. Their king was a god. As being holy was more fun for him than everyone else, he let his people also take up Buddhism and Hinduism. There were other pick-and-mix civilizations (with or without running water) in Korea and Burma.

MEANWHILE...
While the Easter Islanders were heaving hard-faced statues onto empty shelves by the seashore (1100), on the other side of the world Europeans were hauling up smaller hunks of stone to raise the walls of their castles.

Easter Presents
The huge statues (called moai) on Easter Island may have been erected to honor stony-faced ancestors. Similar holy shapes appeared on other islands.

Because they were proud islanders, the Japanese couldn't decide whether to stick to a homemade civilization or borrow bits of China's. In 646, when the Tang were the oriental trendsetters, the Japanese chose the China option. They built a new headquarters (Nara) as a copy of Ch'ang-an and tried to organize their country Chinese-style: All pull together and do as you're told. They even got the Ainus of the north (*above*) – the original Japanese – to behave like everyone else.

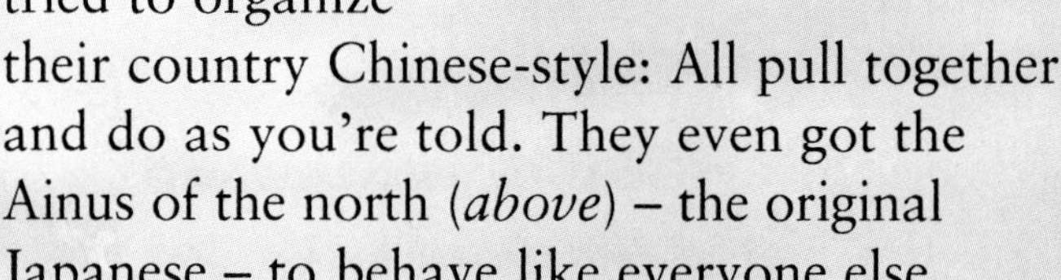

BETTER LETTERS

Chinese writing (a shape for each word) was OK for the Chinese because their words were short – e.g. Tang, bin, dung, etc. It was not so useful for Japanese, which had much longer words – e.g., Yamaha, kamikaze, etc. The Japanese solved the problem by inventing letters that represented sounds (like "Ah").

Chineseification did not really work. In 858, the Fujiwara clan took over and went back to the happy-go-lucky Japanese way of doing things. The headquarters were moved from Nara to Hein-kyo. They still had an emperor, but nobody paid much attention to him.

While knights-in-armor were running Europe, knights-in-padded jackets were taking over Japan. These were the Samurai. By 1170 they had kicked out the Fujiwara and were squabbling to control the emperor. Samurai superstar Minamoto won and got the emperor to make him General No. 1 (*Sei-i tai-shogun* – or "Shogun" for short). The emperor was now a puppet, with the Shogun pulling his strings.

The Chinese objected to the Japanese doing their own un-Chinese thing. Twice (1274 and 1281) Mongol emperor Kublai Khan tried to teach his awkward neighbors a lesson. Each time his ships were blown away by holy winds (kamikaze).

Warring Samurai clans

The Shogun controls his puppet emperor

Kamikaze winds destroy the Mongol fleet of Kublai Khan

ELECTROLYSIS

Electrolysis is a process in which an electric current is passed through a liquid, causing a chemical reaction to take place. The liquid used is called the electrolyte. The wires or plates where the current enters or leaves the liquid are called electrodes. The electrolysis of metallic solutions is useful in putting metal coatings on objects. If you have a look at some car bumpers, you will notice that they may have a nice, smooth, metallic appearance. This is because they are coated with a metal called nickel, in a process called electroplating. This helps to stop the metal underneath from rusting. The same method is used to coat cutlery with silver. This is called silverplating. Michael Faraday discovered the first law of electrolysis. The process is also used to purify metals like aluminum.

COPPER PLATING

1. For this project you will need a glass jar, a copper coin, a paper clip, two batteries, insulated wire, and water. Pour the water into the jar. Place the batteries together with unlike terminals adjacent. Connect wires to the terminals. Attach the copper to the wire from the positive terminal of the battery. The paper clip must be attached to the wire from the negative terminal. Use modeling clay. Do not allow the metal objects to touch in the solution. You could even tape each wire to the side of the jar so that they are suspended.

1

2. Observe closely what happens. Can you see bubbles? Leave them for a few minutes, then remove. Observe any color changes. Replace them for a while. Are there any further changes?

WHY IT WORKS

The copper coin is connected to the positive terminal of the battery – the current enters here. The other, the paper clip, is joined to the negative terminal – the current leaves here. As the current flows through the water from the positive electrode (anode) to the negative electrode (cathode), the copper is carried from the coin to the clip.

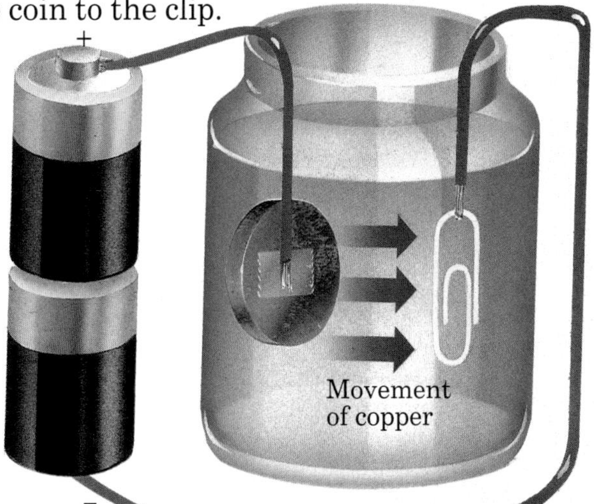

BRIGHT IDEAS

Repeat the project using salt dissolved in vinegar instead of the water. What difference do you notice – if any? What do you observe about the appearance of the paper clip? Maybe your school has scales that can weigh very small objects? If the coin and the paper clip are weighed before immersion in the liquid and their weight recorded, you can check whether electroplating has really taken place. After carrying out the project weigh them both again. Now replace the battery with a more powerful one, or add a second battery into a parallel circuit, to increase the "push" of the current passing through the liquid. (Remember to stop your experiments if the batteries heat up.) Weigh the coin and paper clip a second time. If the weight of the paper clip has increased further, then you have proved the first law of electrolysis – the size of the charge passed through the liquid determines the amount of copper freed.

2

BIG, BAD WOLF?

The wolf, once common in most of Asia and Europe, is now returning to many of its old hunting grounds. It is a hunter and scavenger that sometimes operates in huge packs. Although its normal diet is small wild mammals, it has a fearful reputation because starving packs have attacked children or weakened adults. Russian wolf packs were said to have pursued sleighs to get at their terrified passengers. The grey wolf, "prairie wolf" (coyote), and Arctic wolf (*top*) were less dangerous.

What Big Teeth You Have
The wolf's jaw (below) *can exert a pressure of 36 lb/in^2, twice that of an German shepherd dog.*

HOWLING AND LAUGHING

There is no sound more certain to send a shiver down the spine than the howl of a wolf (*above*). But the wolf howl is not a signal to attack, any more than the hyena's "laugh" (*left*) means that it is enjoying itself. Wolves howl for many reasons, such as making contact, calling a pack meeting, or just out of loneliness. A howl lasts up to 20 seconds and each wolf has its own "voice."

1 2 3 4

Wolf Expressions** – like humans, wolves use their faces to show how they're feeling:* ***1 *= angry,* ***2*** *= aggressive,* ***3*** *= afraid, and* ***4*** *= terrified.*

A Bad Reputation The view of the wolf as a cold-blooded human killer dates from the 14th century, when the Black Death killed a third of people in Europe. Wolves were very common and probably scavenged the remains of the dead. Medieval tales like Little Red Riding Hood (*above*) spread the message: "Don't trust a wolf!" In fact, wolf attacks on humans are very rare. Wolves will even eat worms, insects, and berries when meat is scarce.

Beware the full moon. The myth of the werewolf was once widespread in Europe – and is still popular at the movies (such as this beast from *An American Werewolf in London*, 1983, *above*). The werewolf is a human who changes into a wolf, usually during full moon.

***Native Americans** greatly respected the wolf, which was often a cultural hero and the remote ancestor of some tribes. Its symbol was the Dog Star, the home of the gods.*

Call of Nature American novelist Jack London (1876–1916) wrote many of the finest tales of the frozen world of the husky dog and the wolf. The best-known are *White Fang* and *The Call of the Wild*, made into a movie in 1972 (*left*).

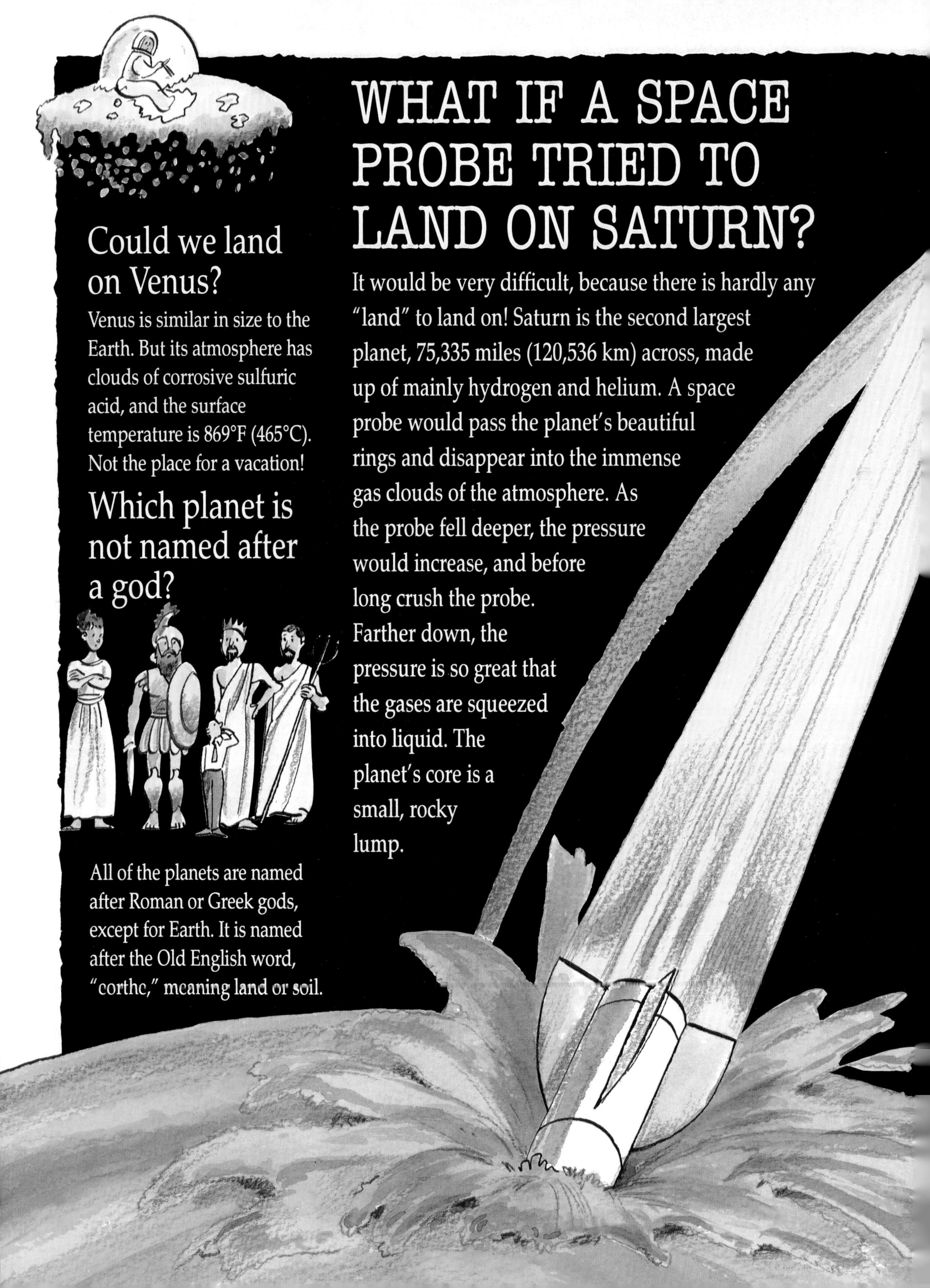

WHAT IF A SPACE PROBE TRIED TO LAND ON SATURN?

It would be very difficult, because there is hardly any "land" to land on! Saturn is the second largest planet, 75,335 miles (120,536 km) across, made up of mainly hydrogen and helium. A space probe would pass the planet's beautiful rings and disappear into the immense gas clouds of the atmosphere. As the probe fell deeper, the pressure would increase, and before long crush the probe. Farther down, the pressure is so great that the gases are squeezed into liquid. The planet's core is a small, rocky lump.

Could we land on Venus?

Venus is similar in size to the Earth. But its atmosphere has clouds of corrosive sulfuric acid, and the surface temperature is 869°F (465°C). Not the place for a vacation!

Which planet is not named after a god?

All of the planets are named after Roman or Greek gods, except for Earth. It is named after the Old English word, "eorthe," meaning land or soil.

The planet of fire and ice

Mercury, the planet closest to the Sun, is only 3,048 miles (4,878 km) in diameter. Its atmosphere has been blasted away by powerful solar winds. This rocky ball has daytime temperatures ranging from over 806°F (430°C) – hot enough to melt lead – to a bone-chilling -292°F (-180°C)!

Stormy weather

Jupiter has a storm three times the size of Earth, about 25,000 miles (40,000 km) across. It's called the Great Red Spot, and drifts around the planet's lower half. A gigantic vortex sucks up corrosive phosphorus and sulfur, in a huge swirling spiral. At the top of this spiral, the chemicals spill out, forming the huge spot, before falling back into the planet's atmosphere.

Are there canals on Mars?

Not really. But there are channels or canyons. In 1877 Italian astronomer Giovanni Schiaparelli described lines crisscrossing the surface of the "Red Planet." He called them canali which means "channels."

What are planetary rings made of?

Saturn has the biggest and best rings – six main ones, made up of hundreds of ringlets. They are 175,000 miles (280,000 km) in diameter – twice the planet's width. They are made from blocks of rocks, ranging from a few inches to about 16 feet (5 m), swirling around the planet, and covered with glistening ice. Jupiter, Neptune, and Uranus also have fine rings.

Which planet is farthest from the Sun?

Pluto. No, Neptune. No – both! On average, Pluto is the outermost planet. This small, cold world is only 1,438 miles (2,300 km) across, with a temperature of -364°F (-220°C). Its orbit is squashed, so for some of the time, it's closer to the Sun than its neighbor Neptune. In fact, Pluto is within Neptune's orbit until 1999.

DRAGONFLY

IF YOU COULD GO BACK IN TIME, before the dinosaurs – 300 million years ago – then dragonflies would be the biggest flying creatures. They were the first large insects to appear on Earth. Some were the size of crows. They haven't changed much since, except to become smaller. Dragonflies are fierce hunters that catch small insects in midair.

ABDOMEN

Inside the long, thin abdomen are the usual insect innards of blood vessel along the top, guts in the middle, and main nerve along the bottom.

BREATHING TUBES

GUT

HEART

WINGS

The two pairs of see-through wings are held out sideways when resting.

EYES

Dragonflies have better eyes than all other insects. Each has more than 30,000 units, ommatidia, for incredible vision. A dragonfly can catch a tiny gnat in twilight (when we could barely see a tree).

FLYING MUSCLES

LEGS

In flight, the legs hang down to form a prey-catching "basket." Their sharp tips grip leaves or twigs when resting.

ANATOMY *AT WORK*
HOW FLIES FLY

The wings are joined to the rigid-cased thorax. This contains two sets of flight muscles. One set pulls the top of the thorax, which clicks down and flips the wings up (1). The other muscle set pulls the thorax in, making it thinner, so the top clicks back up again, flipping the wings down (2).

WHY AM I NOT A FLY?

Many insects called "flies" are not. True flies, like houseflies, bluebottles, crane flies, fruit flies, mosquitoes, gnats, and midges, have two wings. Pretend "flies," like dragonflies, damselflies, mayflies, stoneflies, and butterflies, have four wings.

BEETLE

SOME BEETLES ARE SO TOUGH that even after you step on them they run away unharmed. This is because what looks like the beetle's abdomen (rear body part) is really a pair of wings. These have become hard and strong, like a shield, to protect the body.

FLY ON FIRE!

Fireflies are not on fire, nor are they flies. Glow worms are not worms. They are both types of beetles that glow and flash at night. Usually the female, who is wingless, makes the light – to attract a male, who flies in to mate.

JAWS

The male stag beetle's huge jaws look fierce, but they are only to impress other males. They can hardly move!

HEART

BRAIN

STOMACH

BREATHING TUBES

WING COVERS

Called elytra, these are really the front pair of wings. They fold together over the rear pair of flying wings.

WINGS

The rear pair of wings are large, thin, and flexible. Normally they are folded away, under the wing covers.

LEGS

Each leg is made of five hollow, tubelike sections, with joints between them. Ground beetles have very long legs, for fast running. For their size, they are ten times speedier than a human sprinter.

ANATOMY *AT WORK*

ARMORED WINGS

To take off, a beetle raises its front wings, or elytra. The second pair unfold and flap, to produce flight power. The elytra help by giving some lifting force, like a plane's wings.

The Fall of the Templars

In 1307, the attention of bankrupt King Philip IV "the Fair" of France was drawn to the Templar Knights, a group of crusaders founded to recover the Holy Land from the Muslims.

The Templars (whose seal is shown *left*) were now rich and powerful. They vowed obedience to their commander, held secret ceremonies, and were rumored to have associated with the Assassins. Heresy! cried King Philip. The Templars were rounded up, tortured, and their order dissolved – and all because King Philip wanted their money.

Fiction Mightier than Fact
Hundreds of Templar knights were burned at the stake (left) *after denying a range of false charges made by King Philip. These included spitting on the holy cross, worshiping cats, and secretly killing members who tried to leave the Order.*

Secrecy – or Death

In medieval Europe any group meeting in secret might be suspected of heresy (having opinions different from church teachings). Suspicion of heresy could bring in the dreaded Inquisition, set up by Pope Gregory IX in 1231 to force heretics to change their beliefs. Many suspects were tortured. Those who refused to change their beliefs were burned at the stake. Understandably, many genuine heretics kept their beliefs as secret as possible.

The Witches' Coven
Medieval villagers feared no secret society more than the witches' coven. In the dead of night, when the moon was full, witches (left) *were said to meet with the devil in a ritual of dance and wicked ceremony. How do we know? Because many poor souls confessed to witchcraft, often under torture.*

GRAIL GUARDIANS. The Holy Grail, the cup which Jesus Christ was supposed to have used at his Last Supper, inspired medieval legend – and modern film. In *Indiana Jones and the Holy Grail* (*above*), the Grail is guarded both by an immortal Templar knight and by a secret sect distinguished by a red cross tattooed on their chests.

Faith in the Shadows

John Wycliffe (c.1330–1384, *above*) was an English religious reformer whose Lollard followers were forced by harsh heresy laws to keep their beliefs and meetings secret. The movement survived for over a century.

The Chosen Few?

The Gnostics were a secret cult, not because they feared persecution, but because they wanted to keep their secret route to God to themselves. There were both Christian and Muslim Gnostics. The extreme members of the cult believed in dark magical powers.

The Sign of the "Great Secret"

Verdi the patriot

VERDI
(1813–1901)

MAIN OPERAS

Nabucco
Ernani
Macbeth
Luisa Miller
Rigoletto
Il Trovatore
La Traviata
The Sicilian Vespers
A Masked Ball
The Force of Destiny
Simone Boccanegra
Don Carlos
Aida
Otello
Falstaff

In March 1842 Giuseppe Verdi suddenly found himself famous. His opera *Nabucco*, first performed that month at the Scala opera house in Milan, was an instant success. *Nabucco* (Italian for Nebuchadnezzar) tells the story of the Jewish captivity in Babylon; and the Italians, under the domination of Austria, immediately identified themselves with the exiled and persecuted Jewish people. The opera's stirring chorus, *"Va, pensiero, sull' ali dorate"* ("Fly, thought, on golden wings"), became the theme song of Italian patriots longing for independence. From then on Verdi took his place as the musical spokesman of Italy.

Before *Nabucco*, Verdi had written a couple of unsuccessful operas, as Wagner had done before the success of his *Flying Dutchman* in 1843. The career of the two giants of 19th-century opera show striking similarities and contrasts. Both were born in 1813, both were deeply involved in the political upheavals of their day, and both wrote masterpieces toward the end of their lives (Wagner's *Parsifal* and Verdi's *Falstaff*). But whereas Wagner made his own operatic rules, Verdi built on the foundations of the Italian operas of Rossini, Bellini, and Donizetti. Wagner, like Weber, approached opera through the orchestra rather than the voice. Verdi, far more instinctive in approach, begins and ends with the voice, using the orchestra in its traditional operatic role as accompaniment and support, rather than as commentator on the story.

Verdi was born in the small town of Roncole, near Parma, the son of an illiterate innkeeper. He might have become just another struggling musician but for the tremendous natural resilience and toughness inherited from his peasant family. The personal tragedies that struck him between 1838 and 1840, when his two children and then his young wife died, seem to have given him inner strength rather than discouragement. He certainly needed all his energy to write the 13 operas that separated *Nabucco* from his first masterpiece, *Rigoletto*, performed in 1851. Verdi referred to this nine-year period as his "years of the galley slave." Most of these operas have a nationalistic theme and, although seldom heard today, they established Verdi's reputation as an Italian patriot.

VERDI AND POLITICS

The 1840s saw the rise in Italy of the movement called the *Risorgimento* ("Resurrection"). Its aim was to unify the separate states of Italy under one ruler. Verdi, who based many operas on patriotic themes, was associated with the movement. After a successful first performance of a Verdi opera, the audience used to shout *"Viva Verdi!"*, partly to show how they honored him, and also because Verdi's name spelled the initials of the monarch who eventually became ruler of a newly united Italy, *Vittorio Emanuele, Re d' Italia* ("Victor Emmanuel, King of Italy").

Verdi admired the three very different men who led the *Risorgimento*. The most famboyant of them was Giuseppe Garibaldi, the activist (above). In 1860 he led one of the most brilliant campaigns in military history. At the head of 1,000 red-shirted volunteers, he defeated vastly superior forces in Sicily, and finally took Naples for the Kingdom of Italy.

The thinking behind the *Risorgimento* was evolved by the theorist Giuseppe Mazzini (above). He spent much of his early career in exile, but organized a patriotic movement called "Young Italy" and masterminded risings in various Italian towns and cities. The third leader was the statesman Count Cavour (below), whose diplomatic skills helped bring about Italian unity. In 1861 he set up Italy's first elected government, in which Verdi was a deputy. Although the composer was a patriot, he was not a politician, and hardly ever attended after the first session.

Verdi's opera *Nabucco* (below) included a chorus that became the unofficial "national anthem" of Italians longing for liberation from the rule of Australia.

Unlike Wagner, who insisted on writing his own librettos, Verdi tended to look around for some existing plot to set to music. There is an amazing variety in the subjects he chose. In *Rigoletto* the tragic hero of the title is a hunchbacked dwarf. *La Traviata* ("The Woman Led Astray"), written two years later, portrays the love story and death of a famous courtesan. *Don Carlos* is about a Spanish prince who comes into conflict with the authority of the Inquisition. All Verdi's operas are full of vivid human incident, and many of his melodies are so famous that they have passed into the realm of super-classics. Typical of such tunes is the Grand March from *Aida*, played by military and brass bands, and the even more famous *La donna è mobile* (*Woman is Fickle*) from *Rigoletto*. Verdi himself finally became so tired of the popularity of this catchy tune that he would actually pay organ-grinders not to play it in the streets.

As a great musical dramatist, Verdi worshipped Shakespeare, but apart from his early opera, *Macbeth* (1847), he kept clear of setting the plays until near the end of his life. About 1880 he met Arrigo Boito, who was himself an opera composer and, more important, a poet who had the same love of Shakespeare. In Boito he found the ideal librettist, and their collaboration perfectly rounded off Verdi's lifework. *Otello* brilliantly re-creates Shakespeare's tragedy of love and jealousy, while in *Falstaff* Verdi says farewell to the world of opera in a bubbling and joyful comedy about Shakespeare's scheming knight. The opera, which is based on *The Merry Wives of Windsor*, ends with the words: "All the world's a joke" – the 80-year-old composer's last message to his audience.

Although Verdi was almost entirely an opera composer, he wrote one non-operatic masterpiece, the gigantic *Requiem*, first performed in 1874 in memory of the novelist and poet Alessandro Manzoni, who had died the previous year. Verdi lived on until 1901 as a revered master. He once remarked of himself: "I am not a learned composer, but I am a very experienced one." More than 200,000 people lined the Milan streets for his funeral. As the cortege rolled by, the vast crowd softly hummed the chorus from *Nabucco*, which had electrified their grandparents almost 60 years before.

Giuseppe Verdi (left) at the time of writing his patriotic operas. Verdi's spirit was with the revolution but, when he was not writing, he preferred peace on his farm at Sant' Agata to the turmoil of politics.

This cartoon (above) shows Verdi conducting his *Requiem* in 1874. The death's-head figures are an allusion to the *Dies Irae* ("Day of Wrath") movement.

BODY ARMOR

Armor protects soldiers from enemy weapons. The Greeks and Romans used it extensively, but the development of armor reached its peak during the Middle Ages. With the development of firearms that could penetrate metal, most soldiers stopped wearing armor, although cavalrymen still wore helmets and breastplates until the 19th century. Recently, new types of body armor have been introduced for soldiers and specialist police on riot duty (*below right*).

HOPLITE HELMETS

Greek infantrymen, called hoplites, wore heavy armor and large helmets, which were made from bronze and had a brightly colored horsehair crest. This Corinthian-type helmet (*above*) covered the entire face, so that only the eyes and mouth were exposed.

ROMAN PROTECTION

Many Roman soldiers wore breastplates (*left*). Another type of Roman armor, worn by legionaries in the first to the third centuries A.D., was made up of strips of metal held together by leather straps on the inside. This made it light and flexible.

FROM MAIL TO PLATE

Chain mail armor was made from many iron rings linked together (*below*). Soldiers wearing it could move around quite easily, but it provided only limited protection from arrows, heavy swords, and axes. During the Middle Ages, knights (*above*) began to add pieces of plate armor until, eventually, they wore complete suits of plate armor. These were skillfully made and were not as heavy and cumbersome as they look (*right*).

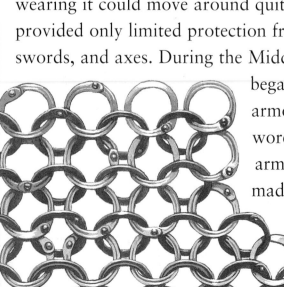

ARMOR FROM JAPAN

Samurai warriors wore armor made from iron and leather (*right*). The armor was usually coated in black lacquer, which prevented the iron from rusting. High-ranking samurai had armor decorated with brass and sometimes even gold. The helmet, or kabuto, had a wide protective neck guard.

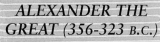

ALEXANDER THE GREAT (356-323 B.C.)

The most famous general of ancient Greece, Alexander was respected by his soldiers because he fought as hard as them – he wore a bright helmet so that his troops could recognize him in the thick of battle.

FROM CIVIL WAR TO WORLD WAR I

During the English Civil War (1642-1646), cavalrymen (*below left*) wore "lobster pot" helmets as well as breast and backplates, underneath which were thick leather coats. After the Civil War, armor began to die out, but during World War I (1914-1918) bulletproof armor was introduced. It was very heavy and was only worn by a few troops on guard duty (*right*).

WEIGHT PROBLEMS?

It has been said that some medieval armor was so heavy that riders had to be lifted onto their saddles using a mechanical hoist. In fact, full body armor weighed no more than about 44 lb (20 kg).

ARMOR FOR TODAY

Modern armor can be made from a new material called Kevlar. This is made of layers of synthetic fibers and is stronger than steel, but is flexible and light (*right*). Different types of Kevlar protect against knives or bullets.

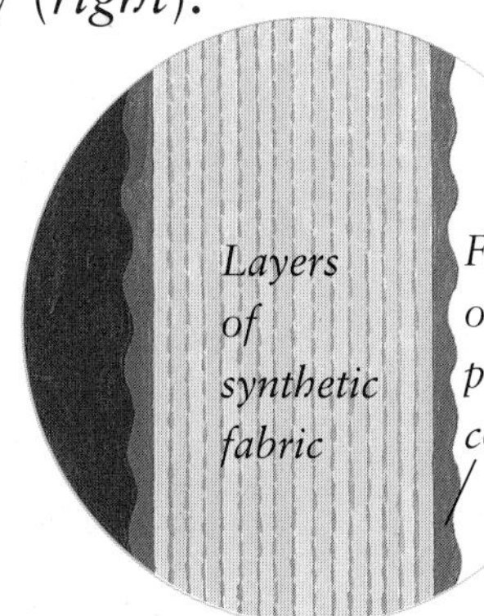

FLIGHT OF BIRDS

The champions of the air, birds can fly faster and farther than any other animals. This has given them a great advantage over other creatures, allowing them to exploit food sources far and wide and escape from danger. Birds fly in different ways. Albatrosses soar and glide on rising currents of air. Hummingbirds hover in front of flowers by beating their wings an incredible 90 times a second. Other birds flap their wings with powerful strokes.

Male Anna's hummingbird hovering

Laysan albatross braking in flight

Flapping flight

In this most common method of flight, huge muscles in the bird's breast contract to push the wing down. Then tendons act as pulleys and pull the wing back up.

Famous flight

The Ancient Greek legend of Icarus has been the subject of many paintings and poems. Icarus was the son of a brilliant inventor named Daedalus. Both were imprisoned on the island of Crete. Daedalus crafted two pairs of wings so they could escape. The wings worked well and Daedalus flew to freedom. However, Icarus enjoyed flying so much that he flew too close to the sun. The wax which attached his wings melted and Icarus plunged into the sea and drowned.

Icarus

Flightless birds

There are 10 families of flightless birds. Scientists believe that some flightless species, such as ostriches and emus, evolved from birds that were never able to fly because they were too heavy. But most of today's flightless birds are thought to have gradually lost the ability to fly because flight was not necessary to their survival. These species are mainly found on islands in the Southern Hemisphere where they have few natural predators. Unfortunately, when many flightless birds came into contact with humans they had no defense or means of escape. The giant moa of New Zealand was an enormous flightless bird that grew up to 13 ft (4 m) tall. It was hunted to extinction by humans some 600 years ago.

Giant moa

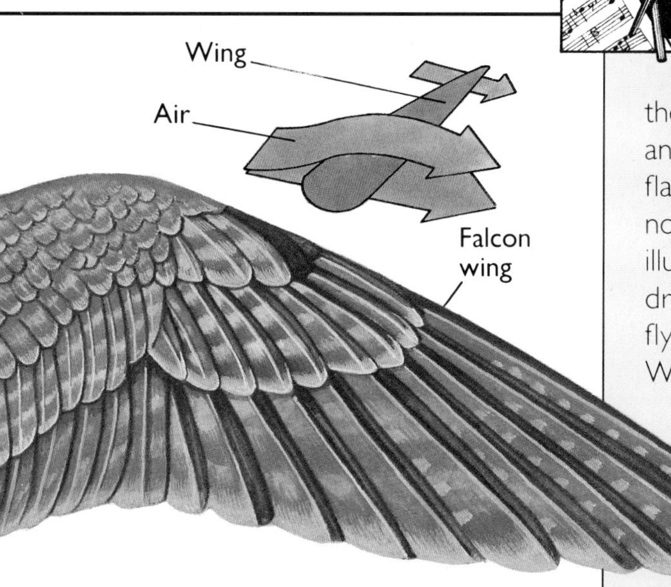

Flip book flight

Animation is a sequence of pictures that, when passed quickly before the eyes, looks like it is moving. You can animate the flight pattern of a bird: swooping, flapping, bouncing, or wheeling. Make a small notebook with blank pages. Choose a bird to illustrate and draw it in flight. On each page, draw the bird in its next stage of flying, like the examples below. When you have drawn each page, flip through the book quickly. The bird will look like it is flying.

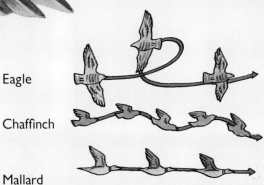

Eagle

Chaffinch

Mallard

A bird's whole body is designed for flight. Its wings are shaped like airfoils, flat underneath and slightly curved from front to back on top. As the bird flies, air flows over its wing. As it does so, the airfoil shape creates an area of high pressure under the wing and an area of low pressure above it. This pushes the wing, and the bird, upward. This design is so successful that it is also used for aircraft wings.

Flightless cormorant

There are many species of cormorants that can fly, but the flightless species lives only on the Galapagos Islands off the coast of Ecuador. Its small wings are useful when it dives for fish.

Kiwi

The kiwi of New Zealand is active only at night. It has no visible wings or tail. To get from place to place, it breaks into a waddling run.

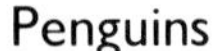

Penguins

Penguins slowly adapted from fliers to expert swimmers. This is because the icy lands of the Southern Hemisphere where they live are barren of life, but the ocean is full of food. Their wings act as flippers which help them to "fly" underwater.

Emu

The emu is an Australian bird that can grow to nearly 17 feet (2 m). Like an ostrich, it has long, strong legs and feet which enable it to run at great speeds. Emus generally run at slower speeds so that they can travel long distances without tiring.

The Legend of the Horse

Priam's Palace

1 The Real Troy?

The Troy that the ancient Greeks imagined from Homer's description was a splendid city of wide streets and beautiful temples (*main picture*). Yet none of the nine cities excavated at Troy had the impressive buildings of the legend. In fact, the city that may have been burned to the ground by an invading Greek army, Troy VIIa, covered an area big enough for just 1,000 people to live in – about the same size as the area within the blue walls near "Priam's Palace."

Although we don't know exactly what Troy looked like, there are four buildings hidden in the picture that certainly wouldn't be there. Can you spot them?

2 Homeward Bound

The *Odyssey* tells how it took Odysseus ten years to get home after thinking up the idea of the wooden horse (*see* page 4). Using the maze (*below*), find a route that lets Odysseus (O) reach Penelope (P), his wife, without meeting the one-eyed Cyclops, Circe the witch, the deadly singing Sirens, the whirlpool Charybdis, or the serpent Scylla. Also, Odysseus can't sail past the blue arrows, which are the bad winds sent by Poseidon.

3 The Wooden Horse

Which of these explanations for the wooden horse legend (*see main picture*) is the real one?

- the horse was a kind of battering ram (*below*);
- the horse was a siege tower covered in wet horse hides that protected it against fire arrows;
- the walls were destroyed by an earthquake, and the horse myth started because the symbol for the Greek god of earthquakes, Poseidon, was a horse;
- the real Trojans were horse breeders, so the wooden horse is Homer's joke on them!

4 Achilles' Weak Spot

Achilles was the greatest of the Greek heroes at Troy, and Alexander the Great's idol. He is famous for killing the Trojan champion Hector in revenge for the death of his friend Patroclus, then dragging Hector's body three times around the walls of Troy.

According to legend, Achilles' mother, the sea nymph Thetis, dipped him as a baby in the magical Styx River, making him invincible but for one weak spot. Can you guess where this was?

Heart • Heel • Eye • Neck • Buttocks!

5 Treasure Hunt

Greek legend tells of the fabulous treasures belonging to King Priam of Troy. Look at these objects below. Can you guess which one might be a genuine Trojan treasure?

6 The Mighty Greek Fleet

In the *Iliad*, Homer lists the ships taken by each Greek hero to Troy (his total is a huge 1,186). However, the ancient Greeks used letters of the alphabet rather than numbers to count with. So:

α = 1, β = 2 γ = 3, δ = 4, ε = 5, ζ = 6, ς = 7, η = 8, θ = 9, ι = 10, ια = 11, ιβ = 12, ιγ = 13, κ = 20, λ = 30, μ = 40, με = 45, ν = 50, ξ = 60, ξη = 68, ο = 70, π = 80, ϙ = 90, ρ = 100.

Can you work out how many ships the following kings brought: • Agamemnon = ρθ • Ajax = λβ • Nestor = πζ • Menelaus = ξε • Odysseus = ιδ?

Answers: 1 Pyramid, pagoda, teepee, igloo. 2 Odysseus must turn right, right, right then left, left then left again above the Sirens, right then right again, 1st right, around the corner to avoid the whirlpool, 1st left, right before the arrow marked (x) then right again – and then he's home! 3 No one knows, but all of these theories have been put forward! 4 His heel. Doctors today still refer to the tendon in the heel as the "Achilles' tendon." 5 Only the helmet might be a real treasure. The vase and the map can't because the ancient Greeks didn't know about America or China. The coin can't because the first coins weren't made until 750 B.C., and food quickly rots and would not survive. 6 Agamemnon = 109, Ajax = 32, Nestor = 86, Menelaus = 65, and Odysseus = 14.

Tsunamis

"The wave, like an enormous hand crumpling a long sheet of paper, crushed the houses one by one." *Eyewitness,* tsunami *in Chile, 1960*

In 1960, an earthquake in Chile started a *tsunami* that swept across the Pacific to Japan. Huge waves washed over many coastal towns, destroying 50,000 houses and killing hundreds of people.

Tsunamis are huge waves up to 100 ft (30 m) tall that are set off by underwater volcanoes (*right*) or earthquakes. Scientists use earthquake-monitoring devices called seismographs to predict when a *tsunami* will hit a particular coast.

The waves can travel at 480 miles (800 km) per hour and are devastating when they reach shallow water. They crash onto the land, washing people, animals, homes, and cars away — no sea wall is high enough to stop them. The power of *tsunamis* is so great that, in 1692, one that hit Port Royal in Jamaica threw ships onto the tops of buildings. It is said to have moved mountains and created huge splits in the earth that swallowed people whole.

WHAT ARE *TSUNAMIS*?
Tsunamis *are often called tidal waves, although they are not caused by natural tides. The burst of energy from an earthquake or underwater volcano sets the sea in motion. If the waves reach shallow waters, they bunch up and become one huge — and highly destructive — wave.*

The Japanese artist Katsushika Hokusai (1760-1849) made this print in 1831. It shows a huge *tsunami* tossing boats around like matchsticks.

HOLDING BACK THE WAVES

*Japan suffers from many earthquakes and a large number of storms from regular typhoons. These sea defenses (*right*) are used to minimize the damage caused when* tsunamis *crash onto the shore and to help prevent flooding from storm surges. When the sea hits the defenses, the energy of the waves is reduced by the special shape of the blocks.*

WAVE GOODBYE TO HOME

No, it didn't get there under its own steam — this steamer was swept into the Sumatran jungle by a huge tsunami. *The* tsunami *occurred in 1883 after the Indonesian island of Krakatoa was blown apart by a volcano. Waves 40 ft (12 m) high destroyed coastal villages on Java and Sumatra.*

Huge waves form

Waves become closer and taller near shore

When the *tsunami* hits land, it sweeps away everything in its path

The earthquake forces part of the seabed upward

THE FINAL FRONTIER

"Have you come from outer space?" asked the farmworkers. "Yes!" came the reply.

When Yuri Gagarin landed in a remote field in Asia on April 12, 1961, he had fulfilled a dream that was as old as humankind. Although the official welcoming party wasn't there to greet him, the Russian cosmonaut Gagarin had been the first person to journey successfully into space.

Left *Featuring aliens that live under the Moon's crust, Jules Verne's fantasy* From the Earth to the Moon *was written over 100 years before the real Moon landings.*

SPACE RACE

Orbiting the Earth in *Vostok 1*, Gagarin's mission focused the Earth's attention on the possibility of exploring other worlds. Before the decade was over, NASA had put astronauts on the Moon. On July 20, 1969, a billion people watched in awe as men from the *Apollo 11* mission took their first tentative steps outside the Earth. Science fiction had at last become science fact.

NO CHEAP THRILL

According to some estimates, an *Apollo* mission to the Moon today would cost a staggering $500 billion to fund. Scientists need to find cheaper ways to explore space. They have already sent robot probes to our solar system and beyond. These have brought back spellbinding images of our neighboring worlds. The farthest reaching probe, *Pioneer 10*, is now over 6 billion miles (10 billion kilometers) from Earth. That's roughly 100 times the distance from the Earth to the Sun. In October 1997, NASA launched a new probe, *Cassini*, that will take a closer look at the rings and moons of Saturn.

Below *A two-seater* lunar rover *was folded and packed into one small cabinet on its trip to the Moon in the later* Apollo *missions.*

Right *Scientists on the space station* Mir *have studied how to support life for several months in space. This has help them plan future missions.*

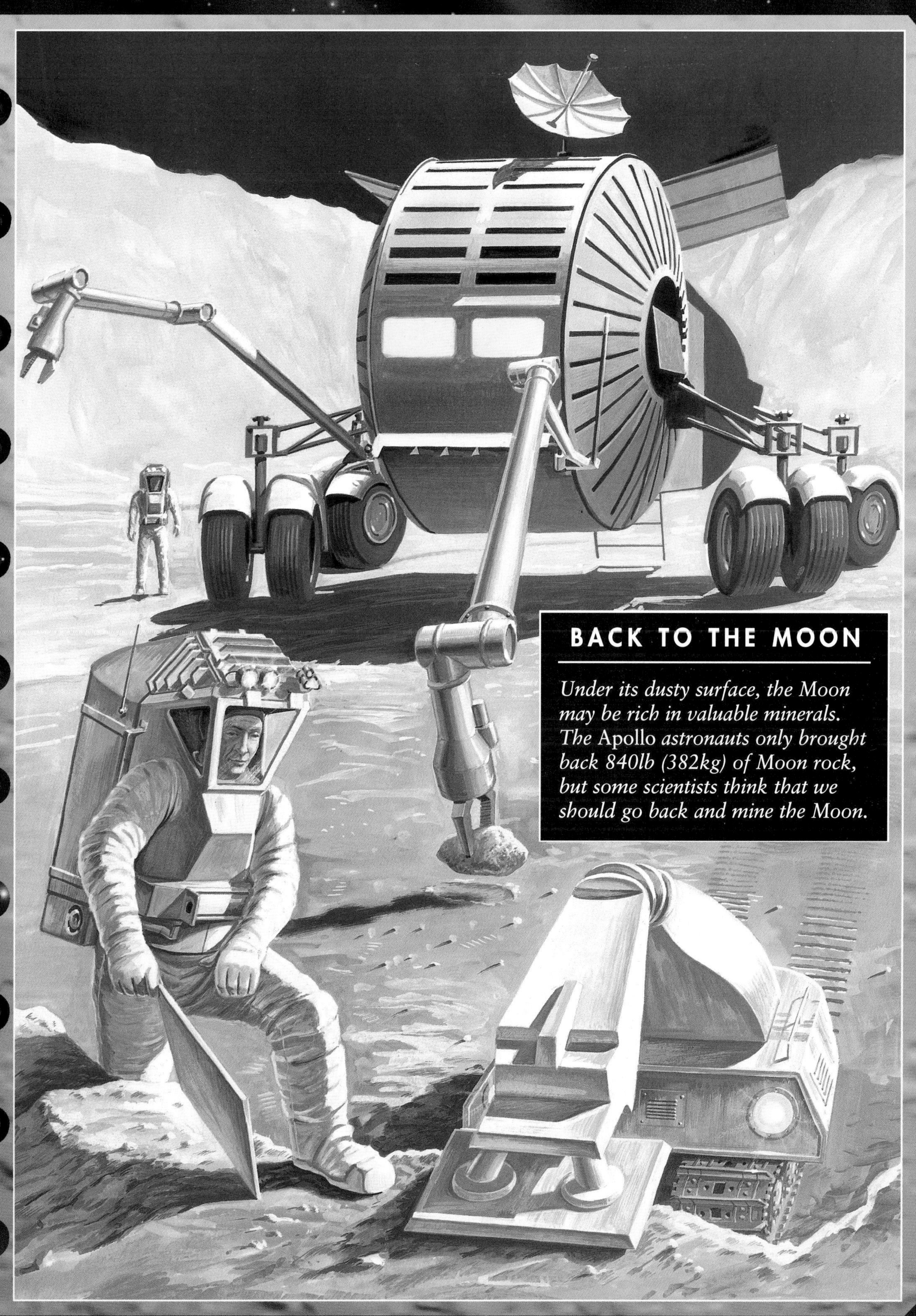

BACK TO THE MOON

Under its dusty surface, the Moon may be rich in valuable minerals. The Apollo astronauts only brought back 840lb (382kg) of Moon rock, but some scientists think that we should go back and mine the Moon.

How does a vacuum bottle work?

The key to this is a double-walled flask made of silvered glass or some other shiny material. Between the walls is a vacuum. Heat can travel in three ways: by radiation (such as the heat we feel from the Sun); by conduction (such as the heat transferred along a poker in a fire); by convection (such as the heating of air by a fan-forced electric heater). Heat does not radiate in or out because it is reflected by the silvering. It is not conducted in or out because the inside wall of the flask hardly touches the outside wall. And the heat cannot be carried by moving air because there is no air in the vacuum.

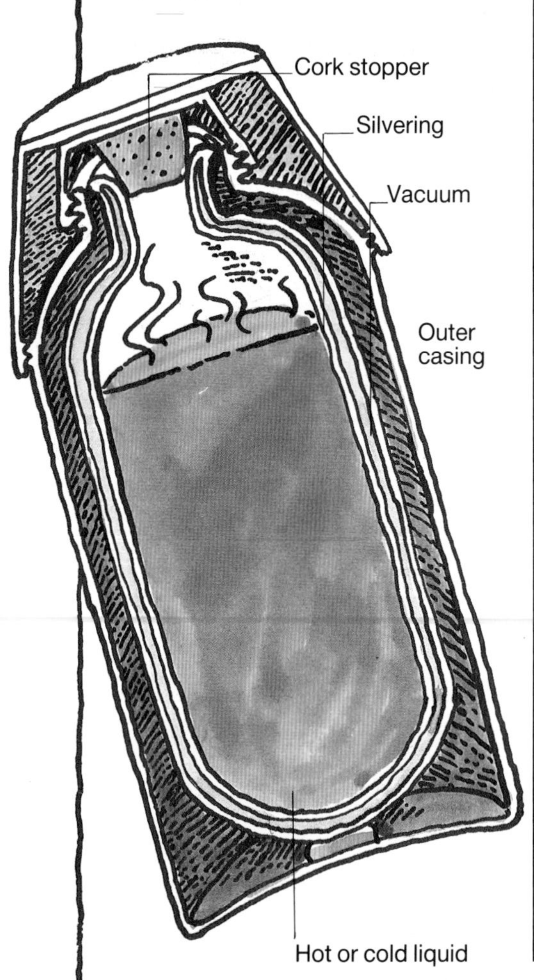

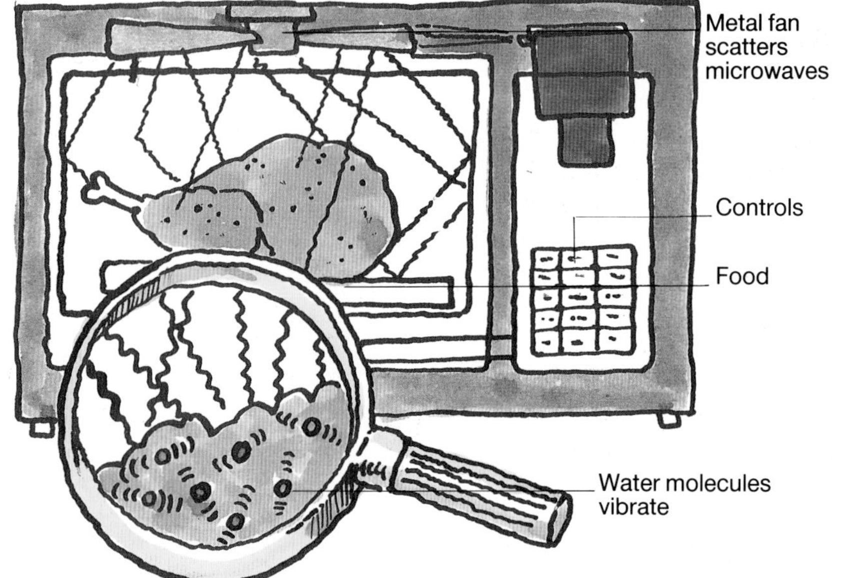

How does a microwave oven cook?

Like any other oven, a microwave oven cooks food by heating it. But it does this in a very different way from a conventional oven. The microwaves (which are similar to radar waves) cause water molecules in the food to vibrate at about 2 billion times a second. This vibration produces the heat that cooks the food. So dried food without water would not get cooked.

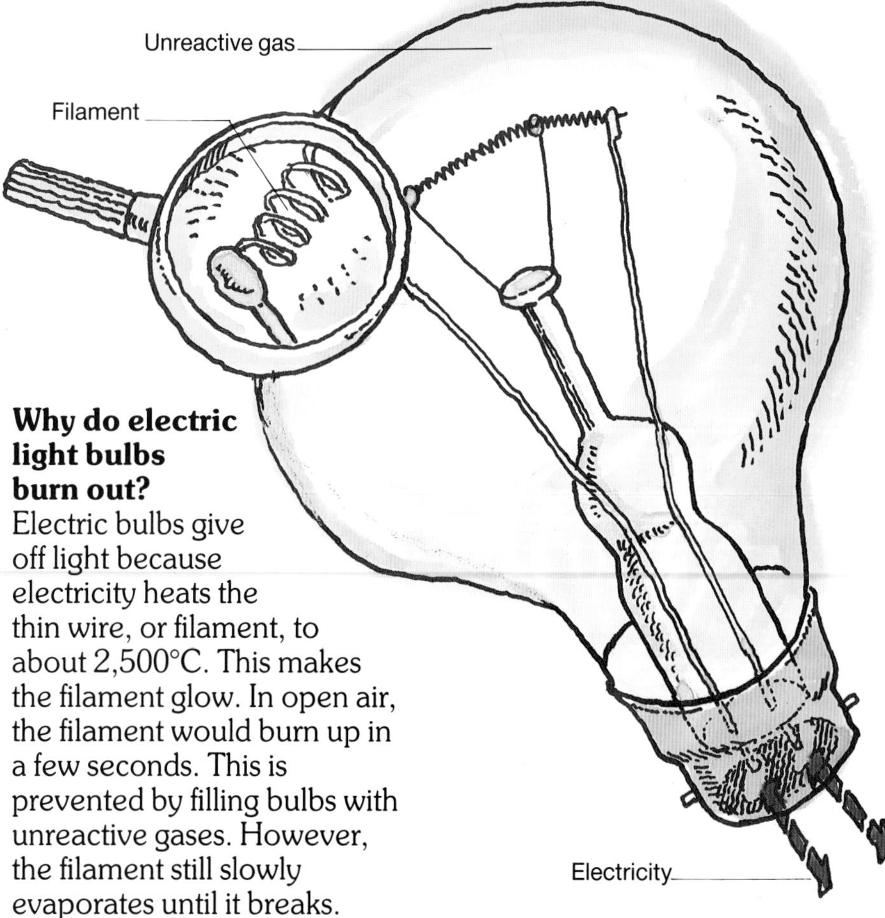

Why do electric light bulbs burn out?

Electric bulbs give off light because electricity heats the thin wire, or filament, to about 2,500°C. This makes the filament glow. In open air, the filament would burn up in a few seconds. This is prevented by filling bulbs with unreactive gases. However, the filament still slowly evaporates until it breaks.

Why don't plastic handles on cooking pots melt?

There are many types of plastic. A large number, such as thermoplastics, melt at quite low temperatures, but some are very heat resistant, for example, thermosetting plastics such as Bakelite. These thermosetting plastics differ from thermoplastics because they are heated a second time during manufacture. Links form in the polymers (molecular chains) to make a permanent structure that is heat resistant. The handles of cooking pots are made of such heat resistant plastics.

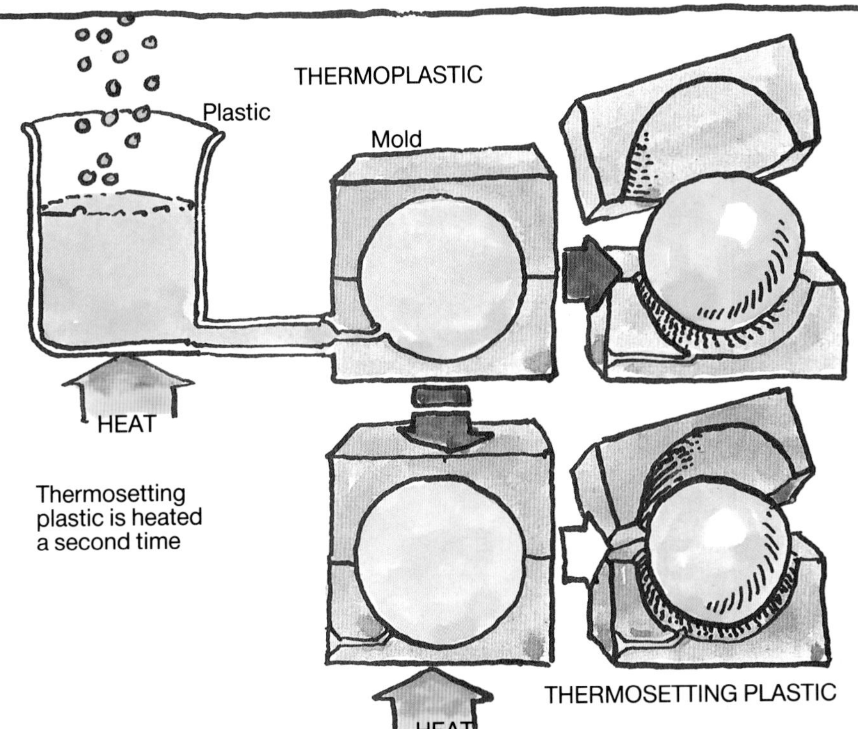

Where is the vacuum in a vacuum cleaner?

There are two types of vacuum cleaner. In an upright vacuum cleaner, the fan sucks up air and dust, then blows it into the bag. In a canister-type vacuum cleaner, the fan sucks air out of the bag, and so dust and air are pulled into it. In both types of cleaners, the vacuum is only partial and is basically in the place where the fan is. But in a canister-type cleaner, there is also a partial vacuum in the bag.

What makes safety matches safe?

Safety matches will not accidently ignite in the box. They only will light if struck against the striker on the side of the box. This is because they ignite by a chemical reaction between the match head and the striker. Heat generated by friction sets the reaction off.

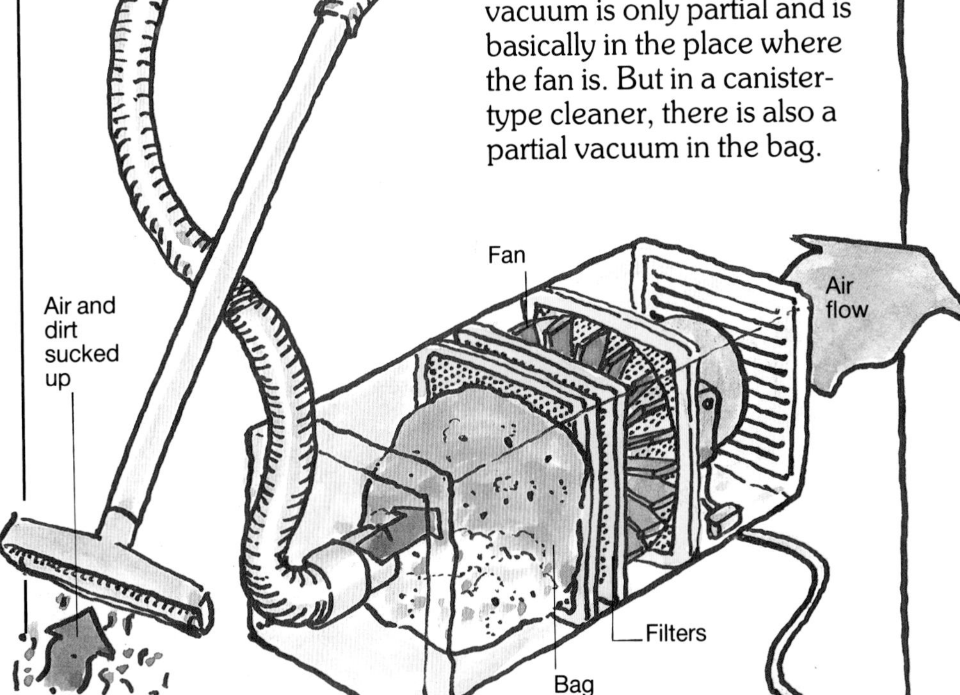

SMALL MAMMALS

Most mammals are quite small. The most successful mammal group, with more species than any other, is the rodent group. Rodents are intelligent, adaptable animals with high reproductive rates. One quarter of all mammal species are bats. The smallest mammal of all is the tiny Kitti's hog-nosed bat which weighs only 1/20 oz. The earliest placentals were insectivores. They are secretive night-time or underground animals.

Rodents and Insectivores

Beavers, squirrels, gophers, mice, rats, voles, hamsters, dormice, porcupines, guinea pigs, and mole-rats are all rodents. They are opportunists who make the most of whatever is available. They are found in every habitat, from lemmings under the Arctic snow to gerbils in the parched desert. Rabbits are not rodents, but are closely related. Long-snouted tenrecs, moles, shrews, and hedgehogs are insectivores.

Rats!

Bubonic plague is caused by a bacterium that infects rat fleas. People get the plague from flea bites and spread the disease when they sneeze. Infected people suffer fever and swollen lymph nodes (called buboes) and soon die. Epidemics have killed millions of people. In the 14th century, belongings were burned in an attempt to control the disease.

A Winter's Tale

When the weather is very cold the dormouse hibernates. First it eats large amounts of food and gets fat, then it curls up in its cosy nest. Its temperature drops to just above freezing, and its heart beat and breathing almost stop. In this state the dormouse uses very little energy and it can survive the winter.

Bats

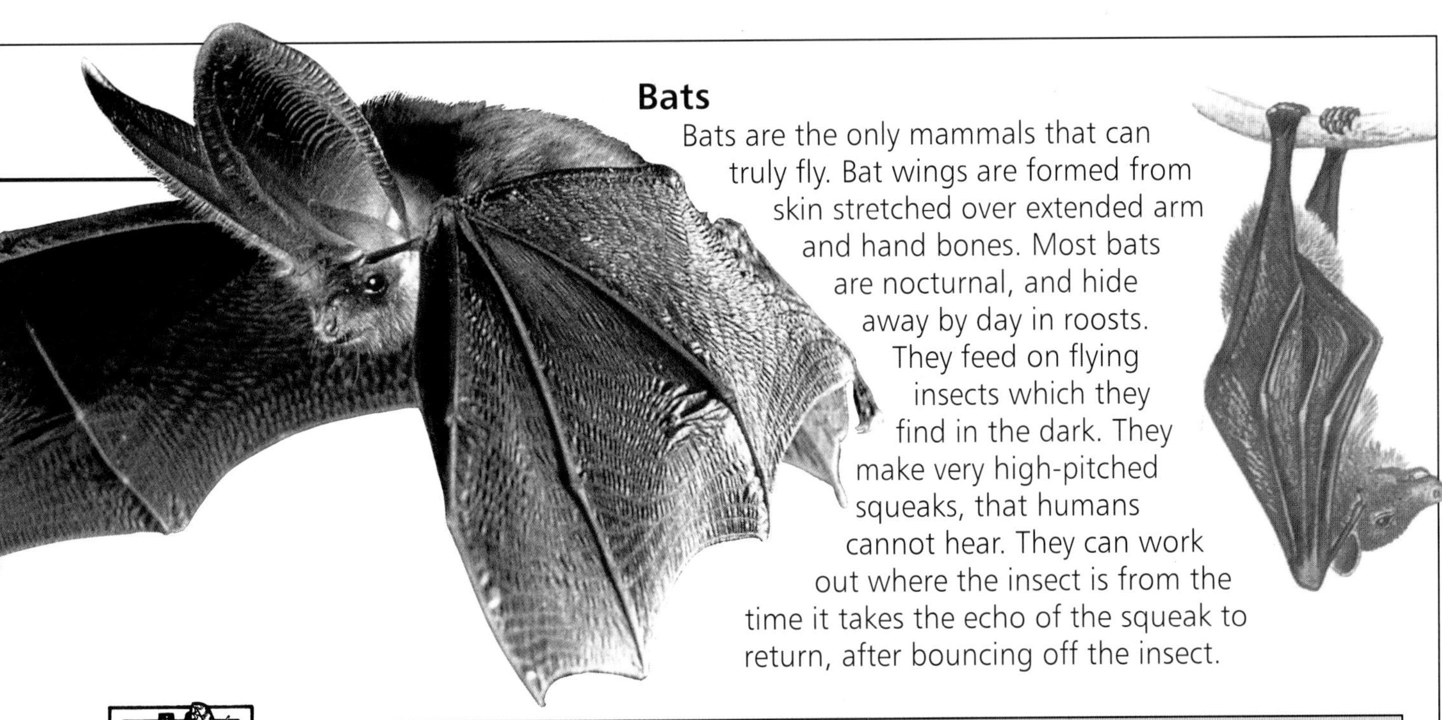

Bats are the only mammals that can truly fly. Bat wings are formed from skin stretched over extended arm and hand bones. Most bats are nocturnal, and hide away by day in roosts. They feed on flying insects which they find in the dark. They make very high-pitched squeaks, that humans cannot hear. They can work out where the insect is from the time it takes the echo of the squeak to return, after bouncing off the insect.

Nocturnal Animals

Many small mammals are nocturnal. They come out only at night when predators that hunt by sight cannot see well. They also avoid competition with daytime animals that feed on the same food. In very hot, dry places, animals like gerbils stay hidden in dark, damp burrows in the day, coming out only at night when it is cool. Nocturnal animals, such as the urban fox (right), have well-developed senses of smell or touch to find their way around.

Animal Sizes

The African elephant stands 13 feet high and weighs six tons. Its heart beats 25 times a minute to pump enough blood for its ponderous movements. The pygmy shrew is only two inches long and weighs just two grams. It hardly ever stops scampering about and its tiny heart beats over 800 times every minute.

Wind in the Willows

These charming stories about the antics of the small mammalian friends Mole, Water Rat, Badger, and the rather pompous but loveable amphibian, Toad of Toad Hall, were first written by Kenneth Grahame as a series of bedtime stories for his son Alastair. The full collection of stories, called *The Wind in the Willows*, was published in 1908.

Knights and Castles

The castle had many purposes. It was a home for the lord, his family, and servants; it was a symbol of his power, dominating all other buildings in the area apart from the church; it was a store for weapons and food; and it was a refuge in times of danger.

In medieval times land was wealth. A castle defended that wealth and so was as important to a king or baron as his knights. The first castles consisted of a keep on a large mound (the motte) surrounded by a walled lower area (the bailey). The walls were wood or stone. From the 1270s onward, all-stone castles such as Harlech in Wales (*main picture*) were built with rings of walls and towers. Before gunpowder, a well-built castle like this could take weeks to subdue.

Castles of Delight

Castles in Japan were built differently from those in Europe. The samurai did not produce the West's advanced siege weapons and techniques, and they were more concerned with individual prowess in the battlefield than with the static slog of siege warfare.

As a result, samurai castles, like samurai armor, were works of art. Placed on hilltops and decorated with sweeping roofs and elegant windows, they were a joy to behold (*below*) as well as useful refuges in times of war.

Guard the Door!
During the 13th century it became common to combine gatehouse (a castle's weakest point) and keep in one massive fortification.

Preparing for a Long Siege
Women and servants are led out while the castle stocks up on food, drink, medical supplies, and ammunition.

***Duffus Castle** in Scotland* (above) *is an example of a Norman motte and bailey castle.*

***Pure Disney** – the castle at Disneyland, Paris wouldn't last long in a siege* (below)*!*

Hoarding
In preparation for a siege, an overhanging wooden hoarding, covered in damp hide for protection against fire, was attached along the tops of the walls and on turrets (top).

This sheltered the defending soldiers. It also allowed them to drop rocks and boiling oil on the attackers below (right).

To Take A Castle:

1. Simply surround it and force the garrison to surrender through starvation.
2. Set it alight with fire arrows. Or fling burning rags over the walls.
3. Dig a mine beneath the walls. Support the roof with wooden props. Set fire to them, to bring down the tunnel and the walls.
4. Knock holes in the defenses with battering rams or siege engines.
5. Storm the walls with ladders and towers.
6. Treachery!

Attacking Strategy
Attackers tried to drain the moat and fill it with dirt to allow their siege engines to get right up to the walls.

Fishy Business

Heddingham Castle's (*right*) system of secret passages beyond the walls enabled the besieged garrison to be supplied with food. Once, when fresh fish was thrown at attackers, they realized the castle would not be starved into submission.

FEELING PAIN

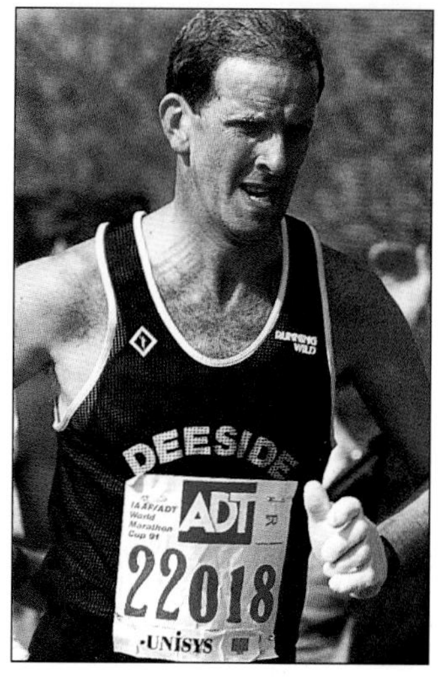

When you stub your toe or bang your head, you might wish that the body lacked its sense of pain. But it is vital for survival. Pain warns you that the body is being harmed, and action is needed to get rid of the danger. Pain causes the body to make fast reflexes or movements called avoidance reactions. There are also pains that happen inside the body, indicating injury, pressure, or disease.

Sometimes, athletes, such as long-distance runners (above right), run into the "pain wall." This is when the body experiences so much pain that it feels that it cannot go on. When this happens, some athletes grit their teeth and continue running to take them through the "wall."

NERVE CELLS
Neurons carry nerve signals (right). Each has a cell body, projections called dendrites, and a wire called the axon. The gap between nerves is called the synapse. Chemicals flood across this gap to the next neuron, to keep the signal going.

REFLEXES
A painful touch causes signals to go from the finger along the arm to the spinal cord. Here, they are sent to the brain, making you aware of pain. But already a reflex arc in the spinal cord has sent signals back to the arm muscles to jerk the finger away.

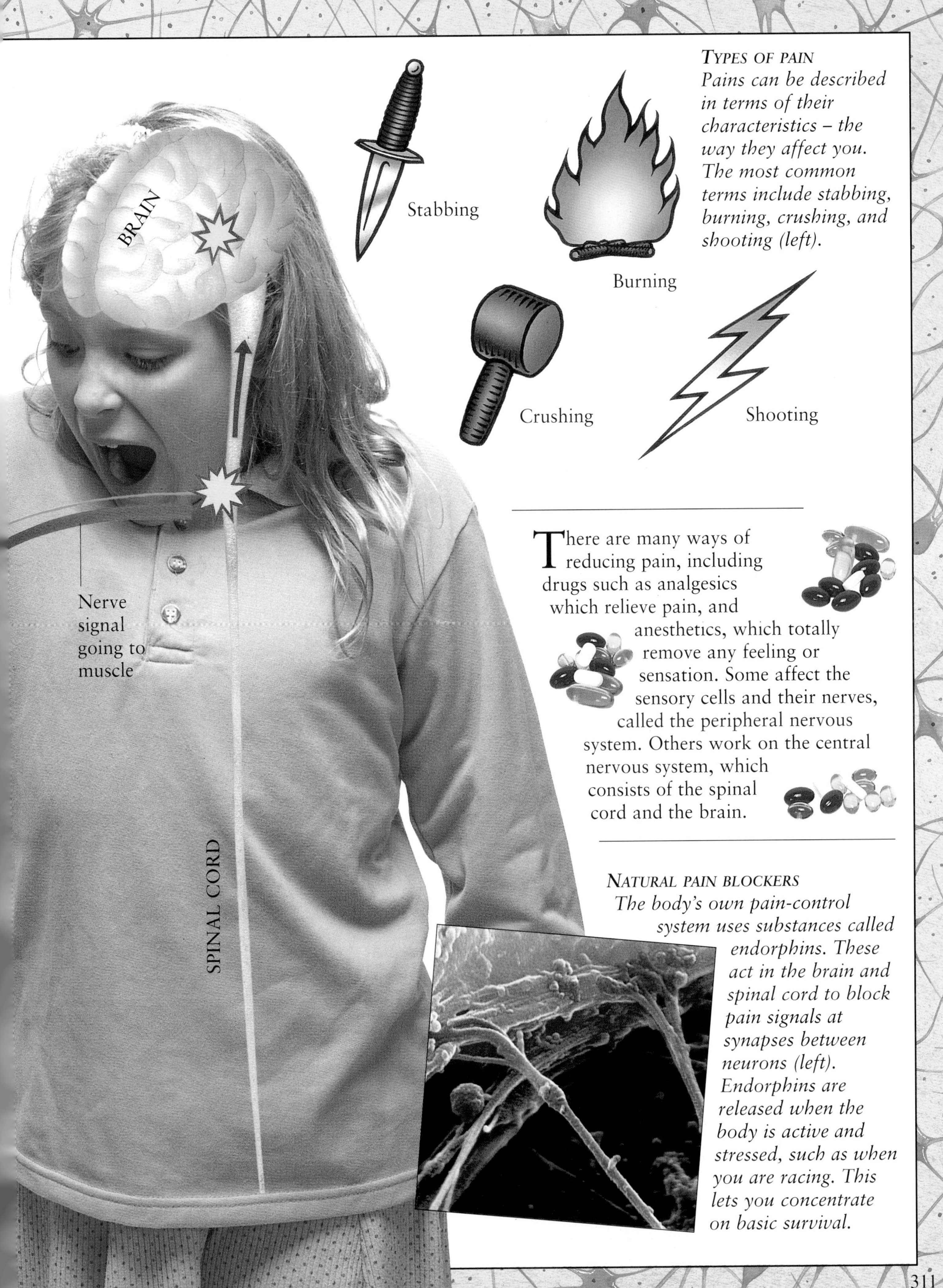

TYPES OF PAIN
Pains can be described in terms of their characteristics – the way they affect you. The most common terms include stabbing, burning, crushing, and shooting (left).

There are many ways of reducing pain, including drugs such as analgesics which relieve pain, and anesthetics, which totally remove any feeling or sensation. Some affect the sensory cells and their nerves, called the peripheral nervous system. Others work on the central nervous system, which consists of the spinal cord and the brain.

NATURAL PAIN BLOCKERS
The body's own pain-control system uses substances called endorphins. These act in the brain and spinal cord to block pain signals at synapses between neurons (left). Endorphins are released when the body is active and stressed, such as when you are racing. This lets you concentrate on basic survival.

Killer Whales?

Under the supervision of Herbert Ponting, the husky dogs were tethered on a large slab of floating ice. Suddenly the ice shuddered. Ponting looked around to see what was happening. Eight orcas had gathered beside them. Some had swum beneath the ice and were bumping it from below.

Ponting was terrified. He believed he knew exactly what was going on: The orcas were trying to get at the dogs by tipping them into the sea. Thanks to reports such as this, the orca got its undeserved reputation as the "killer whale."

Playful Piebalds

The beautiful black-and-white orca – also unfairly known as the killer whale – is a large, highly intelligent member of the dolphin family.

Playful, gentle, and inquisitive, they are famous for poking their noses out of the water to see what's going on. Perhaps this is what happened when the killer whales bumped the ice near Ponting. His tale even led to a U.S. Navy manual stating that orcas would "attack at every single opportunity" – completely untrue!

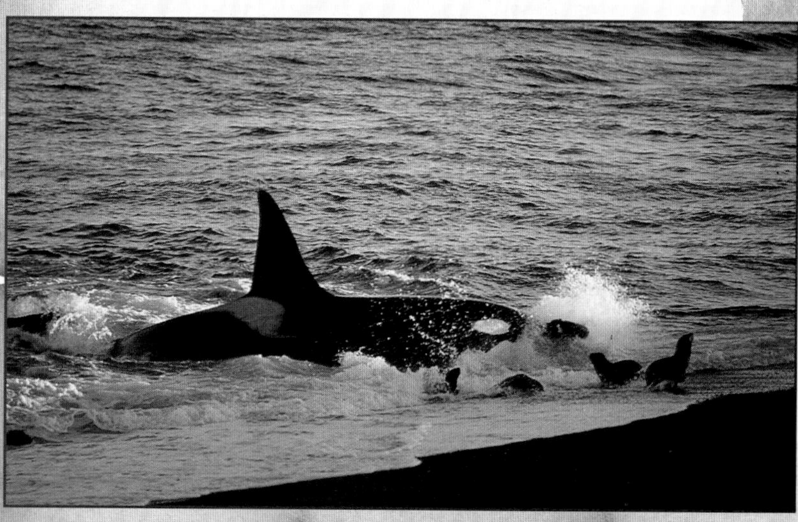

Beachcombers

For the orcas of the Patagonian coast of Argentina, seal pup is a great delicacy. They launch themselves right up onto the beach to grab a tender morsel (left), *ignoring older seals and even a nosey camera crew in the water. There is no evidence of a so-called "killer" ever attacking a boat or a human being.*

A Modern Myth

When Herbert Ponting, photographer on the British 1911 Antarctic Expedition, mistook orca inquisitiveness for aggression (main picture), *he helped create the myth of the creature's murderous nature.*

FREE WILLY? In the 1960s, scientists began to challenge the idea that orcas were man-eaters. When the beast's friendly nature was realized, some were put on display in ocean theme parks and taught tricks.

Further research showed that this unnatural behavior caused the creatures great stress. Though films like *Free Willy,* (1995, *left*) argued for their freedom, many orcas remain in captivity.

Narwhal

Unicorn

HORNY TUSK. The narwhal of the icy Arctic has long been regarded as an exotic creature. In the 10th century, the Vikings sold the narwhal's spiral tusk (actually a single tooth 9 feet long) to European merchants, pretending that it was a unicorn horn. England's Virgin Queen, Elizabeth I (1558–1603), kept a narwhal's tooth under her bed as she believed it had magic powers.

WHALE "SINGING"

Using modern acoustic technology, marine biologists have learned that several species of whales communicate with each other by means of low-frequency sounds ("singing") that carry many miles through the ocean.

Although we do not yet know what the different noises mean, they are further evidence of the creatures' sophisticated intelligence.

A Hard Tusk

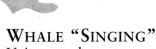

The large tusks of the male walrus serve many functions – fighting other males, breaking holes in the ice, and as an ice pick to heave itself out of the water.

PAPER COLLAGE

Paper is the single most important resource of the collage artist. From tissue paper to newsprint, from picture postcards to typing paper, it's important to get to know the range of papers that are available.

A library of paper

Start your own paper collection. You may be surprised by how much normally gets thrown away. Gather together a stock of paper that you can draw on for this project.

The aim is to find out what paper can do by putting together your own collage of flowers from different papers. Bring in as many textures as you can find. Sandpaper, envelopes and foil are used on the right.

Cut or tear yourself a series of petal shapes from your papers.

Practicing composition

If you pick or buy a bunch of flowers, you will probably want to arrange them in a vase at home. In the same way, your paper flowers need to be arranged in a pleasing way. This process is called composition. One of the great advantages of collage is the ability to practice composition, trying your materials in all kinds of positions before deciding on a final version. When you decide what looks best, stick them down.

▷ ***"Don't forget you can overlap some of your flowers, as I have in the collage on the right. You'll find that using similar shapes will bring out the different qualities and textures of the paper."***

All about paper

Paper comes from trees. It's made from pulped wood mixed with water and pressed flat. Paper can have other substances, flax for example, mixed in with it to give it a different texture. Paper is available in many different weights and textures. Shown here are (1) corrugated paper (2) notepaper (3) tracing paper (4) construction paper and (5) wrapping paper. Construction paper is inexpensive and comes in many colors. Thick watercolor paper and cheap bond paper are also useful.

AIRPOWER

STRIVING FOR STEALTH

Exotic shapes and sophisticated new electronic systems have created a generation of planes invisible to radar. The experience of surface-to-air missiles in wars in the Middle East and Vietnam convinced strategists that in future aircraft would have to elude detection by radar and attack by heat-seeking missiles. The first practical stealth war planes emerged in the 1991 Gulf War – the U.S. B-2 stealth bomber and the F-117A stealth fighter. Stealth technology means making an aircraft hard to detect in every way: by radar, by sight, by sound, or by the heat of its engines.

The engines of a conventional bomber give off a huge amount of heat in producing their 75 megawatts of power, while a modern infrared detector is sensitive enough to track a lighted cigarette at 30 miles. To make the engines of the B-2 less obvious to the detectors, they are designed to be quiet and cool, and are tucked away in the base of the wings. On the F-117A fighter, known to pilots as the "Wobbly Goblin," the two engines are buried in the thick inner portion of the wings. The fuselage and wing are designed as one because the wing root, where wing and fuselage join, can create a very strong radar echo.

(Below) The Aurora – this reconstruction is what some people think the mystery plane looks like. If it exists, it would be able to fly very high, very fast, and for thousands of miles without refueling on reconnaissance missions over enemy territory.

The Northrop B-2 bomber, which first flew in 1989, looks as if it is all wing and no plane. The smooth shape reduces radar echoes by minimizing sharp angles and vertical surfaces. For the same reason, the B-2 has no fin. This would normally make it impossible to fly, so computerized fly-by-wire techniques are used to keep it under control. The B-2 also has complex electronic systems for confusing the enemy, and special paints and materials for a lower radar signature.

CODE NAME AURORA

A HIGH-FLYING MYSTERY

Perhaps surprisingly, no order has been placed for a type of aircraft where stealth is most important of all, the high-flying surveillance aircraft. This has not prevented people from speculating that such an aircraft is being built in secret, under the code name Aurora (see far left), and occasional sightings of the aircraft over Scotland have fed the rumors. Although aircraft have been developed in secret before, concealing an advanced aircraft like Aurora for so long would be a major achievement. However, disappointingly, it looks as if Aurora is just a fantasy.

***The Lockheed F-117A** (above left) does have a tail, but not a vertical one. Its two fins form a V-shape, reducing radar echo. The angles and facets of the plane reflect light and radar in every direction like a cut jewel, confusing defenders. To reduce heat, the two General Electric turbofan engines are deeply buried and not fitted with afterburners, though this does mean a big loss of power.*

***Incoming radar signals** bounce off the panels of the F-117A in every direction. This means that there is no single strong echo bouncing back to give the aircraft's position away. It merges into the background.*

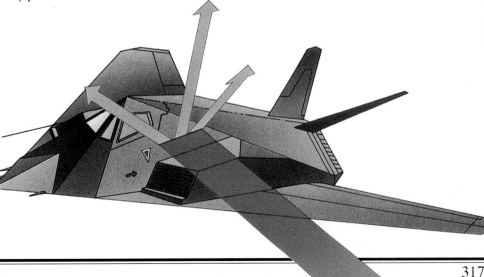

HAIR & FUR

Mammals keep themselves warm with fur or hairs which trap a layer of insulating air. Most have two kinds of fur – a thick layer of soft under-fur, and a thin layer of long guard hairs. Hair is coated with a waterproof substance called sebum which helps keep the animal dry. Hair comes in different colors and patterns which are used for recognition or camouflage, and it must be kept clean. Many mammals use grooming to cement social relationships; hair is sensitive to touch.

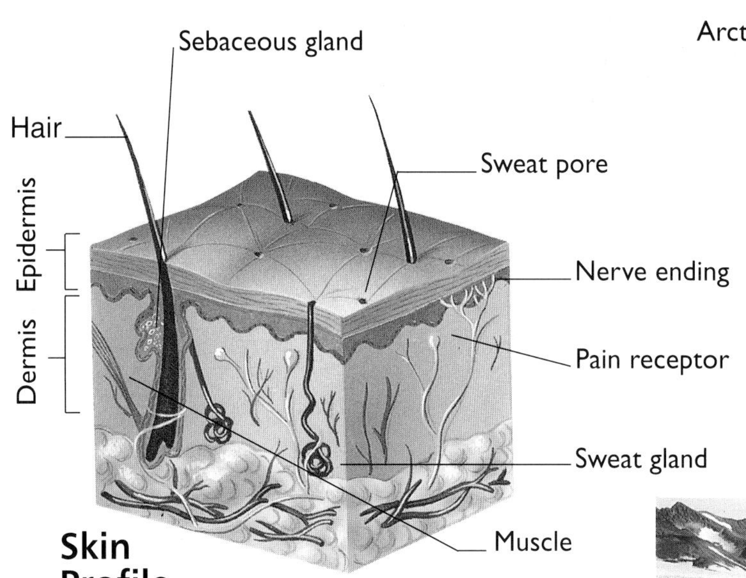

Arctic fox

Skin Profile

Skin is the largest organ of the body. It keeps infections, poisons, and water out. It contains nerves which respond to touch, pain, and heat, and can repair itself when it gets damaged. It is the main temperature-regulating organ. Each hair grows from a tiny hole or follicle, which has a nerve, a muscle, blood vessels, and a sebaceous gland.

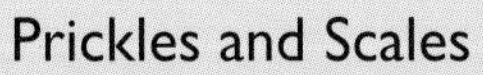

Prickles and Scales

Hair is made from a hard substance called keratin. Some mammals have sharp, rigid hairs in their coats. These spines form an excellent protection from predators. Hedgehogs roll up into a prickly ball when threatened, while porcupines turn their backs on their enemy and run – backward! Pangolin hair is modified to form scales. But the armor plating of armadillos is made from bony plates in the skin. When pangolins or armadillos roll themselves up they are safe from attack.

Armadillo

Fierce Warriors

In Papua New Guinea the native people often argue over territory. Their battles are usually ceremonial, but they dress up in huge headdresses (made from fur and feathers), and pierce their skin with echidna spines to look fierce.

The Arctic fox changes its coat from snowy white in winter to rocky brown in summer, making it difficult for predators to see. It also helps it creep up on *its* prey, the Arctic hare.

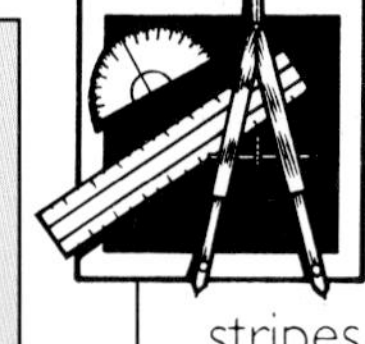

Spots and Stripes

As Rudyard Kipling says in the *Just So Stories*, giraffe blotches, zebra stripes, and leopard spots are a good disguise when the animals are in the dappled light under trees. But how do zebra stripes work out in the open? Some scientists think they might be an optical illusion which confuses or dazzles predators, making it difficult for them to launch a chase. Others think the stripes help zebras recognize members of their own herd, so they can keep together.

Jaguar

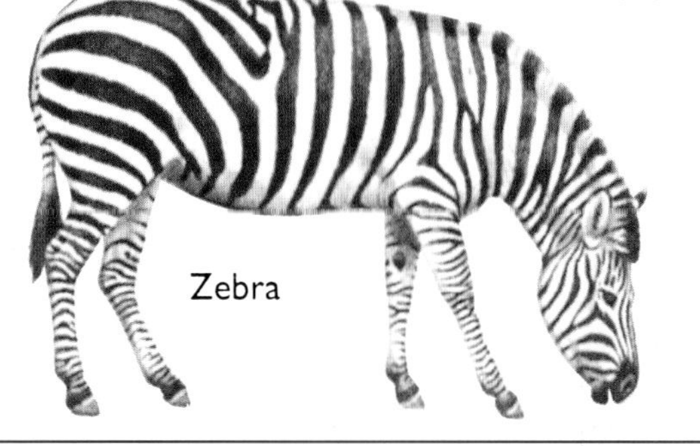

Zebra

Fashionable Furs

In the last century, wearing the furry skins, or pelts, of beautiful mammals became fashionable. Hunting and trapping became big business. Millions of minks, foxes, seals, sea otters, and sables were killed and many, as a result, are close to extinction. Today many people object to killing animals for the sake of fashion (left), and campaign against the fur trade.

Let your hair down!

Rapunzel was a beautiful young girl who had been locked in a tower by a wicked witch. During her captive years the girl's hair had grown to an extraordinary length. Every day the witch climbed up the thick plait of hair with food. Then a handsome prince came by and used the same trick to rescue Rapunzel. They lived happily ever after, but could this story be true? Human hair is stronger than steel fibers and the record for the longest hair is 13 feet, 6 inches. But hair this length is usually very brittle.

Questions and Answers about...

How big was King Kong?
The giant gorilla that crashed across movie screens in 1933 was about 15 inches (45 centimeters) high! Film of the animated model, together with background scenery, was then projected onto a translucent screen from behind. The actors performed in front of the screen. In the 1976 remake, King Kong was life-size, a mechanical monster 18 feet (5.5 meters) tall.

The model is moved one frame at a time

Real actors are filmed in front of a back projection

How old is Mickey Mouse?
The first Mickey Mouse cartoons appeared in 1938. They were Walt Disney's first big success, and Mickey's voice was spoken by Disney himself. So Mickey Mouse was 50 years old in 1988, and he's still going strong!

How did the Oscars get their name?
The Oscars are officially known as Academy Awards. They were first presented by the Academy of Motion Picture Arts and Sciences in 1928. A golden statuette was designed for presentation to each of the winners. When one of the officials of the Academy first saw the statuette, he remarked that it looked like his uncle Oscar. The name has stuck ever since.

Why do people in old films move so quickly?
People in old films—such as *The Keystone Cops*—did not, of course, actually move more quickly than ordinary people. In fact, it was the camera that moved more slowly. Modern cine cameras take 24 pictures (frames) per second, and modern projectors run at the same speed. Old cameras took 16 to 18 frames per second. This means that if an old film is put into a modern projector it runs too fast. And so everything looks as though it moves too fast. It is possible to slow down some projectors, but television works at 30 frames a second. You can't slow down everybody's television set! Recently, however, techniques have been developed that can solve this problem.

One second of a cartoon is made from 24 separate drawings

How does Superman fly?
In the film, Superman usually flies by being held up on a metal arm that is hidden behind him. To make it seem as though he is high up in the air, they use a technique called front projection. A background image is reflected off a two-way mirror in front of the actor. It appears on a screen behind him. The camera films through the mirror. The background image is very faint, so it does not show up on the actor. But the screen is made with glass beads, which intensify the image and make the background bright. You cannot see the shadow of the actor on the screen because he is exactly between the camera and his shadow.

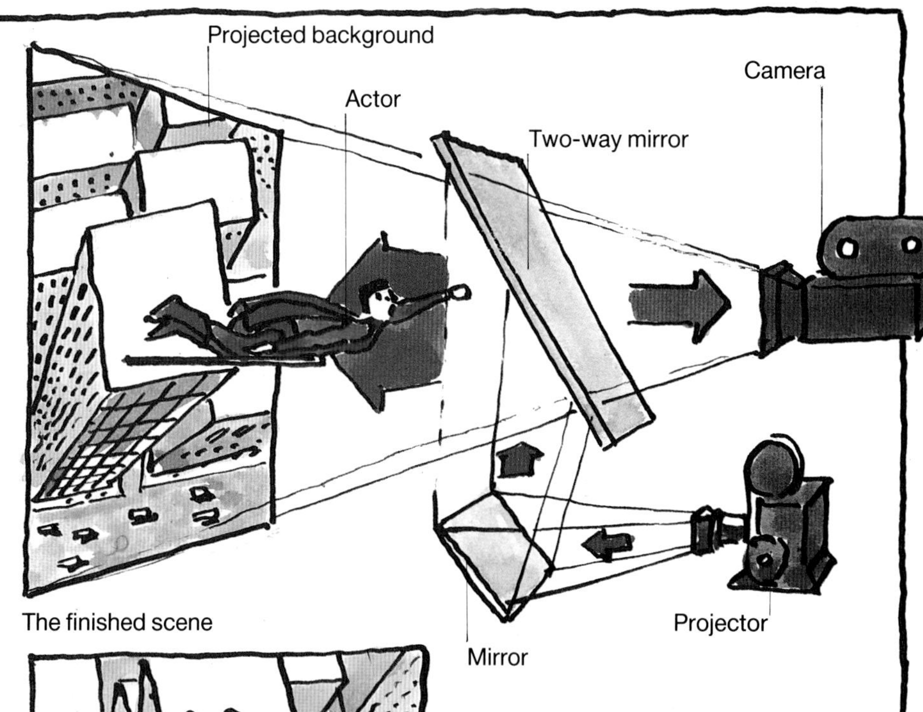

How many drawings are there in a cartoon film?
In a cartoon feature film lasting one and a half hours, there are over 100,000 frames. This means that there are at least 100,000 drawings. In fact, each frame often is made up of several drawings put together. Thus there may be as many as a million drawings in a cartoon feature film. Cheaper cartoons made for television often have many fewer drawings. There may be only a few thousand in a half-hour program.

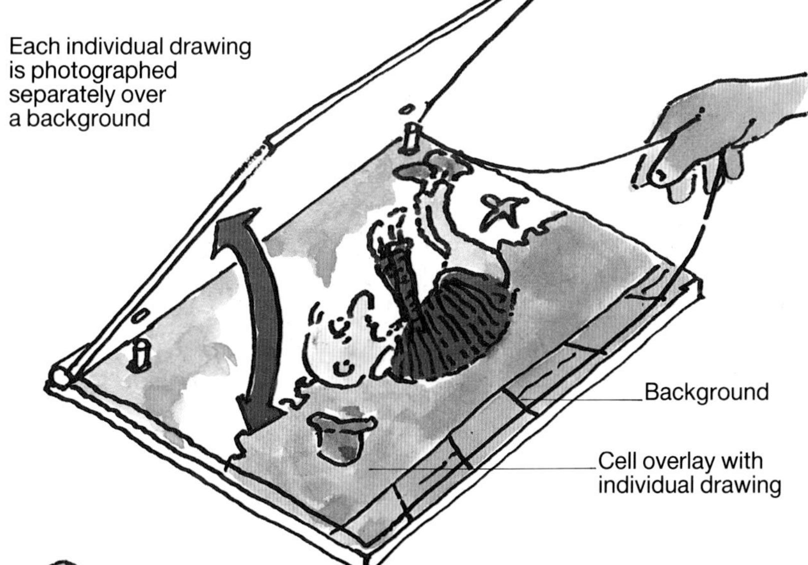

DINOSAUR PLANT-EATERS

Most dinosaurs were plant-eaters. These included the long-necked, long-tailed sauropods, which were the biggest land animals of all time; they could grow up to 20 times the size of an elephant! Then there were the armored dinosaurs: the plate-backed stegosaurs, the bone-headed pachycephalosaurs, the horn-faced ceratopsians, and the armored ankylosaurs. Some of these may have looked extremely fierce, but they were plant-eaters. The two-legged ornithopods, like *Iguanodon* and the crested, duckbilled dinosaurs, also ate plants and leaves from bushes and trees; this is called browsing. They did not graze since there was no grass. Grasses came on the scene only 25 million years after the dinosaurs had died out.

Iguanodon

The second dinosaur to be named was *Iguanodon*, in 1825. Mary Ann Mantell found some teeth of a plant-eating dinosaur in Sussex, England in 1822. Later, her husband, Gideon Mantell, found more bones and realized that they all came from the same animal. He thought the teeth looked like those of an iguana, a modern plant-eating lizard, even though they were 100 times bigger! So, he invented the name *Iguanodon*, which means "iguana tooth."

Teeth

Plant-eating dinosaurs had a variety of kinds of teeth. The giant sauropods like *Apatosaurus* had long pencil-shaped teeth with sharp edges, useful for cutting large quantities of soft leaves. Most of the armored dinosaurs, like *Ankylosaurus,* had leaf-shaped teeth with zigzag cutting edges, specialized for chewing tougher leaves.

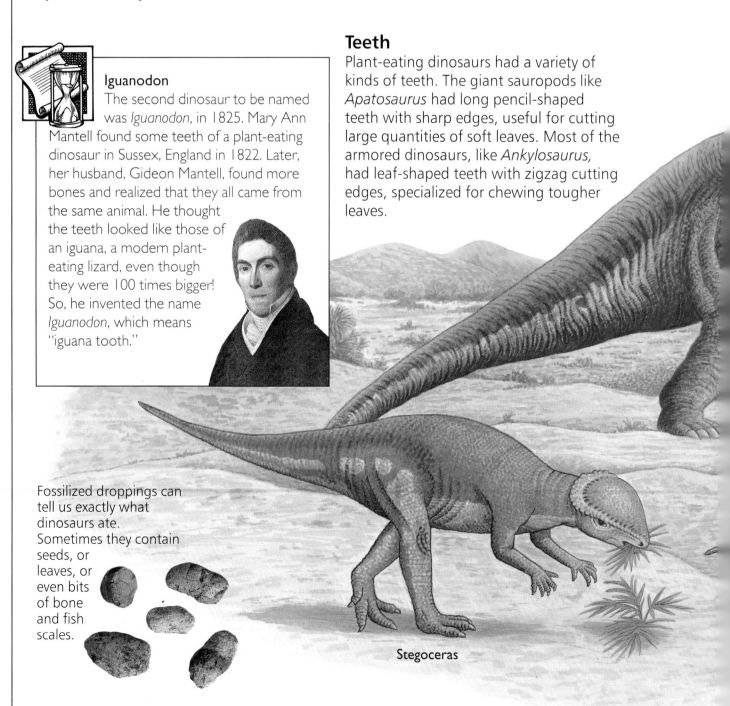

Fossilized droppings can tell us exactly what dinosaurs ate. Sometimes they contain seeds, or leaves, or even bits of bone and fish scales.

Stegoceras

Dinosaur biomechanics
One of the best ways to understand how dinosaurs worked is to think of them like buildings or machines. *Paleontologists* (people who study fossils) may use the principles of engineering in their studies. For example, the huge sauropods had skeletons built like suspension bridges. The massive belly was held up by great ropelike ligaments, fixed to the high spine over the shoulders and hips.

Suspension bridge

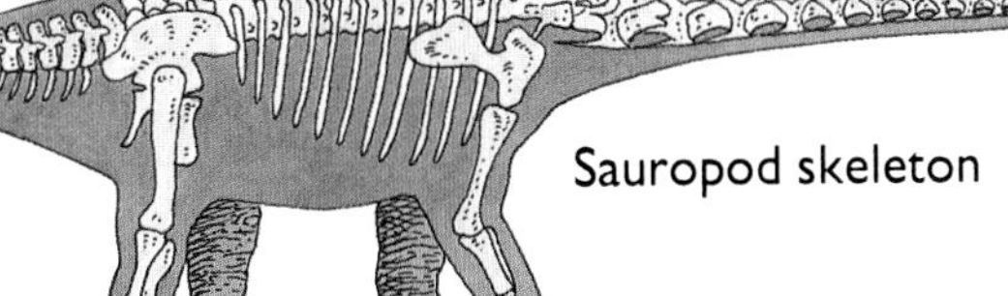

Sauropod skeleton

Apatosaurus

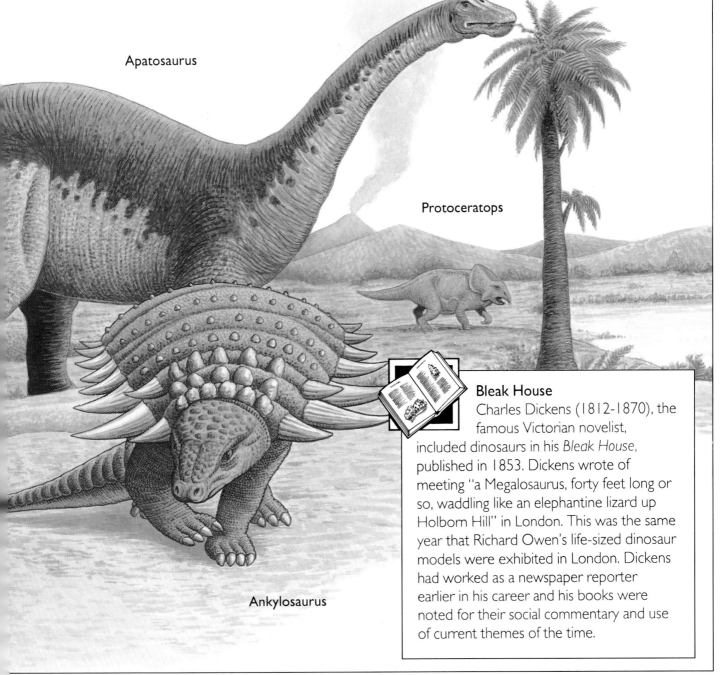

Protoceratops

Ankylosaurus

Bleak House
Charles Dickens (1812-1870), the famous Victorian novelist, included dinosaurs in his *Bleak House*, published in 1853. Dickens wrote of meeting "a Megalosaurus, forty feet long or so, waddling like an elephantine lizard up Holborn Hill" in London. This was the same year that Richard Owen's life-sized dinosaur models were exhibited in London. Dickens had worked as a newspaper reporter earlier in his career and his books were noted for their social commentary and use of current themes of the time.

THE RISE OF THE INCAS

Like the Aztecs, the Incas arrived late on the historical scene. The Inca dynasty was founded around A.D. 1200 by Manco Capac at Cuzco in the Peruvian Andes. For the next 200 years, he and his descendants engaged in local wars. The first emperor to dramatically extend the territories of the Incas was Pachacuti (1438-71). He was followed by Topa Inca (1471-93) and Huayna Capac (1493-1525). At the end of the reign of Huayna Capac, the Incas controlled an area 200 miles wide and 2,200 miles long. This vast empire was unified into a single state with a centralized administration.

Roads

A complex network of roads linked all of the empire. The longest was the Andean road, which ran through the mountains (below). Distances were marked out at regular intervals, while rivers and ravines were crossed using suspension bridges (main picture). Runners carried messages, and kept Cuzco informed of events in different

Peoples of the Inca empire

For more than 10,000 years, different peoples have inhabited the region that stretches from the Andean valleys to the Pacific (left). Since its foundation, the Inca empire defeated and absorbed those still around, including the Chanca, the Colla, and the powerful Chimú kingdom.

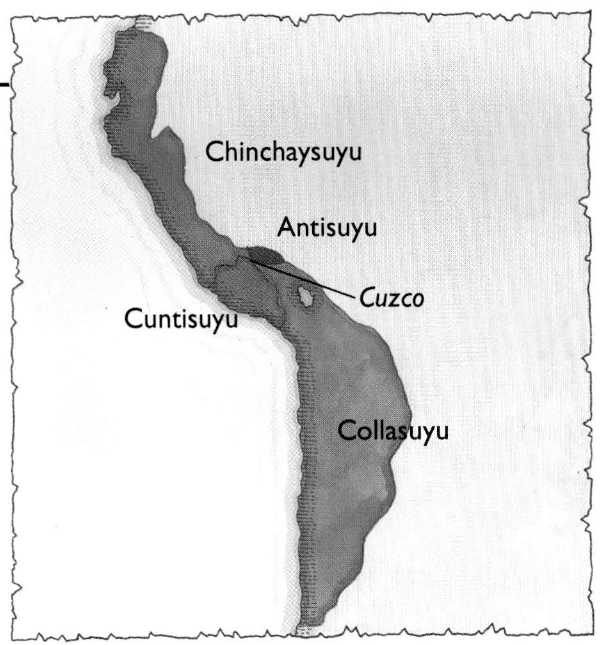

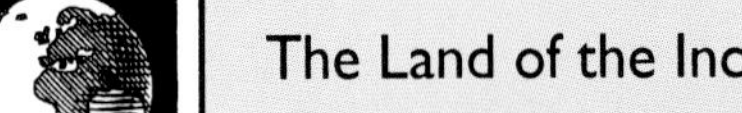

The Land of the Inca

The territories eventually covered by the Inca empire, included all types of climate and landscape. The coastal region is a narrow strip of desert where rain seldom falls (left). From here, the Andes rise steeply to a high plateau that is broken by deep valley basins which offer excellent, arable land. To the east of the mountains lies the vast jungle of the Amazon river basin.

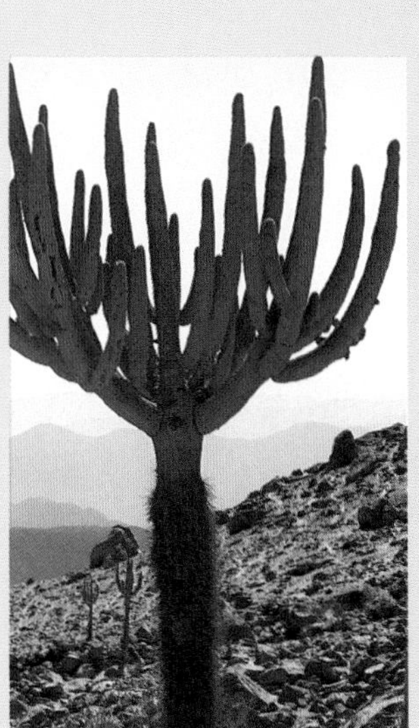

The four quarters

By 1525 the empire stretched from Ecuador to Chile. Tahuantinsuyu, or "Land of the Four Quarters," as it was known, was split into Chinchaysuyu (northwest), Antisuyu (northeast), Cuntinsuyu (southwest), and Collasuyu (southeast) (above), with Cuzco, meaning "navel," at its center.

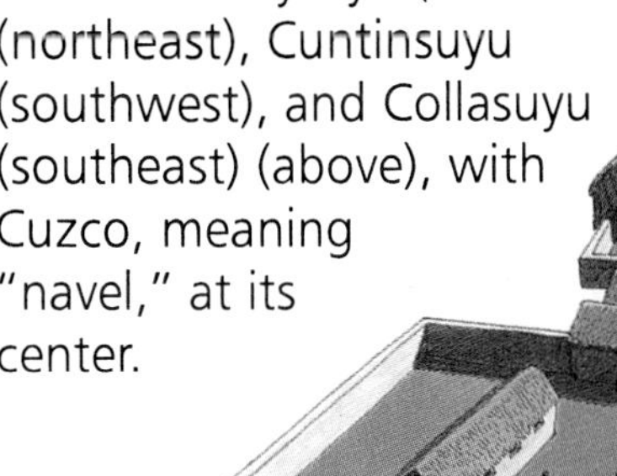

The emperor

The Sapa Inca ("Supreme Inca") ruled by divine right. Worshiped as the "Son of the Sun," his life was governed by elaborate ritual. Each Inca ruler built his own palace (left) in the center of Cuzco. The interior was richly decorated. Its walls were adorned with gold and silver, and hung with textiles. When he died, the emperor's body was preserved and kept in his own palace, while his successor built another.

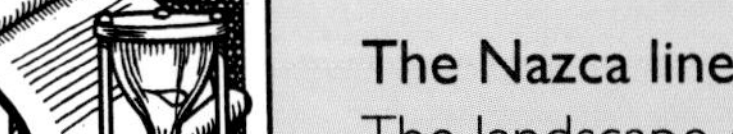

The Nazca lines

The landscape of the Inca empire was filled with the relics of the people who had previously inhabited the continent. Perhaps the most mysterious are the famous Nazca "lines," which form vast figures in the desert. These were made by scraping away the top surface of stones off the desert floor to expose the lighter soil that lay beneath.

These designs include triangles, rectangles, spirals, and even animal or bird forms. Scholars think the lines had astronomical significance, or were linked to cults connected with the sea, sky, and mountains.

Is There Anybody OUT THERE?

Are we alone in our universe? If life evolved (developed) naturally on Earth, as most scientists believe, it has probably evolved somewhere else too. There are so many billions of stars similar to the Sun that many of them must have planets. Among those planets there might be some with conditions like those on Earth. If so, then we are almost certainly not alone. To find other intelligent life, we must constantly listen and observe. For more than 30 years, radio telescopes have been pointed at the stars to try to pick up any radio signals from distant civilizations – but so far without success. The search for life in our universe goes on, and may continue forever.

Is there proof of life in other galaxies? In 1995, British ufologists (people who study UFOs) claimed that they had seen a U.S. government film from 1947. They claimed it showed scientists examining the body of an alien whose craft crashed in New Mexico. Could this solve one of the greatest mysteries of our universe?

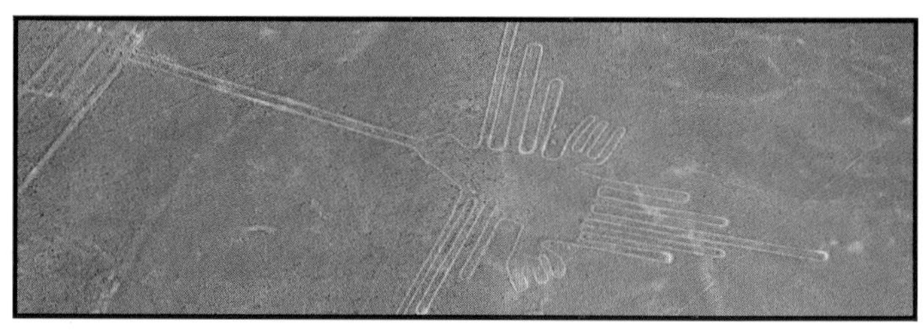

HAVE WE MET BEFORE?
Mysterious lines are clearly visible across the desert in Peru, and are thought by some people to be the work of ancient aliens.

A LONG HISTORY
Throughout history, strange, unknown lights in the sky have made people wonder about other life in the universe.

LIFE ON MARS?
The astronomer Percival Lowell (1855–1916) believed that he could see canals on Mars, evidence of intelligent life there. But these were optical illusions, as photographs by the Viking spacecraft proved.

LIGHTS IN THE SKY
Many people have seen strange, disk-shaped objects in the sky. These have been named Unidentified Flying Objects, *or UFOs. But in spite of many rumors and continuous observation of the skies, there is no hard evidence that they are alien spacecraft. Most UFOs are probably oddly-shaped clouds, or have been cleverly faked in photographs.*

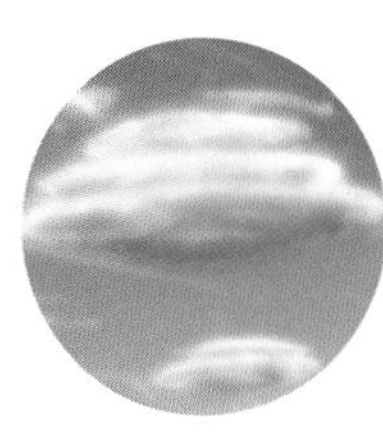

THE FACE OF MARS

Lowell's theories of Martian life were proved wrong, but years later, a picture taken by a Viking probe seemed to show a face carved on the planet's surface.

Was this evidence of an ancient Martian civilization? Unfortunately not. The human eye is so good at recognizing faces that it can easily trick the brain into thinking it can see one – in a rock of roughly the right shape or a landscape covered with shadows, for example.

Little green men?

Most images of aliens have been created in films such as *E.T.* Aliens are often shown as green or gray in color, have large eyes, and talk slowly and carefully. A real alien would probably be quite different, and might think that we look really weird. Or it might look exactly the same as a human!

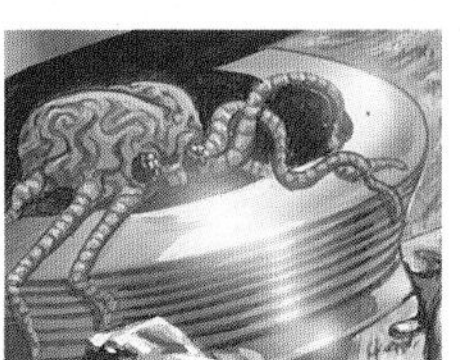

A NATIONAL ALERT

The War of the Worlds, *by the English writer H.G. Wells, describes an invasion of the Earth by Martians.*

The novel was written in England in 1898, and was turned into a radio play in 1938. When it was broadcast, the story was so convincing that thousands of listeners thought it was a real news bulletin, and ran screaming into the streets in their pajamas. Many other futuristic novels have since been written, but none had such a dramatic effect!

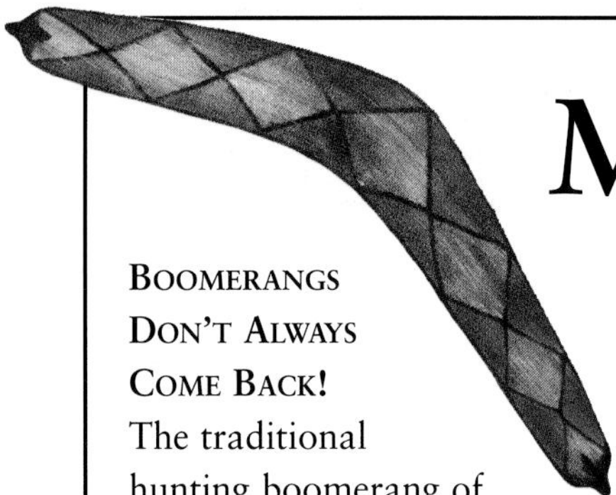

MISSILES AND ROCKETS

Boomerangs Don't Always Come Back!
The traditional hunting boomerang of the Australian Aborigines (*above*) was cleverly designed to return to the thrower if it missed the target. However, the heavier war boomerang was designed to fly straight, and did not return to the thrower.

One of the first times a missile was used in war is recorded in the Bible, when David killed Goliath the giant using a slingshot, or catapult. Such weapons were originally developed for hunting, but their military usefulness soon became apparent. All early missile-throwing systems used the power of the human body (*above*), but the Chinese discovery of gunpowder made possible the development of rockets, which had greater power and far greater range.

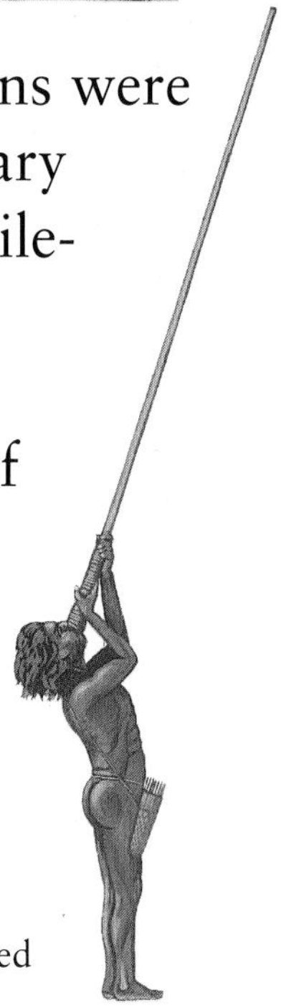

Medieval European lance

Japanese yari

Roman pilum

African spear

Indian lance

Maori spear (from New Zealand)

Air Power
The native peoples of the Amazon region of South America use long blowpipes to hunt animals in the jungle (*right*). A poisoned dart is blown along the tube, and in skilled hands it can be very accurate.

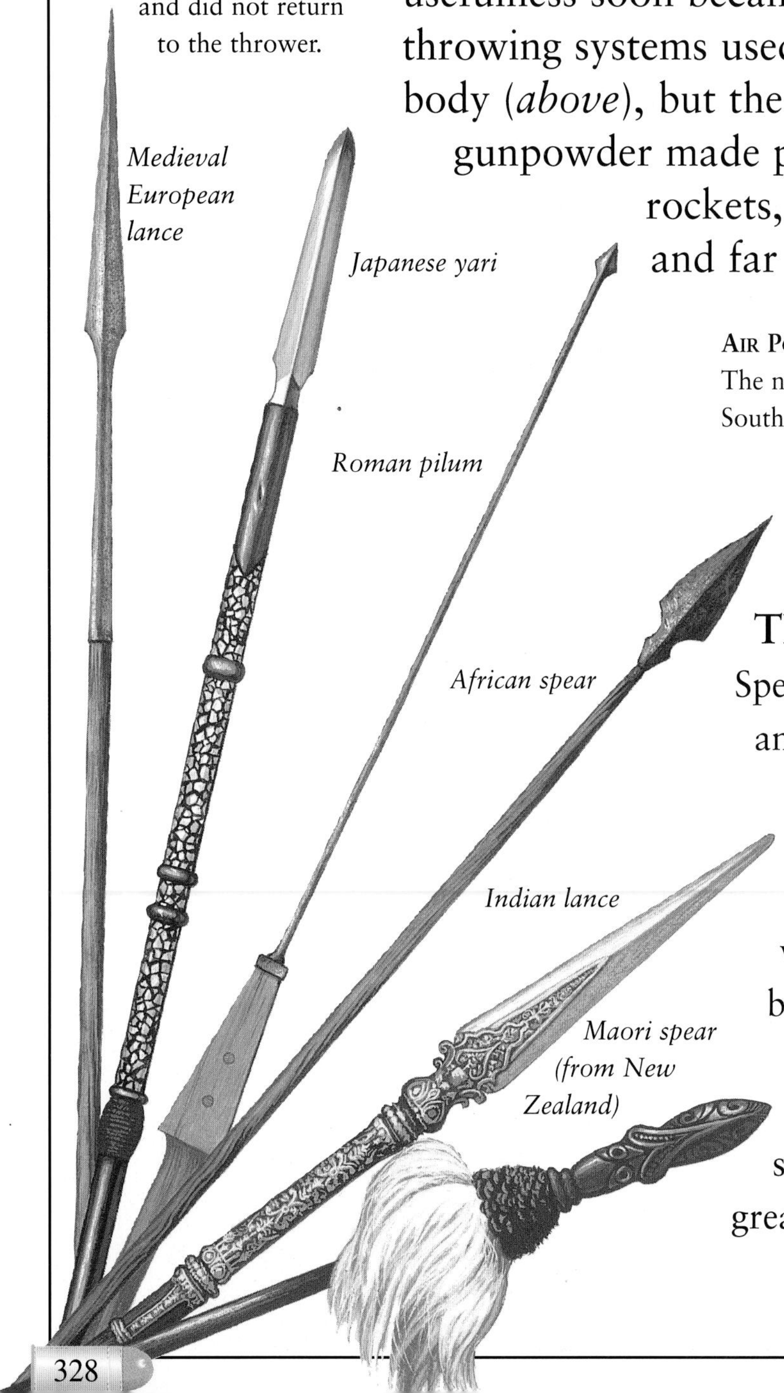

THRUSTING AND THROWING

Spears can be thrust or thrown at an enemy, and there are many variations (*left*). The Roman pilum, for example, had a long iron point that was designed to pierce enemy shields and break off from the wooden shaft, so it could not be thrown back. This Australian aboriginal device (*right*) is attached to the end of a spear to give the user greater force when throwing.

SIEGE CATAPULTS
Invented by the ancient Romans, catapults (*left*) were also used during the Middle Ages to batter down the walls of castles. The throwing arm was attached to a thick cord and winched backward. A large stone was placed in the cup and the throwing arm was then released, hurling the rock forward.

SIR WILLIAM CONGREVE

The British general William Congreve developed rockets during the Napoleonic Wars (1793-1815). Rockets were used against the French at the Battle of Leipzig in 1813 and, although they had a range of 0.8 miles (1.3 km), they were not very accurate.

CHINESE CRACKERS!
The first time a rocket was ever used in war is thought to have been in 1232, when Chinese troops fired gunpowder rockets at a Tartar army (from Russia). These rockets would have been like our modern firework rockets, and they were intended to frighten the enemy's horses.

WORLD WAR II ADVANCES

Rockets became effective weapons during World War II. Germany fired high-explosive warheads with a range of 4.5 miles (7 kilometers) from a multi-launch system called a Nebelwerfer. The United States and England used a hand-held antitank missile launcher (*left*) nicknamed the "bazooka" after the comic-strip character Bazooka Joe!

UP AND AWAY!

The Stinger surface-to-air missile (*right*) makes it possible for a single infantryman to shoot down low-flying jet aircraft. Developed in the 1980s for the U.S. Army, the Stinger has a range of 3 miles (5 kilometers) and can hit aircraft flying up to 3 miles (5 kilometers) high. After the soldier has pulled the trigger, the missile is guided to the target by an infrared homing device, which locks onto the heat produced by the aircraft's engine.

REPTILE SCALES

One of the typical features of a reptile is its scaly skin. On most reptiles the scales are numerous, small, and overlapping. Like a suit of armor made from linked chain mail, they form a tough but flexible covering over almost the entire body. This allows the reptile to bend its body and limbs, so that it can move about. At the same time, the scales give good protection against drying out, and from the teeth and claws of enemies. In most reptiles, the scales are replaced singly or in patches as they wear. In snakes, however, the whole skin is usually shed at once, a process called sluffing.

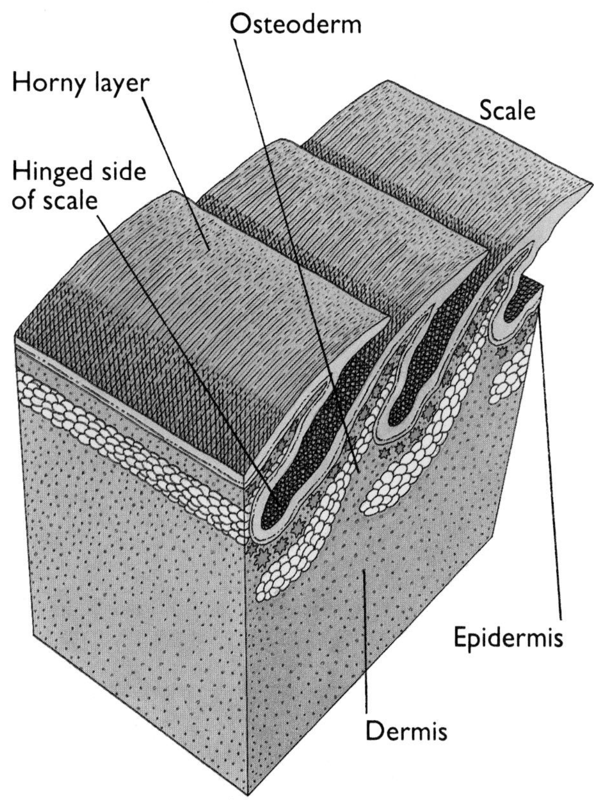

Scale structure

Each reptile scale is made of a hard, horny material called keratin, the same substance that forms your own nails. The scale is a thickened plate of keratin set within the outer skin layer, or epidermis. It has a flexible hinge area along one side, so that it can tilt and twist slightly when the animal moves. In crocodiles and many lizards, there are additional plates of bone called osteoderms, set deeper in the skin. These strengthen and reinforce the scale layer above. Below is the dermis, containing blood vessels and nerves.

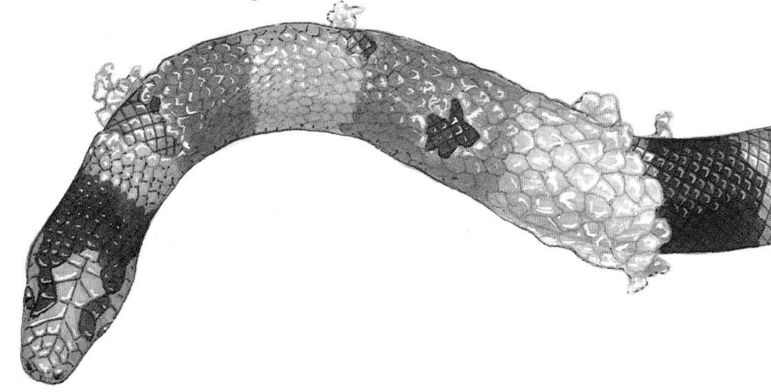

Useful skins

Since prehistoric times, people have used the tough, strong skins of reptiles for many purposes. They made the skins into hard-wearing purses, belts, boots, shoes, and coats.The colors and patterns of reptile skins are very beautiful. In some countries people believe that they gain strength by wearing the skin of a powerful animal such as an alligator. However, the reptile skin trade caused many species to become rare. Today it is controlled by laws.

New skin for old

As with your skin, reptile scales wear away. They are replaced as cells in the base of the epidermis multiply, forming new scales. When sluffing its skin, a snake rubs itself against rocks and twigs to pull off the old layer, revealing the ready-formed skin beneath.

Suits of armor

Through the ages, people have tried to make suits of armor that give the same all-over protection as reptile scales. However, the armor was rarely as light or as flexible as the natural reptilian version. In Europe, suits of armor were made from plates of metal, as shown here. In China and Japan, it included sheets of thick leather. Perhaps the most effective armor was chain mail, formed from small metal rings looped together.

The gila monster is a lizard with curious rounded, bead-shaped scales.

The armadillo lizard has big, spiky scales for protection and can roll into a ball to defend itself from predators.

The rattler's rattle

The poisonous rattlesnake shakes its tail rattle very fast to make a buzzing or rattling noise, that warns other animals to keep away. The rattle is formed from large tail scales that have remained behind when previous skins were shed. The scales are linked loosely together, the bent-over end of one fitting into a circular groove in the next. There is a story that the longer the rattle, the older the rattlesnake. However, scales sometimes break off the rattle by accident. So rattle length is only a rough guide to the snake's age.

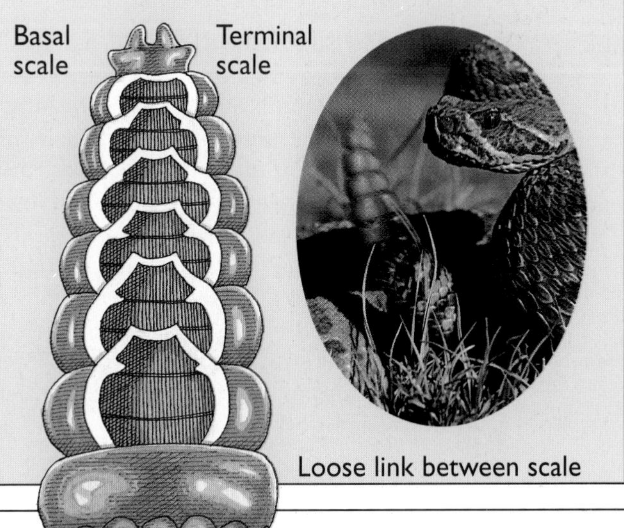

Debussy shows the way

DEBUSSY
(1862-1918)

MAIN WORKS

ORCHESTRAL

Prélude à l'après-midi d'un Faune
Nocturnes (3)
La Mer
Images (3)

OPERA

Pelléas et Mélisande

FOR PIANO

Suite Bergamasque
Pour le piano
Estampes (3)
Images (6)
Children's Corner
preludes (24)
studies (12)

SONATAS

cello and piano
violin and piano
flute, viola, and harp

many songs

IN DECEMBER 1894 a concert of new orchestral works was given in Paris. Among the pieces of music by Glazunov, Saint-Saëns, Franck, and a number of composers forgotten today was a short piece by Debussy, the *Prélude à après-midi d'un faune*. The critics called it "interesting," but otherwise took no notice of it. Based on a poem by Stéphane Mallarmé, it opens with a fluctuating, wayward tune played on the flute by the mythical faun of the title, leading into a short, delicately orchestrated movement, in which horn calls and swirls on the harp evoke the heat of a summer's afternoon. What was revolutionary about it was not the subject matter – atmosphere scene painting was nothing new in music – but the way in which Debussy dissolved classical harmony into a fine haze and shimmer of sound.

Claude Debussy was born in 1862, and as a boy saw the horrors of the Franco-Prussian War of 1870-71 at first hand. His father was put in jail for his part in the short-lived Commune – the democratic uprising in Paris that followed France's defeat by Germany. Two years later, at the age of 11, Claude became a pupil at the Paris Conservatoire, where he stayed for the next 11 years. He was in constant trouble with his composition teachers for writing what seemed to them outrageously modern harmonies. On one occasion, when he was playing some wild progressions on the piano, a teacher asked him what rules of music he followed. *"Mon plaisir"* ("My pleasure"), answered Debussy. All the same, he could keep to the rules when he chose to do so. In 1884 he was awarded the top composition prize for a cantata on the theme of the Prodigal Son, which Gounod, who was one of the panel of judges for that year, described as "the work of genius."

During the next few years Debussy came under a vast number of influences, many of them nonmusical ones. In the 1880s France was swept by a mania for Wagner, and he became enthusiastic about Wagner's operas. He made settings of poems by Verlaine and other leading poets; he studied the paintings of the pre-Raphaelites and of Whistler; he read the supernatural stories of Edgar Allen Poe. At the Great Exhibition in Paris in 1889, he listened to the strangely exotic sounds of gamelan music from Java. In the course of his travels, Debussy became the household pianist Madame von Meck, who was Tchaikovsky's patron. More than any other composer before or since, he had an intense curiosity about all the other arts apart from music. He was also very much a man about town, and was at his happiest sitting in a Montmartre bar with a group of friends, listening to the latest witty café singer, or discussing theories of art and poetry far into the night.

Erik Satie (left) was a musical eccentric, who gave his pieces strange names, like *Pieces in the Shape of a Pear*. In recent years his music has been taken seriously by modern composers.

Maurice Ravel (right) was the only French composer to rival Debussy during his lifetime. He wrote brilliant piano music, orchestral works, short operas, songs, and chamber music.

Debussy has often been described as an Impressionist and, like the painters Monet and Renoir, he was more concerned with mood and atmosphere than with rigid structure. But he did not like being labeled, and when he was composing his orchestral *Images* in the early 1900s, he told a friend: "I am now writing something which the fools will refer to as Impressionism." This was not long after he had reached the height of his fame with the opera *Pelléas et Mélisande*, which is a somber love story full of half-lights and mystery, set in a twilight medieval world. First produced in 1902, *Pelléas* is Debussy's only completed opera, although he worked on and off at other possible themes, among them Shakespeare's *As You Like It* and Poe's *The Fall of the House of Usher*. Soon after *Pelléas* Debussy became involved in a tragic scandal, when his first wife tried to shoot herself after he had left her.

Debussy (left) outside his Paris home in 1910. At this period he was writing some of his finest works, such as the 24 piano preludes and the orchestral *Images*.

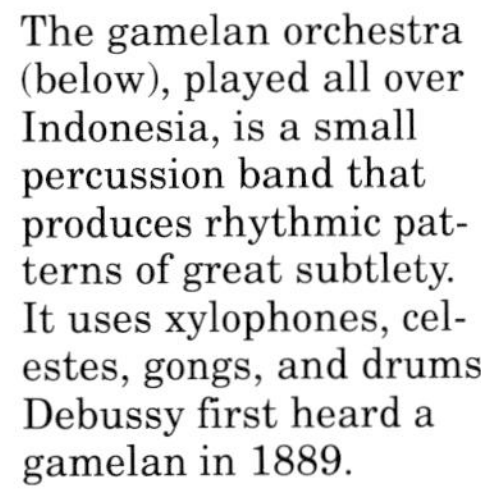

The gamelan orchestra (below), played all over Indonesia, is a small percussion band that produces rhythmic patterns of great subtlety. It uses xylophones, celestes, gongs, and drums. Debussy first heard a gamelan in 1889.

Edgar Allan Poe (above), the American writer of supernatural tales, was popular in France in the 19th century. Debussy left sketches for an opera based on Poe's *The Fall of the House of User.*

This time of emotional turmoil saw the creation of Debussy's finest orchestral work, the three symphonic sketches called *La Mer*, which was completed in 1905. As the cover for *La Mer*, Debussy chose a print by the Japanese artist Hokusai, which is sharp-cut and threatening in outline. Like the print, the music is all clarity and sparkle, with no Impressionistic woolliness or vagueness about it.

Most typical of all his works are the short piano preludes. Like Chopin, Debussy wrote 24 of them, but whereas Chopin's preludes are untitled, each of Debussy's creates a scene of a mood. The banjos of the café entertainers appear in *Minstrels,* and a Breton legend in *La Cathédrale engloutie* (*The Submerged Cathedral*). Others depict fireworks, yachts becalmed on the sea, and even an ancient Greek vase. They form a kind of musical autobiography, in which many aspects of Debussy's character find a place.

Toward the end of his life he struck up a friendship with Stravinsky, who was in turn an enthusiast for Debussy's works. But his last years were made wretched by disease and by the outbreak of World War I, which he saw as the end of civilization. As a patriotic gesture, he added the words *musicien français* to the title page of his last works. He died in March 1918, as the Germans were bombarding Paris in their final gamble of the war.

Debussy's only opera, *Pelléas et Mélisande* (left), is a tragic love story with a legendary medieval setting.

GLASS-FIBER

OPTICAL CABLES

Glass-fiber cables are at the heart of today's communication revolution. Thousands of miles of glass-fiber cables are being installed around the world, creating "data highways" along which a variety of information and services can travel. Glass fiber was first introduced to replace copper telephone cables. Capable of carrying 40,000 calls at the same time, the first long-distance glass-fiber telephone cable went into operation in 1983. Today, glass fiber carries far more than telephone calls. It is used to link up computer systems so that large amounts of data can be sent around the world, and to carry signals for cable T.V. Recent developments in technology mean that glass fiber can potentially carry 500 T.V. channels.

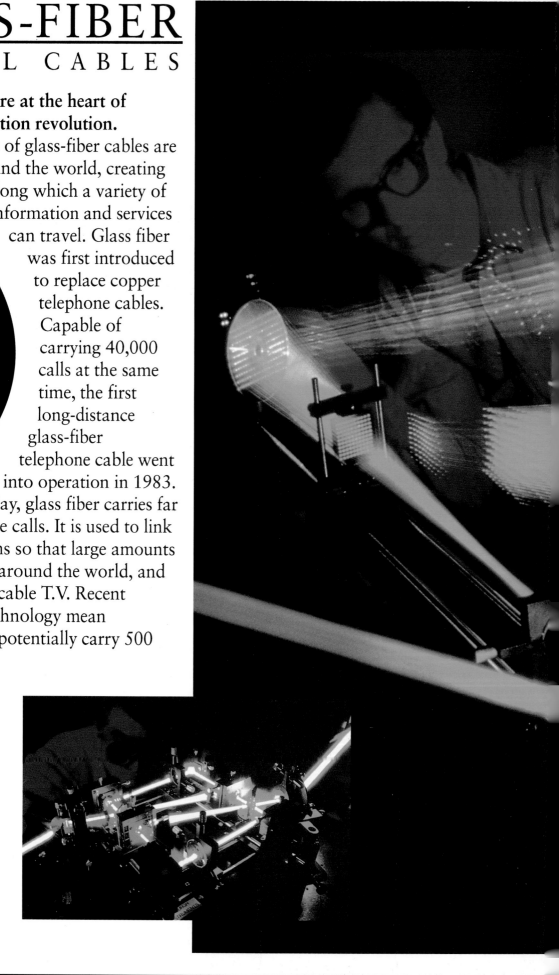

The cables (right) are made of fine fibers of glass. Although glass is usually a brittle, fragile material, the quartz glass used for the fibers is tough, flexible, and cheaper than copper. Many fibers are spun together to form cables. These are clad in a tough plastic sheath to protect them from damage.

The first transatlantic *glass-fiber cable was laid in 1988, linking Britain and France with the United States. Special ships (left) are used to lay cables. The cables are payed out slowly over the stern of the ship and come to rest on the seabed.*

Glass fibers are used to link *together computers so that they can communicate with one another, locally or nationally. Japan plans a glass-fiber system that will link virtually every home and office by 2015.*

Cables are brought *ashore at each end and are linked into the telephone network. Communications satellites share the market with undersea cables, but have yet to replace them.*

Undersea cables *have to be armored to protect them from accidental damage. In shallow water they are buried to avoid damage from ships' anchors.*

GLASS FIBER
HOW IT WORKS

A caller's voice, picked up by a microphone inside the telephone, is converted into digital signals. These turn a laser on and off, sending light pulses along the glass fiber. Each fiber consists of a core of glass surrounded by an outer layer of glass with a lower refractive index. This reflects light at a slightly different angle and stops the light escaping from the fiber. The receiving phone decodes the digital signal. Computer information is transmitted in the same way.

ANTS AND TERMITES

Ants belong to the group of Hymenoptera, like bees and wasps. Termites belong to the order of Isoptera, meaning equal wing. Nevertheless, ants and termites have very similar life-styles. They are mainly social insects, living in huge families or colonies, where each insect has a particular job to do. Most do not reproduce; their lives are devoted to caring for their sisters and brothers. Only the queen mates and lays eggs. Her many young, the workers, build, repair, and defend the nest.

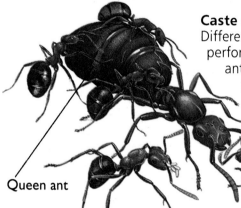

Caste of thousands
Different kinds, or castes, of ants or termites perform different jobs in a colony. Worker ants tend the queen (left), the grubs, and pupae (right). Others clean the nest (above right) and go out in search of food. Soldiers defend the colony.

Queen ant

Workers

Pupae

Social ants

Most ants have poor eyesight, but a good sense of smell. They communicate with nest members through touch and through scents called pheromones which they produce. When foraging ants find food, they lay a scent trail for others to follow. Worker ants produce a different scent if they find a damaged part of the nest, which brings others to help with the repair. Ants from one colony recognize each other by their smell, and will attack an intruder from a different colony. They defend themselves by biting and squirting stinging formic acid into the wound they have made. Ants feed on many different types of food. A column of army ants will tear apart and carry off any small creature in its path. Each ant can lift a load many times its own weight.

Making an ant home
You can study ants more easily by building an ant home from a glass tank or plastic box. Cover the outside of the tank with dark paper. Half-fill the tank with earth, and stock it with small black or red ants from the garden. Add damp soil and leaves. After a few days, remove the paper, to see the tunnels built against the sides.

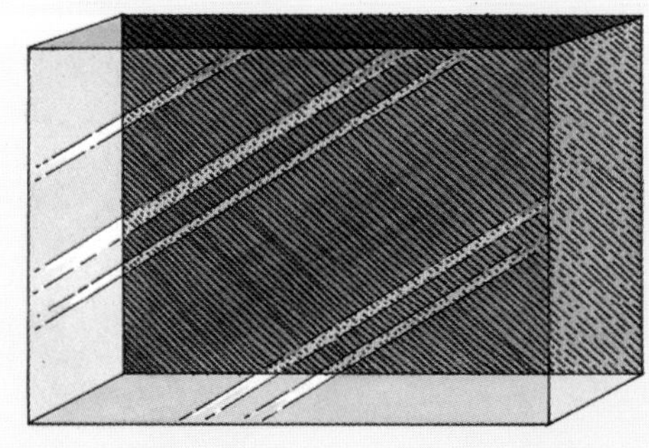

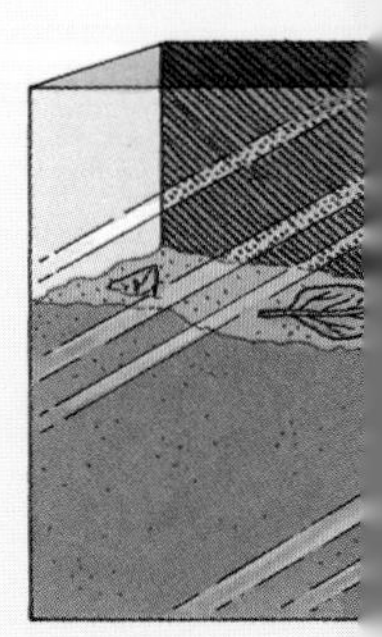

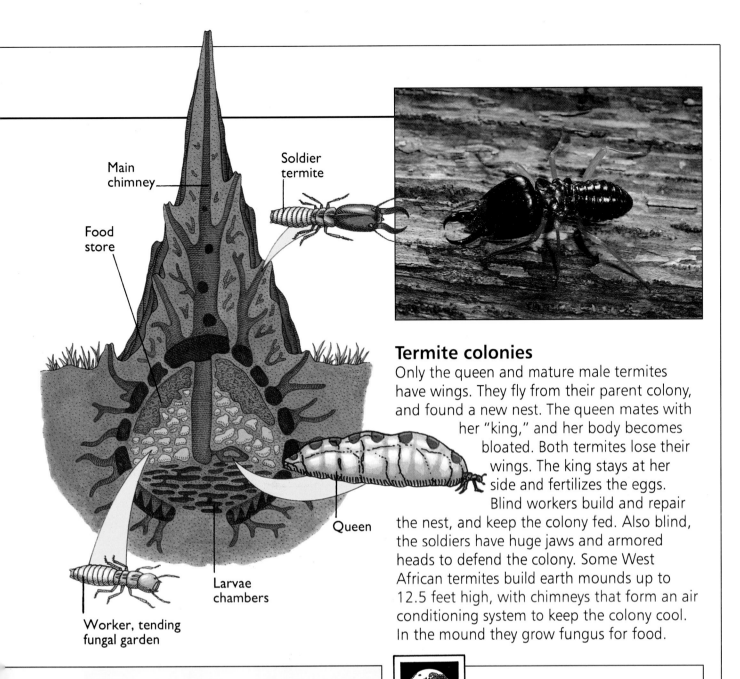

Main chimney

Food store

Soldier termite

Queen

Larvae chambers

Worker, tending fungal garden

Termite colonies

Only the queen and mature male termites have wings. They fly from their parent colony, and found a new nest. The queen mates with her "king," and her body becomes bloated. Both termites lose their wings. The king stays at her side and fertilizes the eggs. Blind workers build and repair the nest, and keep the colony fed. Also blind, the soldiers have huge jaws and armored heads to defend the colony. Some West African termites build earth mounds up to 12.5 feet high, with chimneys that form an air conditioning system to keep the colony cool. In the mound they grow fungus for food.

Feed ants on ripe fruit, meat, or jam, and provide fresh leaves and water on damp kitchen paper. Keep your tank in a cool place, and cover it when you are not studying ant behavior, so air can get in, but the ants can't escape. If you have managed to catch a large queen with your stock, the colony should go on indefinitely, and may even produce a swarm of winged ants in the summer. Let them go to produce a new nest.

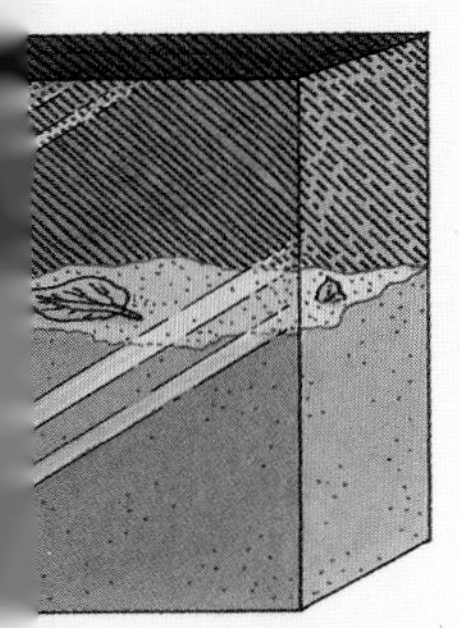

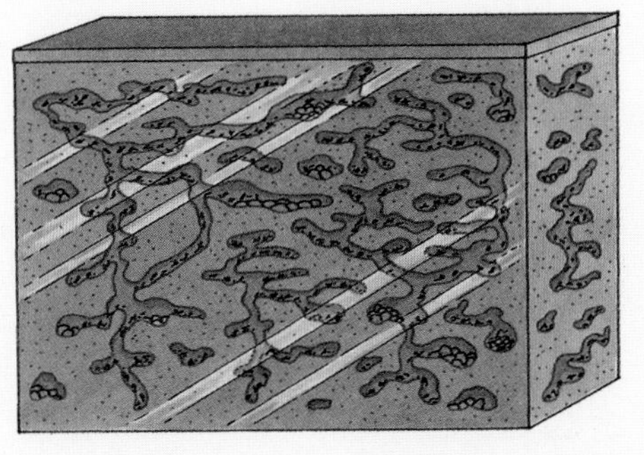

Anteaters of the world

Ants and termites are food for any animal with strong claws to rip open the nests, and a long, sticky tongue to lick the insects out. In Central and South America, armadillos and giant anteaters (below) live on the savannah, and collared anteaters are found in the forests. The aardvark lives off the same diet in South Africa, and the pangolin in Asia. The spiny anteater lives in Australia.

COWBOYS OF THE WORLD

American cowboys were only one of many groups of famous herdsmen who relied on horses for their work. They are the best known, not because they were any more skilled than other riders, but because their way of life has been made famous by hundreds of novels and films. Humans first learned to tame and ride the horse thousands of years ago. The invention of the stirrup in the 4th century A.D. gave riders extra control of their mounts. Until the widespread use of tractors in the mid-20th century, the horse was the indispensable friend of farmers around the globe.

Cowboys and mounted shepherds were found where animals grazed on wide open pastures, such as the Australian Outback or the Hungarian Plain. And cowboys can still be seen today on some of the more remote grazing lands.

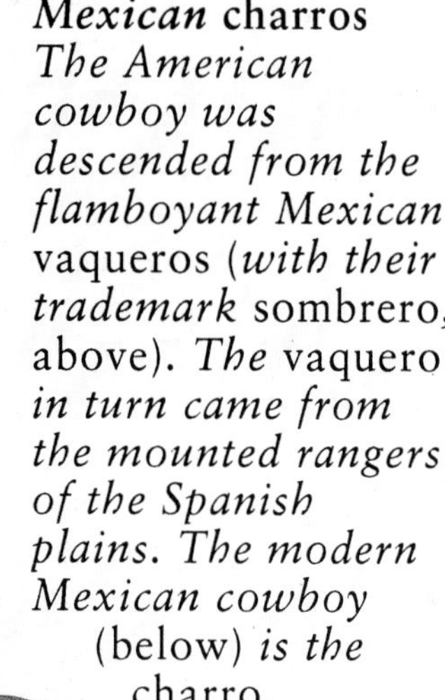

***Mexican* charros**
The American cowboy was descended from the flamboyant Mexican vaqueros (*with their trademark* sombrero, above). *The* vaquero *in turn came from the mounted rangers of the Spanish plains. The modern Mexican cowboy* (below) *is the* charro.

***The South American* gaucho**
(below *and* right) *was a cattle herder working on the broad* pampas *of Argentina and Uruguay. They were famous for catching cattle with the* bolas, *a short rope or chain with weights at either end.*

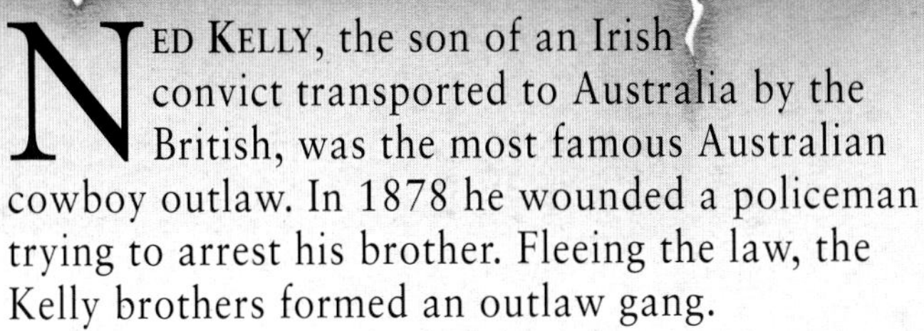

NED KELLY, the son of an Irish convict transported to Australia by the British, was the most famous Australian cowboy outlaw. In 1878 he wounded a policeman trying to arrest his brother. Fleeing the law, the Kelly brothers formed an outlaw gang.

They settled on the border between Victoria and New South Wales, where they made several daring robberies before being tracked down and captured. Ned was hanged in Melbourne at the age of twenty-five. However, like many young American outlaws, he became a folk hero, and numerous stories – usually untrue – grew up around him.

***Hungarian* csikosok**
Hungarians are descended from the Magyars, daring horsemen who swept into Eastern Europe in the 9th century. The csikosok *cowboy* (third from left) *of the Hungarian Plain keeps alive his ancestors' tradition of brilliant horsemanship.*

***Camargue* gardian**
For centuries horsemen have roamed the Camargue, the marshy area at the mouth of the Rhone River in France, famous for horse and cattle breeding. Today, mounted gardians (below) *can still be found there.*

Australian stockman
Although four-wheel-drive vehicles now churn across the Australian outback, some stockmen still prefer to round up their cattle on horseback (first horseman on right).

Like America, Australia had no cattle until they were introduced by settlers in the 19th century.

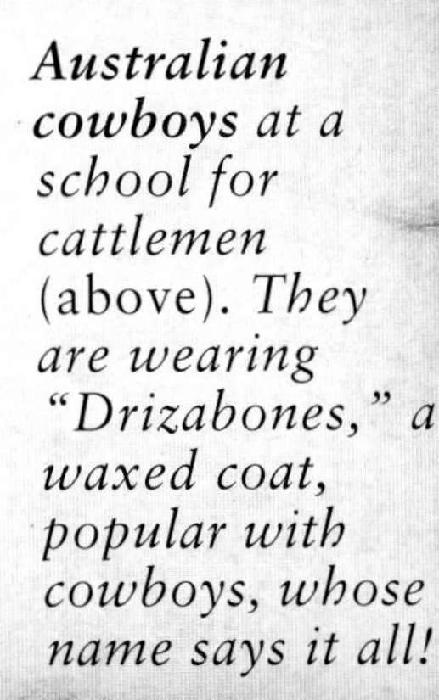

***Australian* cowboys** *at a school for cattlemen* (above). *They are wearing "Drizabones," a waxed coat, popular with cowboys, whose name says it all!*

WHAT IF HUMANS COULD GRIP WITH THEIR FEET?

You could hang upside down from a tree, and do all kinds of other exciting activities. But you might not be able to run and jump so easily. Human feet are designed for walking, and human hands for holding. Our monkey and ape cousins spend most of their time in trees, so they don't need to walk. Instead, all their limbs can grip like hands. Some monkeys are even able to grip with their tails!

Orangutan

These great orange apes live in the densest, steamiest rainforests of Southeast Asia. They rarely come to the ground, and they can bend their legs at almost any angle from the body.

What if apes could stand upright?

One close cousin of the great apes spends most of its time upright. That's us! The true great apes, however, are not able to stand for long. The gorilla spends much of the day on the ground. It usually walks on all fours, on its feet and hand-knuckles. Males sometimes stand upright and charge, if they are threatened by an intruder. Chimps and orangutans can walk upright in order to carry things like fruit, sticks, or rocks. But they can only keep this up for short distances.

Gibbon

The gibbons of Southeast Asia are the champion tree-swingers. They hang from branches by their hooklike hands and powerful arms, and move by swinging from tree to tree with astonishing speed. Because of this, their arms are much longer and stronger than their legs.

Potto
This primate from Africa looks like a small bear. It moves very slowly through the trees.

Tarsier
The tarsier's huge eyes show that it comes out mainly at night. It can leap by its back legs to another branch 7 feet (2 m) away! It feeds on small animals and insects.

Flag-waving primate

Lemurs are primates from the large island of Madagascar, off the eastern coast of Africa. They can run across the ground or leap through trees with equal ease. When they aren't leaping about or searching for food, lemurs like to bask in the warm sun.

The ring-tailed lemur (below) signals to its troop by sight and smell. It waves its black-and-white, ring-patterned tail, like a flag. This is covered with a special scent that the lemur produces from glands on its shoulders.

Spider monkey
The spider monkey has a gripping tail, to help it move through the trees. Without it, the monkey might slip and crash to the floor.

What if apes could use tools?

Humans are not the only animals to use tools, many others use them as well. The great apes are tool-users, especially the chimp. It makes a tool by stripping the leaves off a twig, then pokes the twig into a termite mound, to dig out the termites for a snack. Animal tools are natural objects like leaves, stones, and twigs. They haven't figured out how to use any power tools, yet!

A firefighter burns an area of forest scrub to provide a barren area that breaks the advance of a serious forest fire.

TACKLING LARGE-SCALE FIRES

*Water bombers (*below*) are airplanes that carry large tanks of water that can be released over a wide area of burning woodland. It takes seconds for the tank to be emptied, after which the crew takes the airplane back to the airfield to be refilled. Some types of water bombers can fly over lakes or seas to scoop up extra water.*

The biggest risk of forest fires occurs following a dry spell when the wood and vegetation are tinder dry. The fires start in a number of ways: Human carelessness accounts for many, although they can also be caused by lightning or by the sun's rays magnified through discarded glass.

Hoses

Water tanks

OUT OF CONTROL

In 1997, fires raged through forests in Indonesia, encouraged by drought thought to result from a weather condition called El Niño. The whole area was clouded in thick, choking smog. The southern hemisphere was further plagued by a ring of fire around Sydney, Australia. Drought, heat, and high winds created the worst bush fire conditions in 30 years. Temperatures soared as firefighters struggled to contain the lightning-sparked blazes.

Forest fires

"It came in great sheeted flames from heaven."
A survivor describing the Lake Michigan fire, 1871

Forest fires are both terrifying and lethal. Giant flames leap from tree to tree, beneath huge clouds of smoke (*right*). They move erratically, leapfrogging some areas to ignite the trees beyond and then returning to destroy the small islands they missed. Animals flee ahead of the pursuing wall of flames; people try to escape the heat by hiding in water tanks or wells, or by sheltering under wet blankets.

One of the world's worst forest fires was in Illinois in 1871, when a wall of flame swept rapidly along the shores of Lake Michigan, destroying over a million acres of forest and killing more than 1,000 people. Survivors describe a whirlwind of flames that rose above the treetops. Some people were killed by breathing in the super-heated air.

Fighting forest fires requires a two-pronged attack. First, specialized crews fly over the blaze in water bombers. Then, once the blaze is under control, regular firefighters attend the scene. Hundreds of extras from the army or civilian populations may be called in as reinforcements.

A helicopter hovers above a forest fire, ready to drop water from its bucket (*above*).

THE AFTERMATH
Firefighters move in to beat out a forest fire (above). *These fires can be extremely difficult to deal with because of the speed at which they move and the enormous temperatures that are reached. In Australia, the heat of a bush fire twisted huge steel girders and machinery as if they were toys.*

Face markings
There are often white hairs (below) *growing down a horse's face that can be used for identification. The marking may extend over the entire face or just be a fleck on the forehead.*

Measuring a horse
Horses are measured from the highest point of the withers to the ground. The unit of measurement is a "hand" (4 inches).

Interrupted stripe

Star

Blaze

Points of the HORSE

No one horse or pony is the same. Each has her own individual temperament and look, from color to the patterns of the markings. Each face marking *(see above)* is unique to the horse or pony, just like a human "fingerprint" is to a person. A horse's overall shape is called her conformation, and is often the result of her breeding. When you care for and ride horses, you need to learn the terms that are used to identify and describe them. These include the names of the colors, from skewbald (white and another color) to piebald (black and white), and the names of the markings and the different parts, or points, of the horse's body.

The picture shows the most important points of the horse. You may know a few – but try and learn them all!

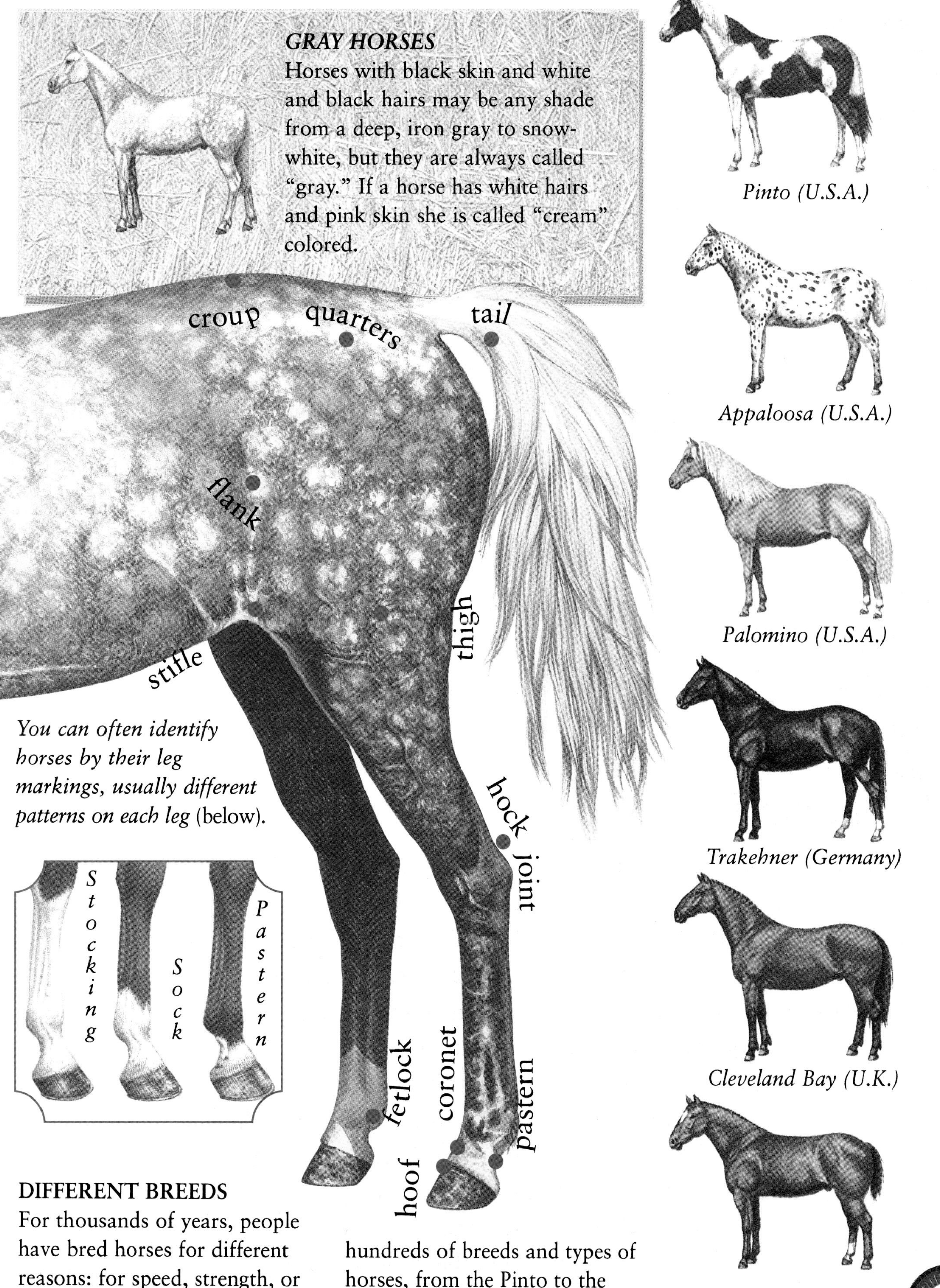

GRAY HORSES

Horses with black skin and white and black hairs may be any shade from a deep, iron gray to snow-white, but they are always called "gray." If a horse has white hairs and pink skin she is called "cream" colored.

You can often identify horses by their leg markings, usually different patterns on each leg (below).

Pinto (U.S.A.)

Appaloosa (U.S.A.)

Palomino (U.S.A.)

Trakehner (Germany)

Cleveland Bay (U.K.)

Quarter horse (U.S.A.)

DIFFERENT BREEDS

For thousands of years, people have bred horses for different reasons: for speed, strength, or good looks. There are now hundreds of breeds and types of horses, from the Pinto to the Palomino *(see right)*.

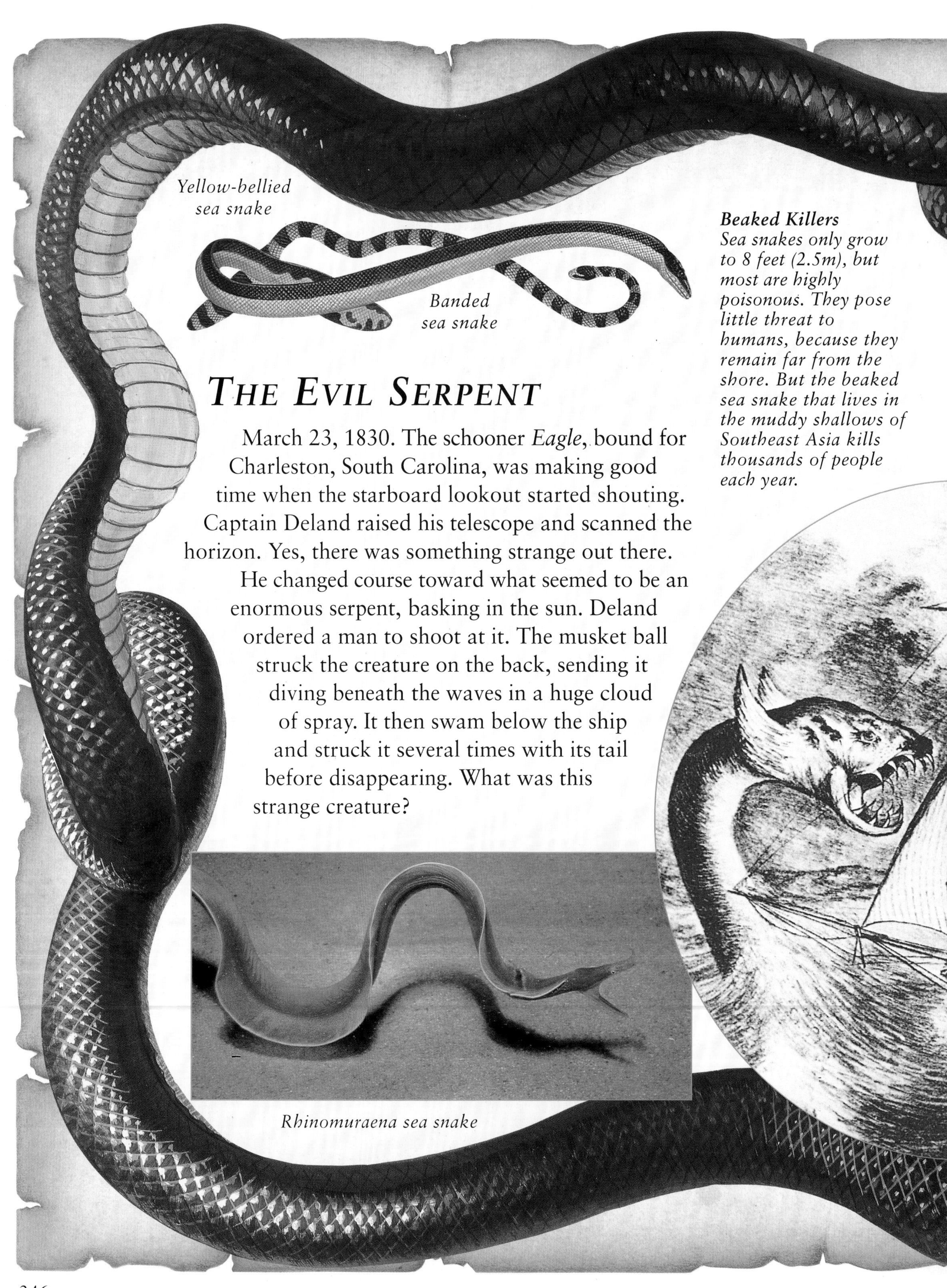

Beaked Killers
Sea snakes only grow to 8 feet (2.5m), but most are highly poisonous. They pose little threat to humans, because they remain far from the shore. But the beaked sea snake that lives in the muddy shallows of Southeast Asia kills thousands of people each year.

THE EVIL SERPENT

March 23, 1830. The schooner *Eagle*, bound for Charleston, South Carolina, was making good time when the starboard lookout started shouting. Captain Deland raised his telescope and scanned the horizon. Yes, there was something strange out there.

He changed course toward what seemed to be an enormous serpent, basking in the sun. Deland ordered a man to shoot at it. The musket ball struck the creature on the back, sending it diving beneath the waves in a huge cloud of spray. It then swam below the ship and struck it several times with its tail before disappearing. What was this strange creature?

Rhinomuraena sea snake

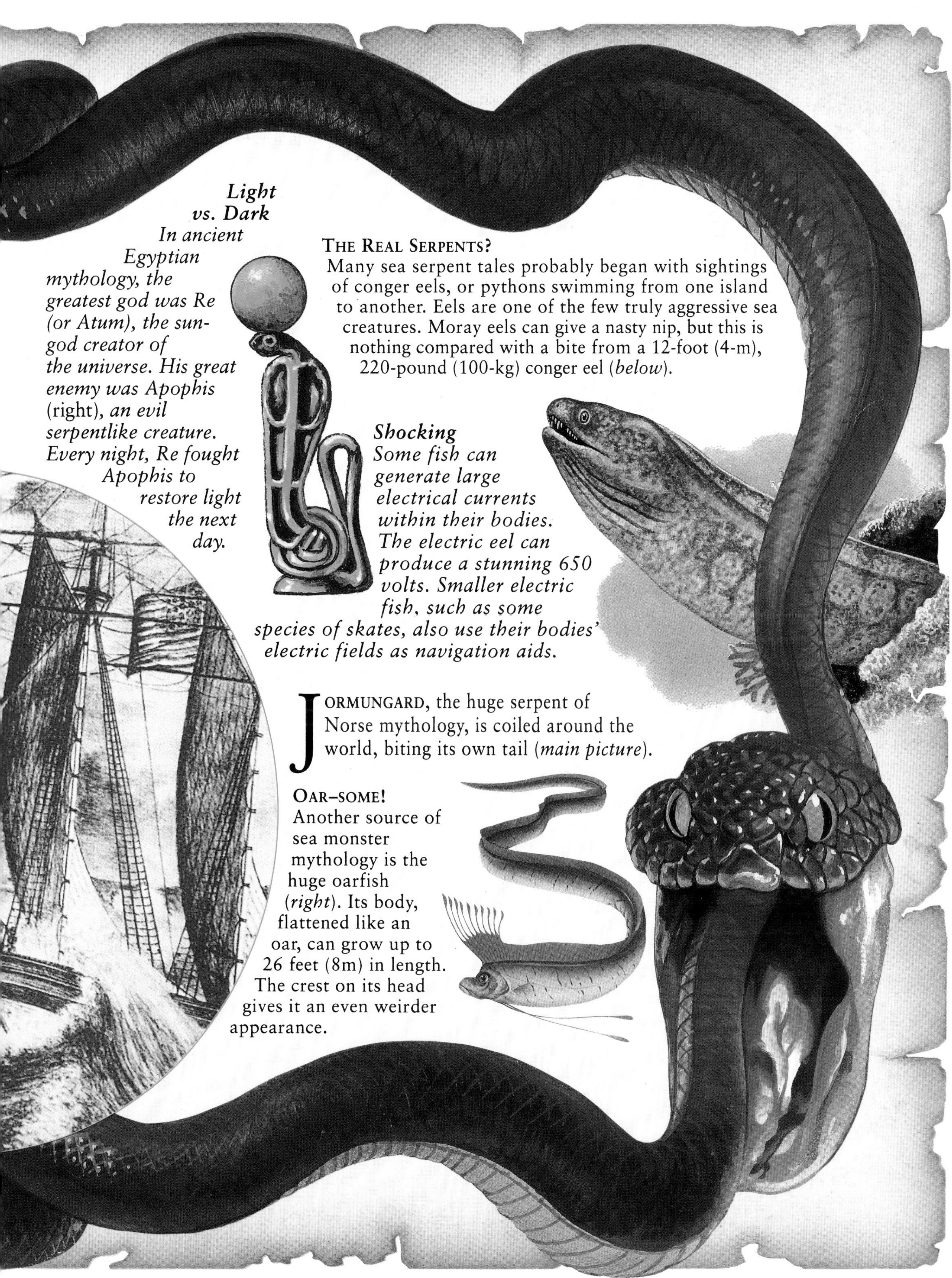

Light vs. Dark
In ancient Egyptian mythology, the greatest god was Re (or Atum), the sun-god creator of the universe. His great enemy was Apophis (right), *an evil serpentlike creature. Every night, Re fought Apophis to restore light the next day.*

The Real Serpents?
Many sea serpent tales probably began with sightings of conger eels, or pythons swimming from one island to another. Eels are one of the few truly aggressive sea creatures. Moray eels can give a nasty nip, but this is nothing compared with a bite from a 12-foot (4-m), 220-pound (100-kg) conger eel (*below*).

Shocking
Some fish can generate large electrical currents within their bodies. The electric eel can produce a stunning 650 volts. Smaller electric fish, such as some species of skates, also use their bodies' electric fields as navigation aids.

JORMUNGARD, the huge serpent of Norse mythology, is coiled around the world, biting its own tail (*main picture*).

Oar–some!
Another source of sea monster mythology is the huge oarfish (*right*). Its body, flattened like an oar, can grow up to 26 feet (8m) in length. The crest on its head gives it an even weirder appearance.

INDEX

INDEX

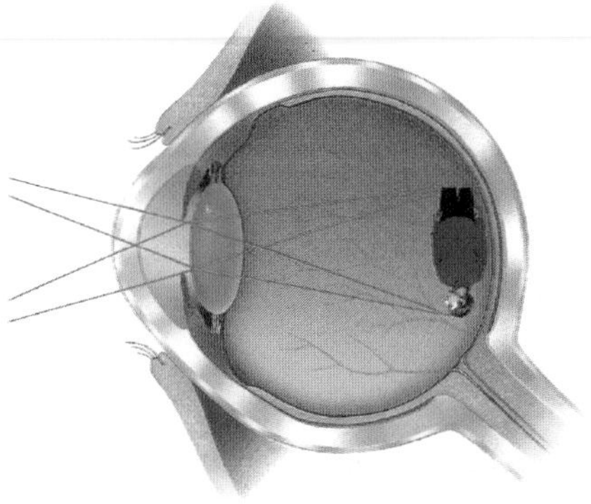

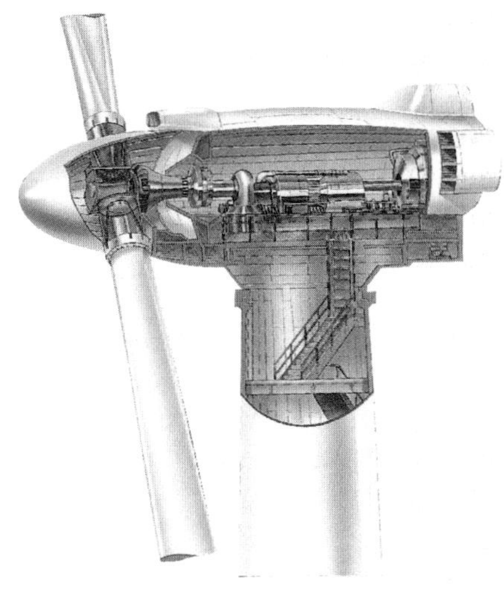

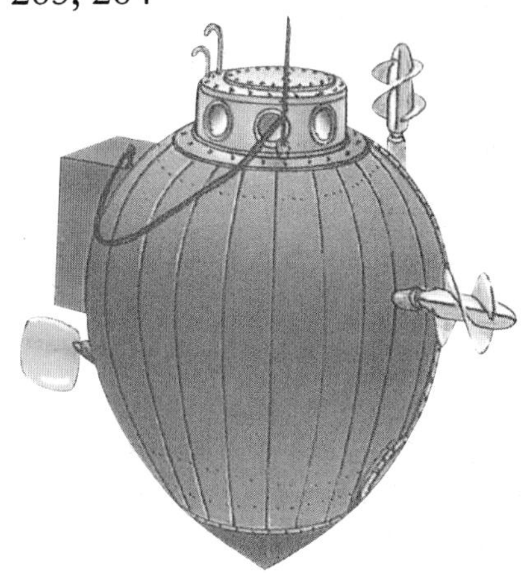

INDEX